American Spy

American Spy

My Secret History in the CIA, Watergate, and Beyond

E. Howard Hunt

with Greg Aunapu

Foreword by William F. Buckley Jr.

John Wiley & Sons, Inc.

Published by John Wiley & Sons, Inc., Hoboken, New Jersey
Published simultaneously in Canada

Photo on page 172, courtesy of Hollis Hunt

Wiley Bicentennial Logo: Richard J. Pacifico

Library of Congress Cataloging-in-Publication Data:

Hunt, E. Howard (Everette Howard), date.
    American spy : my secret history in the CIA, Watergate, and beyond / E. Howard
  Hunt ; with Greg Aunapu and Eric Hamburg.
        p. cm.
  Includes index.
  ISBN 978-0-471-78982-6 (cloth)
    1. Hunt, E. Howard (Everette Howard), date. 2. Presidents—United States—Staff—
  Biography, 3. Nixon, Richard M. (Richard Milhous), 1913–1994—Friends and associates.
  4. Watergate Affair, 1972–1974. 5. Spies—United States—Biography. 6. United States.
  Central Intelligence Agency—Biography. 7. United States—Politics and government,
  1945–1989. I. Aunapu, Greg. II. Hamburg, Eric. III. Title.
  E840.8.H86A3   2007
  973.924092—dc22
  [B] 2006023009

Printed in the United States of America

10 9 8 7 6 5 4 3 2 1

*With deep love, this book is dedicated to
my extraordinary wife, Laura; my children;
and my fallen comrades*

Contents

Photographs follow page 164

Foreword
by William F. Buckley Jr.

I met Howard Hunt soon after arriving in Mexico City in 1951. I was a deep cover agent for the CIA—deep cover describing, I was given to understand, a category members of which were told to take extreme care not to permit anyone grounds for suspicion that one was in service to the CIA.

The rule was (perhaps it is different now) that on arriving at one's targeted post, one was informed which single human being in the city knew that you were in the CIA. That person would tell you what to do for the duration of your service in that city; he would answer such questions as you wished to put to him; and would concern himself with all aspects of your duty life.

The man I was told to report to (by someone whose real name I did not know) was Howard Hunt. Howard was ostensibly working for the State Department in the Mexican embassy as a cultural affairs adviser, if I remember correctly. In any event, I met him in his office and found him greatly agreeable but also sternly concerned with duty. He would here and there give me special minor assignments, but I soon learned that my principal job was to translate from the Spanish the huge and important book by defector Eudocio Ravines.

Ravines had been an important Communist in the Peruvian party, and he defected in the forties. He had brought forth a book called *The Road from Yenan*, an autobiographical account of his exciting life in the service of the Communist revolution and an extended account of the reasons for his defection.

It was a lazy assignment, in that we were not given a deadline, so that the work slogged on during and after visits, averaging one every week, by Eudocio Ravines to the house I and my wife had occupied in the region that used to be called San Angel Inn—postrevolution, Villa Obregon. (We lived and worked at Calero #91.) It is a part of Mexico City on the southern slopes, leading now to the university (which back then was in central Mexico City).

It was only a couple of weeks after our meeting that Howard introduced me to Mrs. Hunt. Dorothy was a striking presence, witty and sharp, devoted to her husband and to their firstborn child, Lisa. The Hunts became frequent visitors to our house, and we went to theirs from time to time.

I learned that Howard had graduated from Brown University, and he was exercised by left-wing activity there, by the faculty, the administration, and the students. His own interest in alumni affairs made him especially interested in what I had to say about my own alma mater. My book *God and Man at Yale* was published in mid-October 1951, and I shook free for one week's leave to travel to New York to figure in the promotion that attended the book's publication.

My book attracted a great deal of publicity, and two publications offered me jobs. One was *The Freeman*, the highbrow fortnightly edited by Henry Hazlitt, Forrest Davis, and John Chamberlain. The accent there was heavily on economic issues. *The American Mercury* was owned and edited by William Bradford Huie, a veteran journalist and novelist, and he also asked me to join his staff.

But I went back to Mexico and to my project with Ravines, and persevered in my friendship with the Hunt family. In the early spring of the next year, 1952, I yielded to the temptation to go into journalism. The project with Ravines was pretty well completed when I called on Howard to tell him I had decided to quit the agency.

Our friendship was firm, and Howard came several times to Stamford, Connecticut, where my wife and I were camped down. I never knew—and he was very discreet about—what he was up to, but I assumed, correctly, that he was continuing his work for the Central Intelligence Agency. I was greatly moved by Dorothy's message to me that summer—that she and Howard were joining the Catholic communion, and wanted me to serve as godfather for their two children (daughter Kevan was now born). Later, the invitation extended to serve for their son, St. John, though by now the family had moved to the Far East, and years passed without my seeing Howard.

But then came Watergate, and the dreadful accident over Midway Airport in Chicago that killed Dorothy in December 1972. I learned of this watching television with my wife, and it was through the television that I also learned that she had named me as a personal representative of her estate in the event of her demise. I consulted with a veteran lawyer and close friend. He recommended that the Hunt family's wrongful-death lawsuit (which had to be brought in my name) be turned over to the attorney who was representing other victims of the crash of the United Airlines airplane.

That terrible event came at a high point in the Watergate affair, and it was in November (as I recall) that I received a phone call from Howard, with whom I hadn't been in touch for several years. He asked to see me.

He came with his daughter Kevan, a student at Smith who would soon be going to law school. He startled me by saying that he intended to disclose to me everything he knew about the Watergate affair, including much that (he said) had not yet been revealed to Congressional investigators.

What especially arrested me was his saying that his dedication to the project at hand had included a hypothetical agreement to contrive the assassination of syndicated muckraker Jack Anderson, if the high command at the Nixon White House thought this necessary. I remember especially his keen surprise that the White House hadn't exercised itself to protect and free Hunt and his collaborators in the Watergate enterprise. He simply could not understand this moral default. It was left that I would take an interest, however remote, in his household of children, now that he was headed for jail. (Neither he nor Dorothy had any brothers or sisters.)

Soon afterward, Howard told me that his lawyer had quit because Howard could no longer pay for his services. I called a very distinguished lawyer in New York who served also as my personal attorney. He was vastly informed on the international struggle against the Communists, and he volunteered to handle Howard's appeals free of charge.

A singular piece of good fortune was that Howard came upon William Snyder, a young and resourceful attorney who became not only his advocate but his close friend to this day.

Howard was soon in jail, and I visited him once in Washington. I thought back on the sad contrast between Hunt, E. H., federal prisoner, and Hunt, E. H., special assistant to the U.S. ambassador to Mexico—and his going on to a number of glittering assignments but ultimately making that fateful wrong turn in the service of President

Nixon, for which his suffering has been prolonged and wretchedly protracted. I prefer to remember him back in his days as a happy warrior, a productive novelist, an efficient administrator, and a wonderful companion.

Howard Hunt now has a new family, who love and dote on him. I can say of his two oldest daughters that they are exemplary human beings and citizens and represent the best of their two parents.

Introduction

I've been called many things since the foiled break-in of Democratic National Committee headquarters at the Watergate complex, including a criminal mastermind, a bungling burglar, and even a bad spy novelist. I don't know which accusation hurts most. Two are outrageous overstatements and one is a matter of opinion. Need I explain which is which? Whatever the case, none of them describes the whole man, and all disregard over two decades of service to the United States, first as a sailor in World War II, then as an OSS (Office of Strategic Services) operative, segueing into many years as a CIA agent.

While I occasionally consent to do the odd interview about the Watergate era, the early 1970s is not a time that I like to remember. I have barely entered my study, written a word, or looked at any mementos in years. But recent blockbuster headlines shouting that former FBI deputy director Howard Felt was Bob Woodward's secret source—known worldwide by the shameful title of Deep Throat, which I believe he deserves—have stirred a wasps' nest of negative memories for me that I have otherwise learned to suppress from day to day.

The revelations prompted me to delve through some old files, where I found my prison diary covering thirty-three months in prison. The contents are terse and abbreviated, the handwriting as small as I could scribble in order to conserve precious ink and paper, which was in short supply. In it, I describe the many trials (literally) and tribulations that were my reward for trying to protect my president.

If I had known that the president and his staff were deriding me as a bungler, I might have behaved differently and not tried to take the blame for my superiors, ending up with a thirty-five-year provisional sentence by perjuring myself in front of the grand jury. I wouldn't find out about the insults heaped upon me by the rats in the president's sinking ship until the White House tapes were seized and made public under the power of subpoena.

In addition to these slurs, Nixon had some other interesting asides. In one famous conversation, he opines that my involvement in Watergate will open up "the whole Bay of Pigs thing," which will be "very bad for Hunt and bad for the CIA." What did he mean by this? Why did he complain that "this fellow Hunt knows too damned much"? These are questions that roiled around in my brain for a while but whose urgency has diminished over the years. It is time to explore them now.

It isn't going to be easy to relive my life by writing this book. As a result of Watergate, my wife was killed in a plane crash, during a flight she would never have been on if the failed Watergate operation had been aborted as I had requested several times. My children were left almost as orphans for three years while I was on my "government-sponsored vacation," doing hard labor along with murderers. My two oldest daughters blamed me for the catastrophes in their lives, while my two older sons had difficulties before straightening out their lives in recent years.

Ultimately, some good things happened, too. While in prison, I met Laura, who has become my second wife and second life. After I was released from prison, we lived in Guadalajara, Mexico, for several years, where I resumed writing some of my better works, before we moved back to Miami. We have two children, Hollis and Austin, who live with us and are supportive of this effort to explain and analyze the past.

As I reflect on my life and career at age eighty-eight, it is hard to believe that I have crammed so many dramatic and historical events into one lifetime. I have learned many—too many—lessons about service, honor, loyalty, and betrayal, and the meaning of love and family. At times, I did things that I am not proud of. But I did them believing that what I was doing was in the best interests of my country. I have no regrets.

But I do have a story to tell.

1

World War II

B y the summer of 1943, the tides of World War II seemed to be turning ever so slightly to the Allies' side. Earlier in the year, Hitler had been forced out of Stalingrad and Tunisia. The Allies landed in Sicily, bombed Rome, sent German troops scurrying out of Italy, and arrested Mussolini. But it was a tug of war. Hitler countered by invading Allied-occupied Italy, where he rescued Mussolini in the middle of September. If we were going to win this war, Uncle Sam needed every man he had, but I was twiddling my thumbs as a briefer to a paper-pushing general in sunny Orlando, Florida.

A lot of enlisted men would have envied my position. Life was, in many ways, gentle as the Florida breeze. I woke up each balmy dawn, read a few intelligence reports in the morning, briefed the general as succinctly as possible, then usually spent the rest of the day at the Officer's Club on the lakeshore, falling in love with various girls at night. But when a particularly dramatic love affair ended in September, there was nothing to keep me from joining the action.

My expectations to jump into the fray were crushed, however, when my application for overseas duty was refused because I had already served twice.

As a graduate of Brown University in 1940 with a B.A. in English, I had already done a stretch in the navy as assistant first lieutenant on the destroyer *Mayo*, where I scouted German U-boats, manned the range finder on the topmost part of the ship, and saw action as our fleet guarded shipping in the North Atlantic. Unfortunately, I was injured in a fall on an icy deck and, much to my disgust, offered two vile alternatives—shore duty as a supply officer or a medical discharge.

I had lost a lot of my Naval Academy classmates in Pearl Harbor and Wake Island, so I wanted to continue serving in the fray, but I was also very action oriented and felt that others could handle the easy supply job better. So, with regrets, I accepted the medical discharge and recuperated at my parents' home in Albany, New York, where my father, a lawyer, was an insurance industry lobbyist at the State Capitol.

By the shores of the Hudson River, I purged my repressed energy by banging out my first novel, a fictionalized account of convoy duty in the North Atlantic titled *East of Farewell*. When the manuscript was finished, I sent it to Knopf, the publishing house that had once employed a Brown University mentor of mine named Dr. Kapstein. Amazingly to me, the work was quickly accepted and became the first book published about World War II by an American who had actually served in the war. The reviews were all I could have hoped for, but I couldn't compete with the real-life war blaring in the newspaper headlines and newsreels. Sales were not good enough to escalate me to full-time author.

The publication did lead to employment working on navy training films in New York City, where I enjoyed a good salary and many girlfriends, and nightlife was swinging at the 21 Club and the Copacabana.

But those horrible headlines never quit. In March 1943, German U-boats sank twenty-seven merchant ships in the Atlantic. Newspapers published photographs of the doomed liners, plumes of smoke billowing out of frame as their smokestacks disappeared under water. I became obsessed with finding a way to get back into the war and found an opportunity as a war correspondent assigned to the Pacific fleet for *Life* magazine, actually seeing my share of action and narrowly escaping death a few more times. I left after getting on the bad side of General MacArthur when I asked him the wrong question at a press conference and was subsequently blackballed.

I was a navy man through and through, but there was no place for me at sea anymore. I took a brief job at *Fortune* in New York and wrote my second novel, *Limit of Darkness* (okay, so maybe I wasn't a genius with titles), about airmen based at Henderson Field in Guadalcanal. But living a safe civilian life still rankled me. So one day, I trudged through the crowds of off-duty sailors in the streets, where I made my way to Grand Central Station and joined the army air force as a private.

But the army air force was counting my duty as a reporter in the Pacific as a second tour and notified me that I was destined to serve out my sentence in safe, lovely, boring Orlando, Florida.

It was then that I started hearing whispers of a mysterious new organization whose importance to the war effort was becoming greater every day—the Office of Strategic Services. Little was known about it, and it sounded more like a bunch of paper-pushing bureaucrats than anything else. Maybe some unit that supplied our boys with chocolate bars or got the mail delivered during battle.

I soon learned that there were three officers on base looking for volunteers for the new service. It seemed hush-hush—not everyone was even told they were there. All I could ask was, "Why are they here? Why would you want to work for them?"

An officer who knew that I was dissatisfied with my duty called me into his office and told me, "I don't know much about it, but I think you should meet with them. They've got some kind of connection with General Donovan."

If Donovan was involved, I was more interested. Although "Wild Bill" Donovan had originally earned his nickname on the football field playing for Columbia University, he had lived up to the name as a soldier, becoming a World War I legend by garnering a Medal of Honor, the Distinguished Service Cross, and three Purple Hearts.

I did a little digging and found that I was wrong about the OSS outfit. It took me some effort, but I found out that they weren't a bunch of paper pushers. They were involved in some kind of unconventional, behind-the-lines warfare. Now I really wanted to meet with the recruiters, but they had already left the base.

My obsession with action tuned into this opportunity. It called to me in the night. I couldn't get it out of my mind.

I knew that my father and Bill Donovan had been friends in western New York and had similar political tastes. They were both lawyers and supported the Buffalo Athletic Club.

I picked up the phone and dialed my parents' number. "Father," I started when he answered the phone, "I need you to get in touch with Bill Donovan for me. Find out what this outfit he's connected with is up to, because I'm so bored here I can't bear it anymore."

As a lobbyist, my father had become adept at navigating the political morass. It didn't take him long to get in touch with General Donovan's office. Within twenty-four hours, I had a FAGTRANS (first available government transportation) order for Washington, D.C.

I was met at the airport by a stoic man in plainclothes who wouldn't answer any questions. He took me to an ordinary-looking apartment in a D.C. suburb, which I would later know as a safe house, and advised me that I had an appointment with General Donovan the next day.

"What's he like?" I wanted to know.

The man could have had a great career as a department store mannequin for all he had to say on the subject. That night, I ate a quick dinner out, shined my shoes, and prepared mentally for the next day's meeting.

In the morning, my taciturn driver showed up bright and early and whisked me away to an office near the Potomac, where I didn't have to wait long to meet the war hero.

Most of the generals I had known wore ties and shined shoes and generally looked like they had a twenty-four-hour crew keeping their uniforms creased. They were brusque and authoritative around subordinates. Donovan, renowned for being unpredictable and unorthodox, however, was relaxed, didn't wear a tie, and greeted me warmly. He put me at ease, saying that he remembered me as a child and recounted a funny anecdote about my father, whom he liked. He was about sixty at this time, and his hair was white and short-cropped in sharp angles to go with his square Brahman jaw. He had gotten a bit plumper than I remembered, but his remarkable blue eyes sparkled with energy and intelligence. He would live until shortly after his seventy-sixth birthday in February 1959, and, at that time, he still looked like a man you wanted next to you in a fight.

His handshake was so firm it almost hurt, and after a few minutes of cordiality, he got down to business. "So tell my why you're here," he said.

I thought it was pretty obvious why I was there. But he was doing what men in power often do. They don't just grant you what you want, no matter how obvious; they make you ask for it, state your exact intentions—earn it.

"Well, sir," I said in a strong, clear voice. "I've seen a lot of service in the North Atlantic and the Pacific and feel like I'm a Florida retiree in Orlando. I'm here to volunteer for your organization."

His eyes settled on mine for a moment, gauging my mettle, I suppose. I wasn't the first or the last young man who felt a bit withered and awed by the gaze. My heart was beating, as I thought that I might be rejected.

"Well, we've got the manpower we need in Europe right now. Things may be winding down there," he said finally. "But there's still a lot of activity in Asia. I have a billet right now in China, if you're willing to go there?"

"Yes, of course," I reacted with enthusiasm. "Absolutely, General. Wherever you want."

"Okay," he said at last. "I'll have you assigned to OSS."

So far so good.

Now he continued with the fine print. "But it's temporary, you understand. You know I'd love to have you in this organization. But this is an elite force. You're going to have to qualify for it like any other candidate."

Qualify? That was new to me. Uncle Sam would have taken a cross-eyed, one-legged man at that point. Any willing body to throw at the enemy.

"Qualify?" I repeated. "Of course. I wouldn't have it any other way."

My new orders arrived in Orlando before I did. I barely had time to pack and phone a girl for a last good-bye kiss before I had to return to Washington.

From tiny sparks a bonfire is made, I guess. Only in hindsight can you see the string of coincidences that make up a life, each step leading inexorably to the next. President Roosevelt picked Donovan to head OSS. My father happened to know Donovan; otherwise, I would probably never have joined the service. But all the connections were there. Thus began my long, tumultuous career in the U.S. clandestine services and my various—some would say nefarious—connections to historic events that have reshaped international and domestic politics.

2

OSS

In many ways, the Office of Strategic Services was an elite force made up of the country's crème de la crème. Donovan was a Phi Kappa Psi alumnus of Columbia University Law School. Most of the volunteers he found were savvy Ivy Leaguers—sons of America's upper class—and I'm sure the Brown University degree in my records did not go unnoticed.

Even today, Yale prides itself on graduating more students who go into the field of intelligence than any other university. Princeton, however, is no slouch, counting former CIA chief Allen Dulles among many CIA alumni.

At the time, Donovan had become one of the most powerful antitrust lawyers in the country and had gained the confidence of many Washington politicians. As early as the Woodrow Wilson administration, he had been a member of a group of Columbia intellectuals who advised the president on foreign affairs and was sent on an early mission across the Atlantic to report on a Russian uprising in Siberia. He served as attorney general during the Coolidge administration, from 1925 to 1929; he supervised and made an enemy of J. Edgar Hoover, head of the fledgling FBI. By 1941, he had become an important adviser to Franklin D. Roosevelt—a former classmate from Columbia—and was shortlisted to become the next secretary of war. Ultimately, he was passed over for the position, but FDR sent Donovan to England in June to assess the country's chances against Germany.

By all accounts, Winston Churchill had no illusions that his valiant little country had any hope of prevailing against the scourge spreading across Europe. The host wined and dined the general and gave him access to a wealth of British military intelligence. Of everything that he saw, the wily Donovan was most impressed by Britain's covert intelligence operations. At the time, America's own intelligence network was primitive at best, a function of the military and the State Department, with little funding, training, or coordination. The general returned home determined that the United States needed this type of weapon in a world at war and should immediately build a counterpart to what he had seen in England.

In July, FDR responded by naming Donovan chief of the Coordinator of Information Office, which by 1942 evolved into the Office of Strategic Services (OSS). Most experts believe that the service I became part of in 1943 was a determining factor in winning the war. OSS helped destabilize Hitler's regime with groundbreaking strategies to undermine the German economy and morale, going so far as to try to flood the enemy country with counterfeit deutsche marks and stamps.

The main branches of OSS included a nine-hundred-member team of scholars in Research and Analysis (R&A), Secret Intelligence (SI), Special Operations (SO), and X-2, the counterintelligence branch. They used every means available to research the enemy's capabilities. An early founder of data mining techniques, OSS discovered that some of the most important information could be siphoned out of public sources—in libraries and newspapers. They soon learned that insurance records provided the blueprints for bomb and aircraft factories and showed the most vulnerable targets to bomb.

Then, after Luftwaffe plants were wrecked, for instance, their aircraft would no longer be able to guard against an attack against Germany's oil facilities.

But I knew nothing about this then. My training was just about to start.

I ensconced myself in a small apartment at the elegant Wardman-Park Hotel for several days during my first examinations, which included not only a complete physical but IQ tests as well. Then, one Sunday morning, I was ordered to report to the old Christin Heurich brewery near OSS headquarters. A dozen green volunteers were loaded aboard a shrouded military transport truck and taken on a long drive to a secret training facility—a farmhouse in the middle of nowhere—called Area E, where we would be tested by a cadre of civilian psychologists.

Each member of the training group was assigned a room, as we were scheduled to stay for a week of intensive testing. The head of the facility entered the room after dinner. He was an innocuous middle-aged man who could easily have been an actuary or a school dean. He spoke in measured, cultured tones.

First, he congratulated us on being chosen as volunteers, adding that our admittance to the service would be based on our evaluations here. But, he cautioned us, "Never divulge your true identity to anyone here, even the staff, and use only your assigned alias." It all seemed simple enough. My alias was easy to remember—William, which was my grandfather's name. "Oh," he added nonchalantly. "By the way, one of you is a ringer, an OSS plant, who will help in your evaluation. Good luck, everyone." Then he smiled and left.

His ploy worked. Paranoia set upon us immediately as we looked around at one another trying to gauge who was the spy among us.

To further throw us off, tests began immediately after dinner, when our energy was focused on digestion in the stomach rather than puzzles in the brain. The group was led into the basement, where a simulated hotel room had been constructed. It looked like something out of an Eastern European movie, complete with faded drapes, a threadbare bedspread, and a rusting radiator.

It looked like whoever had rented the room had left in a hurry. Strewn across the bed were a railway ticket for a trip between Vienna and Belgrade, money from various European countries, a set of keys, and a torn address book. There was a coat in the closet and an over-turned chair by a desk.

"You will each be given three minutes alone in the room," our facilitator told us. "Then you'll be brought into another room, where you will write down what you remember about the contents, and most importantly, any deductions you can make from what you have recorded."

Accordingly, after a couple of other candidates, I was let into the semidarkened room, where I was able to search through the closet and the bureau drawers and make a cursory mental catalog of the items on the bed. Later, it appeared that each volunteer had come up with wildly varying stories to account for the tableau.

My scenario focused on a foreign agent traveling from Belgrade to Vienna, who, assuming that he had arrived safely at his destination, where he would attempt to change his identity, had been surprised by an intruder just as he had started to empty out his pockets. Even with my writing experience, it was the best story I could come up with in such a short time.

Once everyone had submitted their papers, our facilitator took over, pointing out the inconsistencies in each person's report. "The train ticket runs between Belgrade and Austria, but no one noticed that there was no money from those particular countries," he observed. "The coat in the closet is heavy, but the radiator isn't on, because it's not cold outside. In fact, it's summer. The phone on the table has a nonexistent exchange, so who knows where you are. . . ." But then, just when we were each feeling that we had failed our first test miserably, he chuckled.

"It's all right," he continued. "There is no proper answer to the riddle. The room has built-in inconsistencies to confuse you. What we are really interested in in this test is to see how many of the items on the bed you were able to remember and weave into your conclusions."

This was my first lesson in the true deviousness of clandestine operations, and it made my brain instantly start functioning on a higher level. It got everyone else's attention as well, and you could see the wheels start working differently inside each person's head. If this was the first test, what lay ahead?

The tests would indeed grow more perplexing. After breakfast the next day, we were brought down to a partially frozen creek.

"Your mission here," we were told, "is to devise a means to cross the stream. Only this isn't a stream, men. Consider it to be a bottomless chasm. The use of wood will not be permitted."

The evaluator dropped a length of rope on the ground and shuffled off to sit against a nearby tree, where he would observe and evaluate us, writing his conclusions on a pad.

Among us was a large navy lieutenant, whom despite our aliases I knew to be Jay Rutherfurd, a Golden Gloves boxer and a graduate of Princeton. He was in the best shape of any of us, and I could see him gearing up to make a massive leap across the bank.

"Wait a second," I said. "The rope may be a ploy, or it may be for something. Let's see what we can do with it."

"It's too short for anything," came the group's consensus.

"Lift me up," I suggested to Jay.

I got on his shoulders, from where I could just reach an overhanging branch to tie the rope to. From there, we each swung easily across the supposedly bottomless chasm. Our evaluator gave us a brief, light applause.

"So what do you think this test was for?" he questioned.

"To evaluate how inventive we could be," was the popular answer, including my own.

He shook his head. "Not in the least. The test was to determine which one of you would take the initiative to lead the group to success."

Another test must have been conceived by a sadist. Here we were taken into a barn and introduced to two "army privates" and a pile of broomstick-size poles with holes drilled into them.

The supervisor said, "You will each be brought inside individually, where your task will be to instruct these two gentlemen how to assemble these poles into a house. You cannot use your own hands in any way. The time limit is five minutes."

When my turn came, I found the two privates lounging on the floor, paying absolutely no attention to me. I examined the poles, figured the problem wasn't too hard, and instructed the men to assemble four of the sticks into a rectangle on the floor before raising the uprights at the corners. It was kind of a large version of a child's play toy.

The two men didn't seem to hear me.

"Excuse me, gentlemen," I urged. "Can we do this today?"

They looked at me with disgust. "I think the officer wants us to do something, Joe," one said.

"Can't officers lift a finger themselves?" the other countered. "Do this, do that. It's always us privates gotta do the grunt work."

They slowly got up to their feet.

"I don't always like how officers treat enlisted men, either," I said, trying to get on their good side. "But I'm not one of them. You know I can't touch this stuff. Now can we get on with it? I only have three minutes left!"

With deliberate sluggishness, they sabotaged my efforts at every turn. When the uprights were finally raised to my liking, one man stumbled drunkenly against them, scattering the poles across the floor. He didn't apologize; instead, his laughter indicated that he found my plight rather humorous. The other looked at me and started laughing, too.

"This isn't a joke," I said. "Now put it back together."

The stumbler looked at me with a bovine intelligence. "I forgot how," he intoned.

"Forgot how?" I asked, then saw what I was up against and slowly repeated my earlier instructions. Checking my watch, I saw that four precious minutes had slid by during this exercise and nothing had been accomplished. I snapped my fingers to hasten the men's efforts.

"Officers!" the stumbler scoffed with malice.

"I suggest you get back to work immediately or you *will* get a dose of officer from me," I finally said.

Instead of placing the fourth upright into its hole, the man stared brazenly at me and broke the pole across his knee. Both men laughed hysterically.

The buzzer sounded.

I left the room in dejection, furious that the men had undermined me so badly. The staff supervisor looked inside the room with a grim expression. But before I could explain what had happened, a smile spread across his face. The two truculent privates came out of the barn, noticed my surprise, and started laughing along with their supervisor.

"The experiment wasn't to evaluate your command abilities," the psychologist told me. "But to see how cool you stayed trying to finish such a frustrating task!" He clapped me on the shoulder and turned to the privates—really two staff psychologists. "Has anyone ever managed to get you guys to build the house in the last year?"

They shook their heads. "I imagine there're more than a few guys who wanted to tear us a new one," the stumbler observed.

The two men went back into the barn to await their next victim—Jay Rutherfurd. Within two minutes, the barn door burst open. The two "privates" scurried out, pursued by a red-faced Jay brandishing a pole. If the two men had been a little slower, they might have needed a medical discharge. As it was, we were able to calm Jay down enough to explain the situation, though he brooded for the rest of the day.

Every task had complex layers that seemed unfathomably mysterious when we were first confronted with it, but became obvious once it was finished. By Friday, our brains were truly fried, and we were ready for the steak dinner that we were offered. Even a full bar was set up in a corner of the room, with several cases of liquor stacked nearby. The "headmaster" informed us that we had been "a very good class of candidates," adding "The staff has learned as much from you as you have from us. It will help us hone our tasks in the future. Now, you'll all be very glad to hear that you've finished all the requirements and you can return to Washington in the morning."

A cheer rang through the room as he told us that we were now off duty and free to celebrate. The group rushed to the area where a cheerful staff member tended bar.

We hadn't been allowed a drink all week, so I figured that it would be wise to pace myself so that I didn't arrive in Washington with a hangover. I slowly sipped two satisfying cocktails and cut myself off, nursing the melting ice the rest of the evening. Still, the room felt increasingly hot, as if a furnace was blasting overtime, making us all feel groggy. I had just decided to go to my room when the chief of Area E made an appearance.

"Oh, gentlemen," he said. "I seem to have forgotten one little item. You still have one final test. We are going to have a debate. Half of you will debate in the negative and half in the positive of the proposition. The topic is: President Roosevelt had no right to get us into this war."

An eerie issue, considering that over the next sixty years similar debates could have occurred that over Korea, Vietnam, Iraq, and others.

I slipped out of the room into a nearby bathroom and dunked my head into a sink full of cold water to clear my head. When I returned to the room, I found that I had been assigned to the negative team, although I would certainly have preferred to argue for the positive. It didn't matter, though. The debate proved ludicrous, as no one in the room was sober enough to stand on his feet, let alone reason a point intelligently.

After the drunken argument, however, it became clear that the subject of the debate held no importance whatsoever. During the test, it turned out, a few staff members had been able to get some of the besotted candidates to divulge their true identities.

Before leaving the next day, we were all asked to write down which person in our group we suspected of being the OSS spy. When the consensus was tallied, the overwhelming majority favored me, which I took as a compliment and a tribute to nascent talents that would later be cultivated in the CIA. We were never told who the real agent was, if there even was one—that piece of information might have been just another layer of *dis*information set to work against our psyche.

We were driven back to Washington in the covered truck and let off at the brewery. I would never see most of the dozen candidates I had spent the grueling week with at Area E again. Only four of us passed.

After a few days' rest, I was called into General Donovan's office. As before, he was hearty and casual, paternal even.

"Well, son, you will be glad to know that you won't be heading back to sunny Florida anytime soon," he said. "You are now a member of the OSS and relieved of any further air force duties."

I communicated my gratitude and enthusiasm to be a part of the new service.

"So which combat theater would you prefer?"

"Wherever you need me, sir," I replied.

He sat back in his chair and thought for a minute. "Well, the war in Europe is winding down, and we've been shifting personnel to the Far East. A man who wants to be noticed would probably volunteer for the China-Burma-India theater."

"Sir, you know much better than I do," I said.

His blue eyes bore into me for a moment, then shifted into some distant object that only he could see—perhaps my future. He nodded his head, thinking to himself before he turned his attention back to me.

"I think you might be good in China," he divined.

China! I never thought I would end up there. At that point in history, very little was known about that vast territory. It was truly a world away, incredibly exotic, romantic, and extremely difficult to get to.

"Yes, sir," I said. "China will be fine."

"China it is, then," Donovan said. "You'll need a lot more training, of course. We have a class starting in a few weeks, so I'd like you to work around the office. Every day we prepare a situation report from intelligence we've gathered around the world for President Roosevelt—a bit like what you were doing in Orlando but much more complicated, so I'll put you on that duty."

The reports were edited by a team of agents who siphoned the volumes of material into a readable summary. Then they were typed on a special typewriter with a large presidential-size font. My job was to edit the final report before Donovan signed off on it and had it sent to Grace Tully, FDR's private secretary. So, while it wasn't that different from the job I had just left, it was a step up, as I was now the quasi-editor of the first national intelligence brief ever submitted to a U.S. president.

Although the job might have been similar to my past duty, the ambience was not. Orlando was laid-back—sun and fun at the Officer's Club; "good ole boys" in military uniforms, telling blue jokes and recounting lurid nights with local girls—true or not. At OSS, everything was ceaseless activity; conversation was more intellectual, as many of the officers had been attorneys before the war. One navy lieutenant, James Donovan, later defended Soviet spy Colonel Rudolf Abel and was instrumental in exchanging his client for the famous U-2 pilot Gary Powers, who had been shot down over Russia. Another officer, Lawrence Houston, would later become the first general counsel at the CIA.

I had scarcely settled in when I was ordered to the West Coast to begin training with a group of OSS war veterans who had seen action in France, Italy, Scandinavia, Yugoslavia, and Greece. As General Donovan had promised, the effort was indeed being shifted from Europe to the Far East. But before we left, we would have to face a punishing six-week crash course on Catalina Island.

Our group was ferried across the channel in a speedboat on a rough, blustery day, sending the spray up across the bow and occasionally slapping our faces. I loved the ocean and always had, ever since my father had taken me fishing in Florida in the winters when I was a kid. During the Depression, fishing was more than a means of relaxation—it put dinner on the table.

We were taken to a former boys' school, owned by William Wrigley (of chewing gum fame), who lent it to OSS during the war. I roomed with an OSS officer, Ed Welch, who had already served in France and was friendly with many of the men in our group. Among us was Jack Singlaub, who would later become an army general and supreme commander of all forces in Korea.

The training proved to be as rugged as I had feared—and hoped. First, we were rousted for calisthenics every morning before dawn. Then the commanding officer, a young colonel, gave us the day's orders before breakfast. The elite staff of OSS—these lawyers and scions of industry—did have a few perquisites that normal troops would have killed for. Rumor had it that our chefs had worked at the

Waldorf-Astoria and that General Donovan drew double ration money for every member of OSS. No matter how tough our training, we did it on full and satisfied bellies.

Spy movies have now filled the world with images of covert training and combat techniques first instituted at OSS. In the morning, we were instructed how to subdue or kill an enemy in seconds. This training was based on a radical new approach to hand-to-hand (H2H) or close-quarter combat (CQC), which we were taught by the team of William Fairbairns and Rex Applegate.

William Ewart Fairbairns was a British soldier who joined the Shanghai Municipal Police in 1907, becoming one of the first Europeans to study martial arts from Chinese masters. At the time, the city was a dangerous Asian version of America's old Wild West, with shootouts and criminal mobs raiding and lording over the city. Tensions between Europeans and locals turned into daily riots in the streets.

Whereas Asian martial arts took years of training to master, Fairbairns boiled down the essentials to an explosive down-and-dirty method of disabling or disarming an attacker, which could be taught in a matter of weeks. When he became head of the Shanghai Police Department in 1927, he instructed his troops in his methods of self-defense, eventually bringing peace back to the dangerous and lawless city. On the long boat trip back to England in 1940, he penned a book called *Get Tough* (still in print today), outlining his commando fighting skills, which he first called "Defendu," focusing on holds, pressure points, and a merciless quick-kill, "either-or" philosophy, including eye gouging, biting, chops to the carotid artery, groin hits, and kicks.

During World War II, Fairbairns and another former Shanghai officer, E. A. Sykes, taught the techniques to elite Allied forces in Scotland, then drilled British and Canadian operatives on a base in Canada, where they came to the attention of Wild Bill Donovan, who sent some OSS officers to train there, including Colonel Rex Applegate.

Applegate adapted the techniques for OSS agents, turning the simplified combination of judo, jujitsu, and kung fu into a ruthless and lethal survival method with which a weaker agent could overpower a larger opponent, even in close quarters where they were likely to be attacked, such as in train cars, hallways, elevators, and theater boxes. Applegate published his adaptations in 1943 in the classic combat textbook *Kill or Get Killed*, which is also still in print today.

We trained with knives—some of which were designed by Fairbairns—and bayonets, learning how to disarm an assailant. From there we practiced rapid fire with handguns, the operation of Japanese mortars, machine guns, rifles, and pistols. The Applegate methods of point shooting were taught for close combat, a technique stressing how the eye and the brain can immediately calculate where to aim if you point your finger, even from the hip, while discharging multiple rounds.

Later in the day, we were instructed in the clandestine arts of the spy—how to pick locks, how to open envelopes without leaving a trace, cryptology, Morse code—and were introduced to some top-secret tools and weapons being manufactured by OSS's Research and Development branch, operated by a Boston chemist, Stanley P. Lovell—think Agent Q from the James Bond movies.

R&D's products and other items manufactured for the army and given to OSS included an amazing array of weapons and gadgets: pencils that hid a thin, sharp knife inside (also included in POW packages to help prisoners escape), an easily concealable silenced pistol, tiny limpet mines, and something called "Aunt Jemima," an explosive powder packaged to look like Chinese flour. Additional items included a uniform button with a secret compass inside, a deck of cards in which the back of one card could be soaked off to reveal a hidden map, and a tiny Kodak 16mm camera hidden inside a matchbox.

Since we would need to infiltrate certain regions on the sly, we were taught mountain climbing and nocturnal amphibious operations with special transportable kayaks produced by R&D (these were so useful that even the British bought a hundred or so units). Once we were in enemy territory, we would be equipped with fabricated identity papers, ration cards, work passes, even paper currency printed by R&D to the most exacting and up-to-date standards. Our clothing would be sewn to exactly match the fashions worn by people in the geographic area in which we were operating; and for special assignments, even our dental work, toothbrushes, razors, and eyeglasses would be made exact so that they could be examined under a microscope to fool the most paranoid enemy.

We might be called on to blow up bridges and sabotage factories, so we learned how to use dynamite, C-3 plastic explosives, and other demolition products such as "Aunt Jemima." We had drills in disabling a vehicle, setting the limpet mines, and various field techniques to turn common objects into weapons. Lastly, we learned to live off the land and not consume poisonous plants.

As in one of today's TV reality shows, we were later divided into four small groups and set loose, without food, to survive on separate parts of the island for a week. We were each weighed, given a Springfield rifle with a clip of shells, and told we should return without losing more than ten pounds.

At first, we weren't too worried. We had trained in archery and laying animal snares. Goats ran wild, and large abalones nested on rocks just below the shoreline. But, like everything in OSS, it wasn't so simple. Our instructors scared the goats into the surrounding hillsides and carried off the only animal we were able to kill before we could retrieve it. We were reduced to diving for abalone, which we baked on an open fire, doused by rain. We huddled cold and miserable while it poured for two nights, but we were able to keep the fire going and the tough, chewy abalones baking. We were unable to find any edible tubers, so the abalone was our lone food for the week. Still, none of us lost more than five pounds, so we guessed our mission was a success.

But now we had a field test of a different sort. Our survival teams were issued $5, some civilian clothing, and a suitcase radio, then ordered to get into Mexico and transmit a message back to headquarters in Catalina. Besides the $5, we were given no documents or identification of any kind.

We discovered that the border was porous and busy enough to allow us easy access, with the sweaty border guards waving us through without asking for documentation. We rented a room in a squalid Tijuana hotel, plugged the transmitter into an outlet, stood the bedspring by the window, and transmitted a somewhat rude message back to Catalina. That was actually the easy part, as we could quickly be arrested trying to return to the United States sans identification.

Somehow we had to get money and documentation. We each placed collect phone calls to friends in the United States and implored them to wire $10 to the names we had registered under at the hotel. After the money arrived, we split up individually and started for the border. Crossing with the spylike radio suitcase during wartime security was a worry, but the customs inspector had apparently seen our black fiber cases before and passed our radio man through without stopping him.

Our Mexican task had evolved from an earlier test when trainees for the European theater had been schooled in the Baltimore area. The former agents had been given orders to get hired at a defense plant and steal classified documents or a blueprint. The primary target became the Martin Aircraft Company, where the incipient agents gained brief employment on a bomber assembly line and pilfered a few pages of classified aircraft designs.

Having graduated our training class, most of the members took transport from California to Calcutta, India. I was allowed to go back to Washington, then given leave to visit my parents in Albany for a couple of days before heading out on my first assignment.

I had wanted and pleaded for action, and now I was going to get it. A couple of months before, I had been lounging in Orlando. Now I found myself taking an Air Transport Command plane from Newfoundland to the Azores, then Dakar. From there I flew overnight across the Mediterranean to Karachi, before getting a ride to Calcutta, where I was unceremoniously dumped off at Dum-Dum Airport after dark.

And so began my adventuresome life as a secret agent. What should have a dull stopover on my way to China turned out to be my first accomplishment: revealing a double agent at our OSS branch in India.

3

China Station

I hailed a Calcutta version of a taxicab—some tin-can contraption in which mud splashed through rusty holes in the floor—and took a miserable two-hour drive to the OSS Calcutta office, where I found staff officers and secretaries involved in a raucous office party, drinking and dancing like they were at a New Year's Eve shindig. No one paid a modicum of attention to the unshaven, dirty, tired second lieutenant who entered their midst.

The billeting officer could not be found, and no one cared enough to help me search so that I could get a room. Finally, the staffer in question emerged from an upstairs room, lipstick smeared on his cheeks, and became coherent enough to find me the address where I could lodge with other transient officers. This was certainly not what I was expecting from the "elite" OSS agency I had come to know.

Finding a taxi along Chowringhee Road, then a quiet area of Victorian-era buildings in northern Calcutta, with the homeless bedded down in alleys, would not be easy. I walked through standing water, feeling things squish under my shoes that I preferred not to think about, until I found a lonely cab that would take me to the safe house where I found a bed.

If I wanted something exotic, I had found it. Sitar music from the house next door was my morning alarm clock. The music blended with the ululations of a muezzin from a nearby minaret. The sweltering air smelled of chicken excrement wafting from a coop next door.

The following morning, I found an ancient, nearly toothless Indian woman in the downstairs kitchen who served me strong coffee, Indian bread, and a tiny egg fried in rancid ghee. Luckily, a few other officers stumbled downstairs and made me feel a little less like I had entered some surreal dream.

Besides myself, there were several others waiting for transport over the Hump—the dangerous flight over the Himalayas to China—so we joined the Calcutta Swimming Club to cool off from the heat, dined at Firpos, a swanky place nearby with a three-piece string band, and drank at the bar at the Great Eastern Hotel, where Mark Twain had once stayed.

Time passed slowly in India, each second seemingly imbued with heat and humidity, so we had plenty of time to get to know one another. One of the other agents waiting transport to a far-flung post was an irascible hunchbacked Indian, a Morale Operations (psychological warfare) expert who had attended university in the United States, a country that he often maligned after getting a bit drunk. At first, I tried to avoid him, as every conversation turned into an argument. He despised our capitalist society, seemed to think we were all stupid and bourgeois, and had some bizarre notion that Americans looked down on Indians because we sat in chairs and most Indians sat on carpets.

My suspicions were doubly aroused when I saw him exit from a large storage room that he had no reason to enter. On the pretext that I was looking for a new mattress, I entered the room, and after scrounging through some old boxes, found a pile of papers with secret and top-secret classification stamps.

Heart beating hard, I found that the papers were lists of OSS agents in Burma, India, and China. I put them in my musette bag and immediately caught a taxi for OSS headquarters downtown, where I turned them in to the officer in charge. An investigation proved that the sour Indian had stolen them from the office, and given his predilection against capitalism and the United States, probably planned to hand them over to unfriendly hands. I was congratulated by the commanding officer, but little could be done to the spy, as he was a civilian.

Later, he staggered up to a table where a few of us were playing cards, looked at us in disgust, and berated us for being "white, bourgeois, capitalist officers."

"If you say another word," I growled, "we'll kill you and toss your body in the Hooghly River. That's the way we usually get rid of spies."

He paled and whirled away.

I never learned what became of the man, as a cholera outbreak swept through the city and we were quarantined for our safety before being transported to the airport to board a C-47 for our high-altitude flight.

Flying over the 530-mile section of 15,000-foot-high peaks was no one's favorite trip, but it was just about the only way into China since the Japanese had bombed the Burma Road. Additionally hair-raising was the fact that it was better to fly during inclement weather to avoid ravenous Japanese bombers operating out of their base in Myitkyina, Burma. It was said that "if you can see the end of the runway through rain and mist, then a takeoff is expected." From 1942 to 1945, a thousand men and six hundred ATC (Air Transport Command) planes were lost during the crossing.

It was a harrowing ride, with the engines hacking and coughing from lack of oxygen. Sometimes we fell a stomach-dropping hundreds of feet at a time, only to smack into a brick-hard updraft that made the plane shudder. I was extremely relieved to make it alive to Kunming Airport, where Lieutenant Ed Welch was waiting to inform me that, from what I told him, we had enjoyed a very uneventful trip.

"At least no one was shooting at you," he tossed off casually. "By the time I got here, our plane looked like it was made of Swiss cheese."

Welch took me to the OSS compound, Detachment 202, to report to the commanding officer before escorting me to downtown Kunming for my first authentic Chinese meal. We topped this off with a bottle of Tiger Jack's Home Brew, a revolting drink with high grain-alcohol content produced from who-knows-what that could have easily doubled for a laxative, a fact almost instantly proved by me. The only other drink available, I found out, was a locally produced mulberry wine that usually had similar effects. A bottle of scotch was apparently worth its weight in gold.

The commanding officer was a genial colonel named Dick Heppner, a Princeton alumnus and a peacetime member of General Donovan's law firm. Our field commander was Captain Walter Mansfield, also a member of Donovan's law firm, who became a New York judge after the war. Other members included Jack Singlaub, then a captain, who became a lifelong friend. Many people, including me, believe the eventual general should have become chairman of the Joint Chiefs or even taken a run for president later on. Additionally, we had Paul Helliwell, who would become OSS Secret Intelligence chief and later

a CIA agent before becoming involved in the Castle Bank scandal of
the 1970s, which laundered and moved secret funds for the agency,
and Lieutenant General Peers, who would later head the My Lai investigation during the Vietnam War. All in all, a pretty impressive roster.

On a lighter note, the chief of our small graphics unit was Paul
Child. His secretary, whom he later married, became the television
cooking sensation Julia Child and the subject of a best-selling novel
by Elizabeth MacDonald, *Undercover Girl*.

Under Chiang Kai-shek's reign, most of China was sectioned into
areas governed by warlords who enjoyed near autonomy. Our province, Yunan, was ruled by Tu Li-ming, whose common characteristic
with other such regional warlords appeared to be a reluctance to engage the Japanese.

It was a very complicated atmosphere. The Japanese at this time
were content to occupy major cities and towns in China, leaving vast
rural areas untouched. Mao Tse-tung was barely on our radar, heading a small Communist force based in Yenan, in northern China, where
he made occasional forays into the countryside to scavenge weapons
abandoned in the battlefields. Our role here was to operate outside of
Japanese strongholds, dynamiting convoys and bridges, infiltrating
Chinese agents into coastal cities to gather intelligence, and recovering
and returning Allied pilots shot down on the mainland or offshore.

OSS China was divided into four units: Secret Intelligence (collection), Special Operations (sabotage), Morale Operations (psychological warfare), and Operational Groups (commando units). Additionally,
we staffed a liaison office with the Chinese Nationalist army and
manned forward bases in Chengtu, Hsian, and Chihkiang. We also
liaisoned with the French army on Indonesia problems and with the
British about Malaya and Singapore.

One of our major problems was logistics. As Kunming was also
headquarters for the Fourteenth Air Force, the military was given top
priority and monopolized supply flights over the Hump. OSS received
our supplies secretly over what was left of the arduous 1,100-mile
Burma Road, running through three countries, from soggy, sweltering jungle to the famed 21-curve section snaking across arid, high
mountain ridges where drivers had to fend off hijackings and evade
Japanese bombings, landslides, and crumbling roadbeds. A month
after my arrival, the rest of my Catalina group arrived after they drove
trucks over the Burma Road from Bhamo to Kunming rather than
wait indefinitely for transport over the Hump.

I was soon dispatched by Colonel Helliwell to Hsian in central China to assess the work of our Korean asset, General Li Bum Suk, who was being maintained lavishly by OSS. General Li was an interesting character who spun a colorful yarn about the many intricate operations in which he planned to infiltrate his supporters into Korea, but it soon became clear to me that he was quite satisfied to preserve his current lifestyle, had done virtually nothing, and had not obtained any worthwhile intelligence.

My negative report enraged Colonel Helliwell, who was a great supporter of the general, and resulted in my first dressing-down. As punishment, I was soon dispatched to the Chengtu base, where scalding daytime temperatures often hit 120 degrees, melting insulation from aircraft wiring and forcing us to shave our heads, work at night, and sleep in a heat-induced stupor during the day.

From there I was sent back to Hsian with a team headed by Captain Bob Rodenburg—who would go on to own the Baltimore Colts football team—on a futile mission to encourage the local warlord to fight the Japanese. We surprised a half-dozen Japanese soldiers camped by a riverbank. We fired on them from a nearby bluff, killing all but one, who managed to flee. The following day, we were summoned to the enraged warlord's palace.

"If you weren't Americans," he sputtered, "I would have you executed. You have upset a very tenuous cease-fire with the Japanese. At any moment, they could sweep down on my forces and destroy us all."

Our intelligence differed from his. We knew that the warlord wasn't worried about getting routed by the Japanese. He was making a fortune selling them smuggled radios and electronics, for which he was paid in untraceable gold bars—local paper money being almost worthless except in major urban areas. Gold coins and gum opium were the preferred currency. In fact, when OSS agents parachuted into Indochina, they were issued bags of counterfeit French Louis d'or coins, newly minted by the U.S. Treasury. The coins were so heavy that the bags often split on impact, scattering treasure all over the ground.

This was to be the war's last summer, and we went on many missions, some successful, many not, as our efforts were often frustrated by the warlords who we were trying to help. One of the last operations, however, will always stick in my mind.

I volunteered to take part in an operation to reprovision an OSS station a few miles from Changsha that was suffering because it had not been resupplied in over a month. As we finished loading cargo aboard our C-47 under the supervision of a Captain Blackwell, we were joined by a lieutenant from the Fourteenth Air Force whose mission was to photograph the airdrop. Our pilot also hailed from the Fourteenth, but the copilot-navigator was an OSS officer.

As usual, we flew very low to the ground to avoid Japanese radar until we saw the markers spread on the ground by the team. Blackwell and the photographer both wore parachutes, but there weren't enough to go around, so I gripped the static line as the plane circled, and we kicked cargo out of the open door. We circled long enough to make sure the team found the containers before heading back.

Then our OSS navigator exited the cockpit carrying a tommy gun and addressed Captain Blackwell.

"How about we give the enemy a scare?" he said. "I'm itching to get some target practice with tommy here."

Blackwell wasn't too enthusiastic about the idea.

"C'mon, Captain. Just one magazine. The pilot's up for it," he implored.

Blackwell caught the bug and allowed the plan to continue. The pilot climbed several thousand feet to begin our run on the Japanese stronghold. Black and gray puffs of smoke exploded from the ground, and flak burst around us.

I sat down on the deck, my back against the forward bulkhead, and crossed my fingers as the plane went into a steep dive. Blackwell and the photographer were silhouetted in the open doorway. Just then a burst of flak rocked the plane. Blood spurt from the photographer's chest. He fell out of the doorway and pulled his ripcord. There was another spurt of flak; the captain took a bullet in the head, spun around, tried to catch the door frame, but fell out of the aircraft.

The plane roared over the rooftops with the navigator popping his tommy gun, then gained altitude. When we were out of enemy range, the navigator stalked aft with his weapon, chuckling. Then his face fell into a look of despair.

"What happened to the others?" he queried.

"What the hell did you expect?" I said. "Flak happened."

"That wasn't my fault," he replied.

I could barely look at him, because I did think it was his fault.

Back at base, I wrote a detailed account of the incident, which, along with the pilot's report, was used in a court-martial of the irresponsible OSS navigator. Sometimes the Ivy Leaguers did the stupidest things.

To add insult to this painful injury, we learned that due to the close proximity of the ground, our comrades' parachutes had not opened fully and they had plummeted to the street. They were seriously injured, and Japanese soldiers had flayed them alive, tying their skinned bodies to bamboo poles and parading them through the Changsha streets. When I thought back on it, I realized that the lack of additional parachutes had saved my life. As the flak exploded around us, I had been utterly convinced the plane was going to crash and would no doubt have parachuted out of the door after the other two men.

I was overdue to be rotated back stateside or even discharged under the army's point system when coded news came over our radio that the Enola Gay had dropped the first atom bomb and obliterated Hiroshima. There wasn't time to think about the moral implications of the strike. I volunteered to go with a team to Nanking, where we knew that the Japanese had committed one of the great atrocities of modern times, killing an estimated 250,000 to 300,000 men, women, and children, and where we had intelligence that they had murdered thousands of people in tests of biological warfare. We needed to get to Japanese strongholds like this before the enemy could enact some kind of brutal retaliation against the Allied prisoners of war.

4

The End of War

We were amazed that the Japanese did not immediately surrender after the destruction of Hiroshima, and we had no idea what kind of reception awaited us when we landed at Nanking Airfield between several rows of smoldering Japanese aircraft blistered with holes from Allied fire. We taxied and stopped to unload our plane far away from a large tent where a line of guards stood at attention outside the Japanese command.

After a while, a lone Japanese interpreter tentatively approached us. While the Japanese hierarchy had not yet capitulated, it was plain from the interpreter's message that the military ranks were awed by the stunning display of America's new nuclear weapon. In American-accented English, the man informed us that his commanding officer would be pleased to offer our unit some cold beer on this scorching August day.

Our commanding officer, Colonel Al Cox, still not knowing how things would shake out, made a disgusted sound, then replied as if we had a battalion of armed soldiers backing us up.

"Tell your commander that we do not drink with the enemy. He will provide us immediate transportation into the city and an escort to guarantee our safety and will find us suitable lodging."

The ruse worked, as the interpreter came rushing back in a few minutes with a small detachment of unarmed escorts to show us to a hastily evacuated barracks near the airfield. We created a base there, established headquarters in a hotel, then fanned out to various POW camps.

I will never forget the moment that we opened the gates at the first camp. The starving prisoners knew nothing about how the war was going. They stood frozen and incredulous when they saw our American uniforms and were told that the Japanese had been defeated. We immediately distributed rations to the emaciated men and women and their hungry children, many of whom had actually been born in the camps during the war.

A couple of days later, I was ordered to return to Kunming to join another team that hoped to repeat our success in Shanghai.

Shanghai was the largest, most Westernized and cosmopolitan city in China, home to thousands of English, French, and American traders who had begun appearing in the late 1800s, after the Opium Wars. As such, it also had more POW camps than anywhere else in the country.

Fresh with visions of nightmarish Nanking, our team, Sparrow II, filled two C-46 aircraft with supplies for the mission. We evicted Japanese soldiers from the American Club, took it over as head-quarters, mounted a radio antenna on the roof, and forced the reluc-tant Swiss consul to show us the camps, at which he was supposed to be protecting the rights of Allied prisoners.

We could instantly see what kind of job the ineffectual man had been doing. Conditions in the Shanghai camps were more dismal than anything we could have imagined. The incarcerated populace included thousands of military prisoners, as well as civilians. The camps stank of human waste and mountains of garbage and teemed with rats and flies. Food in the camps had been limited to thin soup and a couple of pounds of fish or meat per week per thousand or so inhabitants, who had been reduced to catching and eating rats, kit-tens, and puppies that had somehow squeezed through the fences.

Our army rations were much appreciated gourmet fare. Many children had never tasted milk other than their mothers' and relished the powdered stuff that we abhorred. The staggering amount of their deprivation caused our supplies to run out, so we raided the stores of the Japanese army to continue the relief effort.

Our small unit, working nearly around the clock, was soon ex-hausted from the effort. Luckily, now that OSS had proved it safe, General Wedemeyer's China troops arrived, followed by the navy cruiser, Nashville, which sailed into the harbor. We were summarily and happily relieved from most of our duties and became free to bask in the euphoric bacchanalia that marked postwar Shanghai.

But danger came in other forms. A group of OSS officers spent a small fortune buying a large stash of prewar scotch whiskey, filled their hotel rooms with cases of the precious commodity, and boasted about the money they would make from the fleet. Unfortunately, their plans were thwarted when one of the first drinkers of the scotch died in agony outside the American Club bar. In one last desperate act of a defeated army, the Japanese had poisoned random bottles of liquor before departing the city. Of course, all liquor became immediately suspect and worthless, as no foreigner dared partake. Accordingly, the black marketers went bankrupt, much to the general satisfaction of those of us who had not been invited to participate in the promising enterprise.

One night, I was visited in my quarters at the American Club by an older Russian woman and her adult daughter, who apparently wished to offer me a measure of gratitude for my part in saving her mother. While the mother had been incarcerated, the young blonde, Marusha, had been secreted outside of the city, where she had been spared the ordeal of the concentration camps. She would have looked beautiful to me even if I hadn't been cut off from female companionship as long as I had been.

The young Marusha confessed that she was married to a Russian but that it was just a wartime convenience and she didn't love him. Her gratitude to me resulted in a discreet affair, but the husband, Valantin, a Soviet spy working for the Tass news agency, was not easily tricked. The jealous man followed her and started shouting at us outside of our covered rickshaw one night. Glancing outside, I saw the enraged husband nearby, brandishing a fist at me. I told the rickshaw runner to get moving, dropped Marusha off where she could not be seen, and continued down the street.

The brawny Russian agent pursued the rickshaw until traffic slowed us to a stop. He whipped back the curtain and was stunned to find only me. He turned red with embarrassment and muttered an excuse, saying that he wanted to thank me for helping his mother-in-law and wanted to buy me a drink sometime. I hastily agreed, and he left looking a bit perplexed. From then on, Marusha and I continued the affair more clandestinely.

* * *

Once free, Shanghai quickly came back to life, and even the Shanghai *Post* started back into operation. Reading the paper one fateful day, I was shattered to see a headline proclaiming that President Truman had disbanded OSS. This was the culmination of a scathing internal battle in the highest echelons of government and geoglobal politicking to which we were not, at the time, privy.

It was all extremely complicated, as over the course of the war, OSS and the Russian secret police, the NKVD (People's Commissariat for Internal Affairs), had worked closely in Eastern Europe against the Nazis. The alliance soured, however, near the end of the war. For one thing, Donovan's second in command, Princeton alum Allen W. Dulles, was associated with the powerful Wall Street law firm Sullivan & Cromwell, which represented numerous German businesses that supported the Third Reich. Dulles personally handled many of these clients. Second, Stalin was outraged that OSS had made a decision to support and fund a former Nazi general, Reinhard Gehlen, helping him set up ratlines to assist thousands of high-ranking Nazis under the general's control to exit Germany after the war. In return, OSS gained control of the general's voluminous knowledge and secret files on Soviet agents. Gehlen would go on to become West Germany's spymaster during the Cold War.

The Gehlen affair divided the Roosevelt administration and the Donovan/Dulles duo. Presidential advisers wanted to reduce Germany to an agrarian society unable to wage war again; OSS was more worried about Stalin's expansionist plans—preferring to allow ex-Nazis to rebuild much of the German machine as a levee against the rising Crimson Tide. Adding to OSS's PR problems was a pervading congressional paranoia that the agency would become a sort of American gestapo, which they could abort by cutting funds to the money-hungry department.

In the end, Roosevelt died of a brain hemorrhage on April 12, 1945, and Harry Truman, elevated to the presidency, quickly disbanded OSS as soon as the war ended.

Before we were even able to digest the news and discuss it among ourselves, General Wedemeyer's headquarters ordered our group to report for duty in the regular army. The war was over, we had done our part, and we had other plans. We radioed Kunming and requested an air transport to evacuate us forthwith. Two planes airlifted us out the next day, flying across China to return us to base.

At Kunming, we were greeted by a much larger contingent of personnel than had been there when we had shipped out, as teams that had been operating far afield had been straggling back. Some had hiked hundreds of miles on foot. Others had been lucky enough to catch a plane or commandeer some Japanese vehicles. Among the arrivals was Captain Robert G. North, who had been operating commando style for several months in the North China countryside.

We packed our confidential files into cargo containers and filled the courtyard with our weapons, which were supposed to be turned over to Chiang Kai-shek's Nationalist forces. Instead, we later learned that Captain Helliwell's favored asset, General Tu Li-ming, swept through, stole the weapons, and sold them to Mao Tse-tung's communist forces, which were becoming braver now that the Japanese had been vanquished.

Soon the white peaks of the Himalayas emerged in the distance as we made our final trip over the Hump, where so many of our comrades lay in unmarked graves beneath the snow.

While I was offered the chance to join one of OSS's successor organizations, the Central Intelligence Group, I decided on other plans.

On my return to the United States, I first went to stay with my parents in Albany, where I found that I had a difficult decision to make between a Guggenheim fellowship in creative writing and a Rhodes scholarship, both of which I had been awarded. Weighing the two was difficult, but I opted against the idea of bad food and worse weather in England, accepting the Guggenheim stipend, somewhere between $1,500 and $2,500 a year, which could fund a grand lifestyle in Mexico, where I hoped to use the time to write another book.

Before I left, my father suffered a near fatal heart attack, so I stayed an extra six weeks, helping my mother care for him. Once assured that he was on the road to full recovery, I acquired a difficult-to-find postwar automobile from a state trooper who lived next door and drove the long haul down to Acapulco.

Acapulco was still just a sleepy seaside village, a virtually unknown, undeveloped paradise. My room at a quiet pension boasted an expansive view of the sparkling turquoise bay. I lounged and swam on Caleta beach in the mornings, and in the afternoons, after feasting on a lunch of fresh fish, plaintains, and exotic fruits, I finished my third novel, *Stranger in Town*.

A former OSS comrade, the commando Bob North, had also found a career in writing and was out in Hollywood banging out B-movie scripts for a producer named Sol Wurtzel. Bob urged me to team up with him to write original screenplays.

After I sent my book off to a publisher, I drove up to L.A. and joined North at his rented apartment near the Lakeside Country Club, where the scratch golfer earned almost as much playing as he did writing. OSS had recruited from America's brightest, and North was no exception. From an old California family, Bob had graduated Stanford—a year late, after being suspended for a prank—and had many close contacts he could draw on in the area.

He introduced me around town, where I met with agents, flirted with pretty young starlets at parties, and wined and dined with the best of them at the Brown Derby and Chasens. The fatal flaw in the plot was the unfortunate circumstance that the screenplays Bob and I churned out did not find a home. Several were optioned for small sums, but nothing was green-lighted (at which point you were able to really cash in), as the market had slowed down in response to a greater audience drifting toward television. Also, our scripts were, admittedly, not of the highest quality. Bob's income dropped as well, when Sol Wurtzel became involved in a dispute with 20th Century Fox and cut production on the films that Bob was working on.

Having caught a common Hollywood disease, EEI (expenses exceed income), I reluctantly paid respects to my friends and made a strategic retreat to Albany, where I hunkered down and wrote my fourth book. The result was a compact action-adventure novel set in the Bahamas, called *Bimini Run*, published by Farrar, Straus & Co. The advance was adequate enough for me to join the Fort Orange and Albany Country Clubs, where I enjoyed playing tennis, squash, and golf in good weather; I migrated to skiing and hunting when the seasons changed. When spring melted the snow in 1948, however, I started to dream of Paris and decided to figure out some way to move there. Yet another vague inkling that when turned into action, would prove to become a major milestone that would alter my life and become a stepping stone into a new agency called the CIA.

5

The Marshall Plan

To further my obsession to live in Paris, my father introduced me to his friend Paul Hoffman, who had been appointed by President Truman to head the Marshall Plan, a program to help Europe recover from the ravages of war. Hoffman suggested that I apply as a staff member to Ambassador Averell Harriman, who was the Paris administrator for the Economic Cooperation Administration (ECA), the coordinating agency.

I was hired by Harriman at Washington headquarters, where I noticed an attractive woman named Dorothy de Goutiere. As we conversed on our single Washington date, she proved to be witty and intelligent, and told me that she had spent the war years in Bern employed by the Treasury Department's Hidden Assets Division, which investigated concealed Nazi assets abroad. She had opened the treasury's new office in Shanghai and even served as the technical adviser on a Dick Powell film, *To the Ends of the Earth*, a story centered on the department's role in tracking down international narcotics traffickers.

While in Shanghai, she quit her job to marry a civilian pilot for China National Airways Corporation. Dorothy and her husband briefly led a nice life between Shanghai and her husband's family seat in the French concession Chandernagore, located near Calcutta. But the marriage quickly turned rocky and was now over, and Dorothy had initiated divorce proceedings in Florida. To make sure everything was finalized, she also planned to apply for a divorce in Paris. We agreed to meet again in the City of Lights, where I was scheduled to land several weeks prior to her arrival.

As soon as I arrived in Paris, I was plunged into a maelstrom of administrative and political activity. The personnel, like myself, had mostly been hired through their social or political ties with people in power, and they had varying degrees of competence. My immediate superior was an enthusiastic Democrat named Alfred Friendly, who had been endorsed by the *Washington Post* for a position with the Marshall Plan. His deputy, Waldemar Nielsen, had worked for the Ford Foundation and would later head up the CIA-sponsored Africa Foundation. I became good friends with several people, including Glen Moorhouse, an officer in the CIA Paris station.

Major players also included Kingman Brewster, a member of the legal staff, who would later become the president of Yale. A former chief of OSS operations in Europe, David K. E. Bruce, was the chief of the ECA mission. New Deal historian, Roosevelt confidant, and later speechwriter for John F. Kennedy Arthur Schlesinger Jr. often flew over to write or polish an important speech. We were also visited by Paul Hoffman's deputy, Richard Bissell, an economist from Yale, who would one day join the CIA and make his mark developing the U-2 spy plane program. Years later, I would work for him on the ill-fated Bay of Pigs invasion in Cuba.

Politics was always the main topic of conversation, and I slowly became aware that there was a major dichotomy between my conservative views and almost all of Harriman's Democratic staff. We clashed often on everyday issues such as the Soviet Union, which refused to donate to Europe's recovery fund and was becoming less friendly to American interests every day.

Ideology reared its ugly head when a high-level U.S. State Department officer, Alger Hiss, was accused of passing U.S. secrets to the Soviets. Many of the staff members knew Hiss personally and promoted his innocence; I almost came to blows with a few of the accused man's friends when I refused to uphold their stance. Not knowing the man at all, I argued, "Let a jury decide. That's what trials are for."

Came the angry reply: "You Republicans are so paranoid that you'd see the Red Menace in an apple!"

Sixty years later, the controversy still rages. Hiss, who died in 1996, steadfastly declared his innocence the rest of his life and appealed his case all the way to the Supreme Court. While avoiding conviction on most charges, he was eventually found guilty of perjury in 1950. The crusading young congressman who headed Hiss's trial was a virtually unknown, ambitious politician by the name of Richard Nixon.

Conspiracy theorists who believe Hiss was railroaded say that the prosecution aimed to stir popular support against Communism. The only witness against the accused was Whittaker Chambers, a *Time* magazine senior editor who supposedly received secret documents, which were proven to be typed on Hiss's Woodstock typewriter (which he had given away). *Time*, many people point out, was owned by Henry Luce, a major player in American politics who had ties to Allen and John Foster Dulles and was a champion of America's place as world leader. A popular theory, not beyond consideration now that Nixon's massive paranoia has come to light, is that prosecutors forged the evidence on another typewriter engineered to duplicate Hiss's typewriter. John Dean writes in his book *Blind Ambition* that Nixon even confessed to Charles Colson, "The typewriters are always the key. We built one in the Hiss case," though Colson claims that he has no memory of such a conversation, and it never came out on any tapes. Still, twenty-five years after the trial, Nixon's secret tapes show that he remained obsessed with the case, talking about it frequently.

At the time, however, none of that was known. I admired Nixon for blowing a horn that needed to be heard. Years later, my interest in the case and belief in Nixon's motives would prove to be the fatal link that would mark my introduction to the president, engineering my later downfall. But at that point, the Soviets did have a greater agenda, which was quickly established when Communist tanks isolated West Berlin in June 1948 and tried to take control of the city by cutting off food supplies to the populace.

The Truman administration authorized a continual airlift to the beleaguered city, which became more than a yearlong effort dubbed the Berlin Airlift. I flew on one of the first flights with Harriman, who visited personally to diagnose the city's present and future needs. It seemed like this might be the start of another war. Soviet aircraft buzzed the air corridors, and their soldiers refused to allow Allied convoys to enter the territory. The air bridge continued until September 1949 when the Soviets ended the crisis by lifting the blockade.

This, of course, was one of the many incremental steps leading up to the Cold War, and I noted that attitudes in our office did harden quite a bit toward the Soviets at this time.

Still, Ambassador Harriman called me into his office when he learned that the ECA was scheduled to host Senator John Foster Dulles—a conservative who had been shortlisted as secretary of state if Thomas Dewey had been elected over Truman—who was visiting Europe to help draft a treaty between Austria and the Western powers.

"Hunt," Harriman said, "the senator is going to want to go to several European cities, and I want you to take him around."

"Why me?" I queried.

"Because you're the only Republican I know," Harriman quipped.

Of course, I complied, as I was already quite knowledgeable about Europe, having previously visited many cities with the ambassador and his wife. On one occasion, I happened to meet General Albert Wedemeyer, our former China commander, in Vienna. The general, in turn, introduced me to a member of his party, a deputy assistant of war named Frank Wisner. Wisner was one of the few anti-Communist hardliners I met while in Europe, and a refreshing contrast, I thought, to the views of most of my colleagues. The fortuitous meeting would later become an important ingredient in the cocktail of my life.

Meanwhile, the relationship between Dorothy and me grew stronger every day, and by Thanksgiving—while the two of us and a few guests tried to make due over a ruined turkey—I was pretty sure I wanted to spend the rest of my life with this feisty woman.

The work of the ECA was always in turmoil with bizarre problems needing constant triage. In Vienna, I was ordered to make a documentary film about the Marshall Plan to combat rumors by the Austrian Communist Party that the food we were distributing was tainted. People were starving because they were afraid to eat the food. While in Austria, I became friendly with a man whom I'll call Jordan, a naturalized American citizen, originally from Belgrade. He had illegally smuggled his girlfriend into Vienna using his diplomatic passport and automobile license plates.

On what should have been a Sunday off, I was notified that as a representative of Harriman's office, I needed to go to the local morgue to identify someone who was thought to be Jordan. I had seen a lot of dead bodies during World War II, but was unprepared for this sight.

Jordan's face and skull had been smashed repeatedly, reduced to a jellied, almost unrecognizable mass of flesh. It must have been a painful death, added to by several oozing bayonet wounds in his body. I identified and claimed his body for the legation and reported the incident to the ECA mission chief.

An investigation uncovered the movements of Jordan's last day. He and his girlfriend had left their apartment in the early evening and driven into the Russian zone for dinner. While they were dining in a tavern, Russian soldiers, who had apparently been tailing them, burst inside and dragged the couple into the street, where they were forced into Jordan's car and ordered to drive deep into the Russian zone. The soldiers pushed the girlfriend out of the car within a few blocks, but Jordan was taken to a dark alley, where he was beaten to death with rifle butts before his car was stripped of tires and set ablaze. The flames attracted Austrian police, who brought the body to the morgue where I identified it.

It turned out that Jordan's girlfriend was a Russian double agent whose mission was to marry him and acquire U.S. citizenship. Jordan, however, was married and intended to end the affair when his wife arrived from New York. It was unclear who had ordered his murder— the girlfriend or her Soviet controllers—but this definitely contained the hallmarks of the bloody modus operandi used by the KGB to terminate a failed operation.

The sight of Jordan's cruelly murdered body and the duplicity of his mistress, whom he had brought to Vienna at the risk of his own job, served to heighten my antagonistic feelings toward the Soviets.

This was not an isolated incident, either. Once, the American minister invited me to a gala in honor of the Austrian cabinet minister and a lady deputy cabinet minister. The party waited for hours for the two to arrive, but they disappeared while driving through the Soviet zone, never to be seen again. Another tragedy involved the unsolved murder of an American naval attaché, Captain Eugene Karpe, whom I had befriended. He had come under suspicion by the KGB after visiting an American businessman who was in a Budapest jail, accused of spying. The visit was just one of friendship, however, as the two had attended the naval academy together.

I happened to see Karpe one winter evening in the Bristol lobby as he prepared to go to the opera before leaving on the Arlberg-Orient Express to Paris, en route to Washington for reassignment. He was ecstatic to be leaving three years of Iron Curtain duty and was looking forward to going back to sea. I shook his hand warmly and wished him well.

His brutalized body was found in a tunnel near Salzburg the next day. His face was pulverized so badly that he could only be identified by the passport in his pocket. Karpe's murder was every bit as vicious as Jordan's, and I took both personally. From these and several other incidents, my revulsion for everything Soviet took hold.

I wasn't the only one who felt this way. An American army private marched into a hotel adjacent to the Bristol that was occupied by Soviet officers, snatched a submachine gun from a guard, and rushed into the lobby, where he emptied the magazine indiscriminately on men and women before he was killed by return fire. No one ever learned what set him off.

On a more positive note, my relationship with Dorothy was going well. She continued to work with Harriman in Paris, however, so we phoned constantly. The only problem was that there were so many Cold War taps draining power on the line in a dozen stations across Europe that every time we talked, our words became increasingly inaudible until we were forced to hang up.

For Christmas, she met me in the Tyrol for skiing. We stayed at the wonderful five-star Zurserhof hotel—still among the world's finest resorts—with several young married couples from Paris and Vienna. We had a blissful holiday, marred only by my breaking my thumb while skiing. The thumb was badly treated by a doctor who I later learned hated Americans, and it never healed properly.

While life in Vienna was enjoyable, I missed Dorothy so much that I decided to rejoin her in Paris, turning down a promotion that would have kept me in Vienna.

When I returned to my former office, I found that Friendly's staff had increased and that my duties were being carried out by a half-dozen new arrivals. There didn't seem to be much of a job for me; with the reelection of President Truman, it appeared that the ECA office had no place for a token Republican.

After the war, a great wave of expatriate writers, artists, and students overflowed the streets of Paris. So did spies. At one point, I realized almost nobody was who they said they were. Case in point: I set

up my friend, Pinky Walsh, from OSS China days, with my former
secretary, Barbara Rurup, after which the two became an item, often
double-dating with Dorothy and me. Walsh was in Paris ostensibly to
study for a doctorate at the Sorbonne, but I soon figured out that he was
establishing cover in the French student milieu. He was probably one of
many dozens of spies from different countries attending the university.

Somewhere around Easter, Frank Wisner visited Paris and took a
temporary office at the embassy. Apparently remembering our mutual
agreement over Communist intentions, he asked to meet with me.

Wisner, born in 1910 in Laurel, Mississippi, could not hide his
Southern accent. He had a patrician look, was a bit stiffly postured
and thin lipped, but his natural expression made him look like he was
perpetually smiling to himself about something he knew and you didn't.
His anti-Soviet stance, it was said, bordered on obsession, and Arthur
Schlesinger is quoted as saying about Wisner, "He was already mobi-
lizing for the Cold War. I myself was no great admirer of the Soviet
Union, and I certainly had no expectation of harmonious relations
after the war. But Frank was a little excessive, even for me."

"I know you've been with OSS," Wisner said after some small
talk. "And I've heard good things about you from mutual friends. I'm
setting up a new organization inside the CIA called the Office of Policy Coordination, and it'll be something different, maybe something
up your alley. OPC won't just gather intelligence. We'll be what
America needs in this Cold War, an action arm. You're a man of
action. Aren't you, Hunt?"

I told him the idea was appealing but that I had gotten my fill of
government service in ECA. "It's very frustrating," I said. "So many
levels of red tape to cut through to get anything done!"

Wisner made a dismissive gesture with his hand. "It won't be the
same in OPC. You'll have a lot more freedom to be proactive. We
need people with initiative, people like . . ." He went on to mention
several of my OSS colleagues who had already joined. "Now, if you're
happy at ECA . . . ," he intoned.

"You know I'm not, sir," I said.

I was tired of ECA's ambivalent attitude toward Communism, of
the Al Friendly and Arthur Schlesinger Jr. types, of seeing my friends
beaten to death and being unable to do anything more about it than
lodge an official protest that was, no doubt, greeted with laughter.

Wisner said that my field clearance would take as long as three
months, and I would have to resign from ECA before I could offi-

cially file my application. I did have Dorothy and my somewhat enjoyable lifestyle to consider, however, so we parted after I told him I would give his invitation serious thought. I also didn't like the idea of having to spend a quarter-year without drawing an income.

The possible problem of how to spend three months without earning a paycheck was solved, however, when my Guggenheim Fellowship novel, *Stranger in Town*, became a paperback best-seller, affording me the freedom I needed to tender my resignation. I had hoped to spend the three months in Paris but instead learned that it would be better if I returned to the United States.

Dorothy was resentful that I could even think of leaving, and our parting at Orly Airport was strained.

"I don't know why you won't take me with you. . . . Or don't you love me?" she asked.

I didn't like it any more than she did, but she couldn't understand. Additionally, I was not allowed to tell her or anybody what I was doing. "Honey, you know I love you," I told her. "But without a steady income, I can't support a wife."

She crossed her arms petulantly. "If you loved me, you would take me with you."

"It's not that simple. I don't have a job. I can't promise security when I can't even foresee it. Maybe after I . . ."

"'Maybe after' could be too late. It's not just money. Is it, Howard?"

"That's the only reason, darling."

"Then I'll take the first plane tomorrow. If you can't find a job, I'll keep on working."

I kissed her reluctant lips and raised her chin to make her look me in the eyes. "We're both used to luxuries," I told her. "You know that. What would our life be like jammed together in a one-room efficiency—with your dog?"

Her body tensed. "I don't care about that," she said stubbornly. "I just want to be with you. If you loved me enough, you'd be willing to take a chance. I am."

A French voice crackled unintelligibly over the loudspeakers but was unquestionably calling my flight. I kissed Dorothy again. She was unyielding. "Are you willing to have it end like this?" she asked.

"I don't want it to end at all," I told her. "But I don't know why you can't see things my way."

"Perhaps because I'm in love and you're not."

I shook my head. "Maybe it's because I'm practical and you're not."

"You know that isn't so," she insisted. Then she gave me a desperate hug and flung herself away.

"Will you write?" I called to her back. But she didn't answer.

I boarded the plane like so many men before and after me, knowing that their heart, their mind, their duty, and their wallet were all on divergent paths.

I completed my final processing out of ECA in Washington and joined my parents in Albany. I figured I would use the three months wisely and sat down at the typewriter. When I was several chapters into a new book, my Hollywood agent called to say that Warner Brothers had bought *Bimini Run* for the small fortune of $35,000. I ran to the Western Union office and sent off a short cable to Dorothy: "Will you marry me?" I then went to meet with Warner Brothers in Los Angeles, where I stayed with Bob North and his new bride, Maxine.

Amazing what a good sale will do for a man. The world of motion pictures was suddenly much more receptive to my talents than it had been when I had been forced to leave town with the dreaded EEI syndrome. Warner Brothers paid me good money to do rewrites on some unremarkable films, while Dorothy put her affairs in order to join me from Paris.

While staying with Bob North, I mentioned Wisner's new organization, which interested him immediately, so, of course, I told him that I would recommend him to my new bosses.

After I finished with a few of my projects, I flew back to Albany. Soon afterward, Dorothy and her dachshund, Coffee, arrived at Idlewild Airport via Air France. I dreaded introducing her to my parents who were opposed to the marriage because they didn't know Dorothy. She was a divorcée and, worse still, a Catholic. But as an only son, I felt that they would never like any woman I brought home, even if she was a virginal Mayflower descendant offering a huge dowry.

I told my father, "You and Mother are going to have to accept the inevitable. Why not do it now and cut down on all our suffering?"

But my parents couldn't get past what they considered Dorothy's fatal flaws. Instead of having a joyous wedding in Albany, we married in Millbrook, New York, and spent our first night at the Sherry-Netherland Hotel in New York. From there, I drove my recently acquired white Cadillac convertible to Sea Island, Georgia, where we enjoyed our honeymoon.

Of course, our splendid time was interrupted by an official government cable ordering me to report immediately to CIA headquarters in Washington, D.C. Grudgingly, my new wife and I sped north, where I began a career in intelligence that was to occupy me for the next twenty-one years.

6

The CIA

The CIA did not come into existence in a full-blown capacity. It evolved bit by bit after Truman fired "Wild Bill" Donovan and his pack of adventuresome OSS "amateurs." Before the bloodbath, however, Donovan had submitted a proposal for a new agency to President Roosevelt that would have operated under the supervision of the president to "procure intelligence both by overt and covert methods," and "at the same time provide intelligence guidance, determine national intelligence objectives, and correlate the intelligence material collected by all government agencies." But his plan also envisioned that this new agency would be a civilian affair that would have "no police or law enforcement functions, either at home or abroad."

Arguments for and against the proposed agency raged in many political arenas. The military, the State Department, and the FBI all vied to have power over this powerful new department.

With no solution in sight and the United States in sad need of collated intelligence in a complicated postwar world, Truman bypassed the arguments by establishing the Central Intelligence Group in January 1946 with a directive to coordinate and supplement U.S. current intelligence from various departments but not to supplant it. To this end, Truman created the National Intelligence Authority, a junta comprised of the secretary of war, the secretary of state, and a presidential representative. He then appointed the deputy chief of Naval Intelligence, Rear Admiral Sidney W. Souers, as the first director of Central Intelligence. Just over a year and a half later, both groups were dissolved.

Then, effective on September 18, 1947, Congress ratified the National Security Act, which established both the Central Intelligence Agency and the National Security Council. Essentially, Congress followed Donovan's original concept, charging the CIA with the responsibility of coordinating, gathering, and disseminating national intelligence that affected the nation's security.

By 1949, the troubled position of director of Central Intelligence (DCI) had devoured both Souers and the charming, well-connected air force lieutenant general Hoyt S. Vandenberg, settling on the third DCI, Admiral Roscoe Hillenkoetter. Hillenkoetter, however, emphatically opposed covert action, believing that the deliberately vague mandate from Congress did not grant him the appropriate authority.

Such qualms did not extend to the Kremlin, however, which had riddled the FBI with spies and maintained operations in theaters throughout the world. To fight the ensuing Cold War, George Kennan, head of policy planning at State, proposed the creation of a bureau that would oversee actual covert operations. The agency would be directed by the State Department, which would appoint its director; but during wartime, the agency would report to Defense. In order that the government could disavow any embarrassing political fallout, this new bureau was to be housed inside the CIA.

Under Kennan's guidance, State nominated Frank Wisner, a powerful Wall Street lawyer and a good buddy of Kennan's, to head this new department of covert activity, whose nonthreatening title was the Office of Policy Coordination (OPC), which I was set to join. From inception, the CIA had been a quagmire of inner-agency politicking, and it became immediately obvious that Frank Wisner's Office of Policy Coordination would not get much cooperation from directors in other sections. In many ways, for instance, this new department encroached on the turf of the Office of Special Operations (OSO), which stoutly resisted OPC's development. The difference was, however, that the OSO was mandated to *gather* covert intelligence, and OPC was formed to *utilize* it against the enemy, which, of course, was considered to be international Communism in all of its worldwide manifestations.

Additionally, as OPC had been designed in great measure by Secretary of Defense James Forrestal, Wisner had amassed a great amount of political clout, more so than his nominal boss, Admiral Hillenkoetter, whom Wisner regarded as a weakling. In addition to Forrestal, Wisner's powerful backers included Averell Harriman, John J. McCloy (assistant secretary of war, later president of the World Bank and Chase Manhattan Bank), General William S. Draper (undersecretary of war), and Secretary of State George C. Marshall (of the Marshall Plan).

At headquarters, among the government buildings astride Washington, D.C.'s Reflecting Pool, OPC established three subdivisions: Paramilitary Operations, Political and Psychological Warfare, and Economic Warfare. I was assigned to the Political and Psychological Warfare staff, headed by Joseph Bryan III, a navy veteran and a writer. Besides me, Bryan gathered an interestingly eclectic staff, including writer Finis Farr; Philadelphia investment banker Gates Lloyde; Lewis "Pinky" Thompson, a New York and New Jersey financier; and Carlton Alsop, a former movie producer and Hollywood agent. All except Alsop and myself were Princeton alumni. The staff was soon joined by artist-illustrator Hugh Troy, who then formed another small coterie of political cartoonists and polemicists who would generate a large amount of material that found its way into newspapers around the world.

Wisner quickly established stations in various overseas embassies, another move destined to generate inner-agency friction, as they often paralleled previously existing OSO detachments. The embassies also had a negative attitude toward this continuing invasion of agents they were forced to host. But since no one wanted to openly oppose Wisner, given his political status, resistance eventually proved futile.

As far as OPC was concerned, there was no time to waste trying to reverse Communist incursion into Europe and Asia, and we hit the ground running. A top mission in Rome was to stop Italy's leftward trend and defeat the Communists at the polls in the imminent Italian elections.

Al Cox, late of Kunming, was ordered to Taiwan to advise Chiang Kai-shek's shaky nationalist government, which had recently fled there to evade Mao Tse-tung's Communist forces on the mainland. Later, Cox became the president of Civil Air Transport, the CIA-owned and operated nationalist airline.

While a high-level agreement with the British forbade the CIA from conducting unilateral operations in the United Kingdom, one of our agents, Merritt Ruddock, was dispatched to London to work with the British equivalent of OPC. For obvious reasons, no such agreement was made with any other European power, where our efforts were aimed at destroying Communist influence in labor organizations, in the press, and among college students. We funded pro-Western political and labor union candidates, founded front groups to counter long-established Communist organizations, and even started Radio Free Europe, complete with a board of distinguished directors. Such operational expenditures grew so large that Marshall Plan funds, known as candy, were required to supplement our efforts.

Over the next couple of years, Hillenkoetter ended up spending almost as much time testifying in front of Congress about CIA blunders as he did directing them. His anemic leadership came to an abrupt end after North Korea surprised U.S. intelligence by attacking South Korea. Lieutenant General Walter Bedell Smith, a hardened battlefield veteran who had been chief of staff to General Eisenhower—now the president—in World War II, took over as DCI on October 7, 1950. Smith—so different from his predecessor—instantly antagonized Wisner by trying to wrest control of covert ops from OPC and bring it under direct CIA management. To cement his power base, Smith brought in the ever-present OSS opportunist Allen W. Dulles as his deputy. Together the two would win the internal power struggle and eventually transform the CIA into the agency it has become today.

At the time I was hired, however, Wisner's OPC was still a powerful entity. During World War II, a presidential edict had made Latin America an FBI protectorate, tasking the agency with guarding against Nazi or Communist incursion in the territory. After international espionage was taken over by the CIA, most of the station chiefs just switched over from the FBI to the new agency. These FBI retreads, as we called them, continued to conduct business as usual, collecting secondhand intelligence through the local police, and were openly hostile to the idea of conducting any kind of covert operations. Similarly, OSO was generally satisfied to peruse and file the intelligence without action. Wisner, however, was eager to put that intelligence to work.

Luckily, my OSS experience allowed me to be excused from the more routine courses that most new CIA agents had to pass after being hired. Instead, I was able to study advanced techniques of counterintelligence and agent handling, learning techniques about how to debrief a friendly source, such as one of our own, or how to interrogate an enemy agent. This included instruction about how to analyze a person's type of character—each of which had a dominant trait, such as aggression, obstinacy, greed, self-centeredness, guilt-ridden, and so forth—then determine his or her specific goals to alter our questioning and personality to suit the situation.

After that, Joe Bryan asked me to set up the first OPC-style training courses in covert political and psychological warfare. At one point, in the spring of 1950, I shared an office with a marine colonel, Bob Cushman, who had been assigned to the CIA. Much later, he would go on to become a commandant of the Marine Corps and come back into my life as a peripheral figure in the Watergate scandals.

At OPC, I also met and frequently consulted with Dr. James Burnham, a former philosophy professor and a prominent 1930s Trotskyite who had been one of Joe Bryan's Princeton classmates. Burnham, however, had gone through an ideological metamorphosis and in 1941 published *The Managerial Revolution*, a best-seller detailing his "science of politics," which theorized that a new ruling class of "managers" would usurp the dominance of both capitalists and Communists alike. The critically acclaimed book was widely discussed and gave him access to intellectual circles around the world. By virtue of his former Communist background, current fame, and, of course, OSS employment during the war, Burnham had extensive contacts throughout Europe and was a particularly astute authority on domestic and international Communist Party front organizations.

Through Burnham, I was eventually to meet a young Yale graduate, William F. Buckley Jr., whose seminal work, *God and Man at Yale*, stirred great controversy within Eastern academic circles and marked the emergence of one of the most influential conservative thinkers of our time. Like myself, Buckley was recently married and a committed and articulate anti-Communist. He was, Burnham told me, looking for the optimum way of working against the Stalinists. Moreover, Buckley was trilingual, speaking English, Spanish, and French. These were all impressive traits, and I was determined to find a way of utilizing his talents.

Life was extremely chaotic, and I juggled the difficult work and family life with as much agility as I could. Luckily, Dorothy, having been exposed to the sort of work I was doing in her former job, understood the demands that it put on me. We were overjoyed when she became pregnant soon after our wedding, and grief-stricken when she miscarried. Her French maid hated the isolation of Alexandria and threatened to leave, so we bought a house on Dent Place in Georgetown and soon acquired a mate for Dorothy's dog, Coffee, named Kuchen.

We enjoyed entertaining when possible, and Dorothy put together a very nice home to do so. In addition to being descended from the presidential families of Adams and Harrison, she was one-eighth Oglala Sioux and brought to our home numerous Sioux artifacts handed down from her mother's family.

Our above-average lifestyle was augmented by my writing habit, which continued to bring in a paycheck when the Fawcett Publishing Corporation began publishing paperback originals under the Gold Medal imprint, signing me to write several books at previously unheard-of guaranteed rates. I banged out the lucrative books in record time and asked for more contracts.

It was OPC's intention to break the OSO stranglehold on Latin America, so I volunteered to open a station in Mexico City, as I had lived in Mexico before and was fluent in Spanish. My suggestion was accepted in late summer of 1950, forcing me to back-burner the book I was writing and start forming an operational plan for Mexico. The first thing I did was process myself into the Department of State as a Foreign Service reserve officer and begin interviewing recruits to work for me as agents outside the embassy.

My premier candidate, of course, was Bill Buckley, who readily agreed, so I set about working out the details of his cover. I also hired several other agents, including a woman. I was assigned a bilingual Puerto Rican secretary, Isabel Cintron, who had previously worked for Naval Intelligence.

By this time, my wife was pregnant again, and her doctor assured us that we should expect a normal delivery. Meanwhile, our French maid became increasingly difficult, so we decided to fire her, offering her return passage to Paris. Instead, she joined the household of Hugh D. Auchincloss, the stepfather of Jacqueline Kennedy Onassis, across the Potomac in MacLean, Virginia.

As news of OPC's new office in Mexico leaked out to the rest of the agency, Wisner was given clear signals that we were not welcome. He called me in for a meeting one day, looking shaken after an argument with a colleague.

"Looks like you're not going to have clear sailing down south," he told me bluntly. "Seems like Hoover's jealous and dead set against us going into Mexico. Thinks we'll be stepping on his toes."

I knew the FBI had a large and active station operating out of the Mexico City embassy under the title of Office of the Legal Attaché.

"Well, we pretty much haven't expected an engraved invitation to join the party," I said.

Wisner smiled. "That's what I like about you, Hunt. Always ready for a challenge. But we shouldn't have to expect trouble from players on our own team. They've already had a lot of problems between them and the OSO station chief there who's a former bureau agent, and they apparently hate each other, so you're walking into a snake pit."

"I guess I'll have to practice speaking in tongues," I joked.

I took his warning seriously, though, as I waited for a letter to codify my specific instructions and the terms of my mission in Mexico.

About then, my OPC group conceived what we thought was a splendid idea to covertly subvert Communist propaganda around the world. We had our Hollywood team of Finis Farr and Carlton Alsop negotiate film rights to George Orwell's book *Animal Farm*, a satire about a group of animals that stage a workers' revolution, taking over the farm from their human owners. Their initial euphoria and collective zeal is eventually crushed by the power-hungry pigs, leaving the animals as badly off as they were under their former drunken human master. The work is a barely concealed anti-Communist fable written by Orwell after he became disillusioned with Soviet Communism.

Our plan was to produce an animated film version, carefully tweaked to heighten the anti-Communist message, and distribute it throughout the world in the hope that it would be seen by parents and children alike. Rights were successfully obtained from Sonia Orwell, but the difficult production, made slower by the albatross weight of accountants, budgeters, and administrators from within and outside OPC, would eventually take four years to complete. Additionally, to compete with Disney fare, jokes and a happy ending were introduced, somewhat dulling the message. Still, the film—unknown by anybody to be CIA-sponsored propaganda at the time—was a critical and box-office success, paving the way for other CIA-sponsored films. Following the success of *Animal Farm*, the CIA would also fund a live-action film of Orwell's *1984*, another antitotalitarian screed.

Nonoperational OPC bean counters and administrators made work increasingly harder, resulting in the resignation of our creative thinker, Joe Bryan, who eventually left in disgust.

As my move to Mexico became imminent, I was ordered to take various courses on station administration and fiscal management, writing reports and current studies of the international Communist government, which made me worried about just how assertive and daring OPC was going to be allowed to be. It seemed like the bureaucrats and paper pushers were going to take this over, as they had so many levels of government—exactly what OPC had been styled against. It seemed like they were trying to turn me from a secret agent into a secret midlevel manager.

Our trip to Mexico was moved up because Dorothy's doctor advised us that given her previous miscarriage, she should not travel beyond a certain date. I forwarded this information to my superiors and quickly started looking for a renter to take over our house. Typical government bureaucracy slowed our diplomatic passports, which arrived so late that we almost missed our flight.

The chaotic day was made more difficult by the sudden arrival of two insurance investigators who questioned us about the mental health of our former French maid, who had become so unhappy at the Auchinclosses' estate, Merrywood, that she tried to commit suicide by jumping off a balcony. She was being cared for at Georgetown Hospital, and the investigators were trying to figure out the precipitating events for her actions. We told them what we could, cut short our interview as the taxi arrived, and departed for National Airport.

We changed planes in Dallas and flew south to Mexico City, where we would spend the next three years and where our two daughters would be born.

7

Mexico

In Mexico City, we rented a small furnished apartment on a some-what busy commercial street not far from where the embassy was located, then I presented myself to the OSO station chief and to Chargé d'Affaires Paul Culbertson at my earliest opportunity. Since I was ostensibly a part of the foreign office, my wife, even in her advanced state of pregnancy, made the necessary social calls on the other embassy wives.

While Culbertson was pretty amiable, telling me that he and his wife were "as easy to get along with as a pair of old shoes," the embassy itself was short of space, and I was shown an ugly storeroom that was to be OPC's office. True to J. Edgar Hoover's instructions, the former FBI station left nothing usable when they vacated their offices to make way for the CIA. My secretary and I cleaned up our new space, then borrowed some chipped government-issued metal desks, file cabinets, and threadbare chairs to make it serviceable. I hoped the arrangement would be fairly transient, as the entire delegation was scheduled to move into a new building downtown along the Paseo de la Reforma.

The embassy was in a state of transition, expecting the arrival of a new ambassador, William O'Dwyer. O'Dwyer was a charismatic and somewhat controversial figure who had been born in Ireland, then worked his way up from day laborer to become a New York City policeman before entering law school. As a lawyer, he built up a successful practice in Brooklyn, New York, eventually serving as a judge and later as the district attorney, becoming a national celebrity after his prosecution of "Murder, Inc.," the cadre of vicious hit men who worked for organized crime. He was elected mayor of New York City in 1946, in which capacity he served for four years, until he resigned after a major police scandal that included accusations that he had associations with organized crime members. Among his lasting accomplishments was getting the newly formed United Nations to make its home in New York City. O'Dwyer cashed in some political chips after his mayoral resignation, and Truman appointed him ambassador to Mexico, where he would have a short tenure until his mob ties caught up with him.

At the time, however, O'Dwyer's Irish extroversion and ex-model wife were well received by the Mexicans and embassy staff. Interestingly, during my bachelor days in New York City, I had actually dated his wife, Elizabeth Sloan Hipp Simpson, among several models I had been going out with at the time. We did not broadcast the past relationship, and there was no direct fallout, but my wife often found reasons for us to turn down social invitations from the couple.

Little by little, my outside agents began to trickle into town. Among the first was Bill Buckley, who arrived with his pregnant wife, Pat. She and my wife got along well and became great friends, as did Bill and I. We frequently found excuses to exchange information over lunch at the only decent French restaurant in the city, La Normandia.

I soon became accustomed to recruiting assets to help gather information. I hunted for prospects at embassy functions, which were generously stocked with leading American businessmen in Mexico. If they were involved in an area of industry that might prove useful, I would draw them into conversations, steer the subject toward this or that political view, possibly find out whom they had voted for or how they viewed America's position in the world. I had those whom I deemed useful name-checked in Washington, D.C. If no abnormal associations or legal hassles were uncovered that might make them a security risk, I asked for permission to contact them as informants.

Once a person had been recruited, he was often able to help identify other Americans and Mexicans who could prove useful. A casual meeting would be arranged, during which I would go through the usual steps. This procedure permitted me to acquire a large group of external assets in a relatively short amount of time. Most of the informants were businessmen, but occupations varied. There was even a popular Catholic priest who worked in the anti-Communist movement at one of the universities.

I met one asset on the tennis court, a businessman from Pheonix, Arizona, named Stanley. After a routine name-check with headquarters, I invited Stan to work with me against Communism in Latin America. He agreed, and we began bird shooting together: ducks and an occasional goose. Stan was great at introducing me to his friends who might qualify as agents, which added to my now fully staffed station.

Over the years, Stan remained a friend and a shooting companion while he worked for successive station officers. In retrospect, Stan was one of the most responsive and productive agents with whom I ever worked, and he set a high standard of performance.

Dorothy's due date approached, forcing us to start looking for a more comfortably sized home in the Lomas de Chapultepec district overlooking the city from the west. Our belongings had finally reached Veracruz by ship, from where they were trucked to Mexico City. The gorgeous white convertible Cadillac I had splurged on with the *Bimini Run* film money, however, was conspicuous by its absence.

It took an investigation from the consulate and a conference with the Mexican customs chief to locate the car, which was hidden at the rear of a customs shed. Whatever official had sought to purloin the vehicle had apparently caused a load of sand to be dumped on it out of spite. From under the sand, the tattered remains of the top fluttered in the wind. The white paint had been blasted from the surface by a few days of bad weather.

After bailing the sand out of the car, finding a new battery, and filling the tank with a few gallons of Pemex gas, I was surprised to find that the engine started readily. Under a sweltering sun, I drove the car slowly back to Mexico City, stopping frequently at roadside stands to drink cold bottled beer to avoid the parasites I had found prevalent in many of Mexico's nonalcoholic drinks. I reached my destination after dark and left the car in a commercial garage next door to our humble apartment.

I reported the news to Dorothy, including the dismal fact that the damage was of such a nature that our U.S. insurance would probably not cover it. The next morning when I went to retrieve the car to bring Dorothy to our new house, I turned the corner to find that the poor

Cadillac had received more insults to its injuries. The night attendant had decided to test the merchandise but had been unfamiliar with driving an automatic transmission. Unable to stop the car, he had headed for the exit and rammed it against the lamppost across the street.

The misfortune turned in our favor when the garage's insurer had the car repaired at the Cadillac dealership, where the front end was fixed, the car repainted, and a new top thrown in.

Dorothy and I now had another domestic dilemma—stay in our apartment until the baby arrived or move to our new house, which needed work before we could move in, with the concern that the new addition might catch us only half unpacked. Our decision was soon made easy, however.

Below us was a club that played mariachi and samba music until late at night, making it hard to sleep. But one evening the jukebox must have been broken, for in the relative silence, we suddenly heard the sounds that the music had previously disguised—the unmistakable rhythmic creaking of beds with the accompanying grunts, gasps, and other sounds of men and women together.

"Oh my God," Dorothy said. "Is that what I think it is?"

I had to laugh. "I think we're living over a cathouse!"

By the next evening, after a long day of unpacking, we were sitting exhausted in the single bedroom that we had managed to put together in the new house—and just in time. Suddenly, Dorothy gave me a strange look.

"Honey . . . ," she said, and stopped.

"Yes, what?" I asked, perplexed.

"I'm afraid you're not going to get a good night's sleep tonight, either."

"No? Do you hear something?" I asked, striving to listen to whatever noise was disturbing my wife.

She smiled a bit shyly. "No, sweetheart. But you're going to be up all night because you've got to get me to the delivery room—right now."

Like any expectant father, I drove my wife at breakneck speed to the hospital—the British Cowdray—and waited anxiously in the anteroom until a pink light signified that we had a daughter: Lisa Tiffany Hunt.

Relations between me and some of the other personnel started to become a bit strained when I learned that the OSO station chief had basically been spying on me by having our radio handler show him all of my dispatches before they were sent. My division chief in Washington complained that my requests for name-checks were too numerous for his staff to handle (to which I pointed out that my OPC station and its projects were breaking new ground). Relations with the local FBI staff were frigid at first, too, but warmed up after a few of the bureau agents realized that I shared their enthusiasm for hunting and fishing. Our friendship was cemented when I helped finance and form a largely FBI duck-hunting club about forty-five minutes from the embassy. The OSO bureau chief could only simmer with jealousy noticing the new cooperation between OPC and the FBI.

Still, the cooperation did not extend to some delicate operations. At one point, one of the FBI agents inquired if I knew the whereabouts of the former Spanish Republican guerrilla General Valentín González, known by the name "El Campesino." The FBI had been charged with locating him to testify before the congressional subcommittee investigating the international Communist movement. A member of the Communist Party, the general had fought in the Spanish Civil War against the nationalist army. A rough, untutored peasant, he was famed for conceiving brilliant guerilla tactics and was notorious for his brutality. When the Communist side capitulated and the war ended, the Soviets welcomed El Campesino into their country, along with thousands of refugees, and more importantly almost all of Spain's gold reserves, which the general had helped capture in Madrid.

Like so many others, González became disillusioned with Communism, especially after he had been imprisoned and forced into hard labor digging subway tunnels in Moscow. The wily guerilla genius engineered his escape to Iran and eventually surfaced in Paris, where our station identified him and suggested that the born-again capitalist write his autobiography. Unbeknownst to the FBI, OPC considered this a great opportunity to help discredit the Communist movement, and I had him squirreled away in a Cuernavaca safe house, where he was telling his life story to a writer, Julian Gorkin.

After all this effort, we did not want to see González testify in front of Congress, where the glare of Washington publicity might diminish his credibility. His location remained secret until after the book was published by G. P. Putnam's Sons in 1952, under the title *El Campesino: Life and Death in Soviet Russia*, one of the first personal revelations of Soviet and Stalinist terror and barbarity. It was translated into many languages and found a great Spanish market, selling well throughout Latin America. Later, after Castro took over Cuba, I noticed *La Vida y La Muerte en la URSS* prominently displayed in Havana bookstores, but copies were quickly confiscated and destroyed.

Another such book program adopted by OPC was the case of Eudocio Ravines, a Chilean Marxist intellectual and follower of Mao Tse-tung. While he had once helped install the Popular Front regime in Chile, the first Communist Party rule in the Western Hemisphere, he had become disenchanted with the ideology. This had come to the attention of the CIA, which contacted him and sent him to live under an alias in Mexico City, where he was writing a book about Communist plans to take over the world.

This, I felt, was finally a great project worthy of Bill Buckley, whom I assigned to help Ravines finish the book, *The Yenan Way*. Bill dove into the mission, and Scribner's accepted the English translation several months later. After that, Buckley decided to leave Mexico and the CIA. He told me that he was considering the purchase of *American Mercury* magazine—the popular intellectual publication founded by H. L. Mencken that had been on a downward track for the last several years—or he was going to start his own magazine.

I tried to talk him out of it, but his mind was made up, especially as Pat was not enthusiastic about staying in Mexico much longer. It was hard to see the couple go. Not only had Bill done a superlative job, but he had become such a good friend that we had named him the godfather of our daughter. Bill went on to edit *American Mercury* for a year, before founding the influential conservative political magazine *National Review* in 1955, and later the television political staple *Firing Line*. Additionally, he has had a fine career as a journalist and an author. Besides being godfather to three of my children, he is considered by many to be the godfather of American conservatism.

Meanwhile, my station agents had established anti-Communist front organizations that embraced the core of Mexican life, including students, women, churches, and laborers. We recruited several journalists who wrote for some of Mexico's most respected newspapers and were able to penetrate the Communist Party of Mexico and a Trotskyite offshoot, both of which could muster fairly good-size demonstrations on a moment's notice.

While most of the work was covert, some of it was obvious, a bit sophomoric, and, admittedly, a bit fun, such as when we sent agents to disrupt a major speech by the artist and Communist supporter Diego Rivera, using CIA-manufactured stink bombs and itching powder.

Another campaign included the creation of weekly anti-Communist posters, which we pasted throughout the city to educate the Mexican public about the menace of international Communism. Reports were that the posters, appearing under the guise of a reputable organization, had a considerable amount of influence among the populace.

We were constantly on the lookout for ways to discredit Communist rhetoric. I learned that Bob North, posted in Bangkok, was trying to establish a Thai film industry, hoping to make a movie about an epic Thai legend. Maxine North, Bob's wife, apparently was enjoying life undercover, learning the language and honing an already skilled golf game. On route to Washington for consultation, Bob flew into Mexico for a few days, and we came up with a complicated operation to discredit a prominent Mexican Communist who was visiting Peking. The plan required critical timing and the top-notch printing work of the CIA's Technical Services Division in Washington.

North flew back to Asia, where he airmailed me a copy of a Chinese newspaper with an article about the Mexican Communist Party leader's visit. I quickly wrote a fabricated story in which the man was quoted as deprecating Mexicans, saying among other things that Mexican peasants could never hope to achieve the cultural level of the superior Chinese. I cabled my fictitious story to headquarters, where a special font was created to reproduce samples of the original newspaper. My fabricated story was set in the duplicate typeface and the entire front page re-created by the technical staff. I was sent a dozen copies by diplomatic pouch, which I received before our target returned to Mexico.

I made the doctored papers available to our contacts in the news media, who believed the story to be true and published translations in Spanish. When the target protested the story, technical tests on the CIA-manufactured newspaper proved that the paper matched other type samples of the same newspaper, and so proved its authenticity.

Mexico City was a sort of Latin American version of Casablanca: a large city full of conflicting ideologies, with agents from different countries spying on one another; peasant uprisings with big business trying to control them; gun running, drug running, money laundering; people hiding out, people seeking the people hiding out; and every other permutation of a vast international power struggle imaginable. One day we would be handling an Eastern European defector, the next trying to keep a spy from giving away U.S. secrets. It was constant, exhausting work.

Amid this, I was also keeping up a family life. In the fall of 1952, Dorothy and I welcomed another daughter, Kevan, into the world. Dorothy's mother came to town to help out during the event, followed for the first time by my mother, who flew in to see her two grandchildren, a visit that signaled a family détente.

About this time, the priest I had recruited came to visit me. He was a charming and handsome Notre Dame graduate who had played football in school and gained a sizeable congregation in Mexico, led no doubt by adoring females. According to Mexican law, he was not allowed to wear an abbot in the country, so he was dressed in civilian clothing. I had met with him several times and never seen him disturbed before.

He explained that his church had been sending religious delegations to Guatemala.

"The last group we sent," he told me, "were seized by police, beaten up, and thrown out of the county."

We both knew that one of the first things that happened in Communist-leaning governments was a power struggle between government and the church. This was not good news.

"I'll send someone to assess the situation," I told him.

I did as I promised and sent a delegation of Mexican anti-Communist students to visit their counterparts to the south. They fared worse than the religious group had. They were rounded up and tortured by the police of the left-leaning president Jacobo Arbenz, their testicles electrocuted and water forced up their noses and rectums.

Arbenz was a man of modest intellect; the true power behind the thrown was his strong-willed wife, Maria Cristina Vilanova. They seemed an unlikely couple to be championing the underclass. Arbenz, the son of a Swiss immigrant, was a handsome man with a high, intellectual forehead, thin lips, and small, almost feminine features, who taught science and history at the Guatemalan Military Academy. His wife was the beautiful daughter of a wealthy San Salvadorian family, with a movie-star smile that lit up the room. The couple dressed well, and was well educated and glamorous.

Yet Maria, the real brains of the two, organized socialist political discussions with two like-minded friends, the Chilean Communist leader Virginia Bravo and a Salvadorian Communist in exile, Matilde Elena Lopez. Meanwhile, she guided Arbenz up the military ranks to the presidency (Arbenz was widely rumored to have killed his predecessor) while indoctrinating him with Communist philosophy.

I reported the beatings of the Mexican students to headquarters but heard nothing in return. Part of the reason for the puzzling and frustrating silence was the new American ambassador in Guatemala, who had insisted that all CIA messages from his embassy be approved by him before they were sent to headquarters in Washington. This was because the previous ambassador had been embarrassed when it was discovered that the CIA had bugged the headquarters of the Guatemalan Communist Party. So, at a time when the Communist Party was rapidly consolidating power in Guatemala, the CIA station there was unable to supply Washington with the intelligence.

I dispatched more Mexican students over the border to gather information, and as a result of the alarming reports that I forwarded, was soon summoned to headquarters for a consult with the director of Central Intelligence, Walter Bedell ("Beetle") Smith, a few staff members, and my division chief, during which I assured them that there was indeed a Communist link to the events.

Finished with my debriefing, I visited some old friends on the staff, then stopped into the security office for a standard polygraph test covering sex, money, and foreign contacts that was periodically required of all agents. With that unpleasant ordeal completed, I dropped in on the security officer who, among other things, reviewed materials that had been written by agency employees before they were allowed to be published.

I had forwarded the CIA and the State Department a copy of my latest manuscript. I thought that as long as I was in the neighborhood, I would take it home with me. But when I inquired about the book, the security officer's face reddened and he had trouble clearing his throat. "There's a little problem," he said finally.

"Did I let something slip?" I asked, thinking that I must have inadvertently committed a security breach.

"No, nothing like that," he said. "It's just that . . . well . . ."

"Well, what?" I queried. "I can't think of any protocol problem. Is there some operation going on that I don't know about that's similar to the book?"

His face got redder. "It's this way, Mr. Hunt. My secretary took it home to read it and somehow lost part of it."

"Lost it?" I exploded. "The CIA lost my manuscript?"

"On the good side, she says she couldn't put it down. I liked it, too, and didn't see any security problems." He fished a bundle of pages from a desk drawer. "You can have these, and I'll get you the rest if she finds it."

I told him that I wasn't writing for the amusement of his staff. And, "If the Office of Security doesn't take the review procedure seriously, then I won't, either. From now on, I'll publish what I want, and you can lodge a complaint after the fact."

I had not made and retained a carbon copy, as I had been under the misapprehension that I was sending the manuscript by diplomatic pouch to the most secure office in the world, so I naturally assumed that it would be safe until I arrived. The missing pages were never found, so I had to reconstitute them from my longhand notes and drafts from which Dorothy had typed the original. Despite my remarks, I did submit some of my future works—especially nonfiction—to the office before publication, a few of which were held up for long periods of time before they could be printed. The agency still reviews all books published by former agents, though recently it has issued guidelines saying that a book won't be edited strictly because it portrays the CIA in a negative light. Usually, just names, places, and dates need to be changed if they may be associated with an ongoing operation or can be used to deduce the true identity of a current agent or assets.

Back in Mexico City, I received a visit from the chastened Guatemala chief of station. He turned out to be an older FBI retread who acted like the ambassador's lapdog, seemed to be having a grand old time living in the tropics, and was not inspired to exercise any operational responsibilities. He knew that I had been called to Washington about a problem in Guatemala and hoped that I could be persuaded to stop rocking the Central American boat.

"Everything's the same as it always is down here," he said. "The Communists are organized but contained."

"Tell me you haven't informed the ambassador about my meeting in Washington," I said.

He shook his head.

"Promise me you won't." I told him about Arbenz's move toward a more Communist ideology and about the student beatings. He was visibly shocked by my revelations, but I could tell he was just counting the days until retirement. This was more action than he was prepared for. I made a mental note that he would give me problems until he was replaced. Per my expectation, I soon learned from a visiting branch chief that despite my reports, no initiatives were being taken in Guatemala.

Interagency gossip slowly filtered down to my station that Beetle Smith was trying to merge OPC and OSO stations around the world, and that Wisner and the OSO chief were negotiating which stations the local OPC chief would take over and which the OSO would run.

The OSO chief in Mexico had seniority by virtue of his career in the FBI but had already received orders to take charge of a station in Europe. I figured that my position would be predicated on the seniority of his successor.

One morning I was called into Ambassador O'Dwyer's office with the OSO chief and the legal attaché. For some reason, I thought that this was something to do with the CIA power struggle, but I was confronted with a different situation entirely. The Fuchs-Rosenberg-Gold atom spy ring had been making headlines, and it turned out that the FBI had kidnapped a Rosenberg associate, Morton Sobell, who had been hiding in Mexico City (more shades of Casablanca), and spirited him back across the border. The ambassador rebuked the FBI bureau chief for making an illegal arrest on foreign soil, but the agent did not even apologize.

During the exchanges that followed, it became clear that the FBI had advance knowledge that the fugitive was hiding here and that the Soviets had promised to provide him passage out of Mexico.

"This should have been a CIA matter," Ambassador O'Dwyer declared. "Can you imagine how embarrassing this would have been if the Mexicans found out that the FBI made an arrest here?"

While I was embarrassed that the CIA had not known of Sobell's presence, I had to remind O'Dwyer that the CIA had no arrest powers either.

Twenty years later, I learned that what the bureau had done to Sobell, they routinely did to fugitives whom they were able to locate abroad.

I had not been involved in a surreptitious entry operation since my OSS experience in China. And some of those were hardly secret. Once, in Shanghai, for instance, we raided the office of the Italian counsel, sending two jeeps' worth of uniformed men bursting into the building, where we set up a camera and photographed records without caring about whether the counsel appeared.

But now I decided on the most daring mission during my Mexico posting. The Guatemalan embassy in Mexico City was located a scant two blocks from the U.S. embassy. From our CIA offices, we had an overly enticing line of sight to the front windows of the other building, and I occasionally amused myself by watching the office workers with binoculars. In a later decade, technology probably would have permitted me to read the papers on the desks, but at that point even a good telescope wouldn't have given me much more information. Now I would get my chance to see what they were up to as I determined that we should penetrate the embassy. We consulted with the National Security Agency (NSA) to fix a date to enter.

A team of CIA safecrackers flew into town a week before the scheduled operation. We cased the target and mounted twenty-four-hour surveillance on the building and its embassy officers, and equipped several vehicles with high-frequency transmitters then unknown in Mexico.

One of the prime steps in the plan was to recruit the embassy's maid, who secreted a microphone in the ambassador's office that broadcast to a listening post in an apartment we rented in the building. This installation supplemented several wiretaps that had been active for some time. We pulled blueprints for the building from local records and paid the maid to give us a description of the safe and make a putty imprint of its keyhole. For an additional sum, the clever woman even supplied us with a key to the embassy service door, which we duplicated.

Now we were ready for action. We selected a Friday night for the entry, as our surveillance revealed that the Guatemalans were not the hardest workers, customarily departing their offices early in the afternoon and not returning until midmorning on Monday. That afternoon, I watched the offices through my binoculars and alerted our surveillance team as each staff member exited the building. As the staffers left, our agents tailed them back to their home or apartment (or to a house of ill repute or a bar), keeping them under constant watch until it was reported that everyone seemed to have settled in for the evening.

The bug in the office had stopped broadcasting noises after everyone left, but I still asked someone to call the embassy from a pay telephone before I gave a green light for the operation. We could hear the unanswered phone ringing through the pickup.

"It's a go," I said into my transmitter.

The entry team gained access through the service door with the duplicate key, and the leader's voice whispered through the walkie-talkie, "Everything is dark and quiet."

I told him to proceed.

Once they had penetrated the embassy office, we could hear the team on the microphone, and they didn't even have to communicate with us over their transmitters, as we could hear their conversation through the bug.

The first thing they did—as in all such operations—was cover the windows with opaque black muslin to make sure that no one outside could see their flashlights. As an added precaution, we had subverted the night watchman, who was drinking tequila and playing cards in the basement with one of our agents who had cultivated the friendship during the prior month.

The specialty team went to work on the safe, pushing a type of soft metal putty into the keyhole, from which they could fashion a key. Before actually opening the safe, they applied an amplifying device to listen for such things as the tick of a time bomb or another kind of booby trap.

When the team opened the safe, they snapped a Polaroid picture of the contents so that everything could be replaced exactly as it had been found. Then, in a small room off the ambassador's office, the entry team set up a special camera that the CIA had designed to photograph documents, plugged floodlights into the embassy's electrical system, and spent the next three hours documenting the entire contents of the safe.

Besides the papers, the team also found $30,000 in U.S. currency but were ordered to leave it in place. When the mission was completed, the team packed up and withdrew from the target area in reverse order, finishing with the black drapes.

Within hours, the entry team was on a flight to Dallas, where they changed identities and flew on to Washington. The photographic evidence was pouched separately to headquarters, where it was developed and examined by various sections of the CIA, and the codebook film was handed over to the NSA. Some of the results were soon sent back to our Mexican station. Among the information were lists of Mexicans whom the Guatemalan embassy had subverted, as well as the names of some prominent citizens who were targeted.

It turned out that among the team's take were the ambassador's notes covering his efforts to buy weapons in Mexico, a physical description of the ambassador's contact in the Soviet embassy, and, quite interestingly, a series of profiles in which the ambassador appraised senior officials of the U.S. embassy.

While we might have been satisfied with the outcome of our burglary, it was apparent that Mexico City was home to some of the world's most brazen thieves. An FBI agent and his wife were chloroformed and their dog killed while Mexican thieves ransacked their house and took everything away in a moving van.

Our own home was looted twice, with the resulting loss of my wife's jewelry, my trusty typewriter, our sterling silverware, a radio, and other valuables. While these items were insured, most of the jewelry pieces were Dorothy's family heirlooms, which she was heartbroken to lose.

With a lot of prodding from the embassy's legal attaché and the promise of a nice insurance award, police soon located one of my wife's distinctive sapphire earrings in the downtown Thieves Market. One arrest led to another, and soon I was summoned downtown to identify a strongbox full of jewelry, which thankfully held most of my wife's treasured belongings.

Instead of allowing me to leave with the merchandise, however, the police official smiled and closed the box.

"We will need these as evidence to prosecute the thieves, of course," the man said in Spanish.

"But they will stay locked up, and we will definitely receive them later?" I queried.

"Yes, señor," he answered. "Tell your wife not to worry. She must be very attached to these fine pieces. Is she not?"

I conceded that she was.

"And she would like to see the men in jail?"

"We'd just like to have the jewelry back."

"It shouldn't be too long," the man continued. "Justice works fast in Mexico."

I consulted with the insurance company, which had a slightly different story, saying the jewels should be released directly after the reward was paid. After this occurred, I was summoned downtown, where I was once again allowed to see the jewels.

"But this case has taken many man-hours," the official told me. "And the insurance reward does not really take care of all the detectives who participated."

"I think the insurance company has given you a very generous reward."

His slimy smile dropped simultaneously with the click of the closing strongbox.

"What kind of extra reward do you have in mind?" I asked.

His vulpine grin returned as he opened the box, allowing me to glimpse my wife's sapphires and diamonds. "My men would love to rejoice in the return of the lady's jewelry. Five cases of scotch would be a fitting reward for such fine detective work. Don't you think?"

I felt like shooting the man but instead tried the more diplomatic approach that was expected of me. "The detective work was very good," I admitted. "But it is difficult to find so much scotch here. Perhaps the detectives would be satisfied with three cases."

He acted as if the weight of the world were on his shoulders but finally said, "Because you are such an esteemed member of the community, perhaps three cases would be enough." He held his hand out to shake.

The official delivered the strongbox to our home the following day and carted off the three cases of scotch that I procured. I knew that his men would never see a bottle of it and that he would sell it on the black market for three or four hundred dollars—a very suitable ransom at the time. It was a lesson about the traditional way to deal with Latin American police that I would never forget.

The interagency wheeling and dealing finally came to a head. A dispatch issued to the OSO station and me from Beetle Smith informed us that the two stations were scheduled to merge and that the new OSO station chief who was scheduled to arrive would be named the overall boss. I was named the deputy. It was difficult to swallow the bile that rose in my throat, but I accepted the change with what good grace I could muster—and asked to be reassigned. Both the new station chief and my replacement reported to the embassy, marking the end of my tenure.

There was a little overlap and free time at this point, so Dorothy and I took the opportunity to enjoy Mexico's culture and be remarried in the Catholic Church, and have our daughters baptized as Catholics. I knew I had to keep this fact from my parents, as it could easily rupture the uneasy truce that had been established between us. Then, after a month of farewell parties, purchases, and packing, our household was trucked away. We flew to Florida, where Dorothy's mother had given us a vacation cottage.

As my leave drew to an end, I traveled to Washington to find out about my next assignment. I was told to find a house nearby for me and my family. True to what must be unpublished government specifications to hire the worst person for a job, I found out that my new position was as chief of covert operations for an area of the world that I knew absolutely nothing about—the Balkans.

8

The Balkans and Operation
PB/Success

After a sweeping victory, the Republican Dwight Eisenhower took office about the time I was transferred to the Balkans in 1953. Ike promised a paradoxical agenda to not only stop Soviet expansion in Central and Eastern Europe but to slash the country's military spending to boot. To serve the opposing gods of thrift and military might, he proposed a new policy of the bargain-basement war, with covert action agents manning the sales floor.

Eisenhower's election was bad news for Beetle Smith. Ike's secretary of state, John Foster Dulles, was the brother of Smith's deputy, Allen Dulles. A quick coup d'état took place, Smith was sent packing forthwith, and the "daring amateurs" of OSS took back their command. Secret operations were no longer to be squashed under the supervision of skeptics but championed by enthusiasts. Under the new regime, men like Frank Wisner, whose power had diminished under Smith, surged to the forefront, and the old romantic ideals of covert action came back into play.

My new station was known as the CIA's Southeast Europe Division, which was responsible for all of the Eastern bloc Communist "ia" countries, such as Albania, Yugoslavia, Bulgaria, and Romania. An added bonus was the problematic country of Greece, which had barely escaped Communist domination during the Greek Civil War. The fate of thousands of children from the northern part of the country who had been taken to Bulgaria was still unknown. While our operations were confined to these countries, we also manned small bases in Frankfurt, Paris, and Rome.

I would spend nearly a year in this troubled part of the world, complicated by ancient enmities glossed over by a thin veneer of Communism that kept the tremulous harmony intact. Trying to piece together a jigsaw puzzle of various populations and get them to work together to overthrow the Communist overlords was extremely frustrating. Here we joined forces with some jaded, burnt-out, rarely sober British MI-6 agents who seemed to come from the pages of Graham Greene novels.

Most of our operations involved sending C-47 cargo planes into Communist territories such as Albania, where they dropped anti-Soviet leaflets and occasional relief packages containing such things as flour and razor blades, which we cleverly branded from their "friends at the Albanian Liberation Front," the leaders of which were living the good life in Rome, making little progress toward fulfilling their agenda.

Final clearance on all of our flights had to go through the CIA deputy chief, air force general Charles P. Cabell, a stocky, aggressive Texan who did not seem to bring a huge amount of creativity to his job. He was more interested in the freshness of the flour and the quality of the razor blades in our supply drops than in how our pilots would evade Communist antiaircraft fire.

Under these conditions, my assignment had become fairly dull and routine when I was summoned to Washington to meet with C. Tracy Barnes, another of the cabal of Wall Street lawyers that had taken over the CIA. He had worked with Frank Wisner at the New York law firm of Carter Ledyard, joined the U.S. Army the day after Pearl Harbor, and was later recruited by OSS. Perhaps there was a personality gene that these lawyers shared that translated into valor in the field and also made them gravitate to secret service. All of these Wall Street boys had parachuted behind enemy lines for special assignments, risking their lives and manicured fingernails before ending up behind desks in Washington.

You would never have guessed it by his appearance—he wore thick black glasses and the customary bow tie—but Barnes had been awarded the Silver Star after parachuting into France in August 1944; he and a French officer, armed only with carbines, held off and killed several hundred enemy soldiers by means of guerilla tactics, constantly changing their firing positions to convey the impression of a larger force. This action brought him to the attention of Allen Dulles in Switzerland, who wrote the London OSS chief, David Bruce, "I have met Tracy Barnes here today and am anxious to get him to Switzerland as soon as possible. . . . We can find useful work for him."

Barnes worked for Dulles until the war ended, then returned to Wall Street for a stint before being recruited to the CIA by his old buddy Frank Wisner as deputy director of the Psychological Strategy Board.

In Washington, Barnes swore me to secrecy before revealing that President Eisenhower and Vice President Nixon had ordered the National Security Council to overthrow Guatemala's Communist-leaning regime. I was told that this was currently the most important clandestine project in the world, and that if I accepted the position, I would be head of the project's propaganda and political action staff.

Obviously, my former position in Mexico and the reports I had written about the situation in Guatemala made me a prime candidate for the job. But whereas my briefs had initially provoked interested concern before being back-burnered for a time, new issues had brought Guatemala into the spotlight.

While a confluence of factors, including the business interests of the United Fruit Company, would doom the unfortunate President Arbenz, prime among them was fear of Communist aggression in our own backyard. The paranoia overwhelmed President Eisenhower, Secretary of State Dulles, many members of Congress, and virtually everyone at the CIA, including Allen Dulles, Tracy Barnes, and Frank Wisner.

The State Department had been consumed with the Guatemala problem for months, but Arbenz was a democratically elected leader, so any overt action against him, including a range of economic sanctions, would anger other governments in the hemisphere. "This situation," officials concluded, "tests our ability to combat the eruption and spread of Communist influence in Latin America without causing serious harm to our hemisphere." So far, a policy of "firm persuasion" had been hardily rebuffed by a defiant Arbenz administration. Unfortunately, covert action came with the same danger as overt action and would cause major problems among U.S. neighbors should the cover be blown, as the United States, under Roosevelt's Good Neighbor Act, had promised not to interfere in the domestic affairs of the countries in the Americas.

In 1947, the Organization of American States had been founded, creating a treaty between the countries to support each other in case of armed attack. Any recognition that the United States was involved in the invasion of one of the member states could cause an uproar.

The State Department and Eisenhower's aids finally decided that Guatemala would be an important test of any and all new methods to eradicate the Communist virus before it could infiltrate Western society and that future allegations of covert action could be met with plausible denial.

The fear of Communism coincided brilliantly with the objectives of the powerful United Fruit Company, America's largest corporation in Guatemala. Called El Pulpo (the Octopus) by locals, the main body of the company owned hundreds of square miles of Guatemalan territory, while its tentacles bought up controlling interests in the railroad, electric power, communications, passenger and freight lines, and the administration of the nation's only port. Its banana plantations employed some forty thousand Guatemalan workers, who were paid low wages and ruled with an iron hand.

The company had gained this power through the support of the corrupt former president, Jorge Ubico, who had given United Fruit most of the land, allowing them to pay almost no taxes on it. Arbenz, however, took back thousands of acres and reallocated them to the indigenous population.

I asked why Guatemala had become such a concern now, when it had not caused such an uproar eighteen months earlier when I had made my reports. Well, apparently the intelligence had generated more action than I had realized. In September 1952, Truman had authorized Beetle Smith to launch Operation PB/Fortune, a plan implemented with Nicaraguan president Anastasio Samosa and a Guatemalan military exile, Carlos Castillo Armas, to destabilize and take over the Arbenz government. There had even been a hit list of assassination targets generated to help a new anti-Communist coup take power.

The operation lasted about a month, when Smith terminated it because of blown cover. Now, under a new administration, the Guatemala problem had raised its ugly head again. The situation was also extremely incestuous. Allen Dulles was a former United Fruit Company trustee, and his brother, Secretary of State John Foster Dulles, had been the company's lawyer at Sullivan and Cromwell. Additionally, the United Fruit president was a good friend of John

Foster Dulles's, who had a sympathetic ear to the company's growing concerns over Arbenz's agrarian reforms.

The connections were further bolstered by Ed Whitman, UFC's top public relations officer, whose wife, Ann Whitman, served as President Eisenhower's private secretary. The company hired Thomas "Tommy the Cork" Corcoran, Washington's first "superlobbyist," to drum up support in Congress against the Guatemalan president. Corcoran was a Harvard lawyer who had clerked for Oliver Wendell Holmes and served as an adviser to Franklin D. Roosevelt's New Deal. He claimed to know every U.S. president since Coolidge and every congressional leader. He was the puppet master of Washington, D.C.—far more influential than today's Jack Abramoff ever was. He knew everything about everyone, and when he twisted an arm, the Capitol Building screamed. Corcoran's efforts were finalized when the National Security Council was given the order to effect a regime change by whatever means necessary.

Still, it wasn't a done deal, as the State Department was worried that a blown operation would reflect negatively on the United States.

While I did not enjoy thinking of myself as United Fruit's lapdog, the bigger picture of stopping the spread of Communism had to be considered. My only concern about becoming involved in the operation was personal. Dorothy was undergoing a difficult pregnancy with our third child, and I didn't look forward to a lengthy separation. Barnes told me that he really wanted me on the project and that he was confident that an appropriate accommodation could be arranged.

I was surprised that when I transferred out of the Southeast Europe station, two other men inexplicably tendered their resignations, leaving the station shortstaffed. Years later, I learned that their routine polygraphs had detected homosexuality despite the fact that one was a married father of two. Interestingly, such tests would not uncover the affairs of the men involved with MI-6 agent Kim Philby, whom I will discuss later.

The administration's request for "plausible denial" meant that this operation would be a true need-to-know operation, with buffers between us and the rest of the agency. So PB/Success, as the operation was named, was set up as a semiautonomous unit with its own funds, communications center, and chain of command within the Western Hemisphere Division. I was issued appropriate forged documentation from the Central Cover Division, such as nonfunctioning credit cards, bank references, and other identification for pocket litter.

The first two letters of a CIA code name such as PB/Success designated the geographical or organizational area of the operation. Here, PB was the diagraph for Guatemala. The following words, such as "Success" and "Fortune," were creative descriptions planting the seeds of optimism among team members, though often an operation was deliberately given a cryptic or arbitrary code name to mask its true objective in case of leaks.

The project's senior staff briefed me on the political situation. There were three Guatemalans around whom a new government could be formed: Lieutenant Colonel Castillo Armas, Colonel Idigoras Fuentes, and Juan Cordova Cerna.

Our top candidate at this point was Cerna, a judge whom I had once had a meeting with in a squalid YMCA room in Mexico, where he had informed me about Arbenz's Communist tendencies, about which I had advised Washington. The consensus was that a distinguished civilian was preferred to military rule. Unfortunately, Cerna was soon diagnosed with throat cancer in New Orleans and would not be able to serve. By default, U.S. support was then thrown to Armas because Fuentes was considered to be a right-wing reactionary. So, but for a medical fluke, the country's history might have been quite different.

I did not meet Armas personally but was given his dossier to study. He was a refugee in Honduras at that time and seemed like an extraordinary fellow, someone who had the personal history and charisma to draw supporters. While he had a bit of a patrician look, with delicate features, he had proven himself to be an extremely durable man.

Although Armas's father had been a prominent landowner, he had abandoned his wife and son to a life of poverty. Despite the hardships of his upbringing, Armas had attended military school in Guatemala and shown enough officer potential for further training in the United States at Fort Leavenworth, where he became friends with high-ranking members of the U.S. military.

Back in Guatemala, Armas was part of a coup that brought down president Jorge Ubico and General Federico Ponce in 1944, after which Armas was appointed to the prestigious position of director of the Escuela Politecnica. When the new president, Juan José Arévalo, began steering the country toward more liberal reforms, Armas again participated in an attempted coup before the election of Jacobo Arbenz, in which he was wounded and thrown in jail. After a short time, he tunneled out of prison with his bare hands and in 1951 escaped to Honduras, where he worked as a furniture salesman and attempted to organize a military force to oppose the Arbenz government.

Field headquarters was set up in a two-story barracks at a former U.S. Navy training camp at the Opa-Locka Airport, in a suburb of Miami, Florida. This was the airfield that Amelia Earhart had taken off from on her ill-fated attempt to circumnavigate the globe in 1937, shortly after the place was founded as an aviation camp. It would eventually play important roles in PB/Success, the Bay of Pigs invasion, and the Cuban Missile Crisis.

We worked and slept at the sparsely furnished building and took our meals at a marine mess hall nearby. We tried to camouflage the operation by having several of our officers who happened to be military reserve wear their uniforms on base, but the installation of a complex communications network and the presence of attractive female secretaries from the CIA pool sparked basewide interest right away.

PB/Success did have a precedent that we planned to duplicate. In August 1953, Operation Ajax had successfully deposed the Iranian premier Mohammed Mossadega in a bloodless coup after carefully preparing the minds of the target government and the population for such an event.

Therefore, we felt that some of the most important weapons would not spit out bullets but words. The man in charge of our propaganda unit was a Spanish-speaking agent named David Atlee Phillips, whom I basically recruited from the CIA's station in Santiago, Chile, where he had been a contract agent running a small English-language newspaper.

While still an embryonic field at the time, psychological warfare was going to be one of the main ingredients of PB/Success. The foundation of the campaign would be guerilla radio broadcasts blared over frequencies close to the Guatemala national channel. Relatively few Guatemalans actually owned a radio at the time, but it was considered to be an authoritative source of information, and we knew that wherever interested ears tuned in, gossiping lips would soon follow, spreading the message.

The channel, stationed across the Honduran border, broadcast a blend of popular music and humor, peppered with significant portions of anti-Communist propaganda tailored specifically to the country's five thousand military fighters and officers, who we hoped would lay down their arms, desert their units, or even change sides, as they outnumbered Armas's combat force by more than ten to one.

On D-Day, the station would direct a powerful blast directly at the Guatemalan government's radio beacon, overriding their transmitter with prerecorded fictional radio broadcasts in which nonexistent Guatemalan military officers would spread terror by announcing that battalions of soldiers were streaming across the border. Additionally, we hired a group of Guatemalan newspaper reporters to bang out reams of anti-Communist articles for publication in Latin American countries. They wrote pamphlets that were passed out in the streets and leaflets that were airdropped to remote towns and villages in the mountains and the jungles. Phillips also devised another interesting anti-Communist technique in Chile that we duplicated in Guatemala, in which housewives were taught to riot in the streets, banging pots and pans to protest Communist programs.

Our propaganda writers soon started to catch cabin fever in the barracks and threatened to strike if their girlfriends were not flown in for some R&R. So the project's security officer arranged to bring the women to Miami, where they were installed in a safe house off-base. While the crisis was averted, the security officer had to deal with good-natured teasing from his colleagues, who dubbed him the project's pimp. He was kept busy in myriad ways, fixing traffic tickets for CIA personnel and bailing out of jail stray Guatemalans who had been arrested for not possessing immigration papers.

Since the time of PB/Fortune, Colonel Armas had been receiving about $3,000 a month to train a small force of about 140 soldiers in Honduras. Now we started running airlifts of supplies to him from the Opa-Locka station.

The battle for the hearts and minds of the people continued when we encouraged a Guatemalan archbishop to issue a pastoral letter urging the populace to rise up against Communism. The letter was published widely in Latin America, and thousands of leaflets were airdropped throughout the remote regions of the country.

Other internal propaganda programs were also taking their toll. Perhaps one of the first graffiti campaigns in history was started during PB/Success. In this program, we got students to paint the number 32 across buses and building walls alluding to Article 32 in the constitution, which banned international political parties, such as the Communists, from operating in the country. This, in turn, sparked considerable amounts of media attention on the issue.

We stayed up late at night devising the most devious strategies we could. One plan was to increase tension in the capital by having our local agents place stickers on the doors of Arbenz supporters that read "A Communist lives here." Another idea could almost have bordered on the realm of a practical joke: we sent out fake death notices for the president and other high-level officials to be published in local newspapers.

In order to keep the populace on his side, Arbenz continued his reforms, expropriating 173,000 acres of United Fruit Company land, adding to the confiscation of 234,000 acres a year earlier. The infuriated company responded with a rigorous PR campaign, encouraging *Time*, *Newsweek*, and the *New York Times*, among other news organizations, to send staff to report on Guatemala's Communist activities.

Arbenz was feeling so much heat that he began sweeping arrests of students and other possible subversives. The crackdown only succeeded in reinforcing the basis for our propaganda efforts, proving that the country was in the hands of a repressive regime. In January 1954, Arbenz somehow got wind of the ensuing operation (later traced to Russian bugs and spies placed in the notoriously lax U.S. embassy), accused the United States of planning an invasion, and began widespread arrests of anti-Communist subversives. In February, the pressure continued when a prominent *New York Times* reporter, Sydney Grusen, was expelled from the country. While Grusen's removal was made to look like it was generated by Arbenz, in reality the CIA leaned on *New York Times* editors to remove a reporter who we thought might be sympathetic to Arbenz's liberal policies.

But time was of the essence. We had gathered provocative intelligence that Arbenz emissaries were busy behind the Iron Curtain searching for quantities of Czech arms and munitions to combat Armas's small band of men. A CIA officer, disguised as a European businessman, was dispatched from Opa-Locka to try to get one of

Arbenz's senior officers to defect. The officer was successfully turned and gave us continuing intelligence on government troop movements.

PB/Success's blown cover led to a full-scale investigation of the project's security lapses, which put us in limbo by shutting down all of Opa-Locka's black ops flights.

Every so often, I was lucky enough to be ordered to Washington to give progress reports or consult on the project and was able to stay overnight with my wife and young children. Dorothy was always worried about me, a problem exacerbated by the fact that she was kept completely ignorant about my activities. She had no idea if I was organizing a project from a desk or putting myself in danger somewhere. I worried constantly about her well-being, too, especially as she was having a difficult pregnancy. We solved the problem by bringing Dorothy's mother to Washington to help take care of the house and keep her company. By luck, I was in Washington when my first son, Howard St. John, was born, late in March 1954.

At this point, our Guatemalan defector confirmed the impending arrival of a Czech munitions ship in Puerto Barrios. With that in mind and heartened by an Organization of American States (OAS) condemnation of Communism in Guatemala in March (spurred by convenient U.S. promises of aid to Nicaragua, Honduras, and El Salvador), the Dulles brothers gave the green light to proceed on April 17.

A barrage of new developments took place starting in May. On the first, our radio campaign went full force with a shortwave radio broadcast named *La Voz de la Liberación*, which proclaimed to be broadcast from deep in the jungle of Guatemala but was actually recorded at our base in Miami, flown to neighboring countries, and broadcast over the border. A team of four men and two women mixed popular music and ribald humor with antigovernment propaganda urging soldiers to reject foreign ideology, asking wives to keep their husbands from attending Communist rallies, and warning government officials that they would have to pay for their crimes. The antigovernment theme struck an immediate cord with a rabidly receptive audience that had been suppressed from denouncing the government and believed the broadcasts were being made by a brave cadre of rebels in hiding.

This operation has been called the "finest example of PP/Radio effort and effectiveness on the books." By happenstance, a few weeks into the broadcasts, Guatemala's government radio station shut down for over three weeks to install a new transmitter, handing *La Voz* a monopoly over the airwaves, with no effective way to counter anti-Communist propaganda.

On May 15, the SS *Alfhem* successfully evaded an oceanwide search and delivered a thousand tons of Czech weapons at Guatemala's Puerto Barrios seaport. As noted by former CIA researcher Nick Cullather in his book, *Secret History: The CIA's Classified Account of Its Operations in Guatemala 1952–1954*, the U.S. government issued dire warnings that the shipment exposed Russia's plans to expand Communism in Latin America. The U.S. media upped the ante, with the *Washington Post* proclaiming that "the threat of Communist imperialism is no longer academic, it has arrived." The *New York Times* agreed that the weapons would soon "find their way to Communist rebels throughout the Americas." Congress added fuel to the fire, with congressmen such as House Speaker John McCormick proclaiming that "this cargo of arms is like an atom bomb planted in the rear of our backyard."

On the twentieth, five days after the infamous shipment hit the shore, Armas's commandos tried and failed to sabotage a train carrying the weapons to the capital, resulting in the deaths of one soldier and one rebel. While this was a victory for Arbenz, it served as proof that the Soviets and Guatemala were indeed cooperating, and any fears that the State Department might shut down our operation because of blown cover subsided. The U.S. Navy began a sea blockade of Guatemalan ports to make sure that no more weapons were delivered, boarding French and English ships bound for Guatemala without regard for legality.

Despite antiaircraft guns included in the Czech shipment, Armas's pilots were able to penetrate Guatemalan airspace with impunity. One plane buzzed the Presidential Palace and dropped leaflets across the capital with the message that the *Guardia Nacional* should "Struggle against Communist atheism, Communist intervention, Communist oppression. Struggle with your patriotic brothers! Struggle with Castillo Armas!"

Reports came in that Arbenz was feeling increasingly stressed and had holed up in the palace in a depression. He even communicated with the U.S. ambassador, offering to meet with Eisenhower to allay his fears. The State Department did not respond to the request.

Desperate to hold on to power, Arbenz's police rounded up some four hundred eighty anti-Communist subversives operating inside the country, torturing many at military bases, killing about seventy-five, and effectively netting almost all of Armas's clandestine network.

Liberación radio broadcasts exhorted military officers to defect and offered rewards to Guatemalan pilots who fled the country in their planes. While no one seemed to be taking us up on our offers, it made Arbenz so paranoid that he grounded the air force, which cleared the skies for a ragtag group of mercenary pilots (one a Chinese flyer from Taiwan who spoke no English) hired by the CIA to buzz the country trying to sabotage various military targets. Bombs were in short supply, and we didn't want to hurt civilians, so in order to make it seem like the planes were laying large flurries of bombs, the pilots threw out Coke bottles that made terrifying whistling noises before exploding on the ground. An agency memo prepared for Eisenhower explained that the operation relied "on psychological impact rather than actual military strength."

Finally, on June 4, we had a huge propaganda success when one Guatemalan pilot, Colonel Rodolfo Mendoza, defected to El Salvador in a private plane. Unfortunately, he was too scared to go on the radio to implore his colleagues to follow him, so agents in El Salvador got him drunk one night, recorded his conversation about the negative impact of Communism on Guatemala, and broadcast it without his consent.

Tracy Barnes joined us in Opa-Locka and assumed charge of the final stage of the operation. He took over an office and called me in one morning. I expected to be briefed on the latest developments in Guatemala.

He looked up at me, his eyes magnified by thick glasses, put down a sheaf of communications that he had been thumbing through, and wiped some sweat off his brow with a handkerchief.

"Hot down here," he said. "The cherry blossoms are just coming out in Washington, and down here, it's full-blown summer already."

"After Mexico City, it seems cool, sir," I told him, wondering where things were going.

"Speaking about cherry blossoms . . . ," he said. "You ever seen the cherry blossom festivals in Japan when you were in Asia?"

I shook my head. "No, we were too busy saving POWs," I said. "Don't know if I ever noticed a flower anywhere. Besides, I was on mainland China. Never actually got out to Japan."

"Well, I hear they're beautiful," Barnes said. "The trees blossom in Tokyo until sometime in June."

"Yes, sir?"

"You're going to be seeing them soon, Hunt," he said. "You've been doing an impressive job, and you're being reassigned as chief of covert operations for North Asia Command. That means Tokyo. Congratulations."

This was not the positive news that it might have been for another operative. I explained that my war memories of the Japanese were extremely negative, with the added weight that so many of my friends had died fighting them. I knew Dorothy would not be pleased, either, as her stepfather had been killed during the Bataan Death March.

Barnes held up a hand to stop any further conversation. "The die's been cast, Hunt," he said in a clipped tone. "This is an extremely important position, and you have been approved at the highest levels."

After that meeting, I was called to Washington to confer with Allen Dulles about my appointment to Japan. I reiterated the concerns I had described to Barnes, namely that I had no sympathy for or real understanding of the Japanese.

"I'm sure there are other people available, sir," I said. "Surely you can let me off the stick."

Dulles, speaking in a blue-blooded patrician accent, tried to mollify me. "Well, the admiral has been yelling to have you or someone like you go over there, because he believes that big things could be accomplished. I'll tell you what. If you go over there for six months and find that it's intolerable, we'll make a change. But make no mistake, you are going over there."

I gritted my teeth, knowing that the agency considered this a reward for the Guatemalan project. "You can't imagine how this is going to uproot my family, but I can see in your eyes that this is an offer that can't be refused," I said.

So Dorothy and I moved our three children to postwar Japan, where I was covered as a Department of the Army civilian adviser to General Matthew Ridgeway's Far East Command. Based in Japan, my domain encompassed a huge territory—all of North Asia. I was now responsible for trying to change the mind-sets of millions of people who harbored quite negative viewpoints about the United States.

We had barely debarked when I received a cable that D-Day had been initiated in Guatemala.

On June 15, Castillo Armas was ordered to invade. He divided his band of just under five hundred men into four small groups that crossed the border in the dead of night on the seventeenth. The divided force was supposed to seem like a large contingent of troops that would strike fear into any opposition. On the day of the invasion, *La Voz*, as part of the disinformation campaign, reported to the populace that large numbers of well-armed rebels had crossed the border to engage the army. In reality, Armas led his band of a hundred or so men across the muddy border in a rusty old station wagon. It took a couple of days, but the rebels finally captured the barely defended town of Esquipulas.

The attack almost ended in tragedy when Armas's other three rebel forces were destroyed trying to take over Puerto Barrios and Zacapa. Armas himself then came under siege by the national forces that had defeated his other men.

Trying to regain an upper hand, rebel aircraft flew incursions into Guatemalan territory, blowing up railroad tracks, bridges, and a small oil tank. Hopes that the populace would rise up against the Communist oppressors, however, were not realized. World opinion, which had seemed to be siding with the United States at one point, shifted suddenly, with headlines across the world accusing the Eisenhower administration of trying to fan the flames of the Cold War, which many had hoped to see die to embers with the passing of Stalin in 1953.

By the twenty-third, prospects for Armas's success looked bleak. The better-equipped army had reinforced key garrisons and was ready for attack, making it look as if Armas would soon be rounded up and captured.

At the darkest moment, luck inexplicably turned our way.

The propaganda efforts had finally had an effect: Guatemalan officers believed that the United States was going to invade the country because of Arbenz and his Communist ideology, and they were reluctant to defend the president. An adviser told Arbenz that the soldiers would soon change sides—a prediction that came true a few days later when a small garrison capitulated to a rebel group without a fight.

After warning civilians that air strikes were imminent, rebel planes attacked the capital with old World War II bombs, many of which did not explode, though here and there the old bombs did their duty. A run on the Matamoros fortress caused a chain reaction of secondary explosions in their weapons cache. Another casualty was a British ship unloading at Puerto Barrios, which was mistaken for the SS *Alfhem* and sunk. During the attack, our powerful transmitter in Honduras overrode the Guatemalan national radio channel, broadcasting the sounds of fictional battles and nonexistent victories to confuse the enemy, saying that large columns of insurgents were closing in on the capital.

Under pressure from the rebels and his own army, Arbenz resigned on June 27, handing over executive power to Colonel Carlos Enrique Díaz. While we hoped that this was a positive turn, Díaz formed a junta with two other military leaders, who kept most of Arbenz's cabinet in power. The United States pressured Díaz to resign, which he did. Over the next eleven days, five different juntas came and went, until a Castillo Armas–headed government was finally brought into power.

During this time, Arbenz and his wife took refuge at various embassies, then with a general assembly of other officials who appeared at the airport hoping to board planes to flee the country. In Japan, I was cabled for my advice by the senior man on the scene watching the defeated Guatemalans milling around, women crying, men looking fearful and dejected, sure that they were all going to be put up against the wall and shot by the new regime.

If it had been up to the new Armas government, the airport refugees probably would have seen their worst nightmares realized. I advised that we should halt any kind of bloodshed, worried that it might turn into a nationwide bloodbath. Instead, the former president, his wife, and other officials were strip-searched, then allowed to board the aircraft and leave the country into exile. I would certainly regret my decision to allow an asthmatic Argentine medical student named Che Guevara to leave with them. He was granted political asylum in Mexico and joined up with Fidel Castro. The presidential family flew to Czechoslovakia but popped up several years later in Uruguay, where I would meet them again.

The Eisenhower administration and the CIA were ecstatic about the outcome of the operation. Wisner was so pleased that he sent an uncharacteristically jubilant cable saying that the plan had "surpassed even our greatest expectations." The new style of clandestine warfare, leveraging small amounts of U.S. dollars into highly productive amounts of fear and propaganda, seemed almost magical in its effectiveness.

Armas finally took charge of the country. Since I had been involved in his selection, I was extremely interested to see the outcome of his leadership after he took over the Presidential Palace. Unfortunately, instead of carefully guiding the new government into a model of democracy for the rest of Latin America to follow, the United States promptly forgot any responsibility for continued direction in the country. Armas was popularly elected but assassinated by one of his bodyguards three years later. This, in turn, led to decades of iron-fisted military rule, under which some one hundred thousand mostly impoverished Guatemalans died.

Following the overthrow, General Walter "Beetle" Smith joined the United Fruit Company board of directors.

Because thousands of files were confiscated from the Presidential Palace, no direct link between Arbenz and the Soviets ever emerged, although a few letters were found espousing a pro-Communist theme. Most important, the fallout resulted in a lasting legacy of anti-American bias throughout Latin America, most significantly in Cuba, Brazil, Argentina, and Venezuela.

The heady success of the cheap war, fueled by capitalist propaganda, expecting a country's populace to rally around the American ideas of capitalism and democracy, would lead to many unfortunate years in which successive administrations would try to duplicate unsatisfactorily our perceived success in Cuba, Chile, Vietnam, and most recently, Iraq. This is not unlike a gambler winning a huge bonanza early in his career, only to become a habitual gambler losing everything the rest of his life.

One reason that there has never been another success of this magnitude is because revolutionaries such as Che Guevera and Fidel Castro learned more from the Guatemalan defeat than did the United States, having been taught to strike quickly and decisively at the enemy before help arrives from abroad. Five years later, I would prove this theory when I was brought in to help with U.S. efforts to wrest control of Cuba from Fidel Castro.

From an operational standpoint, however, PB/Success lived up to its name. Almost everyone involved in the action received commendations and awards. For the first time since the Spanish Civil War, a Communist government had been overthrown—in the geographically important "Good Neighbor" area of Central America to boot.

9

Japan

As I had predicted, convincing my wife that she would enjoy Japan was a world-class effort in propaganda worthy of our efforts in Guatemala but hardly as effective. She wept silently as we gathered our two young daughters, infant son, and two squirmy dachshunds aboard the sleeper jet to Tokyo, where we arrived in the evening after a very tiring trip. But her attitude perked up on our ride from the airport when we entered the posh Ochanomizu (Tea Water) District of Tokyo close to the Imperial Palace. The neighborhood had once housed Japan's most notable nobles and wealthiest businessmen and was so named because it was near the river where the Shogun's tea water was extracted during the Edo period.

There was a lush park nearby, as well as a noted university. The home we were assigned was the nicest we had lived in yet, built by Frank Lloyd Wright while he was designing the nearby Imperial Hotel, still one of Tokyo's finest. Drawing from local influences, Wright designed the place in a charming blend of European and Japanese styles, complete with a customary moon gate, a courtyard, a garden with shrines, and a lovely lily pond so big that we were able to convert it into a small pool for the children.

Befitting the prestige of my cover, Japan being exceedingly class conscious, we hired a staff of Japanese servants, including a nanny for our infant son, and enrolled our two girls in a school run by elderly French nuns. Most of our children's classmates were Japanese, however, so they soon learned the language from their new companions.

My office at the Far East Command was located about ten minutes away from home in the CIA building at Pershing Heights. Our geographic area of responsibility was mind-boggling, encompassing all of mainland China, North and South Korea, Taiwan, Okinawa, Hong Kong, a forward base in the problematic Philippines, and, of course, Japan.

The Soviets were very active in the region, so there were hundreds of people working in and around Tokyo for the North Asia Command office. I soon found, however, that I was the only person in the entire group who had any field experience on the China mainland, as none of my former OSS comrades who had joined the CIA were stationed in the region. This was a major lapse in judgment by my superiors, as China was certainly our principal enemy in the Far East, and North Korea was simply a puppet regime of Red China.

This office was also quite a bit different from my previous assignments. In Mexico, being the boss of a small station, I could be almost as courageous and daring as I could imagine. We broke into an embassy, turned defectors, and came up with plots that would have done Graham Greene proud. Resourcefulness and imagination were prized during PB/Success. But in the decade since the war, the CIA had evolved into a government bureaucracy like any other, and the Far East Command embodied the worst of it. It was rife with paper pushers and analysts with no sense of action or initiative, completely lacking in vision—perhaps the same attributes that have hindered the agency during recent years.

When I joined the CIA, the spirit of OSS was still alive. We entertained a notion of group elitism, of daring spirit, of complete confidence that you could trust your comrades with your life. But in the Far East Command, I found the various units and personnel mired in a toxic work atmosphere of mistrust, backbiting, and competition.

This was due to the rapid expansion of the agency, which needed to absorb and train mass numbers of personnel. As a result, the CIA soon had to dispose of hordes of inadequate workers, who often found cozy niches where they could hide away from the light and draw a paycheck. Allen Dulles was a kindly man and did little to acknowledge and deal with the problem. When Richard Helms took over, however, one of his first major programs was to clear out the deadwood from the organization.

The CIA is popularly called "the company" these days, and that's exactly what I found at my new office. An intelligence-gathering company, but a company all the same. Like that of a corporate officer, my job entailed many days of exhausting travel, visiting various stations similar to branch offices from Korea down to the Philippines. Despite the mind-numbing lack of enterprise, I still managed to start various print and radio campaigns with subtle anti-Communist, pro-West messages in Japan.

But that was a bright spot in a sea of mediocrity. In Japan, I found that my predecessor, with typical lack of imagination, had gone the subsidy route to gather information. There was an enticingly titled project called Samurai, in which a Japanese warlord and his son—who spoke very good English—collected an enormous paycheck from the CIA every month to conduct a broad political and psychological warfare project. They, by virtue of their position, had promised the CIA access to political intelligence, anti-Communist labor unions, and student groups. But I could find no concrete accomplishments.

I met with the two Japanese assets in question, who resisted the revelation of any pertinent information, saying they couldn't discuss such sensitive matters.

"We've paid you hundreds of thousands of dollars," I told them. "And I want some progress report showing where that money is going. Let me see some action on behalf of the United States against the Russians."

"You should speak to your superiors about that," was the measured response.

"Oh, that I will," I responded.

Later when I met with my boss, things did not go as I had planned. "Admiral, I don't see us getting anything for our money. Don't you think we can do without this project?"

The admiral's face reddened, the veins in his neck bulging. "No!" came the answer. "This is one of Allen Dulles's favorite projects, and nobody can touch it!"

When I cabled Washington about the project, they promptly replaced the senior case officers with new ones. I thought that this was the last I would hear about Project Samurai, but the new case officers fell in love with the Japanese father and son, and lost all objectivity as well. My complaints and suspicions about the project finally reached Frank Wisner, and even he cautioned that this was a pet program of Allen Dulles's. Wisner cabled me to "keep an open mind" about the project.

I had definitely struck a nerve here. The situation became ever more mysterious when Mr. Dulles visited the station a couple of months later. After a luncheon with various other people from the office, I got the DCI's attention. "Mr. Dulles, you've heard from the case officer about the Samurai project, but I can't get any solid information from them, and I don't know where this river of cash is going. I think if there was ever a candidate for elimination, this project meets the criteria, but when I mentioned it to my superiors, they went crazy, saying it was a favorite project of yours."

Dulles said that he was aware of the project, but he waved away its importance with a flick of the hand. "That's ridiculous. It should meet the same standards as any other project that we endorse."

With this ammunition, I was able to bring the project to a halt. During a final meeting with the father and son, the CIA case officer issued profuse apologies, begging them for their forgiveness. The father and son looked at me without the rancor that I expected. Instead, the father actually smiled and said, "We've been wondering how long it would take for you to catch on."

Samurai's abrupt termination did not make me a popular commodity around the office, as a remarkable number of officers and lower staff members seemed to have their entire careers entwined in this useless project, and many of them were no longer needed after its demise. But if the CIA was going to be run like a company, layoffs were to be expected.

Other projects that I felt had some benefit were run out of Taiwan, where we maintained a large station under navy cover from which we flew clandestine flights over the China mainland, took pictures, dropped leaflets, staged agent infiltrations (the agents usually met their doom), and broadcast anti-Communist radio propaganda over a powerful transmitter.

Hong Kong was always an interesting station to visit, as I could always count on a nice influx of high-powered defectors from the mainland. Since the island was British territory under the authority of Scotland Yard, the CIA ran no independent operations but conducted joint debriefings of the refugees.

One of the more important stations was South Korea, which I enjoyed visiting because I could take time off for the best pheasant hunting in my life. Apparently, the Koreans didn't know these magnificent birds were edible, so they were generally not hunted here. The ones I shot were fat and tasty.

Taking a more aggressive stance than my predecessor, I initiated a propaganda campaign over North Korea. It was a difficult proposition, however, as leaflet flights over the border were strictly forbidden, so I had to come up with a more imaginative method of gaining access to the country. Since prevailing winds were in our favor, I tweaked an old method pioneered by the Radio Free Europe staff in Germany during the war and ended up launching balloons from a Corvette-size ship. Leaflets, set off by time release, offered a magnanimous $5,000 reward to any North Korean pilot who delivered a MIG-15 to the West.

I had great hopes for the project, but after several months without producing a single defector and with the winter weather setting in, I decided to terminate the project, just as I had Samurai. Just as all hope had died, I received an urgent cable from the South Korea station saying that our efforts had paid off—a North Korean pilot and copilot had landed a plane, emerging from inside clutching one of our leaflets. When I cabled back excitedly, I could almost hear the laughter in the station chief's memo in return. Apparently, we had not secured our coveted MIG-15 but a rust-bucket with wings, some kind of Yak trainer.

The initial disappointment wore off a bit when it was discovered that the pilot had flown MIGs during the Korean War and had even operated advanced models of the fighter plane. He and his copilot were given asylum, debriefed extensively, and allowed to fly American jet fighters to compare them with Soviet aircraft.

That was the peak of the project, which was closed down thereafter. The personnel of the project were pink-slipped or reassigned. The captain of the balloon-launching ship, Colonel Luke, was sent back to the United States. I would meet him again in early 1961 on a secret airfield in Guatemala, where he was one of the soldiers training a parachute battalion of the Cuban invasion brigade.

It was during this time that I received a sad cable from Maxine North in Thailand, in which she informed Dorothy and me that Bob, my old OSS comrade and writing partner, had died after coming down with meningitis. I had a hard time reconciling myself to a world without my great friend and would often think about him in later years, considering what kind of advice he would have given me to get me through dark times to come. Maxine was, of course, heartbroken by the loss but eventually rose above it to become one of Thailand's leading businesswomen.

Despite our initial resistance to the Japan assignment, Tokyo turned out to be one of the finest cities in which we ever lived. Our standard of living was exceptionally high, and we were able to entertain a good deal. While this was the first time we had ever had military cover, we still made friends with the local diplomatic corps, and my wife was able to get a job as a part-time speechwriter for the Argentine ambassador.

Juan Domingo Perón, with his charismatic wife, Eva, was the dictatorial power in Argentina, with consequent strained relations with the United States. Dorothy soon became so trusted that the ambassador started using her to code and decode his classified cables. She, in turn, repaid the trust in the manner that any dutiful wife of a CIA agent would do—one weekend, she brought me the embassy's entire stock of codebooks, which we gratefully photographed and returned.

My children also learned to love Japan. I could give them the equivalent of twenty-five cents and see them return from the store with arms full of toys. They loved the famous tigers, pandas, and flamingos at Ueno Park Zoo, the swans in the moat at the Imperial Castle in downtown Tokyo, and taking various day trips to other islands such as Nikko, Nara, and Kyoto.

Any animosity that we still harbored for the wounds of World War II were healed one cathartic evening when we returned home to find our entire staff of servants watching a television program. We were about to reprimand them for the unauthorized use of the set, when our eyes adjusted to the darkened room, and we saw that the women were weeping uncontrollably. Even our most inscrutable older houseman had wet cheeks. The program they were watching was about the long-awaited wartime films taken by Japanese photographers, which had been sealed in the Imperial War Museum.

This was the first time the Japanese public had seen the atrocities perpetrated by their military, by their husbands, sons, and fathers under pressure from the ruling elite. Three of the four women had been widowed by the war, and the family of the fourth had been incinerated at Hiroshima. We knelt beside them and watched the jarring program to the end. Then my wife embraced each of the women, attempting to console them for their losses before sending them off to bed.

From then on, our compassion for the Japanese grew, and we both let go of our deep-seated cravings for vengeance. Dorothy even started studying Japanese culture and dressed our daughters in adorable little Japanese kimonos and zori. By this time, all three children spoke fluent Japanese, sang Japanese songs, and played with Japanese children in the neighborhood.

From the time I arrived, I had problems with the admiral who had lobbied so intensively to have me or someone like me assigned to the CIA station. In a typical scenario, I once dictated a detailed fifteen-hundred-word report to headquarters, which he refused to sign off on and send. When I asked him why, he nudged the papers on his desk and said, "Suppose you tell me what it's all about."

I didn't know how anyone could get to be an admiral without reading thousands of reports, but I quickly summarized the cable for him, which he signed. He was also not careful about security, often talking about intelligence matters in front of personnel who were not qualified to hear them. Perhaps the admiral needed someone like me because he ran a fairly loose ship and mostly looked forward to lunch at the Officer's Club.

He was replaced by his deputy, Lloyde George, who, thankfully, was not only a detail-oriented, seasoned intelligence veteran—formerly chief of OSO's Far East Division—but also a charismatic, intelligent man with a broad range of interests. Morale improved, and the station's communication with military hosts and subordinate stations flourished.

The Cold War was a constant chess match, with one of the most important strategies involving the turning of defectors and the catching of spies on both sides. At headquarters, one long-lived situation that hung on like a bad cold was a continuous review of the Fecteau-Downey case: two young agents who had been captured by the Chinese after their aircraft had crashed on the mainland and sentenced to long prison terms after a long series of vigorous interrogations.

The Chinese also captured a B-29 bomber and its pilot, a Far East air force colonel who often liaisoned with the CIA in Tokyo. The pilot was privy to sensitive information and high-level clearances that the enemy would have dearly loved to obtain. From an operational standpoint, when agents have been captured, assumptions must be made that all of their information has been compromised; that no matter how well trained, they have performed an aria worthy of the great Caruso. This certainly proved to be correct in the cases of Fecteau and Downey.

The situation did not improve when the Chinese returned the colonel and his crew through Hong Kong a few months later. A damage assessment proved the rule, and orders were immediately handed down to keep personnel with sensitive clearances from traveling in hazardous areas. These orders included even me. From here on, I was allowed to visit Kowloon but no longer permitted to drive within several miles of the New Territories or within sight of the armed border with mainland China, as I might be kidnapped by a roving gang of Chinese infiltrators.

Spies were indeed everywhere.

Befitting my status in Japan, I had joined the prestigious Tokyo Lawn Tennis Club as would have been expected of me if I was truly a civilian. I didn't know it, but a Soviet KGB agent, Yuri Rastvorov, under cover as the second secretary of the Soviet Mission, had done the same thing in an attempt to recruit an American. His efforts had proved fruitless, however, and he was recalled to Moscow. Unproductive agents were dealt with severely in the Soviet Union, so he defected to the British embassy on a cold winter morning.

MI-6 was happy to take him in and planned to fly him to Hong Kong immediately. Unfortunately, the aircraft could not take off because of bad weather. Rastvorov requested and was issued identification by MI-6 personnel, who drove him to downtown Tokyo, where they allowed him to depart without a guard. The Soviet was unimpressed with his treatment and wondered whether to proceed with his resolution, so he decided to try his luck with the United States. He telephoned the only American he knew, his tennis teacher, who worked for the army's Counterintelligence Corps (CIC). I have long forgotten her name but *Washington Post* reporter Serge F. Kovaleski identifies her as Maud Burris in his absorbing January 15, 2006, article, "The Most Dangerous Game." As Yuri was a suspected agent, she had been assigned to befriend him and had very subtly encouraged him to defect. She called the CIA station, which immediately sent a car to pick up the Russian.

The agent proved a bit elusive, however, wandering away from the telephone booth to drown his anxieties in a nearby sake bar, where an agent finally found him and hustled him away in a car. To prove his worth, while still in the car, the Soviet immediately identified three Japanese assets who were under KGB control.

The defection, while welcome in principle, nevertheless had a cataclysmic impact on the station, which, despite its size, was unprepared for such a major event. We consulted the procedural notebook, which proved useless, as it was Europe-oriented. So, Chief of Station Lloyde George brought the senior staff together at a long conference table, where we came up with a new course of action.

As it was after dark, we had our liaison officer call on his Japanese counterpart and inform him that the U.S. government was planning an extra nighttime flight. It was only a formality, because the Japanese were well aware that we kept three airfields active and could use them as we chose. Fifth Air force HQ had to be notified and put a C-47 aircraft on standby at Tachikawa Airfield.

At this point, someone remembered Ms. Burris, but for whom the station would not be engaged in its unusual burst of activity. So Burris was woken up, filled in on the case, and brought into the holding room where the nervous Russian was waiting.

Rastvorov, overjoyed to see a familiar face, jumped up and hugged her, exclaiming, "What do I do now?"

Burris told him that everything would be all right and introduced him to the Russian-speaking case officer, Gil Hoonan, who was familiar with Rastvorov's file. They were joined by another station officer, who was to act as conducting officer to Okinawa, where Yuri was to be debriefed.

The weather, however, was steadily deteriorating, forcing the pilots to call in and warn Lloyde George to get the party on board before the airfield shut down.

I accompanied the defector and the handler aboard the plane; the rain had turned to snow, coating the windows white and making ice form on the wings. The control tower advised the crew that takeoff was now extremely risky, so it was postponed.

Rastvorov decided that God was against him and tried to leave the plane. "I shouldn't have tried to defect," he said. "If I don't get out of here, the Japanese will find out and hand me back to the KGB."

I wasn't about to let him leave and pushed him gently but firmly back into his seat, strapping the belt tight around his waist. "We won't let that happen," I told him.

Meanwhile, the crew was fending off sharp questioning from the tower. While weather forecasts were increasingly pessimistic, Lloyde

George feared that Yuri's fears would come true and Japanese officials would intervene to take charge of the defector. He conveyed his concerns to the flight crew, ordering them to take off as soon as it was safe.

Rastvorov was becoming unruly, so Burris was brought back in to calm him down. Cabin temperature plummeted, as the pilot declined to expend fuel for such niceties as heat because the distance over water to Okinawa was a thousand miles with no opportunity to refuel. Even with Burris there, the Russian soon started to complain how much he regretted his decision to defect. His demeanor made it quite clear that if he was allowed the favor of a warm Japanese hotel room, he would probably disappear. The only alternative was to keep him liquored up on the aircraft and wait out the blizzard. By 3 a.m., the Russians had noticed their missing "second secretary" and notified the Japanese to begin an investigation. Luckily, the weather had cleared sufficiently for takeoff, and after a rather harrowing flight to Okinawa, Rastvorov was turned over to the debriefing team.

The Russians made a big stink with the Japanese Foreign Ministry, claiming that they suspected foul play in the disappearance of their citizen. The U.S. embassy was also questioned and finally had to admit that the agent had defected. This provoked a strong reaction from powerful Japanese left-wingers who were angry that the United States had infringed on Japanese sovereignty. The same party also proved a vocal opponent when it was revealed that American U-2 planes had been spying on the Chinese and the Russians from bases in Japan.

Whatever minor embarrassment was occasioned by the Soviet agent's exfiltration was made up for by the wealth of knowledge that he divulged during months of interrogation by a team of skilled Russian-speaking specialists who wrung out every last drop of intelligence the man possessed. Indeed, our Yuri proved to be one of the most important defectors the United States had during the Cold War, identifying three to four thousand KGB agents across the world, for which he was given a commendation by the CIA. Additionally, we were able to further extend his usefulness by having a writer pen three articles for *Life* magazine, ostensibly by Rastvorov, about the horrors of life in Soviet Russia. In the United States, he assumed the name Martin Simons, living a good life, even remarrying after a Mexican divorce from his Russian wife and enjoying many years of tennis, cigars, fancy suits, and sports cars until he expired at the age of eighty-two in 2004.

According to reporter Kovaleski, while Yuri was living the good life in the United States, his Russian wife was exiled to five years in Siberia for her failure to report a betrayal of the motherland.

By the summer of 1956, I was looking forward to a new set of initiatives, more creative problem solving, and greater latitude to conduct sophisticated operations under our new administration, but I received surprise orders appointing me the chief of station in Montevideo, Uruguay. I had to look it up on a map to figure out where it was! I was at first deeply concerned that I was being demoted for some reason to this tiny, innocuous country way down in South America—a little wedge between Brazil and Argentina.

Washington cabled me back that this was an important station because it was host to over a half-dozen embassies from Communist countries and was a tiny linchpin in the Communist strategy. Argentina and Brazil had evicted the Communist ambassadors, so they were all now concentrated in Montevideo.

By this time, my family had become very acclimated to Japan, and we were all more reluctant to leave than we had been to arrive. It was a good lesson for us, though, and we decided to think positively about our new assignment. We packed and made reservations on a big Pan American Stratocruiser that offered comfortable bunks for the long transpacific flight. Before we left, the airline informed us that there weren't enough bunks on board to accommodate us, which necessitated a departure on another flight.

I had barely escaped death by airplane accident during World War II, and would now do so again. When we arrived in San Francisco on a later flight, we found our friends all grieving for us. The plane we had originally reserved bunks aboard had gone down in the Pacific, and news reports indicated that among the dead were a Foreign Service officer and his wife and children. I didn't know then how airplane accidents would affect my life and those I loved so much in later years. At that point, we could only feel relief for ourselves and sorrow for the poor people who had not been so lucky.

We flew on from San Francisco to Sarasota, Florida, where I left Dorothy and the children in our seldom-used home there before reporting to Washington to be processed back into the Foreign Service reserve.

As if I had never done any of these things before, I was required to take various courses in station administration, wiretap management, mobile surveillance, and surreptitious entry, and a seminar on KGB operations in Latin America, some of which even proved worthwhile. I started looking forward to the new post, remembering how much freedom and creativity I was allowed in Mexico when I had been chief. I thought that Montevideo would allow me to continue the progress I had achieved in Mexico City.

After my courses and the necessary hobnobbing in Washington, I was utterly exhausted and was given a few weeks leave to spend with my family in Sarasota before dragging everyone down to the lower hemisphere. In the end, I would find Montevideo to be everything I expected and more. If Mexico City had been a never-ending carnival of spies, a Latin American Casablanca, Montevideo was even more intense and concentrated—a riotous circus of spies, complete with sideshows, high-wire acts, and trick ponies.

10

"Play It Again, Sam"

With my training courses complete, I first worked at the Uruguay–Argentina desk in Washington, studying all current dossiers on the main political figures in the country. I didn't enjoy working in D.C. anymore, as headquarters had a different feel to it than when I left to go to Japan—definitely more bureaucratic than in past years. Despite the tenure of Allen Dulles, the esprit de corps from OSS was almost negligible here, too. I paid the necessary visits to Dulles, of course, then to General Cabell, Frank Wisner, and Tracy Barnes. The new chief of operations for Clandestine Services turned out to be a man named Richard Helms—a former United Press reporter who had been in the navy and joined OSS during World War II—with whom I formed an enduring friendship that would last until my name was broadcast in connection with Watergate in the summer of 1972.

In Washington, I boned up on various Soviet agents and their suspected Communist assets in my new area and readied myself for a meeting in Havana, Cuba, of all the Latin American station chiefs. Havana was a rip-roaring city—a Mafia-riddled, spy-infested, booze-addled, women-crazy city with the world's best nightlife. There was nothing else like it in the hemisphere. When a meeting between the station chiefs and the U.S. ambassador was interrupted at the embassy by an aide with the news that President Batista's forces had just engaged and slaughtered a small force of rebels in the Oriente

Province, none of us could have envisioned how the almost insignificant incident would form the seeds of a massive revolution that would change world politics.

In an almost offhand manner, Ambassador Gardner remarked that the leader of the radicals was a former University of Havana agitator named Fidel Castro who had arrived by boat with a group of about eighty supporters to overcome Cuba's experienced army of thousands. But it was of no matter, as Castro had been killed.

The other chiefs and I looked at one another and nodded with relief. We all knew that Castro posed a danger and had been involved in the infamous Bogotazo coup attempt in Bogotá, Colombia, in 1948, so we were quite satisfied to hear that he would no longer be a threat. Unfortunately, the information furnished by Batista was gravely erroneous. While most of the eighty-two occupants in the boat had indeed died, the dozen principals who had escaped into the Sierra Maestra mountains to fight another day included Castro, his brother Raul, and Ernesto Che Guevara, whom I had given safe passage to leave Guatemala with Colonel Arbenz two and a half years earlier.

We sailed for Uruguay on a modest Argentine liner in early 1957, with a brief stopover in Rio de Janeiro and São Paulo, Brazil, before entering the harbor at Montevideo. My children cried when they saw our new city: bleak, gray, and dirty. The air stunk, the beaches were polluted, and the city seemed bereft of architectural creativity. We would later find a more inviting old town, and a few nice shopping boulevards, but after Japan, even postwar Japan, the city was clearly a step down.

We stayed in a hotel near the embassy before settling into a rental home in the suburb of Carasco. This was where the wealthy elite had moved over the years. It was much prettier than the city and the beaches along the ocean considerably more inviting for the children, who attended a French lycée across the street from the house. For transportation we had the Cadillac, which had traveled with us aboard ship to avoid problems similar to the ones we had once had in Mexico.

As this was one of the only nice neighborhoods in which to live, I had no doubt that every spy in town had taken residence here. I soon learned that my MI-6 counterpart lived a half block from me, and his children attended the same school as mine—all dressed up in white uniforms and floppy black bow ties.

While Uruguay boasted a stable, somewhat socialist-democratic government that had been in place for some ninety years—governed by the same Colorado Party—the country turned out to be a bit more turbulent beneath the surface. The ruling party was made up of a base of urban laborers, while the minority Blanco Party was primarily supported by outlying landowners and their workers who tilled the soil and exported meat, wool, and hides—the primary sources of trade with other countries. So there was a bit of a class struggle going on, but from the bottom up, rather than from the top down as in most of Latin America—a perfect little niche for the Communists to gain a toehold in the Americas.

The Uruguayans made that easier by maintaining friendly diplomatic relations with most Communist countries, excluding only Albania and China. The Soviets were extremely strong here—with the largest embassy south of Mexico City—because they had been thrown out of Brazil and Argentina, and now ran all their clandestine operations in those countries from the convenient venue of Montevideo.

I was assigned to the foreign desk, and my new ambassador was a nice, stolid yet ineffectual administrator, handicapped by an unfortunate stammer that made him difficult to understand in English, let alone Spanish—although he had a good understanding of the language. His deputy, the counselor, had been cut from completely different cloth. He was high-strung and paranoid, always fretting about the status of his career Foreign Service job. It didn't help that his wife started drinking her martinis at lunch and could always be counted on to make some kind of scene at almost any function, spontaneously kicking off her heels and executing pirouettes when the mood struck her.

As the ostensible first secretary, I was considered the next-highest-ranking official below them. Since neither Dorothy nor I stammered, nor were we subject to getting drunk or dancing impulsively, we soon became the couple invited to parties where an embassy official was desired. This caused some friction between us and people who had been there longer, but I didn't allow it to bother me, as I was more interested in my CIA operations. Luckily, the ambassador's wife happened to be the sister of one of Frank Wisner's senior aides and defended us at every opportunity.

After debriefing my predecessor, I quickly ascertained the reason why I had been assigned here. He was just treading water until retirement, and the word *ineffectual* could not begin to describe him. He had no contacts to take over, except one retired American—the agent's stockbroker, who had little information to contribute but who seemed mildly amused to be an asset, as if cultivating an attribute he could someday trot out at cocktail parties to make himself interesting. Even the chief of police, a logical asset to acquire, thought so little of my predecessor that he not only refused to cooperate with him, he wouldn't even have lunch with the poor man. I was going to have to build a network from the ground up, just as I had in Mexico.

I immediately identified and began courting the rich and powerful natives and foreign nationals in the country. This included well-placed men in industry, agriculture, and finance. To that, I added a list of government and police officials whom I wanted to have in my pocket, dividing the list into sections of "must-haves" and "would like tos." On the "must-haves" side, I definitely needed agents inside the police department and the presidential cabinet. Top picks on a sort of fantasy team of assets included the president of Uruguay, Luis Batle, and, of course, the chief of police in Montevideo. Perhaps that seemed like reaching for the stars, quite improbable, but with a lot of work, not impossible.

A "coincidental" meeting with the police chief was arranged at a reception at the Argentine embassy, where I was, of course, introduced under the cover of being the first secretary. He seemed brash and macho, qualities made palatable by a healthy dash of Latin charm, and I knew he held a dim view of Yankee imperialism in the region. When I was arranged an introduction to him by an Argentine official, I could see a glaze come over his eyes as we shook hands perfunctorily, and he turned his head to admire a stunning woman on the other side of the room. I could tell that I had less than a second to gain his attention before he made an excuse to leave.

"Just the man I was hoping to meet," I said in good, barely gringo-accented Spanish.

His head snapped back in my direction, and the glaze dissolved from his eyes. "Ah, they finally have someone at the embassy who can speak decent Spanish," he said with appreciation.

I brushed off the insult against my colleagues without comment and continued in what I hoped was a diplomatic matter, explaining to him that my position included the responsibility of security for visiting American dignitaries and asking if we could arrange an appointment.

"I am a very busy man," he said. "But I'm sure our secretaries can find a time that is mutually convenient in the next few weeks."

I knew a few weeks could easily stretch out to a few months in "mañana-land." But I had an ace up my sleeve. "I was hoping you would be my guest at the Jockey Club," I said. "I'm fond of a particular fifty-year-old cognac they serve there. . . ." I let the invitation dangle suggestively.

Gaining admittance to the Jockey Club was particularly difficult, and I knew he did not belong. I could see a silent battle blaze behind his eyes: animosity for the United States—to actually be seen with an American official—vying against the craving to taste the benefits of the elite.

"Perhaps Monday?" I prompted.

Tonight the battle was mine. "One o'clock would be convenient," he muttered, a bit ashamed of himself.

At the Jockey Club, we lunched at a secluded table, enjoying lobster appetizers and white wine, followed by thick local steaks complimented with Argentine Malbec wine. After lunch, the police chief sat back with a satisfied sigh, sniffed the old cognac I had promised, and waved his other hand expansively. "So, tell me, Mr. Secretary, what can I do for you?"

I didn't attack. I allowed the question to settle a moment, let his mind start asking itself questions. I obviously wanted something large, a grandiose action. Was it something he could deliver? Was it something he wanted to deliver?

What I was going to ask was something you'd usually ask in hushed conspiratorial tones. But that would only get his guard up. Instead, I continued in a nonchalantly conversational manner: "What you can do for me is tap some embassy phones."

He coughed, nearly choking on the precious brandy. Any sense of gratitude for lunch, happiness to be here, ideas that he might indeed wrangle more invitations, drained from his face. His gaze grew intense as he leaned forward. "You must be from CIA," he said, his words dripping with animosity.

I shrugged and took a casual sip from my brandy glass. "Chief," I said, "I can make the taps with or without your help, the difference being that if we do it together, we can share the take." I smiled affably. This wasn't something out of the ordinary. We did it every day.

He took a larger gulp of brandy to calm his nerves. At least he hadn't bolted from the table. He considered the proposition for a minute—I could see the wheels turning in his mind—before nodding. "I would have to tell Luis Batle," he said.

"Why not? He's your president, and more than anyone, he should be interested in what's going on in Uruguay."

He shook his head. "This will not be easy. I will have to think about it with care."

We both knew that Batle was staunchly anti-American and was courting the Soviet Union as a trade partner for Uruguayan exports of meat, wool, hides, and rice. Asking the police chief to broach such a subject might mean his job. However, intelligence that might be gained from such a partnership could be essential to the stability of the country.

"You don't have to give me an answer now," I said, promising to meet at another, perhaps even better, venue to discuss our subversion.

I indicated that there might be other perquisites, as well. Perhaps his own admission to the Jockey Club. In turn, he promised to relay the request to the president and get back to me.

The chief would be an important asset, and gaining the president would be a fantastic two-with-one-blow success. It was something I had to steer a little better. Accordingly, on my instructions, one of my station officers recruited the deputy chief of police to give us daily reports on his boss's activities.

The chief did not find an opportune moment to broach the subject to his boss for several weeks, so I got to work adding a couple of Russian-speaking agents and a Communist Party specialist to the station. We quickly launched several mobile surveillance teams to keep tabs on a large KGB group stationed at the Soviet embassy and recruited members of the Uruguayan Communist Party to report on meetings.

Due to various logistics problems stemming from bad communication and long-distance travel, combined with a basic contempt for Latin American secret police, the Soviet agents were particularly careless and did not follow their own rules of procedure. That was fine by us in the CIA office, who were quite happy to capitalize on their lack of security.

If any waiters at the Jockey Club had been spies, they might have had a lot to report, as the restaurant became one of my most valuable bribes for top military officials who ran the power and telephone companies. I made sure to become chummy with the chief of staff of the army and the chief of military intelligence, with whom I became so friendly that I gave him a grand tour of the United States, which was standard practice in the CIA, as it made many of our foreign assets eager to emigrate, something they could hardly afford to do without creating additional sources of finance. These "friendships," along with the chief of police, eventually translated into more than ten high-quality telephone wiretaps.

In those days, the tape recorders were large, often weighing forty to fifty pounds, and reliable only in the fact that you could count on them to break down at the most inopportune moment. As there was no one in the station, or in Uruguay for that matter, who could repair a misbehaving recorder, we had a constant supply of new units being furnished from Washington.

These would be sent to the embassy in mailbags, necessitating our in-house mail service—which, of course, had no idea they were hosting a CIA station—to deliver these awkward parcels upstairs without the use of elevators, which the embassy did not have. So at least once a week, I knew that the mail had arrived when I heard the delivery-man dragging the units upstairs, banging them against each step. It was amazing that any were delivered in working order at all.

As there was no way to destroy the defunct instruments, my only recourse was to take advantage of the occasional moonless night, making a nighttime fishing expedition to conveniently add them to the briny bay, where, no doubt, some future marine archaeologist will excavate them and wonder at the mystery of why so many ancient recording devices found their way to such a desolate watery grave.

Additional complications arose, because there was no outlet to purchase recording tape in the city, the closest store being in Rio de Janeiro. But with so many taps working twenty-four hours a day, we needed an enormous amount of reels. The project was immense, taking three full-time Soviet and Eastern bloc translators working overtime seven days a week typing transcripts of the conversations. While only a small percentage of the tapes held useful intelligence, everything had to be typed and analyzed, as every comment, however innocuous, could easily be a form of code. We also conducted technical penetrations of several of the embassies and the residences of key personnel.

The quantity of information was more than the agency was obtaining from almost any other place in the world. The project was so successful that I was asked to host tours from other stations to instruct them in our operations. The only other CIA post to operate such an enormous network of taps was the Berlin bureau, which controlled a massive surveillance organization.

Our electronics detail was aided by a sophisticated street surveillance of all Soviet agents whom we had identified, which was an amazing percentage of the Eastern bloc embassy personnel. In the long run, it was futile to try to hide our status, however, as each side learned to recognize the agents of the other. At a dinner party, it became almost comical when my Soviet counterpart, a man I knew as Samoilov, would grin devilishly and give me a little nod while his drably dressed wife would admire Dorothy's couture with obvious envy.

To try to keep the Soviets from building a reliable network of intelligence, I employed additional people to keep tabs on our military assets and to report back to me if any of them showed signs of making contact with Communist agents. Our efforts were successful enough to keep the Soviets from gaining the foothold they hoped for.

Not that the Soviets didn't try their best. In the previous year, the FBI had identified a Uruguayan diplomat in New York named Ramirez who was passing information to the KGB. He became our problem when he returned to Montevideo, where we learned he was in contact with a local Soviet agent in the embassy. We found that he maintained contact with his case officer through a dead drop, leaving messages in a crack in a weed-ridden, dilapidated brick wall. Whoever left the message turned over a tin can to indicate that the dead drop was charged. The recipient kicked the can over to indicate that the message had been received.

My predecessor revealed the mischief to an outraged federal police chief, who swore to catch the two *en flagrante*. What no one knew at the time was that the matter was even more delicate than it appeared, as Ramirez was a good friend of President Batle's and his only qualification for the diplomatic corps was his allegiance to the ruling Colorado Party.

When our station and the Uruguayan police staked out the drop to arrest the perpetrator, the police bungled the operation by charging in with their sirens blaring before Ramirez completed the transaction. I suspected that this had been done on purpose, as the *federale* opined that he couldn't arrest Ramirez or even bring the matter to the attention of the president, since there was no proof that the diplomat was a spy.

But luck turned our way. Notified that a local smuggler—specializing in transporting gold bars from Uruguay into Argentina—was also a noted source for real Uruguayan passports, I initiated contact, as obtaining authentic foreign documentation was always something that interested the CIA. Through a contact, I agreed to purchase five blank passports but insisted on learning the identity of the Foreign Ministry official was who was prepared to sell them.

I was happy to learn that the vendor in question was none other than the corrupt Ramirez, whom we were determined to catch this time. When Ramirez arrived to sell the passports, our agent bargained the price down and recorded the entire transaction. We mailed copies of the tapes and the original blank passports to the major newspaper, along with copies to the authorities. The diplomat was disgraced after the headlines broke and was summarily dismissed; yet he still managed to squirm out of any jail time, as he had powerful enough cronies in government to avoid going to trial. The chief of police easily guessed who had been responsible for the operation and must have passed the information to the foreign minister, who from then on treated me coldly at receptions.

I soon had another guest at the Jockey Club, though, as the chief of police was succeeded by a tough young cop of Italian descent. When I called on him, he brought up the Ramirez incident, saying, "I can only admire whoever is responsible for engineering his dismissal."

I laughed, saying that I, too, was a fan, and didn't commit to any further knowledge of the affair. He chuckled knowingly along with me, then clapped me on the shoulder. "I am dedicated to two things," he said: "fighting crime and Communism in my country, and I think we can be friends."

He became a valuable resource who introduced me to the chief of army intelligence, who was also a hard-line anti-Communist. Through mutual cooperation, we formed an effective unit in which the CIA was not only able to gain the assets of the police but very importantly the army as well. My fantasy team turned into a reality that could not have been stronger.

As so many of those Eastern bloc countries don't even exist in the same form anymore, I occasionally wonder if it was all worth the effort. At the time, however, it was the only way we knew to combat the spread of Communism, which our government considered a major threat to world stability. That is what we believed, and it paid off when the Soviet empire collapsed. If private business occasionally used government policy to further its ends, such as in Guatemala, the government often used U.S. business interests as a powerful weapon in our arsenal as well, often making our causes symbiotic. Every foreign country needed to trade, and the United States was a well-heeled customer. American companies often employed thousands of workers in other countries, giving the governments a more stable economic base.

About this time, we at the various CIA stations around the globe started noticing that the stodgy old KGB agents in their trench coats and heavy black shoes were giving way to a younger, slicker generation who we jokingly referred to as "joy boys." These fellows were good-looking and well groomed, assimilating into their target countries with flair, generally wearing tailored suits, speaking a few languages fluently, and easily charming the ladies at receptions with fluid dance moves.

In Montevideo, one such agent named Vadim caused a bit of a sensation in the diplomatic corps, appearing at three diplomatic parties on successive evenings trailing a different blazingly beautiful Russian damsel, introducing each as his wife. No doubt these women were also agents, assigned the role by the KGB station chief, Samoilov, a droll, sorrowful man with dark baggy eyes and wrinkles dripping from his face like a bloodhound. Certainly not one of the new joy boys, Samoilov was distinctly old school and nervous at social engagements.

At one reception, Samoilov sidled up to me and offered a Russian cigarette.

"No, thanks," I said, having smoked one of them before and suffered lung damage for a day or two afterward.

The KGB agent lit one, hacked strongly, and then asked coyly, "You are a friend of the Chernikovs?"

"I am?" I inquired.

"You knew them in Shanghai," he prompted.

Shanghai had been a long time ago. I searched through my memory and finally lit on my treasured Marusha and her husband, Valantin! While the files of my memory might have been faded, the KGB's were quite fresh. Although we all knew each other's spies by face, I didn't suspect that they knew me quite so well.

I smiled. "How are they?"

"Fine . . . fine," Samoilov answered. "They have three fine children now."

"Is he still with Tass?"

"No. He is now a diplomat," Samoilov announced. His lips turned up in an ironic smile. "Like ourselves."

I nodded, knowing what he meant. "Where are they?"

He swallowed, perhaps thinking that he was revealing a bit too much. "In Bangkok," he muttered finally.

I clapped him on the shoulder and raised my glass as a toast. "Then you must give them my regards! Tell them I'm very happy to hear they are doing so well." Then to change the subject, I continued, "Have you had the shrimp tonight? No? Well, they look tremendous. You'll excuse me if I try the buffet?"

While I enjoyed good relationships with the chief of police and the intelligence chief, my original fantasy team list still lacked the quarterback I deemed most important—the president. Unfortunately, since Batle remained staunchly anti-American, there was only one way to get the president on our side: replace him with someone who liked us better.

I expanded my circle of friends until I met one of Uruguay's most prominent families, headed by a man I'll call Amilcar Redondo. He was a well-read, intelligent banker who wielded a certain amount of power in the minority Blanco Party. As his estate was located near my home in Carrasco, he occasionally invited us to his home for dinner, served with great wine and a generous helping of political conversation.

As could be expected, our topics usually ended with complaints about the present administration. Finally, he expressed his desire to find a Blanco candidate who could appeal to enough urban and labor votes to win an election. He envisioned an alliance between the Blancos and a small third party, the Ruralista Party, consisting mostly of farmworkers.

"What I have in mind," Redondo said, "is to find what Los Blancos have always lacked—a man of the people. But now I have found such a man. His name is Benito Nardone."

"And this man is pro–Los Estados Unidos?" I asked.

He winked. "In my experience, people are always pro-whoever helps them, señor. Don't you think?"

"Tell me about him," I answered.

Nardone was the self-educated son of an immigrant Italian cobbler. He wrote popular opinion pieces in support of Uruguay's farm laborers, gaining him a wide following among the Ruralistas. Redondo arranged an informal barbecue to introduce me to the man, who I found liked to ride horses, hunt, and fish. Since I enjoyed those same activities, it was easy to engage him in conversation.

I courted him faithfully for several months, often seeing him for drinks or dinner a few times a week. It wasn't hard work, as he was a likeable fellow, but I certainly had an ulterior motive. I was evaluating him at every level to see if he had the right stuff to pull off a major political upset, eventually deciding that he did.

Of all the political leaders in Uruguay, Nardone had the most charisma, had the best ideas on how to lead the country out of its postwar economic decline, and exhibited none of the emotional self-pity propagated by many of the country's present leaders who complained that the United States had abandoned them after they had sided with the Allies during the war. The country had gone through an economic boom from World War II through the Korean War, exporting all the wool, meat, and grain it could harvest at artificially high prices. Now it had been forced to compete at world prices, and its economic euphoria had settled into a virtual depression, exacerbated by the largess of being one of the most generous welfare states in the world. In one way or the other, the government employed about half the working population, bestowing full-pay retirement at fifty years old and giving other lifelong benefits that were on par with economic giants such as Switzerland.

Uruguay was leaning ever more leftward, with most of the populace supporting Fidel Castro's movement, which was gaining ground in Cuba. From time to time, there were large street demonstrations in support of the revolution, where funds were collected for Castro's emissaries. I made several reports on these rallies, but Washington did not seem at all concerned about what was happening in Cuba. Meanwhile, the environment toward Communism was becoming so fertile in Uruguay that a family from Czechoslovakia moved into my neighborhood. I did a little investigation and found out that it was Colonel Jacobo Arbenz—whom I had helped depose in Guatemala—his wife, Maria, and their two daughters. Amazingly, Arbenz would live longer than his nemesis, Castillo Armas, the rebel who had ousted him.

By chance, I had recruited a diplomat who was a relative of Maria Arbenz's. He was able to cultivate a friendship with the family and give me detailed reports on actions of the former dictator. Another coincidence brought me in direct contact with Arbenz at our golf club, where Dorothy and I met him and his wife at a reception. After all this time, he seemed to still be under his wife's thrall and hardly spoke about anything that she did not instigate. I wondered if I could have brought him out of his shell by divulging that I was one of the engineers of his downfall, but, of course, I said nothing of the sort.

While I did not feel the American ambassador was particularly effective, at least he was a well-meaning, copacetic man. Unfortunately, his ineptitude had finally been acknowledged in Washington, and he was replaced by a career diplomat, John Woodward. Woodward wasn't much of a step up, however, seeing as the extent of his ambassadorial experience had been confined to the challenge of Costa Rica.

Woodward took an immediate dislike to me, having heard that I had been involved in the regime change in Guatemala. At one of our first meetings, he told me that he was against U.S. foreign intervention and hoped that I wasn't planning more of the same in Uruguay. Additionally, he seemed jealous of the extensive contacts that I had made in the country, saying that it looked like the CIA was taking over the responsibilities of the Foreign Service Office.

"We're both on the same side," I told him. "I'm here to make sure the Communists don't take over the country."

Woodward replied in a cold tone, "You won't find any more Communists in Uruguay than you could find in the whole state of Texas."

Before the elections took place, the new ambassador was quite sure that the Colorado Party would notch another win, and never even bothered to meet with Nardone. So when my friend swept to a surprising win I was the sole American invited to his victory party. As no member of the embassy except me was even on speaking terms with the president elect, Woodward was forced to swallow his pride and arrange an introduction through me. My moral victory might have felt good, but it only served to make the ambassador more antagonistic toward me.

After Nardone took office, our friendly relationship paid off further when I was able to advise the new president on various candidates for prominent official positions and in one case keep him from appointing a minister of the Interior who regularly sold information to the KGB to fund his gambling habit. Woodward became increasingly resentful by my connection with Nardone and complained to headquarters that my home was too opulent for a deputy secretary and that the parties we threw for the diplomatic circle were too lavish for my station. Little by little, he tried to get me reassigned.

When President Eisenhower visited the country, Nardone felt that it was a great opportunity to come to my defense.

"When I meet with President Eisenhower," he said, "I will mention that I feel that it is very important for you to stay here for a while. Do you feel like that is a good plan?"

I told him that a vote of confidence would be much appreciated.

It seemed like fate would be in my corner, as well, since I was picked to be Eisenhower's interpreter, pending the arrival of Colonel Walters, who had been delayed. Additionally, as the president was lodged in the embassy, I hand delivered the normal daily intelligence briefing to his chief of staff every morning, just as he would have received in Washington.

On several occasions, I was called into the room prior to Eisenhower's breakfast, where I found a different person from the public persona of the grinning, friendly Ike that was broadcast to America. In private, the president I saw was authoritarian and easily irritated, often insulting or putting down a staff member for some small perceived slight, even muttering something nasty at a secretary because the coffee wasn't hot enough. These incidents not only dulled my enthusiasm for the president but enhanced my conviction that Vice President Nixon might be better suited to the job.

My interest in Ike diminished further after President Nardone personally asked Eisenhower to allow me to stay on. Eisenhower deferred the decision to Ambassador Woodward, asking, "We have a request by the government to keep Mr. Hunt in position. How do you feel about it?"

Of course, Woodward's reply was "We would prefer someone else, sir."

Soon thereafter, I received notice from the embassy watch officer that my father had died, so I flew home to help my mother with the funeral, burying him in the Hunt family plot beside my infant brother.

This was one of the biggest blows in my life, as my father had always been an anchor I could count on to help me brave the storms of life. I remembered how he had taken me fishing when I was a boy, teaching me the value of patience and the love of nature. I wasn't the only one affected by his death. Hundreds of people showed up at his funeral to pay their respects. I felt terrible that I hadn't seen him for several months before he died. The only fortunate aspect of his dying at that point in my life was that he was spared the anguish of seeing my Watergate humiliation and imprisonment, which would have been the greatest disappointment of his life.

Looking back, I see where one of the seeds of Watergate, which was first sown during the Alger Hiss hearings, started to grow. When Vice President Richard Nixon and his wife, Patty, visited Montevideo on a whirlwind tour of South America, I took the occasion to remind him of our coincidental meeting at Harvey's Restaurant in Washington a few years earlier. Still a congressman at the time, Nixon had given a speech at a meeting of the Society of Former FBI Agents and was lingering over dessert with his wife in the restaurant when Dorothy and I found ourselves seated next to them after attending the theater.

I took the opportunity to introduce myself and congratulate him on his prosecution of Alger Hiss, who most people at the time felt was guilty of collusion with the Soviets. The couple invited us to join them, and we spent a pleasant half hour discussing foreign and domestic politics. I was impressed that the Nixons remembered the chance meeting.

While the Nardone administration was definitely pro-American, much of the rest of Uruguay felt a deep resentment toward the United States, especially toward Nixon, believing that his strong anti-Communist viewpoint had taken over the Eisenhower White House, which had originally promised greater détente with the Russians. In fact, there was a lot of friction between the president and the vice president on many issues, and Nixon had scarcely managed to stay on the ticket for Ike's second term. Now he was consolidating power and throwing his weight around in Republican circles in preparation for a run at the presidency in 1960. The prevailing political joke in Uruguay at the time was "The Yankees voted for Eisenhower and got Nixon."

Shortly after the Nixon tour left, I received a cable from Washington, which I had been expecting ever since Woodward's arrival, recalling me to Washington. The missive was signed jointly by Tracy Barnes and my new boss, Richard Bissell, who had taken over Clandestine Services from Frank Wisner, who had been hospitalized for overwork and reassigned to the peaceful London station. Bissell, as mentioned previously, had accumulated a great deal of respect inside the agency after creating the wildly successful U-2 spy-plane program. I thought he would do right by me, as I had had several favorable meetings with him in Washington and a lengthy consultation with him once during a Latin American chiefs conference in Lima, Peru.

I flew to Washington for meetings about my new position. Tracy Barnes, now principal assistant to Bissell, explained that I was needed for an important new project that was similar to the one I had worked on for him overthrowing Jacobo Arbenz.

"I'm all ears," I said. "By the way, you saw my reports that Arbenz moved in near me in Montevideo?" I asked.

Barnes nodded. "Very ironic," he agreed, looking at me through his trademark thick eyeglasses. "This operation is just as important but must be handled even more carefully. There must be absolutely no taint that the United States is involved. That's why we're bringing in the best. I'm reassembling most of the team from PB/Success. It's extremely sensitive. Eisenhower insists on complete deniability."

"And who is the target?" I asked.

"Castro," Barnes replied laconically. "We're taking down Fidel Castro."

I let out a breath. "Finally!"

It seemed like such an easy project at the time.

11

Bay of Pigs

The Bay of Pigs story contains all the elements of a Shakespearean tragedy: An evil but charismatic villain, Castro, wields an ironhanded rule over an inaccessible island and is pitted against a young ruler in exile, the visionary young Cuban Mañuel Artime. The protagonist's ally, John F. Kennedy, promises help but betrays the hero at a crucial hour. I portray myself as the experienced counselor trying to make the different personalities mesh together. There are many complex secondary characters with different agendas for the outcome, including, sadly, the brave soldiers of Brigade 2506, who must fight a much larger force and are doomed by missed opportunities, misunderstandings, and miscommunication. The outcome of this action has been recorded and retold so many times that it need not be a mystery here, but like a classic drama or opera whose ending is already well known, audiences still come to see it played again and again in an act of catharsis.

The tragic Bay of Pigs invasion has been the subject of one of the most intensive self-flagellating internal CIA inquiries in history, several scathing presidential reports and congressional investigations, and an untold number of articles, books, and Ph.D. dissertations. And that was before the Internet.

Blame for the failure is usually heaped on the shoulders of President John F. Kennedy, who championed the exile cause against Castro as an election promise but who withdrew all-important U.S. air support at the crucial hour when men were dying on the beach. A few CIA and government officials have written about the incident in their memoirs, including two Kennedy administration officials and Deputy Director Richard Bissell, who detailed his own shortcomings in his book *Reflections of a Cold Warrior*, mostly blaming himself for taking other people's advice. Scapegoats of the debacle were Director of Central Intelligence (DCI) Allen Dulles, who retired; Deputy DCI General Charles Cabell, who was fired; and Director of Plans Richard Bissell, who resigned. Tracy Barnes miraculously survived the bloodbath and was moved into another section, where I would work for him later.

In any action of this sort, the fault lies in many areas, and no mea culpa, however heartfelt, can bring back the brave men who died that day, many of whom were my friends. The failure would weaken the Kennedy administration and embolden Khrushchev to send nuclear weapons to Cuba, which nearly set off World War III. Sadly, many worthwhile lessons that might have been learned from the disaster, and might have later helped the United States deal better with Vietnam and, most recently, Iraq, were all conveniently forgotten. The operation was expected to take about a year, including finding and training Cuban troops to invade their homeland, with the base of operations initially slated for Costa Rica.

Our children were happy with their school in Montevideo, Uruguay, so Dorothy and I decided that I would go on ahead to set up a household, where the family would join me in July. The Costa Rican government proved problematic, so the base where I was supposed to forge a government in exile from the Cuban leaders was changed to Mexico City, a place even worse than Costa Rica for this purpose, as both the government and the populace were extremely sympathetic to Castro.

Miami, Florida, at this time had three major exile organizations with a few thousand members in each, and several dozen if not hundreds of smaller groups, some composed of just a husband and wife. All were determined to return to a non-Communist Cuba, and each reported to have a solid group of supporters back home who would rally against Castro when the time came. In reality, in a quest for government money, donations, and community interest, even the largest groups boasted many more contacts on the island than they did indeed have.

The Washington headquarters for the operation was in Quarters Eye, an unassuming military barracks along the Potomac, where I met with the task force chief, Jake Esterline, and Gerry Droller, the officer to whom I would report. I was happy to hear this, as I had known Droller for a decade and thought highly of him. He rubbed some people the wrong way with his hearty, effusive personality, and his habit of taking a risky course of action rather than the cover-your-ass way that was beginning to permeate the agency. Esterline later called Droller "insanely ambitious."

Droller was happy to have me aboard and gave me an enthusiastic greeting. The cover that he used when dealing with the Cubans was the name Frank Bender, with a background as an anti-Communist steel magnate who represented a group of wealthy American industrialists, so from now on I'll call him Bender in this narrative.

Adhering to the demands of plausible deniability, the project departed from standard agency procedure and had its own chain of command, starting with DDP Richard Bissell, descending through Tracy Barnes to Jake Esterline to Bender. As far as we were able to determine, DCI Allen Dulles, DDCI General Charles Cabell, and Richard Helms, the chief of operations for Clandestine Services, were privy to the affair but not a part of the operation.

The project, based so much on PB/Success, was divided into three sections: political action, propaganda, and paramilitary action. I was put in charge of political action. The agent in charge of propaganda was my old friend from the Guatemala operation, David Atlee Phillips, who had already begun organizing Cuban students, women, and professional groups around Latin America and had established a radio station on Swan Island off Honduras. The station was so powerful that it could be heard in Cuba and even in Miami.

The paramilitary chief was Colonel Jack Hawkins, a marine officer who had returned to active duty after a period of retirement. I was not happy to meet him, as this man had obviously seen better days physically and had the bloated look of a heavy drinker. He seemed very unprofessional, wearing cowboy boots and speaking in a drawl peppered with slang and curse words. He professed to want to "lead the boys ashore" himself, saying that the next president of Cuba would be decided by military, not political, action. Our disaffection was instantly mutual.

A paramilitary training area in Guatemala had been hacked out of a coffee plantation and an old cargo airstrip resurfaced to handle cargo planes that were currently being purchased around the world to make up the exile air force. To maintain a curtain of plausible deniability, the aircraft in question were old World War II B-25 and B-26 planes, which could conceivably be purchased cheaply on the international market by a rebel army short on funds. Small arms, including some machine guns, were being supplied by a network of European arms dealers, many of which had been rescued from wartime ordnance dumps.

Hawkins said that Castro was far from the revolutionary genius that the world considered him to be; and that he had succeeded only because of Batista's even greater ineptitude and failure to realize how much a majority of the populace hated him. "Piece of cake," said Hawkins. "Our boys will be able to send you a Christmas card from Cuba this year. Castro will be lucky to get away in a rowboat."

"Our boys" were headed by a diverse group of anti-Batista figures, some of whom had fought in the revolution beside Fidel before defecting when the strongman embraced Communism. Returning to my office, I read the dossiers of Mañuel Antonio de Varona, Justo Carillo, José Ignacio Rasco, Mañuel Artime, and Aureliano Sánchez Arango, most of whom had been exfiltrated from Cuba by the CIA Havana station, which ironically had once championed Fidel when he was hiding out in the mountains.

The Cuban operation had taken a while to get into production, as the CIA had been funding anti-Castro activities on the island, but Castro's astute and observant neighborhood watches had fingered the activists, who had been lined up against a wall and shot. To make matters worse, Eisenhower, who had originally greenlighted the invasion concept, left office, hoping to pass the baton to Nixon, who had been the White House point man on the project. Unfortunately, Kennedy won the election and was obsessed with world opinion, only okaying the operation after being assured that the concept of plausible deniability be somehow updated to concrete, written-in-stone, utterly deniable deniability, making our task all the more difficult.

One of my first assignments was to visit Havana and assess the situation in Cuba in the field, trying to determine whether a rebel group could count on help from a popular uprising. I found that while there might be searing hatred for Castro by Miami's dispossessed Cubans, the reason why the anti-Castro movement hadn't taken hold on the island was that the bulk of the populace was either enthralled with their leader or scared to death of him, hoping for some kind of divine intervention to decide their fate. Either way, few would take up arms in opposition.

I certainly didn't like what I saw there. Loudspeakers blasted propaganda radio programs into the streets for hours every day. At one street rally, a live commentator set the crowd on a few of the better dressed members, who fled for their lives. I learned of hundreds of people, labeled as agitators, who disappeared without a trace, others who were festering in dungeonlike prisons because they had uttered a few words against Castro. Many people, accused by the overly efficient neighborhood watches headed by block captains with unknown agendas, had been lined up against a wall and shot as a lesson to others. It was amazing to me that the United States had once supported Castro, and any doubts that I had about the project were resolved during my visit, making me determined to do my best to help rid the country of the bloody dictatorship.

When I returned to the United States, I filed a report that included four recommendations for the invasion. First and foremost, all efforts should be made to assassinate Castro before or coincident with the invasion. This would be a task for a Cuban patriot. Other factors included the destruction of radio and television transmitters and the microwave relay system. All hope that a popular uprising would take place when the people heard that an invasion force had landed should be discarded. I found out years later that Jake Esterline apparently took my advice to heart and recruited Juan Orta, Castro's private secretary, to poison the dictator's drink. Unfortunately, Orta lost his nerve and fled to the Venezuelan embassy right before the invasion.

Of the possible contenders for a counterrevolutionary president, my favorite was Mañuel Artime. At only twenty-seven years of age, he radiated a magnetic aura of leadership that would draw people to his cause. He was extremely intelligent and articulate, having studied medicine at the Jesuit college in Cuba, where he had planned to become a psychiatrist before joining Fidel in the Sierra Maestra. He had proven himself in battle, fighting against Batista troops in several skirmishes, and had been rewarded with a favored command by Castro after the revolution. He had had to escape Cuba, however, after being accused of speaking against Raul Castro and Che Guevera. Now, Artime had joined with Tony Varona, Aureliano Sánchez Arango, and José Cardona to establish the Movement for the Recovery of the Revolution, which had a base of some five thousand followers in Miami, several hundred of whom were already training in the camps in Guatemala.

In order to keep the U.S. presence at a distance—per orders of plausible deniability—I originally set up shop in Mexico City, where I was supposed to forge the Cuban leaders into a government in exile. This group had representatives of the five main exile organizations, including Artime, who belonged to the Revolutionary Recovery Group (MMR): Tony Varona, the Rescate; Aureliano Sánchez Arango, the Triple A; Justo Carillo, the Montecristi; and José Rasco, the Christian Democratic Movement. The diverse members each had slightly to radically different agendas, some fairly leftist, and became a fractious and divisive group we named the Frente Revolucionario Democrático (FRD), the new provisional government.

Mexico quickly became problematic, however, as the government ordered the secret police to harass and follow our members. The situation became so difficult that Eisenhower (who was still in power at this time) finally relented and allowed the headquarters to go to Miami, where I rented a safe house in Coconut Grove. I met a Cuban American CIA asset there, Bernard "Macho" Barker, who had worked for the Havana station for several years, infiltrating the Cuban federal police. Bernie had ties throughout the Cuban community in Miami, and he was an invaluable assistant in maintaining contact with various leaders and recruiting new members for Brigade 2506. Additionally, he had helped smuggle Artime and Varona out of Cuba in a freighter, so he had a good relationship with our favored future leaders. (As an aside, the heroic captain of the freighter was executed on his return to Cuba.)

Barker would later play an important part in Watergate, so it's interesting to look back with twenty-twenty hindsight about how all the pieces of the puzzle fit into place. Another Watergate figure would be Frank Sturgis, known as Frank Fiorini at this time.

Although I did not actually meet Sturgis until the Watergate era, I heard about him, as he had helped pilot a plane from the United States to Havana with compatriot Pedro Díaz Lanz to drop anti-Castro leaflets. While I met Lanz at this time and recommended him to our paramilitary commander as a seasoned pilot who knew Cuba, I was not well acquainted with him. But his name would pop up in future conspiracy theories regarding me and the Kennedy assassination, as well.

From what I understood about Fiorini, he had served in the Marine Corps and the navy, from which he received honorable discharges. Frank was certainly involved in the recommendation of various exiles, whom he knew personally, to be included in the Bay of Pigs invasion, but he was not part of the brigade itself. There's a chance he may have infiltrated the island at one point and scouted the territory, but he was not with the invading force.

There are a lot of conspiracy theories, which I'll get into later, involving Sturgis—whom I first met in 1972—and me, so he's a character to remember. Some of the theories abound because my 1949 novel, *Bimini Run*, involves a character named Hank Sturgis, which has made a lot of buffs speculate that the book is based on Frank. So I would have had to meet Sturgis in the 1940s, long before Sturgis was a person of interest. While he was a U.S. Marine in World War II, he was sent to the South Pacific, far away from where I was at the time. The book is fictional, but the character is based on a very active, tall, thin jungle fighter named Sturgis whom I knew in OSS. That Sturgis contracted tuberculosis in Burma and was sent to a sanitarium in Lake Placid, New York, where he eventually recovered. So the unfortunate coincidence in names has given people hundreds of thousands of hours worth of conspiracy theory entertainment over the years.

As the months passed and the fighting force was being trained, the infighting among the Frente grew ever more intense. There was also a dichotomy between the military force training in Guatemala and the Frente. The political group believed the soldiers should be under their command, with *their* soldiers fighting to install *them* as the leaders. Most of the members of the fighting force, however, had little allegiance to the Frente and basically thought that once they overthrew Fidel's army, they would be in a position to say in whose hands the reins should be held.

The friction between the two groups was so great that my superiors kept them separate, constantly making excuses to the Frente members about why they couldn't visit their troops. There wasn't enough room on the planes, the weather was bad, whatever came to mind at the time.

By April 1961, the U.S. military trainers considered the brigade to be more than ready. Bissell wrote that the evaluations he received from Jack Hawkins indicated that "the brigade had higher firepower per man than a comparable U.S. formation did." The force of approximately fifteen hundred men was made up of mostly students, but there were also farmers, sugarcane cutters, fishermen, mechanics, and even a handful of former Castro and Batista soldiers—men from all walks of life united by the burning desire to kick the Cuba out of Castro.

The brigade commander was Captain José Perez "Pepe" San Roman, a former Cuban army officer who had fought against Castro; the deputy commander was Captain Erneido Oliva, another former Cuban army officer; and Mañuel Artime was named civil leader of the brigade.

The plan called for an initial strike against Castro's small air force before any of his planes could take off, with a second follow-up mission to ensure that any possible resistance from the air had been obliterated. The exile planes would fly from a base in Nicaragua, from where they would only have about an hour's supply of extra fuel before having to turn around. Immediately after Castro's air force was obliterated on the ground, the brigade was scheduled to storm the beach, where it was hoped that they would be able to hold their ground and establish a base from where they could get on the radio and broadcast to the world that the government in exile had returned and make a plea for assistance from other countries. It was also expected from intelligence reports—somewhat erroneously I might add—that 75 to 80 percent of Castro's militia would either defect or refuse to fight. At this point, the United States would be able to openly aid the invaders.

By the time the brigade was nearing battle readiness, however, with D-Day scheduled for April 17, Kennedy had become increasingly paranoid about world opinion and the "noise" that a proposed daytime landing near the large town of Trinidad would bring. Worse, on April 12, he actually promised reporters at a news conference that the United States would not invade Cuba. Somehow he expected the invasion to happen in a vacuum where the world wouldn't notice that fifteen hundred armed men had landed on a Cuban beach.

So just weeks before the operation was to take place, Kennedy ordered that the invasion be moved to a "quieter" destination. Military planners scrambled to come up with another venue, deciding on El Bayo de Cochinos, the Bay of Pigs, about eighty miles from the first site at the port town of Trinidad on the south coast of Cuba. This site had been chosen because it was a hotbed of anti-Castro activity, and CIA analysts believed its citizens would join the brigade forces. The new site was clearly inferior, as it was more secluded, but its merits included a sizeable beach cut off from the mainland by the Zapata swamps. Since the site was accessible by only three bridges, it was hoped that the brigade could easily take and defend the entrances to the area.

The day before the first air strike against Castro, set for April 15, Kennedy, without conferring with military planners—and urged by Secretary of State Dean Rusk—limited the air strike so as to make less "noise." The strike was halved from sixteen to eight planes, which were unable to completely carry out the mission of taking out Castro's forces or blasting the runways into ruins.

The ships carrying the force arrived on schedule and were in sight of the coast on the sixteenth when Kennedy, without warning, called off the all-important second strike until the invasion force had established a position on the ground and taken a local airport from where the B-26s could operate, making it look as if the troops were defectors taking off from Cuban soil. Reactions at Quarter's Eye were emotional. According to Bissell, when Hawkins heard of the command, he banged his fist on the table and yelled, "Goddamn it. This is criminal negligence!"

Further complicating the plan was another Kennedy command to make the invasion after dark, not withstanding that an amphibious attack had never been attempted at night before, even by experienced U.S. armed forces. So on April 17, when Brigade 2506 prepared to launch, the men who set out with a mixture of bravery and gut-wrenching fear had no idea that they were fighting a battle that was almost certainly already lost.

Bissell asked me to bring the six exile government members, all of whom had sons, brothers, or nephews in the brigade, to meet President Kennedy.

"I can't face them," I told my superior. "They trusted me, and I can't face them."

It was Bender who was burdened with the unhappy task.

While Kennedy took the official responsibility for the Bay of Pigs debacle, his administration and the Joint Chiefs of Staff considered it a failure of the CIA, forcing the retirement of the aforementioned officials. Within the agency, anyone involved in the project, even though not responsible for the disaster, was made to feel like an outcast and discriminated against regarding future assignments and promotions. Before his retirement, Dulles assigned me to his staff to help investigate the fiasco.

Of the brigade's landing force of 1,443 men, 1,189 were captured, 114 were killed, and some 150 were able to escape. After months of grueling prison time, with several men dying, the United States eventually paid ransom to get our fighters back.

On Christmas Eve, 1962, I picked up a ringing telephone.

"*Feliz Navidad*, amigo," Artime said. "I'm at Miami Airport."

It felt so good to hear his voice that I cried. Mañuel Artime endured twenty-one months incarcerated in some of Cuba's worst prisons, much of it in solitary confinement, naked, in complete darkness. He had kept his mind sharp by creating and memorizing poetry. During his hardship, I told him, my second son, David, had been born, and I named "Manolo" as godfather, which almost made him break down as well.

"That was my way of promising myself that you'd make it back," I told him.

When I went to prison after Watergate, Artime brought David into his home, where he cared for him as one of his own children. I also owe him an unpayable debt for his active support of the legal defense of myself and my four Miami Watergate colleagues.

A few days later, on December 29, President Kennedy visited Miami, where he met the survivors of the 2506 at a televised ceremony at the Orange Bowl. There, Pepe San Roman gave JFK the brigade's flag to hold for "safekeeping."

Kennedy responded with the faulty promise, "I can assure you that this flag will be returned to the brigade in a free Havana."

Manolo visited me in Washington shortly after the beginning of 1963. We had an emotional reunion, emptying quite a few glasses and getting pretty drunk. He confided in me that the flag was a replica and that the presentation nearly didn't take place because of the animosity of the brigade members toward JFK.

After all his hardship, his spirit had only been galvanized, and he was brimming with plans to take down Fidel. Later, the United States funded his efforts to oust the dictator, resulting in raids against the island from bases in Latin America, but his efforts resulted in mere annoyances, like a mosquito biting an elephant.

A great assessment of the bungled operation and its ensuing repercussions was written by Professor Han J. Morgenthau in an article for *Foreign Affairs*: "To Intervene or Not to Intervene."

> The United States was resolved to intervene on behalf of its interests, but it was also resolved to intervene in such a way as not to violate the principle of nonintervention. . . . The United States failed to assign priorities to these interests. In order to minimize the loss of prestige, the United States jeopardized the success of the intervention . . . and we lost much prestige as a great nation able to use its power successfully on behalf of its interests. . . . It sought the best of both worlds and got the worst.

Or, in other memorable words, the United States was caught up in a miserable catch-22.

I concluded my 1966 book *Give Us This Day*, a nonfiction account of the Bay of Pigs, with this thought about Morgenthau's observations: "For the sake of our country, one can only hope that this analysis of needless failure will be remembered by our national leadership during some crisis yet to come."

Unfortunately, it has become quite clear in recent years that we have not learned the lessons we paid for so dearly. The echoes of the Bay of Pigs have resonated in our international policy ever since.

Like many other people involved, I never recovered psychologically or operationally from the Bay of Pigs tragedy. The top CIA officials were all sent off to pasture, except Dick Helms, who had somehow been prescient enough to foresee the catastrophe far enough in advance to "include himself out" from the beginning. It could also have been his complete lack of interest in Latin America, as he had attended prep school in Switzerland—a schoolmate of the future shah of Iran—and was extremely Eurocentric.

At that point, I might easily have tendered my resignation, as well, but Bissell called me one day to cheer me up.

"The way things are going, I'll be leaving shortly," he told me. "But I want to tell you personally that you need to stay on, continue working in Latin America. You're the kind of guy the agency needs down there."

"You're right, Dick," I agreed. "But what can I do? I'm just one guy and I don't have any political backing, nobody to take up my cause, which I consider the cause of the United States. This administration has an attitude of tolerance for everything. If they tolerate

Castro, he'll export his ideals across Latin America. After the Bay of Pigs, Cuba is a losing cause, and nobody wants to be identified with it, so they look the other way." And I've been right.

It's truly amazing to me how long Castro has maintained power in Cuba. After the invasion, a popular joke on the island went like this: John F. Kennedy falls asleep for thirty years. When he wakes up, the first thing he asks is, "What's happening in Russia?" He's told that all the Communist leaders are dead and it's now a model of Western-style capitalism. "And China?" Same thing. "And Cuba?" he inquires. "We expect Castro to fall any day now," he's told. The joke has progressed through the years, changing U.S. presidents with every new administration. More than forty years later it is now being told with George W. Bush as the latest Rip Van Winkle president.

Another old Cuban joke goes, "Fidel has provided medicine, education, and defense. He still hasn't fixed breakfast, lunch, and dinner." And the final results of Castro-style Communism: "Before the revolution, people died and became skeletons. After the revolution: skeletons first, death later."

While Castro struck a responsive chord in the Cuban populace, he has survived the later disillusionment because his army, secret police, and block spies have been able to keep the isolated citizenry efficiently subjugated. I'm sorry to say that the aforementioned joke will probably be told for several successive U.S. administrations.

A lot of Cuban idealism died with Che Guevara, who was in many ways the romantic soul of the revolution. He was so beloved that Castro realized Guevara would pose a future threat to Castro's one-sided form of government, so Castro encouraged Guevara to leave the country and expand the reach of Communism throughout the Americas.

To that end, in the fall of 1966, Castro managed to have Che and a small band of followers inserted into Bolivia, where they kept in contact with Cuba by shortwave radio. What Guevara didn't know was that the U.S. National Security Agency was monitoring the transmissions of both sides, so we always knew where he was and what he was doing.

Guevara was recognized as a real threat, establishing a guerilla insurgency against the Bolivian government, so the agency sent a Cuban American agent, Felix Rodriguez, to the country, where he was able to pass intelligence to the Bolivian army that Guevara was expected to travel to La Higuera, from where the band of guerillas was tracked down and where Che was ultimately executed in October 1967.

Still, Kennedy did not turn his back on the Cuban problem after the Bay of Pigs. After the failed military action, the CIA did try to resolve the Castro problem through assassination. The project was called Operation Mongoose, headed by William Harvey, a drunk who had been kicked out of the FBI. Balding, with loose jowls and rolls of fat jiggling under his chin and bulging out of a tight collar, he sported a short pencil-thin mustache, trying to give his face some aspect of personality.

Harvey had found an easy spot in which to nest under the CIA's counterintelligence director, James Angleton, a very odd couple, I thought. While I never had any reason to deal with him, I thought he was a strange man who should not be representing the CIA, much less the United States. His supply chief worked for me for a time in Washington, where he told me that he had left the Rome station after working for two months under Harvey.

"The guy is awful," he complained. "You should see what he's up to over there. Harvey's wife is a WAC [Women's Army Corps] officer who looks more masculine than a lot of men I know." He implied that there was some kind of strange sex going on.

Another story I remember is that when Harvey was Rome's chief of station in 1963, every time the large man went to lunch, he would take out his .45 and slam it on the table, making the waiters and the other patrons jump in astonishment, as if to say, "Bring the food fast or else!"

So it was no surprise to me that Harvey's efforts to kill Castro, using the Mafia as the weapon of choice, did not prove fruitful, and the dictator remains stubbornly alive in the Presidential Palace today (or, at least, hospitalized nearby!).

12

The Assassination
of President Kennedy

One of the great mysteries of the twentieth century is whether there was a conspiracy to kill John F. Kennedy. Let me say clearly that if there was such a scheme, I had nothing to do with it. I was not in Dallas on November 22, 1963; I was not part of a plot to kill the president; and I had no knowledge of the planned assassination. The thought of perpetrating any crime against the president, even though I disagreed with many of his policies, is completely against my innermost convictions, as anyone who truly knows me would attest.

But this matter has cost me a lot of hardship and pain, as conspiracy buffs have linked my name to the terrible crime. It started in 1975 with a book that I shall not name here, in which the authors published photographs of three bums who were arrested on Dealey Plaza that day, asserting that two of the men pictured were myself and Frank Sturgis. The resemblance is only visible by somebody with an active imagination or someone examining doctored photos. The FBI was able to track down the bums—Gus Abrams, John Gedney, and Harold Doyle—whom they hauled in and interrogated. They didn't know me and I didn't know them.

I gave a thorough account of my whereabouts in Washington, D.C., that day, sued the authors, and thought that the situation was pretty much taken care of at the time. However, I had no idea about how JFK assassination conspiracies would morph and reconstitute themselves. In a way, it's like the famous Hydra. You cut off one head, and two grow back.

In August 1978, a former CIA agent, Victor Marchetti, put out an article about the assassination in *Spotlight*, a weekly magazine published by the Liberty Lobby, a right-wing group that regularly published articles and advertisements with anti-Semitic, white supremacist, and neo-Nazi slants.

In this article, the author relied on a "1966 CIA memo" from Allen Dulles to James Angleton, which revealed that Frank Sturgis, CIA agent Gerry Patrick Hemming, and I had been involved in the assassination plot. The memo was supposedly in the hands of the House Special Committee on Assassinations (HSCA), which was scheduled to hold hearings later in the month.

The memo, of course, was either fictitious or forged, as it has apparently never seen the light of day and was never published by the HSCA. Nevertheless, I was called in front of the Assassination Committee on November 3, 1978, to give a detailed account of any knowledge I had of the event and about my whereabouts on the fateful day. This testimony, along with that of many other CIA operatives, including Richard Helms, Allen Dulles, and David Atlee Phillips, was finally declassified in 1995.

I read aloud a prepared statement to set the stage:

> Not long after Watergate, it became fashionable in certain quarters to suggest that those guilty of Watergate's heinous crimes might well be guilty of even worse monstrosities, including the assassination of a president of the United States: John F. Kennedy.
>
> Photographs of myself and the other Watergate figures were published widely in this country and abroad. Meanwhile, assassination buffs had developed a number of theories—all at variance with the findings of the Warren Commission—that concentrated on suggested conspiracies. Books appeared, irresponsible headlines erupted in the tabloid press, and the media—ever eager for sensation—gave time and space to proponents of the wildest conceivable theories concerning the identity of the assassin of John F. Kennedy, his sponsors, if any, and so forth. I need hardly take your time or mine to itemize the incredible amount of trash that has been written and televised about that tragic event.

I tried to keep my voice steady and unemotional, befitting a court proceeding; but it proved impossible, and the anger I felt over the following material poured out in bitter tones.

> In due course, a tabloid, the *National Tattler*, sometime around March 1974, I believe, published a story implying that I had been in Dallas when Kennedy was killed and had a hand in his assassination. In response, I sued the tabloid, which promptly went out of business and left me with a default judgment and additional legal costs.

So not only had I been maliciously slandered, but protecting my name against people who were trying to make a buck out of a piece of my flesh, cost me a huge amount of time, money, and aggravation that I couldn't afford.

From here, I spelled out exactly why I could not be a suspect.

> In March 1974—four years ago—I discussed a variety of accusations with the Rockefeller Commission. Although my testimony was not desired, I provided the commission with the following sworn affidavit:
>
> 1. On that date, I was an employee of the Central Intelligence Agency, assigned to the Domestic Operations Division, located in a commercial building in Washington, D.C.
> 2. I was driving with my late wife on H Street near 8th or 9th Street when we first heard of the Kennedy shooting on our car radio. We had been purchasing Chinese groceries at a store named, as well as I can recall it, Wah Ling. . . .

Conspiracy theorists would later point out that there was no Wah Ling store near where I said it was at that time, which gave them ammunition to say that my entire testimony was a lie. They fail to mention that I amended this name just minutes later.

> . . . I do not know how long after the initial radio reports were made that my wife and I first heard the news. [David] Brinkley was the commentator, I remember, because of his having theorized a right-wing plot: i.e., Dallas citizens had abused Adlai Stevenson and the climate of Dallas extremism had caused Kennedy's shooting.
>
> 3. From the Chinese grocery store, we drove out Wisconsin Avenue to pick up our daughter, Kevan, from Sidwell Friends School. On joining us, my daughter told us what we already knew: that President Kennedy had been shot. She had learned this because two of Robert Kennedy's children had been taken from Sidwell Friends School, presumably by Secret Service agents.

4. From Kevan's school, we drove directly to our home on Baltan Road in Sumner, Maryland (off Massachusetts Avenue extended). At home was my newly born son, David (DOB 9/1/63); a maid, Mary Trayner; and my wife's aunt, the late Leona Drexler of Chicago. Our elder son, St. John, a student at nearby Brookmont Elementary School, was probably already home. As I recall, our eldest child, Lisa, arrived soon afterward by bus from Ursuline Academy and joined us at the television set in our basement recreation room, where we stayed long hours watching the unfolding of events: the swearing in of LBJ, the arrival at Andres Field of the presidential coffin, etc.

5. As to why I was not in my office that entire afternoon, I can only presume that I had left early to help my wife shop for a planned Chinese dinner, in preparation of which I normally assisted.

6. I was never in Dallas, Texas, until late 1971, when at the request of Charles Colson [my later White House boss] I flew there to interview General Paul Harkins, former U.S. military commander in Vietnam.

7. I did not meet Frank Sturgis until the spring of 1972, the introduction being performed by and at the office of Bernard L. Barker.

8. I never at any time met or knew Lee Harvey Oswald, Jack Ruby, or any person involved in the Dallas slayings.

9. I was not in Mexico in 1963. In fact, I was not in Mexico between the years of 1961 and 1970.

Of course, conspiracy theorists still have to bring up the following: that I have little but other people's memories of the day to support my testimony, the reasons for which I spelled out now:

> I have no diaries or other memorabilia prior to 1969, having destroyed as many outdated files and records as possible to save weight in the move to my Florida home in July 1974. I retained only such records, bank statements, etc., as are required by the five-year Internal Revenue Service for income tax purposes.
>
> That was signed, notarized, and sworn to at the time.

Then I amended my statement about the Chinese grocery store, which conspiracy buffs fail to remember.

> To that affidavit, I would add only that the name I accorded the Chinese grocery store was mistaken. Since revisiting the site, I have determined that the name of the store was Tuck Cheong.

From here, I contested the so-called photographic evidence of my complicity. I had calmed down somewhat over the last few minutes, but now I could feel the pulse in my throat again. It made me so mad that I had to spend my precious time on this earth repeating my innocence ad nauseam because of the ridiculous accusations of others.

Also in March 1974, I provided the Rockefeller Commission with seventeen different photographs of myself taken during the period 1961–1964. It is my understanding that these photographs were compared with those of the so-called Dallas tramps by an FBI photo analyst, Lyndal Shaneyfelt, who determined with professional finality that the tramp photos were not of Frank Sturgis or myself.

Then in October 1974, assertedly at the request of then FBI director Kelley, I assented to an interview by agents of the FBI's Baltimore office. Their memorandum of the interview was made public last January.

But even that did not end the continuing harassment. Early in 1975, political activist Dick Gregory was given a series of photographs of the Dallas tramps together with several of Frank Sturgis and myself. In press conferences and talk shows, Gregory professed to see unmistakable similarity between the tramp photos and those of Sturgis and Hunt, and pressed the photographs upon the Rockefeller Commission with demands for satisfaction.

Shortly thereafter, in a timing sequence not entirely coincidental, a book by Alan Weberman and Michael Canfield was published, *Coup d' État in America*, which relied heavily on a presumptive likeness of Sturgis and myself to the so-called Dallas tramps. The defamatory intent of the book was so clear that I sued the authors and publisher of the book for libel. The publishing company went out of business, and the publisher returned to his native Nigeria. Litigation against the two authors is active to this day.

That these smears have staying power was reflected during a series of lectures I gave to college audiences last year; invariably some questioner would advert to my supposed involvement in the assassination of President Kennedy on the assumption that I had occult knowledge of the tragedy.

I stopped and took a few deep breaths to keep my temper reined in before continuing.

From time to time, magazine articles rake over the cold ashes of supposed involvement in the Dallas assassination. And the more malicious underground press frequently dwells boldly on the subject, maligning and defaming me to my continuing detriment. Against these injurious falsehoods, I have found myself helpless, for the agitators and profiteers accept no answers save those they prescribe in advance.

Last August, two newspapers—*Spotlight*, published in Washington, D.C., and the *News-Journal* of Wilmington, Delaware—printed similar stories concerning me that I found profoundly disturbing. Their burden was that this committee had received from the Central Intelligence Agency a memorandum purportedly initialed by Director Richard Helms in 1966, stating that some day it might be necessary to reveal that Howard Hunt was in Dallas on the day of President Kennedy's assassination. Copies of both stories have been furnished to this committee together with my request that a copy of the alleged memorandum be furnished to me.

To date, the committee has not responded to my request, and I now renew it: I demand that the committee confirm or deny receipt of such a memorandum, and if the memorandum indeed exists, that it be furnished to me so that I may refute its contents in their entirety.

Because I was not in Dallas on the day President Kennedy was killed, I know that the purported memorandum is spurious. The veil of mystery surrounding it, however, is exceedingly damaging to me. The charge has been made; the committee is said to be the source of the false information, and it is within your power to set the matter straight once and for all.

Fair play demands it, and simple justice requires it.

Thank you.

The committee, of course, never furnished the memorandum.

In 1981, I won a $650,000 libel judgment against the *Spotlight* publisher, Liberty Lobby, which, unfortunately for my bank account, was overturned on a technicality when it was appealed. The case was retried, but a jury decided that the paper had not published the article in "a reckless disregard of the truth," so therefore it did not fit a narrow legal definition of "malice," and the jury ruled against me. There is an entire book to be written about the trial, but suffice it to say that any of the thousands of pages that try to connect me to the killing are utterly wrong, and a few books about the subject leave out many pertinent details and testimony that prove I was not in Dallas on the fateful day.

During the retrial, the defendant's attorney, Mark Lane, trotted out a woman named Marita Lorenz who claimed to have been a former Fidel Castro mistress smuggled out of Cuba by Frank Sturgis under his alias, Frank Fiorelli. Described as a "curvy, black-haired . . . American Mata Hari" by *New York Daily News* reporter Paul Meskil, she was an oval-faced, doe-eyed, innocent-looking woman, sporting a classic Jacqueline Kennedy hairstyle. She laid out a bizarre scenario in which I, Sturgis, Hemming, Oswald, and a few murderous

Cubans drove from Miami to Dallas to perpetrate the crime of the century. The woman was an amazing tale-spinner who could have had a great career as a spy novelist, but her testimony has been widely discredited, with a full account written by Gaeton Fonzi, a staff investigator for the HSCA, in *The Last Investigation*.

Did I get into a car loaded with guns in Miami and head for Dallas, as alleged by Marita Lorenz? The answer is no. Did I know Marita Lorenz? No. I didn't know her, and I wouldn't have wanted to know her. She was the type of person whom Frank Sturgis was accustomed to handling. She and Sturgis did know each other, and he reportedly conceived a plot to send her to Cuba to reunite with Castro, where she was supposed to administer poison pills to the dictator while he was asleep. She claimed that she met up with her jubilant lover but failed to give him the pills, because she had hidden them in a jar of cold cream, and they had melted. But if that's true, Sturgis never told me about it before she told the story, so I would have to assume it never took place, as Sturgis was not a person who would avoid taking credit for an operation as worthwhile as that.

Many theories circle around Sturgis's possible connection with the Mafia. Frank was not a man without a history. He had owned and managed clubs in Virginia Beach, ran guns to Cuba, volunteered for a couple of Central American revolutions, from which he extracted himself without injury, and acted as a petty thief for the Mafia before he eventually straightened out to some extent. Some journalists have connected him to Meyer Lansky and Santos Trafficante, which is entirely possible. He was an amazing individual who could and did pop up in the strangest places when you least expected him.

However, I don't think Frank was part of a plot against JFK. He was a congenial guy who would follow orders but had a room-temperature IQ. He was also very discretionally challenged and would never have been able to keep such a huge secret until his death. He was very incensed by Marita Lorenz's story connecting us to the plot, thus expanding her allotment of five minutes of fame to fifteen. So basically I don't think Sturgis was part of a conspiracy to kill John F. Kennedy, simply because nobody who was intelligent enough to concoct such a wide-ranging plot would have trusted him.

Another name that pops up in JFK conspiracy theories is Cord Meyer. He was a high-level CIA operative whose wife, journalist Mary Pinchot, was having an affair with John F. Kennedy. Meyer was the Yale-educated, blue-blooded son of a wealthy diplomat, who had once been elected the president of the United World Federalists—an organization supported by many intellectuals, such as Albert Einstein—which worked with the United Nations to build a "just world order," hoping to prevent another world war. In 1951, he was recruited to the CIA by none other than Allen Dulles himself, who placed him under Frank Wisner in what has been called Operation Mockingbird, a highly successful project with the objective of having direct influence over the American media (more about this operation later). By the time of the assassination, Cord had been promoted to chief of CIA's International Organizations Division.

Some theorists somehow connect dots between Meyer and Sturgis. This is highly improbable given Meyer's status in the agency. The two just would never have come into contact with each other.

The theorists suggest Cord would have had a motive to kill Kennedy because his wife was having an affair with the president. In 1954, the Kennedys bought an estate just outside Washington, D.C., where they became neighbors of the Meyers. Cord's wife and Jackie apparently became rather friendly and went on walks together.

Then, on October 12, 1964, Mary was tragically gunned down while walking on a towpath in Georgetown. By that time, she and Cord had divorced, and the media did not realize that her former husband was a high-ranking CIA official. Neither did they find out about her relationship with the president, so headlines about the murder quickly disappeared. Ray Crump, a black man, was arrested near the scene. Although he was acquitted of the crime, which remains unsolved, many court observers said that he got off because he had a good lawyer.

Mary had cautioned at least one close friend to grab her diary if anything ever happened to her. Journalist (later editor) Ben Bradlee happened to be married to Mary's sister, Antoinette, who found the diary and letters shortly after the death. But there is an interesting fact here.

When the Bradlees arrived at Mary's house shortly after the murder, they found James Angleton already there, rummaging around the house, looking for the diary and letters. No one has ever mentioned how the CIA official accessed the house, but Bradlee has said that the door was locked when he arrived. So does that mean Angleton broke in?

When Antoinette eventually found the diary, she turned it over to Angleton, who later admitted that the book detailed the affair, talking specifically about how Mary and Kennedy would drop LSD before making love. Mary apparently thought that JFK's murder had taken place because the industrial-military complex couldn't allow his mind to be expanded by the drug. The fact that Angleton was already in the house when Bradlee got there is mysterious, as so little time had gone by since the murder.

Journalist Leo Damore wrote in the *New York Post* that a CIA source told him that Mary's death was probably a professional hit because "She had access to the highest levels. She was involved in illegal drug activity. What do you think it would do to the beatification of Kennedy if this woman said, 'It wasn't Camelot, it was Caligula's court'?"

So I think it probably was a professional hit by someone trying to protect the Kennedy legacy.

I don't think that Cord Meyer killed his ex-wife, and I don't think it was Angleton either, although he did apparently know that Mary and Kennedy had carried on the affair. He died without shedding much light on the matter. Cord Meyer is dead, too, as is Sturgis. No one ever made a deathbed confession about either crime.

As for Frank Sturgis, although he always craved action and felt that Kennedy had betrayed Brigade 2506, this was not the way he would have evened the score. And if he had been involved in the killing, he would have somehow passed the knowledge on to me— hinted at it in the very least. We spent a lot of time together as bunk-mates in prison in Danbury, Connecticut, after Watergate, and I'm quite sure he could never have kept this information from me, as we had a good relationship and he thought of me as his boss in covert affairs.

There has been suggestion in some circles that CIA agent Bill Harvey had something to do with the murder and had recruited several Corsicans, especially a crack shot named Lucien Sarti, to back up Oswald and make sure the hit was successful. Supposedly, Sarti was dressed in a Dallas police uniform and fired the fatal bullet from the grassy knoll behind the picket fence.

However improbable it might be, it is vaguely possible. Oswald was not a great marksman while in the marines, and if he did kill

Kennedy, he got off the most accurate shots of his life. So he may have received some help.

Is it possible that Bill Harvey might have recruited a Mafia criminal to administer the magic bullet? I think it's possible. I can't go beyond that. Harvey could definitely be a person of interest, as he was a strange character hiding a mass of hidden aggression. Allegations have been made that he transported weapons to Dallas. Certainly it is an area that could use further investigation.

Since I don't believe that Oswald had the ability to perform the horrible feat of accurate marksmanship that killed Kennedy, especially with the mail-order 1938 Italian-manufactured Mannlicher-Carcano rifle he used, I think there may have been another shooter behind the fence, although I would like to stress that I have no specific knowledge of who that person might be. I wish I did, but I don't. Again, as technology gets better, perhaps a further examination of film and audio taken that day can formulate new leads.

But I am open to some postulation. While he always denied it, there has been enough speculation that David Atlee Phillips—using the pseudonym Maurice Bishop—met with Oswald in Mexico City before the assassination to have him called up in front of the HSCA to refute the allegations. After the Bay of Pigs, Phillips helped formulate plans to assassinate Castro and was named chief of Cuban Operations in 1963. In Miami, he helped support Alpha 66—an infamous anti-Castro group that made guerilla forays against Cuba—and reportedly told the organization's founder, Antonio Veciana, that he hoped to provoke the United States into interceding in Cuba by "putting Kennedy's back to the wall."

So there are now three CIA agents who have been named in connection with Oswald—David Phillips, Cord Meyer, and Bill Harvey—all with means, motive, opportunity, or some connection to kill Kennedy. Perhaps, one day, a CIA archivist may stumble on some file that connects these operatives together.

If that's the case, Harvey had seniority and would have been the person in charge, with the others taking orders from him. Phillips and I were basically the same rank, so we didn't take orders from each other. But Harvey was senior to both of us by several grades. He had been deputy to Angleton and very deeply involved in counterespionage activities. Having been stationed in Rome, he very well might have come in contact with the Corsican Mafia and heroin traffickers whom theorists claim he recruited for the assassination. Some theorists hypothesize that two other high-profile individuals might have been involved: Richard Nixon and Lyndon Johnson. As far as I'm concerned, as paranoid as he was, Nixon would never have been involved. He would not only have been horrified of the action but would never have trusted anyone to know he was involved.

Lyndon Johnson was an opportunist who would not have hesitated to get rid of any obstacles in his way. He could easily have been in touch with Harvey or Phillips. I think he and Meyer were too different socially to come in contact with each other. I do not know of any specific contact that the two had, but Phillips was a man on the way up and became a significant CIA figure whom LBJ would have wanted to get to know.

Harvey, however, is the most likely suspect. If he felt his position was in jeopardy, he was the type of person who would have taken drastic action to remedy the situation. It is a big leap, because he was a brain-addled pistol-toting drunk and very much under the thumb of his wife, who would have made the perfect concentration camp guard, but there is the slightest possibility that Harvey and LBJ could have formed some kind of thieves' pact between them.

In Washington, there is a caste system in regard to who will talk to whom. Would LBJ have spoken directly to Harvey? Yes, I think he could have done that, as Harvey's rank and position was such that a vice president could talk to him. Harvey may have had an intense personal dislike for the Kennedys and even had a severe clash with Bobby Kennedy around the time of the missile crisis. He posted an old slogan somewhere on the agency premises that read, "The tree of liberty must be nourished by the blood of patriots," which incensed the attorney general, bringing them into direct confrontation.

While it seems that it would be a philosophy Bobby would have embraced, the two argued about it. Some say that Bobby was worried that Harvey was trying to glorify the Bay of Pigs invasion, which he did not himself believe in. Others have simply observed that Harvey was so under the influence of alcohol, he would have argued with anybody about anything. How Harvey had risen so high was a mystery to me. Sometimes the appointments to various CIA positions were entirely baffling, but I just mollified myself by saying that the DCI knew more than I did. The association between Harvey and the Corsicans also stems from a memo he authored when he was running the executive action program (which advocated the assassination of hostile targets), in which he professed a desire to employ Corsicans as hit men, whom he most likely would have used against Castro.

Conspiracy nuts say that the person who had the most to gain from Kennedy's assassination was LBJ. There was nobody with the leverage that LBJ had, no competitor at all. He was the vice president, and if he wanted to get rid of the president, he had the ability to do so by corrupting different people in the CIA.

It has also been said by many LBJ biographers, such as Robert Caro in *The Path to Power*, that the man idolized money, was corrupt and unprincipled, with unlimited ambition—not the type of individual who was content to end his career as vice president (then considered a career-ending position treading water as flotsam in U.S. history, the stuff of future trivia questions). Many people conjecture that Johnson was set to drop even lower in footnote status, observing that he was destined to be cut from the 1964 presidential ticket. He and Kennedy did not get along, and theirs was completely a marriage of convenience facilitated by another power broker, "Tommy the Cork" Corcoran, who had played a backroom part in so much preceding U.S. history.

Having Kennedy liquidated, thus elevating himself to the presidency without having to work for it himself, could have been a very tempting and logical move on Johnson's part. It wouldn't have been hard for him to make contact with Harvey, another ruthless man who was not satisfied with his position in the CIA and its government salary. He definitely had dreams of becoming DCI, and LBJ could do that for him if he were president.

If LBJ had anything to do with the operation, he would have used Harvey, because he was available and corrupt. LBJ had the money and the connections to manipulate the scenario in Dallas and is on record as having convinced JFK to make the appearance in the first place. He further tried unsuccessfully to engineer the passengers of each vehicle, trying to get his good buddy Governor Connolly to ride with him instead of in JFK's car—where theorists observe he would have been out of danger.

Who knows the depths of Harvey's criminal connections? He may easily have known Mafia members who have been named as possible conspirators, such as Johnny Roselli, Santos Trafficante, Sam Giancana, and Carlos Marcello. I don't know if any of these people were involved. But these are names that have come up in connection with the assassination plot on Castro. The flames of the LBJ assassination theory have been stoked into bonfires by a few books citing Billy Sol Estes and Johnson's friend, the powerful Texas attorney Ed Clark, as possible coconspirators.

Other scenarios include the assassination of Kennedy by a Cuban organization angered by the president's failure to go after Castro again. After the Bay of Pigs, I had many of the principals come to me asking, "Eduardo, let me know when we are going to do it again!"

I tried to suppress any hope of reconstituting the invasion, as we had created as massive an effort as we ever hoped for, and its lack of success was probably final. It was apparent that any successful attack would entail the use of a great many U.S. troops, not a brigade of hastily trained adventurers. It was very discouraging news to the Cuban exile movement, which began to hate Kennedy for preventing the needed air support.

When Kennedy compounded his mistake by promising Khrushchev that the United States would not invade Cuba, a lot of exile groups felt that the president had sold them out. The leadership group in the Frente definitely considered him a traitor to the cause and were especially bitter and hostile to the president, whom they had once supported vociferously over Nixon.

Some of those Cuban exiles might have been involved in the assassination, though I couldn't name anybody offhand. It is alleged that Antonio Veciana, the leader of the anti-Castro group Alpha 66, met with Dave Phillips in Mexico City and, at some time, with Oswald. So that is another avenue that could use further investigation.

Interestingly, even Fidel Castro's name has been bandied about as a possible culprit, centering on a grudge against Kennedy for the president's possible complicity with the Mafia to end his life. I suppose this is possible, but I interviewed a Cuban refugee woman in 1971 who happened to have been in Castro's house at the time of Kennedy's murder. She said that a pall of gloom settled over the household because Fidel and Kennedy had been working on a détente to lessen the tensions between countries. While this information was otherwise unverifiable, the woman had an air of credibility, and I furnished my tape of the interrogation to the CIA (from which I had already retired). I don't think that I would have done such a thing if I was guilty of the crime, wishing instead to leave as many unanswered questions in the field as possible.

While many buffs cast a jaundiced eye on Phillips's meeting with Oswald in Mexico City, if it happened, it would have been entirely appropriate for Phillips to meet with the man, as Phillips was station chief, and the station maintained surveillance of the Cuban embassy. Oswald had been spotted visiting there. The meeting may have been completely on the up and up, with Phillips trying to recruit Oswald. The CIA had a general policy that if we came across an interesting figure—and Oswald would certainly have been of interest as a U.S. defector who married a Soviet—he would have been a natural target for any alert CIA officer.

Phillips might have even given Oswald orders for some operation in Mexico, but the bureaucratic steps for something like that were pretty well established, so there should have been a paper trail left behind. If you're dealing with an American who's living abroad, then one set of procedural rules is followed. If the proposed asset is not American, there is another set of procedures and qualifications that come into play. Oswald, of course, would have been considered an American citizen. He had been in the Marine Corps, and so recruiting him, whether in Mexico or the United States, had a fixed set of requirements.

Could Phillips have tried to recruit Oswald on the sly? He certainly had the ability and the knowledge. I mean, we are talking about David Phillips, one of the most effective agents I have ever known. But precisely because of that, I cannot see Philips having anything to do with such an operation. He was a professional's professional who took orders from the top and would have considered the presidency an inviolable position.

While Phillips was a consummate CIA officer, he wasn't above a bit of disinformation. When I was in prison in Connecticut later on, someone mailed me a copy of Phillips's book, *The Night Watch*, which I read with horror, as he used my name in connection with events that I had nothing to do with.

For example, he charged me with taking a group of Guatemalan men to a nightclub and wining and dining them, which never happened. I had an opportunity after I got out of prison to meet with Phillips before he died. He seemed a bit nervous when I told him that I had some questions about the book.

"Dave, you had an interesting story there. Why in the world did you mention me incorrectly in connection with this evening out on the town?" I asked.

He coughed before responding. "Well, my editor wanted some-thing to spice up the book, and you were a well-known name and you were in prison, so I didn't think you'd mind. So I tagged your name onto a couple of things that were fictional."

"Well, you didn't do me any favors with that," I told him. "You could have just made up the name of a fictitious agent like everyone else."

The reason why it was such a negative detail was that if I had been involved in such an affair, it would have been considered a clear secu-rity violation. It didn't happen. I wondered over the years what possi-ble benefit it could have been for him to write that.

I think that was the last time we spoke, and Phillips died fairly soon after our meeting. I have always been a little bitter about being treated that way after everything we had been through, especially as I had been instrumental in forwarding his career. I had heard about the job he was doing as agent in charge in Santiago, Chile, and was one of the officers who asked him up to Washington and Miami for inter-views for PB/Success. On my recommendation, he became a CIA officer and not just a contract agent.

What about Jack Ruby? Was he recruited or pressured by the Mafia to kill Oswald? I think it's possible, because otherwise we are floun-dering around trying to figure out a motive for Ruby to do what he did. At that time, I don't think he was aware that he had terminal can-cer, so that would lend itself to a Mafia plot.

There's only one problem with that scenario. No one has ever talked. With all the top-level Mafia figures—capos, hit men, godfa-thers—who have been arrested and flipped or sent to jail and written books from within the witness protection program, wouldn't someone have used the JFK knowledge as a get-out-of-jail-free card or a ticket to fame and fortune? Even Deep Throat has finally confessed! The Mafia failed to kill Castro and probably wouldn't have been very adept at a complicated scenario like the Dealey Plaza operation, either. Most hits they accomplished were either brutal assaults in a controlled environment, such as a neighborhood street or a restau-rant, using massive firepower, or the quick kidnapping and disappear-ance of a rival. Mafia hit men were not adept sharpshooters using high-power rifles. Also, they probably would have preferred doing the hit in a town where they had more knowledge of the terrain, such as New York or Chicago.

Another reason my name has become involved with the assassination is a notorious letter that was allegedly written by Oswald on November 8, 1963, reading:

> Dear Mr. Hunt:
> I would like information concerding [sic] my position. I am asking only for information. I am suggesting that we discuss the matter fully before any steps are taken by me or anyone else.
> Thank-you [sic],
> Lee Harvey Oswald

In 1974, after my name had been exposed in Watergate, the letter was mailed by the KGB to at least three conspiracy advocates, one of whom published it in a book. Afterward, the HSCA had the document examined by a handwriting expert, who pronounced it a forgery. Most likely, it was part of a clumsy disinformation campaign by the KGB. It certainly doesn't read as if the person who wrote the letter was very conversant in English, even misspelling the word *concerning*. It may have been written by a person with a thick accent, spelling the word the way he pronounced it.

Defecting agents have confirmed that the KGB was involved in many strange and, to us, patently ridiculous propaganda campaigns. Trying to connect the CIA with the assassination of a beloved president may certainly have been on their agenda. The forger may also have been trying to implicate another famous Hunt: H. L. Hunt of Texas fame.

Another CIA person of interest who has been linked to that dreadful day is David Morales. Bill Harvey posted Morales to the CIA's Miami station in 1961, where he became chief of Covert Operations for JM/Wave, an operation to destabilize Castro after the Bay of Pigs. Morales and Harvey could have been manufactured from the same cloth—both were hard-drinking, tough guys, possibly completely amoral. Morales was rumored to be a cold-blooded killer, the go-to guy in black-ops situations where the government needed to have someone neutralized. I tried to cut short any contact with him, as he wore thin very quickly.

It's been written that I was working in Mexico when Lee Harvey Oswald went there. But if he was in Mexico City, I did not know about him at that time. I had no reason to know anything about him, as there was no general alert on Oswald anywhere, and I never heard his name until I read it in the newspaper after he killed Kennedy.

As far as I know, Oswald had no connection with the CIA at all, unless there was some contact initiated by Phillips because of the U.S. citizen's previous defection and return. Someone may have tried to flip him, because it was very strange that he was ever allowed back into the United States.

In that regard, while I don't think that there was ever any evil intent by an official to allow Oswald into the United States to kill the president, I do think that it was typical of the sloppiness and the disregard of the visa people in the Department of State. The official who accepted Oswald's resignation from the United States in Moscow was Dick Snyder, a regular FSO (Foreign Service officer). I don't know if he was ever queried about why he treated Oswald so gently. Snyder should have been sanctioned by the Department of State, but he never was.

Some people have said that there was a false defector program, in which the CIA would send people over to the Soviet Union and bring them back to debrief them. While a program of this type might have proved useful, I think that it credits the CIA with a lot more intelligence than it usually displayed. It never had such a program. It had a program of interviewing Cubans and Spaniards who had been arrested years before and sentenced to work in the Soviet Union. I remember that program because Archie Roosevelt was in Madrid in charge of screening these people. You got the names from the Spanish authorities, and he and his group would have an opportunity to question them about anything hot at that time, but that was the closest to what has been suggested.

As far as a possible connection between Oswald and the FBI goes, I would think that the bureau would have been extremely cautious with him. Oswald would have asked for money, which was in short supply at the FBI. The FBI had trouble flipping people or recruiting informers because they usually didn't have enough hundred-dollar bills to arouse the interest of somebody whom they wanted to use. They were like our poor cousins. Besides, their scope was limited to criminal activity and criminal prosecutions, and I don't know if Oswald had ever had any criminal activities that would have attracted the attention of the bureau.

I think Oswald was actually what he purported to be: a left-wing individual who for lack of any other determining goal had subscribed to the Marxist tenets of the Soviet Union. I think he was attracted by authority, and authority is something the Soviet Union had lots of. They could put people on top of him to hold him down and guide him so that he would do whatever they might want. That whole history of Oswald's defection is a little uncertain as far as I'm concerned, because he came over with too much baggage, and that was revealed later on. Nobody knew it at the time, but I think the bureau was much more cautious of what they did with him.

The CIA never did anything with him and had no reason to. He was a nothing. Oswald was a kind of incompetent dreamer who drifted into Texas politics and then international politics. He got involved with Fair Play for Cuba (a pro-Castro group) and other causes, which limited his scope and limited our interest, if any, in him. I'm assuming that over the years any contact reports between Phillips and Oswald would be a matter of record. You could almost say if there was nothing in the file, then it never existed.

Why would Phillips have a meeting with Oswald? What did he want from Oswald? I think that anybody who had lived in the Soviet Union and had renounced American citizenship to do so would be a natural subject for contact and investigation. Although Phillips was not an investigator, maybe he received direct orders to go after Oswald and see if he could recruit him.

Who could have given Phillips those orders? It seems to me that Bill Harvey is the most likely candidate, because it was an off-key operation. Nothing was being handled through regular channels. But I truly don't know.

Some buffs have even suggested that the mastermind behind the Kennedy assassination was Richard Helms. Again, I would have to say no. Helms was definitely nonpolitical, and he had prospered under the Democratic administration. But Helms was probably the most intelligent of all these people we are talking about. He had a wonderful education at Le Rosey in Switzerland. He worked in Germany, his German was very fluent, and he was a favorite of Allen Dulles—and with good reason, because I think Helms became one of our most effective chiefs of operations. That is what he was to me, and I found him a congenial figure.

But in the end, Helms was an expert in CYA (cover your ass), not CIA. When the time came when he might have been able to help me and come to my defense, Dick said, "Oh, Hunt. . . . Oh, well, I sort of know him. He was a romantic." And that was all he had to say about me. He pretended that he barely knew me when in fact he had known me for years.

During the course of a year, we would have lunch between three and six times. In fact, Helms had made a confidant out of me, once calling me at the office to say, "Meet me downstairs right away. I have something to tell you."

What he had to tell me was that he had broken up with his wife and had moved to a country club in anticipation of a divorce. This was, at the time, extremely privileged information. We had lunch about six weeks later. Helms told me that he had just been summoned down to LBJ's ranch and had spent a wild weekend there riding a jeep at top speed through the property. Out of that emerged the confidence that he was going to be announced as the deputy director of the CIA, which, of course, evolved over time to DCI. So, as far as I know, I was the first person he told about such important events in his life.

LBJ appointed him as director, but he wouldn't play ball with Nixon or comply with Nixon's requests to investigate White House leaks, so the president basically fired him, sending him to Iran during Watergate.

Helms could always keep one thing in sight, and that was his future. He could judge if something was going to be negative, and then he would have nothing to do with it. And if he did, he would lie about it later. He was charged with a federal case of perjury, and he got out of that by paying a fine with money that was raised by people at the CIA who were fond of him. Not that he didn't have money, but his followers were right there raising money, which amounted to about $2,000. A small sum compared to the money I had to pay after Watergate. Of course, I also spent thirty-three months in jail, which he didn't have to do, either. But there were lots of people who got out by the skin of their teeth.

Nixon, on the Watergate tapes, made some famous statements about me. He said, "Howard Hunt, he knows too much. This is going to open up the whole Bay of Pigs thing." He said something about "if you open that scab, there's a lot of stuff that's going to come out." I was extremely surprised to find that out and even more perplexed when H.R. Haldeman wrote in his memoirs that "Bay of Pigs" was code language for the Kennedy assassination. In my mind, this proves that the president was even crazier than anybody gave him credit for. Does this mean he started to believe that he had something to do with the assassination, that I was involved, and that there was some terrible secret to uncover? Well, Ronald Reagan thought that he had fought in World War II, when what he was truly remembering was a movie that he starred in. So anything is possible.

In Nixon's perspective, anyone who was not under his direct authority had to be dealt with very cautiously. And if he thought that I knew things that were only available to limited associates, then that would be cause for alarm on his part. Try as I might, I don't know what he meant by that. The bare facts of the Bay of Pigs simply support the conclusion that we all know—that the United States trained these men, launched them, and that the necessity at the time of concealing the American hand was what in the long run destroyed the Bay of Pigs operation. It's possible, knowing that Nixon was taping himself, that he started to use the Bay of Pigs as a euphemism for Project Gemstone (detailed later) or for the Watergate break-in itself, as the Cubans involved were all BOP veterans. Now that makes sense. I *did* know too much about Watergate. It was something he wanted to hide. It was a conspiracy that would end his presidency.

As long as we are on the topic of assassination, I suppose that this is as good a time as any to set the record straight concerning General Omar Torrijos of Panama (known as the "dictator with a heart") and General Rafael Trujillo, the brutal leader of the Dominican Republic. Both were killed, and some people have suggested that I was involved. I was interrogated about these murders by the Assassination Committee.

A December 1977 syndicated column by Jack Anderson even quoted a supposed "secret memo" by a Miami prosecutor alleging that Mañuel Artime confessed that I had tried to recruit him to help assassinate Torrijos. This was written conveniently after Artime's death, so he could not refute it, and no memo signed by Artime ever came to light.

I had no part in the death of either man. Both had plenty of homegrown enemies who are probably responsible without the complicity of the United States. In fact, Torrijos, while allowing drug smugglers too much latitude to operate in his country—which obviously irritated the U.S. authorities—nonetheless had a stable centrist regime in an area where other countries such as Nicaragua and El Salvador were plagued by unrest. I think that the CIA would have found a more coercive method to influence Torrijos than by sanctioning him.

I will reiterate here, though, that I do not believe the CIA had anything to do with JFK's death. The upper echelon all had prospered under Democratic administrations. The crazier the world was, the more they were needed. The people who were fired after Bay of Pigs would have lacked the wherewithal to accomplish anything like this, even if it had crossed their minds, which it wouldn't have. While there may have been rivalries between divisions over the years, lapses of judgment, and bureaucratic snafus, as there are today, these men had been wealthy power brokers before entering the CIA; they had all persevered through several administrations and were all near retirement age, anyway. If any high-ranking CIA officer had hated JFK enough to do him harm, he would have simply done it politically.

James McCord, a former CIA security officer, wrote lawyer Dan Schultz on December 17, 1976, during the time that I was suing the Liberty Lobby:

> A false allegation was made shortly after March 23, 1973, that E. Howard Hunt and Frank Sturgis were in Dallas at the time the President was killed, and a photograph was circulated purporting to be Hunt and Sturgis there at the time. Persons I know circulated and touted the story to the press, knowing the allegation was false in its entirety, and further that the men in the photographs bore no resemblance whatever to Hunt and Sturgis. I know that Hunt was not in Dallas and had no connection whatever with the President's death. . . . Great anguish and damage has been done to Hunt, and no doubt will be taken into consideration by a parole board considering his release from prison.

I finished my testimony to the HSCA with these words:

> I appreciate the opportunity to appear before the committee and to be interrogated as extensively and broadly as has been accomplished here this afternoon. . . . It is very hard to prove a negative, you know. I didn't have anything to do with the assassination, didn't know anything about it. It is unfortunate that everything I went through in Watergate has bled over into a great national tragedy, and that was the assassination of President Kennedy. And I think that the

nation is willing to forgive Watergate now. I certainly think I have paid my penalty for being involved in it, but to have this new stain attached to me, relatively new—that is, in the last two or three years—this assassination of the President is something really that the nation is never going to forgive. I am afraid I will be forever stained with some kind of suspicion that I had something to do with it. It is very, very unfair.

I did my time for Watergate. I shouldn't have to do additional time and suffer additional losses for something I had nothing to do with.

13

The Great Propaganda Machine

After the Bay of Pigs, I had a couple of interesting jobs within the CIA. While the agency had been established to oversee covert activities abroad, we had a very real public relations problem within the United States. After surmounting many internal problems, Tracy Barnes was able to establish a Domestic Operations Division and appointed me as the new chief of covert action in the division. Most of my work involved publishing and publications, in which we supported an entire division of Frederick A. Praeger titles and subsidized books that we felt the American public should read—for example, Milovan Djilas's *The New Class: An Analysis of the Communist System*, originally published in 1957, a book by a high-level Communist from Tito's Yugoslavia who had become disillusioned with the system.

We also ran a couple of national newswire services and even published a popular series of travel books—the Fodor Travel Guides. Our reasoning behind the guides was that typically most foreigners only got to know Americans through touristic "ugly American" stereotypes. So we hoped to change that impression by getting people in other countries to come visit ours, enjoy life in the United States, and get to know Americans better. I really enjoyed the work and had plenty of energy left at the end of the day to write my own books at home.

Much of what I worked on was exposed in revelations about Operation Mockingbird by a Frank Church–headed Senate investigation in 1975 that divulged a lot of agency dirty laundry about our infiltration of the U.S. and international media. The investigation reported in 1976:

> The CIA currently maintains a network of several hundred foreign individuals around the world who provide intelligence for the CIA and at times attempt to influence opinion through the use of covert propaganda. These individuals provide the CIA with direct access to a large number of newspapers and periodicals, scores of press services and news agencies, radio and television stations, commercial book publishers, and other foreign media outlets.

Church also identified me as an important figure in the operation, pointing out one of my ongoing responsibilities to get certain books reviewed by particular writers who would be either sympathetic or hostile to works we hoped to popularize or suppress. At one point during the Church committee hearings, I was accused of arranging to have a writer under CIA contract write a negative review for the *New York Times* of Edgar Snow's book *Red China Today: The Other Side of the River*, a sympathetic view of Mao's China.

Carl Bernstein published an article in the October 20, 1977, issue of *Rolling Stone* called "CIA and the Media," in which he identified Joseph Alsop (and his brother), a prominent American syndicated columnist, as a Mockingbird operative, writing:

> Alsop is one of more than 400 American journalists who in the past twenty-five years have secretly carried out assignments for the Central Intelligence Agency, according to documents on file at CIA headquarters. Some of these journalists' relationships with the Agency were tacit; some were explicit. There was cooperation, accommodation and overlap. Journalists provided a full range of clandestine services—from simple intelligence gathering to serving as go-betweens with spies in Communist countries. Reporters shared their notebooks with the CIA. Editors shared their staffs. Some of the journalists were Pulitzer Prize winners, distinguished reporters who considered themselves ambassadors-without-portfolio for their country. Most were less exalted: foreign correspondents who found that their association with the Agency helped their work; stringers and freelancers who were as interested in the derring-do of the spy business as in filing articles, and, the smallest category, full-time

CIA employees masquerading as journalists abroad. In many instances, CIA documents show, journalists were engaged to perform tasks for the CIA with the consent of the managements of America's leading news organizations.

Bernstein further identified some of the country's top media executives as being valuable assets to the agency, including Henry Luce of Time; William Paley of CBS; Arthur Hays Sulzberger of the *New York Times*; Barry Bingham Sr. of the *Louisville Courier-Journal*; and James Copley of the Copley News Service. But the list of organizations that cooperated with the agency was a veritable "Who's Who" of the media industry, including ABC, NBC, the Associated Press, UPI, Reuters, Hearst Newspapers, Scripps-Howard, *Newsweek* magazine, and others.

While I worked with some of these organizations and not with others, let me say I know nothing to contradict this report. Many American publishers such as Henry Luce and Phillip Graham were extreme patriots who saw themselves as soldiers in America's war against the spread of global Communism, and they were quick to aid the CIA. Luce, in particular, was a good friend of Allen Dulles's. Additionally, many reporters had been OSS operatives or close to OSS during the war, so they were also friendly assets, ready, willing, and able to share the information they had gathered.

The official use of paid news correspondents ended under the reign of DCI George H. W. Bush, who announced: "Effective immediately, the CIA will not enter into any paid or contract relationship with any full-time or part-time news correspondent accredited by any U.S. news service, newspaper, periodical, radio or television network or station."

Bush, however, allowed that the cooperation of journalists without pay would still be extremely welcome.

The Church committee's report included investigation of some other work in which I had once been involved:

> The Committee has found that the Central Intelligence Agency attaches a particular importance to book publishing activities as a form of covert propaganda. A former officer in the Clandestine Service stated that books are "the most important weapon of strategic (long-range) propaganda." Prior to 1967, the Central Intelligence Agency sponsored, subsidized, or produced over 1,000 books; approximately 25 percent of them in English. In 1967 alone, the CIA published or subsidized over 200 books, ranging from books on African

safaris and wildlife to translations of Machiavelli's *The Prince* into Swahili and works of T. S. Eliot into Russian, to a competitor to Mao's little red book, which was entitled *Quotations from Chairman Liu*.

The Committee found that an important number of the books actually produced by the Central Intelligence Agency were reviewed and marketed in the United States:

- A book about a young student from a developing country who had studied in a communist country was described by the CIA as "developed by (two areas divisions) and produced by the Domestic Operations Division ... and has had a high impact in the United States as well as in the (foreign area) market." This book, which was produced by the European outlet of a United States publishing house was published in condensed form in two major U.S. magazines.

- Another CIA book, *The Penkovsky Papers*, was published in the United States in 1965. The book was prepared and written by omitting agency assets who drew on actual case materials, and publication rights to the manuscript were sold to the publisher through a trust fund which was established for the purpose. The publisher was unaware of any U.S. Government interest.

The Penkovsky book, describing a Soviet intelligence agent's inside information about the Soviet Union's plans to expand its influence militarily over the West, was published by Doubleday and became an international best-seller. Just to be clear, Penkovsky was a real person with real information.

In 1967, the CIA stopped publishing within the United States. Since then, the agency has published some 250 books abroad, most of them in foreign languages. The CIA has given special attention to publication and circulation abroad of books about conditions in the Soviet Bloc. Of those targeted at audiences outside the Soviet Union and Eastern Europe, a large number has also been available in English.

Domestic "Fallout"

The Committee finds that covert media operations can result in manipulating or incidentally misleading the American public. Despite efforts to minimize it, CIA employees, past and present, have conceded that there is no way to shield the American public completely from "fallout" in the United States from Agency propaganda or placements overseas. Indeed, following the Katzenbach inquiry, the

Deputy Director for Operations issued a directive stating: "Fallout in the United States from a foreign publication which we support is inevitable and consequently permissible."

The domestic fallout of covert propaganda comes from many sources: books intended primarily for an English-speaking foreign audience; CIA press placements that are picked up by an international wire service; and publications resulting from direct CIA funding of foreign institutes. For example, a book written for an English-speaking foreign audience by one CIA operative was reviewed favorably by another CIA agent in the *New York Times*. The Committee also found that the CIA helped create and support various Vietnamese periodicals and publications. In at least one instance, a CIA supported Vietnamese publication was used to propagandize the American public and the members and staff of both houses of Congress. So effective was this propaganda that some members quoted from the publication in debating the controversial question of United States involvement in Vietnam.

The Committee found that this inevitable domestic fallout was compounded when the Agency circulated its subsidized books in the United States prior to their distribution abroad in order to induce a favorable reception overseas.

The CIA currently maintains a network of several hundred foreign individuals around the world who provide intelligence for the CIA and at times attempt to influence opinion through the use of covert propaganda. These individuals provide the CIA with direct access to a large number of newspapers and periodicals, scores of press services and news agencies, radio and television stations, commercial book publishers, and other foreign media outlets.

Approximately 50 of the assets are individual American journalists or employees of U.S. media organizations. Of these, fewer than half are "accredited" by U.S. media organizations and thereby affected by the new prohibitions on the use of accredited newsmen. The remaining individuals are non-accredited freelance contributors and media representatives abroad, and thus are not affected by the new CIA prohibition.

More than a dozen United States news organizations and commercial publishing houses formerly provided cover for CIA agents abroad. A few of these organizations were unaware that they provided this cover. The Committee notes that the new CIA prohibitions do not apply to "unaccredited" Americans serving in media organizations such as representatives of U.S. media organizations abroad or freelance writers. Of the more than 50 CIA relationships with United States journalists, or employees in American media organizations, fewer than one half will be terminated under the new CIA guidelines.

The Committee is concerned that the use of American journalists and media organizations for clandestine operations is a threat to the integrity of the press. All American journalists, whether accredited to a United States news organization or just a stringer, may be suspects when any are engaged in covert activities.

Church pointed out with disgust that the CIA campaign allegedly cost American taxpayers some $265 million a year to misinform the world. I would say the money was well spent, and should the operation have continued, perhaps we wouldn't be pouring untold billions of dollars into Iraq right now.

Most interestingly, however, while employed by the CIA, I have to say I *never heard* about a specific Operation Mockingbird, although my projects would certainly have come under its umbrella. But even if there was no official project by that name, we did carry out the basic operations, and I cannot contradict the findings.

Working full-time in Washington, D.C., provided a great domestic venue for my family, since Dorothy's mother had died while I had been involved in the Bay of Pigs operation, and I was now able to spend more time with my wife and kids.

In January 1963, there was quite a shake-up in the world of covert intelligence—the revelation that former MI-5 agent Kim Philby was a Soviet spy. This affected the CIA for a couple of reasons. First, some of the shining lights who had come up through OSS had been trained by Philby in England. Among these notables was James Angleton, who had been tutored by the British agent in 1943. Second, Philby had once been MI-5's liaison with U.S. intelligence agencies in Washington, D.C., and was so trusted that the charming, very British agent might just as well have had a seat in our operations room. He had even helped Angleton set up our counterintelligence unit.

Still, it wasn't the hugest surprise, as suspicions about him had begun years earlier, in 1951, after two senior British diplomats stationed in Washington, D.C., Guy Burgess and Donald Maclean, were exposed as Soviet agents who had been funneling U.S. atomic secrets to the Communists since the 1940s. The moles were old Cambridge friends of Kim Philby's. Philby even roomed with Burgess in the United States, so he came under scrutiny at the time as the "third man," who tipped off his buddies that they had been compromised, allowing them time to flee to the Soviet Union before they could be arrested.

After the 1951 incident, Walter Bedell Smith tasked both Angleton and Bill Harvey with writing separate reports about Philby to help determine if he was also a spy. No doubt, because of Philby's proximity to the U.S. agents, the reports were also ordered to help assess if our own men were double agents.

Interestingly, while Harvey concluded that Philby was a Soviet spy, Angleton came to the opposite opinion, saying that Philby had been duped by his friends along with everyone else, and Angleton advised against taking any further action. Beetle Smith took Angleton's advice, which helped the Soviet agent continue his cover for a dozen more years.

Of course, Philby was a maestro who played Angleton like a violin. Quite a few officers just wanted to socialize with the Brits, and they got in bed literally and figuratively with several of them. I didn't have that sort of social polish and was glad in the later years that I didn't, because I wasn't an attractive subject for the Brits and didn't want to be. Angleton, however, had gone to Yale, and had even written some poetry for one of the Yale publications, so he was someone whom the British found sympathetic. In Angleton's defense, however, the double agent had taken in everyone, perhaps except for Richard Helms, who never liked Philby.

I was not an admirer of James Angleton's. Within the agency, the reclusive figure was known as the Gray Ghost, for his pale white appearance and aloofness, though perhaps that was a by-product of being in charge of counterespionage. Despite his failure with Philby, he was able to maintain enough clout with succeeding directors of the CIA, including Allen Dulles, to be allowed to do pretty much what he chose.

Some people have suggested that maybe Angleton himself was a double agent like Philby, but I don't think so. After Philby was outed, officials looked around for a scapegoat, with some attention lighting on Angleton and his positive report, though he was somehow able to deflect the criticism.

I really only had one contact with him of significance. That came about from one day when I went to a safe house for a meeting in Montevideo, Uruguay, in the late 1950s. Lo and behold, there was one of my local agents talking to a fellow who I learned very quickly was an FBI officer. We had an understanding with the bureau that they didn't do this, and geographically they stayed away. Any FBI officers who came down without notification were subject to sanction. In response, I fired a cable to Washington, saying that I wanted to protest the appearance of the FBI officer. About forty-eight hours later, I was on a plane heading back to Washington.

It was Angleton who met me, and he wasn't very happy that I made this complaint, which surprised me. I asked, "How can we have an agent who's reporting both to the bureau and to me?"

But Angleton was not a pleasant guy to deal with. In fact, he sided with the FBI, saying that he didn't see why I was making such a fuss. That was the side of Angleton that I saw, and he really knew me only from that run-in.

Nonetheless, I was clearly in the right. It was well defined and understood that when a local was briefed and put in play, nobody else was going to use him. We had all kinds of agents and a wide variety of relationships. In the end, the bureau guy was pulled out. His home base was Rio, and why he was down in Monty nobody really knew. But at least I knew he was gone, and I utilized my hollow victory to reinforce my status with other assets who might have been tempted to rejoin forces with the FBI. So I felt a little bit of self-satisfaction about Angleton's mistake about Philby.

In 1964, I became involved in another domestic operation with echoes that would continue into Watergate. After the election-year primaries, Barry Goldwater received the Republican nod. I was disturbed to receive confidential orders from the division executive officer, Stanley Gaines, to have some of my "outside" assets infiltrate and gather information from the candidate's headquarters. This, I was informed, was a White House matter, as Lyndon Johnson had become obsessed with obtaining his competitor's plans.

I was actually a Goldwater supporter—an unpopular position within the agency. But as a professional who had been given orders by his superior—no matter what administration was in power—I carried out the task. My subordinates volunteered inside, collected advance copies of position papers and other material, and handed them over to CIA personnel, who delivered them to Chester Cooper, the CIA officer attached to the White House staff.

This was my first exposure to White House utilization of the CIA to spy on a "domestic enemy." However, as distasteful as I thought it was, I performed the duty, accepting the White House orders without question. This sort of bulldog loyalty would later get me into deep trouble. But it is interesting, if not fascinating, to note that the precedent for Watergate was actually set by a Democrat.

* * *

Around this time, Victor Webright, editor in chief of the New American Library, which had reprinted several of my novels—including *Bimini Run*—in paperback, contacted me with the idea of developing an American counterpart to Ian Fleming's popular James Bond series. The company was a publishing dynamo with huge distribution, so I submitted the idea to Richard Helms, who agreed that this was a magnificent opportunity to boost the image of the CIA. Of course, the editor had no idea that he was working with a current CIA officer who had an ulterior motive to writing the books.

Thus, under the pseudonym of David St. John (the names of my first two sons), I created Peter Ward, a CIA agent whose adventures spanned eight novels. Unfortunately, the Library of Congress somehow published my real name in addition to my pen name on the copyright page. In consultation with Helms and his deputy, Tom Karamessines, the worry came up that there might be some political fallout if Congress should find out, as they were unaware that the CIA was running a domestic operation. Therefore, it became apparent that I should ostensibly quit the agency, get rehired as a contract agent, and be assigned outside of the country.

So until the summer of 1966, I was stationed as a contract agent in Madrid, where I once again established my family and put my children in school. During this time, my assignment, which I have never divulged before (except in classified testimony before the Senate Committee on Assassination in 1978, which was interested in the subject, due to information that Mañuel Artime was in Spain at that time, involved in plans to assassinate Castro—something I knew nothing about), was to develop working, confidential relationships with influential Spaniards who would some day succeed Generalissimo Francisco Franco.

When asked for information about my work in Spain, the CIA told the Assassination Committee that there was none available, classified or not—which of course made the committee suspicious that I was involved in some kind of terrible black-ops work. I speculated at the time that the CIA had been unable to locate my file because it was what was commonly referred to inside the agency as a "bigoted assignment," which was a highly sensitive operation known by only a few people. My direct supervisor was Thomas Karamessines, the assistant deputy director for plans.

Frank Wisner, then retired, wrote that he was coming to Spain, and he asked that I make a reservation at Madrid's Ritz to meet him and his wife for dinner. Strangely, Dorothy and I were stood up and never heard from him. Then a pal of mine in Washington sent me an obituary notice. Frank had committed suicide. We all worked hard hours, Frank more than most, getting only four hours of sleep a night for years. It's hard to keep your mental health under the stress of those conditions.

I became terribly depressed by the news, and wondered how much longer I could take the work myself if this Gibraltar of a figure had succumbed to the pressure. It made me start considering ways that I could retire. We loved Spain, its people, and all it had to offer culturally, but it was extremely expensive to live there. My son David had also developed an illness called celiac disease, which had to be monitored, and medical care was exorbitant. We bid a tearful farewell to Spain, which would be my last posting abroad for the CIA.

Looking back, I wonder how very different our lives might have been if we had stayed in that wonderful country, as the return to the United States would mark the beginning of the period that would make me a household name.

Returning to the States in the summer of 1966, we bought a sprawling horse ranch in Maryland about twenty minutes away from Langley, where I was assigned to the Western Europe Division under Roger Goiran, later becoming chief of covert action for Western Europe. While I got along well with my boss, made a satisfying income, and thought I was doing worthwhile work, the idea of retirement became more enticing. Still stigmatized by the Bay of Pigs, I reasoned that I would not get promoted too much higher. Able to receive a pension after age fifty, I felt I had ample time to find a second career and still write books to supplement my income.

As I was only forty-six, I spent the next four years gradually making contacts in society and in the business world, joining the Brown University Club of Washington, where I was able to renew old friendships and meet other alumni. Through a former classmate, I became friends with a conservative Republican lawyer and Washington player, Charles W. Colson, who had been an administrative assistant to the revered Senator Leverett Saltonstall of Massachusetts.

These might have been good years to look back on with fond memories, except that they were marred by a near tragedy concerning my daughters, who were involved in a car wreck while traveling with friends. Kevan sustained a nasty leg fracture, and sixteen-year-old Lisa suffered multiple injuries including brain trauma. While the girls seemed to recover enough to return to school several weeks later, Lisa developed memory and emotional problems, sometimes forgetting what class she had just left and where she was going. She became so distraught that she tried to slit her wrists and required psychological hospitalization at Sheppard and Enoch Pratt Hospital in Towson, Maryland. One of the most depressing moments of my life was when Dorothy and I sat next to her bed, where she lay unresponsive, gazing at us like we were complete strangers.

We were not permitted to visit her again for three weeks, when the doctors tried to convince us that our daughter was schizophrenic, even though we explained to them that she had suffered organic brain damage from the accident. We faithfully attended weekly family therapy sessions, but Lisa remained confined in the hospital so that she would not harm herself, draining our financial resources.

Dick Helms approved legal and psychiatric counseling from the agency, and he distributed some low-interest loans from a special employee fund, which kept our family afloat until we received a settlement in a civil suit for the accident two years later. Unfortunately, the judgment was for much less money than the cost of Lisa's hospitalization, so it still left us deeply in debt.

When Lisa was deemed sufficiently well, the hospital allowed her to become an outpatient and attend a nearby boarding school. Her doctors turned out to be too ambitious, however, and she had to be institutionalized again after only a few days of school. After keeping her in the hospital for two and a half years, we had hemorrhaged so much money that it had a terrible impact on our family, and we couldn't pay for her to stay at the hospital any longer. This, as it turned out, was a blessing in disguise, as she improved much more at home and was finally able to enter community college.

In 1966, during this exhausting and difficult time, I tried to distract myself by *Give Us This Day*, which was not published until 1973 for security reasons. I became vice president of the Brown University Club in Washington, while Charles Colson was president. I learned in the fall of 1968 that Chuck had joined Nixon's presidential campaign. I mentioned my several positive contacts with Nixon over the years, explained my role in the Bay of Pigs, and described how much I admired the candidate he was working for and hoped that this time Nixon would be elected. At this point, I also made him aware that I was eager to retire from the CIA and work in private industry, where I hoped to become financially solvent again.

Following Nixon's successful bid for the White House, Colson joined the president's staff in the fall of 1969, after which we occasionally lunched and pondered possible employment opportunities for me. I would have to wait a while longer, though, as I had a couple more years to go before I could retire and still receive my CIA annuity; my family could not subsist on a single government salary.

Dick Helms came to the rescue in the spring of 1970, not only agreeing to allow me to retire early but recommending me to the public relations departments of several large companies. Eventually, I was hired by Robert Mullen, a former press aide to President Eisenhower and onetime head of the Marshall Plan's information service, who knew something about my work at the Economic Cooperation Administration and now headed a prominent Washington, D.C., public relations firm. The company had been accused of being a CIA front organization, having run the Free Cuba Committee for the Agency, and it employed several former CIA personnel, so my background was not the handicap it had proved to be with several multinational corporations with which I had previously interviewed.

Prospects seemed bright, as Mullen was looking forward to retirement and hoped to hire two people he trusted to take over the company along with a current employee, Douglas Caddy, who handled their General Foods Corporation account. I was given the HEW account, concerning handicapped children who needed "special education," but I soon learned about backstabbing Washingtonian politics when I saw that Mullen was not taking the promised steps to hand over the company to any successors. Douglas Caddy resigned to take up law (remember his name, as it will come up later), whereupon Mullen announced that he was selling the company to Robert Bennett, son of the Republican senator from Utah. I was offered a minority participation in the firm, but since I would have little control over the company, I chose to remain a salaried vice president instead.

My position deteriorated further when Mullen and Bennett, thinking to broaden the scope of the company, brought in the Democratic son of a Washington lobbyist, Spencer Oliver, as a partner, which I thought diluted the firm's well-known Republican image. Disillusioned with the direction of the firm, I was actively looking for other employment when Charles Colson called me on July 1, 1971, asking what I thought about the Pentagon Papers—the mountain of classified information that the *New York Times* had published in a series of articles the previous month, resulting in the indictment of

Daniel Ellsberg, the leaker, on two counts of theft of government property and the unauthorized possession of documents related to national defense.

The papers were extremely embarrassing not only to the Nixon administration but to Kennedy and Johnson, as well. Ellsberg had been part of a State Department think tank, the McNamara Study Group, which wrote the classified *History of Decision Making in Vietnam, 1945–1968*, extracts of which were now being published. The seven-thousand-page study reported that Dwight Eisenhower had initially gotten the United States involved by secretly aiding the French to defeat the Vietnamese rebellion. John F. Kennedy then turned the aid into a full-blown war by using Asian mercenaries to commit acts of sabotage and to kill and kidnap North Vietnamese in a deliberate "provocation strategy." This eventually led to the controversial Gulf of Tonkin incident, in which the North Vietnamese supposedly fired on U.S. destroyers (but had not; the fire was a faulty instrument reading). President Lyndon B. Johnson spun the nonevent into an aggressive attack against U.S. forces, convincing Congress to authorize a resolution saying the president of the United States could "take all necessary measures to repel armed attack against the forces of the United States and to prevent further aggression." Johnson used this resolution to escalate the war, which the study concluded he had planned to do from the very beginning of his presidency.

Most damaging was the revelation that the government knew the war was unwinnable and predicted that U.S. forces would suffer far greater casualties than they dared admit to the public. I told Colson that I thought it was an outrage to have leaked the documents.

My friend seemed to like my response and continued, "As a good observer of the political scene, what do you think of the Ellsberg prosecution?"

I was a little confused about why he was asking but trusted that Colson was headed somewhere interesting. "I think they're prosecuting him for the wrong thing—possession," I said. "Isn't there some aspect of the law that focuses on the theft rather than just mere possession? Don't you think he should be prosecuted for a more major crime?"

Colson replied, "I don't know. It may be that there can be stiffer charges as the investigation develops. . . ." Now he came to the more interesting question. "Do you think this guy is a lone wolf?"

What he wanted to know was if I thought this was a onetime blast or if this was part of a widespread conspiracy that would keep leaking classified information to harm the president. I didn't have enough information to know that yet, but I told him that I certainly thought the prosecution should go ahead. There was a great deal of unrest about Vietnam, and any breach like this weakened the position of the United States and fueled our enemies.

"Let me ask you this," Colson said. "Do you think with the right resources employed that this could be turned into a major public case against Ellsberg and coconspirators?"

Again, the situation seemed vague. "Yes, I do, but you've established a qualification here which I don't know can be met."

"What's that?"

"Well, with the 'right resources.'"

"Well, I think the resources are there," Colson urged.

"Then, I would say so, absolutely," I ventured.

His voice firmed. "Then your answer would be that we should go down the line to nail the guy cold?"

I replied affirmatively.

The conversation continued, until Colson volunteered, "The case now can be made on grounds where I don't see that we could lose . . . but this case won't be tried in the court, it will be tried in the newspapers. So it's going to take some resourceful engineering . . ." His voice tapered off.

Colson was quite obviously fishing, and I wondered what sort of resourceful engineering he had in mind. I gave him some line to run with. "I want to see the guy hung if it can be done to the advantage of the administration," I told him.

His reply carried a note of optimism: "I think there are ways to do it, and I don't think this guy is operating alone."

"Well, of course he's not operating alone," I said. "He's got congeries of people who are supporting him, aiding and abetting him."

"But I'm not so sure it doesn't go deeper than that," Colson mused. "I'm thinking about the enemy."

The enemy. The Soviet Union? North Vietnam? I was interested and appalled.

"Of course, *they* stand to profit the most, no question about it," I said. "You've got codes and policy-making apparatus stripped bare for public examination, all that sort of thing." I postulated that the

Pentagon Papers were so valuable to our enemies that if we had similar information about them, there would be no reason for the CIA.

Now Colson changed the subject, which he would occasionally do as his mind jumped around, always moving. "What do you think of the idea of declassifying a lot of those old documents now?" He meant classified CIA papers.

Old ones, sure I thought, then said, "I'm all in favor of that and would particularly like to see the Bay of Pigs stuff declassified, including the alleged agreements that JFK made with Castro."

That seemed to satisfy him, and he said we would speak again soon. I put down the phone as perplexed as I'd been in a long time. I would learn much later that Colson recorded this conversation, sending a transcript to Bob Haldeman, the president's chief of staff, with a very interesting covering memo that read: "I think it would be worth your time to meet him [Hunt]. Needless to say, I did not even approach what we had been talking about but merely sounded out his ideas."

On July 5, Colson called me again, this time asking me to meet him at the White House, where he told me that he had been thinking about our conversation and was convinced that the administration needed someone with my background on staff. He had already done a bit of research and found that I could still draw my CIA annuity if I was hired as a consultant. I reminded him that I had a full-time job.

Colson brushed that off as if I had mentioned that I had a cold. "Sure," he said. "And the first thing I want you to do, Howard, is become, let's say, the resident expert on the origins of the Vietnam War. The last administration cleaned out everything, and no one around here seems to know exactly how we got into the damn thing. You and I know it was a Kennedy war, but people, particularly the press, have a closed mind on the subject."

We agreed on a $100-a-day consulting fee, and Colson suggested that I start with the published Pentagon Paper articles, which the White House press office could give me. The money was considerably less than I was now earning, so I didn't want this to have a negative effect on my job. But when I returned to the office, Colson had already phoned Bennett and made the arrangements for my part-time services. Bennett was actually enthusiastic, asking me to mention to Colson that a former employee of his, Clifton De Motte, had some information about the Chappaquiddick tragedy in which he thought the White House might be interested.

Whatever my feelings about the Kennedy clan, I did not like delving into people's dirty laundry. Still, I felt that the Chappaquiddick affair was significant enough to mention.

On July 7, Colson took me to John Ehrlichman's office in the White House for what would be my only meeting with the Nixon adviser. Colson was energetic, talking fast, saying, "Here is the Howard Hunt I've been talking about."

In contrast, Ehrlichman gave me an almost bored nod.

"He's going to work on the Pentagon Papers project," Colson continued enthusiastically.

Ehrlichman gave another nod and asked if I was still with the CIA.

"I retired a year ago," I said. "Since then, I've been working in public relations."

Ehrlichman stood up, shook my hand, and said, "Thank you for coming by."

I thought the introduction had been disastrous, but when we got back to Colson's office, my friend told me that I had just undergone the formality of being interviewed and okayed by Ehrlichman. Now they could start processing my hiring papers.

I filled out some forms, tendered my fingerprints, was photographed by the Secret Service and issued a temporary White House pass. Afterward, I was shown a small office on the third floor of the Executive Office Building, where I was given a typewriter and a safe with a combination set by the Secret Service.

Later I told Colson about Clifford De Motte's information. Colson instantly quivered with excitement, like a hound getting the scent of a fox.

"Does Bennett think he's got inside information?"

"Bob says De Motte worked for the Kennedy entourage back in 1960 and knows the whole gang. Bob thinks he's worth checking out."

Colson cleared his throat. "Could *you* do it?" he asked.

I told him I *could* do it but that I would need some kind of rationale. Who would I be?

"Not a White House staffer!" Colson said.

I agreed.

"You must have done things like this before in CIA, Howard?" Colson insisted.

"Yes, I have, but when you're uncertain of a man—as we are in De Motte—you take precautions," I told him. "In some cases, that means a disguise and certainly false documentation."

Colson thought a minute and leaned back in his chair. "You've got friends at CIA. Couldn't they get what you need?"

"They could, but they wouldn't. It would be too risky for them."

"What would it take to get the things you need?" he wanted to know. He wasn't giving up and appeared somehow enthused about the idea. It seemed like he was interested in more than just the information that might be gained, and he was enjoying the process.

"It's been my CIA experience that a call from the White House always produced whatever the White House wanted," I ventured cautiously.

No need for the caution. Colson was on board. "All right. I'll see what I can do and get back to you."

So, it would all start here. A simple innocuous interview about some dirty laundry. Colson was introduced to covert action by me, however innocently. This first small operation would lead step by inexorable step through the same dreaded process that turns a casual drug user into an abuser. Slowly, as you use more and more, you have to bump up your fix just one notch to get high. In the Nixon administration, information was power, and power was the drug of choice that everyone was high on.

I didn't know that I was working for information junkies and that I would become one of their dealers.

Shown at age three with my mother, Ethel. While I appear to be
quietly attentive here, my later school report cards will claim
that I am "inattentive" and "whisper too much." I received A's in
reading and language and D's and F's in math. In high school, I
was one of the leading musicians, playing trumpet.

I am shown second from the left in the top row. I worked my way through Brown
University as a trumpet player with the Frank Rollins Orchestra. The band played
venues in the United States, Cuba, Nassau, Bermuda, and on a cruise ship.

A buddy and me at Sloppy Joe's
Bar in Havana during a visit with
the Frank Rollins Orchestra.

Having a grand time in Nassau, visiting
with the band.

On military leave, with my father
in Albany, New York.

Posing in navy dress. The uniform no longer fits, but the sword does.

Conversing with George Gay (second from left), the sole survivor of Torpedo Squadron 8 from the Battle of Midway. Gay was later awarded the Navy Cross and the Presidential Unit Citation for his actions in battle.

After surviving my stint in the navy, I rejoined the military to continue fighting in World War II, enlisting in the Army Air Force.

General William "Wild Bill" Donovan, the visionary World War I hero, was the first director of the Office of Strategic Services (OSS), the clandestine agency that helped win World War II. After the war, OSS was dissolved by Congress, which feared that it could become a U.S. version of Germany's SS. The organization was supplanted by the CIA, which employed and was directed by many members of the previous agency.

Dorothy and me in
Montevideo at a reception
for President Eisenhower
in 1959.

Our Man in Montevideo: undercover as first secretary of the U.S. embassy in
Uruguay. Here I am shaking hands with President Eisenhower.

Mañuel Artime (left) and a soldier known as El Guarjiro, while preparing for the ill-fated Bay of Pigs attack in the steamy jungles of Guatemala. The men are standing in front of an aircraft fuselage mock-up that was used for parachute training.

Bay of Pigs soldiers training in Guatemala. Of the brigade's landing force of 1,443 men, 1,189 were captured, 114 were killed, and 150 were able to escape. After months of grueling prison time and several fatal casualties, the United States eventually paid ransom to get the fighters back.

(From left to right) Mañuel Artime, Captain José Perez San Roman, Dr. Antonio Maceo, and Antonio de Varona at the Brigade 2506 training camp in Guatemala.

Tempers were always short in the tense atmosphere while training to invade Cuba. Artime persuades Tony de Varona not to harangue the brigade, while Dr. Maceo mops the sweat off his face.

Laura and me at Pensacola Naval Air Station for the graduation of our son Austin from Officer Candidate School in June 2006.

14

Inside the White House

Colson was quite a character, a big guy who wore oversized glasses and had so much energy that it seemed as if he must be plugged directly into a generator. He had a ready sense of humor, which had created permanent hound dog–like smile wrinkles around his mouth, though he had no patience for fools. Even when he was arrested after Watergate, he could be seen smirking in his police-booking photograph. He was a dynamo around which spun large and powerful wheels, and energy permeated his office so palpably that it almost made your hair stand up. You had the feeling that every moment was filled with a thousand things to do. Phones rang nonstop; there was always a line of people waiting for an appointment in his anteroom; he read papers walking back and forth to the men's room. He was headstrong, a quick decision maker, and devoted to the president, and he expected everyone who was sucked into his maelstrom to be equally dedicated. He was basically a political chess master who some now say was the spiritual ancestor to Karl Rove. In turn, Colson's spiritual ancestor had to be Machiavelli himself.

I admired him greatly, though I realized he was more feared and envied around the White House than liked. No one wanted to be on his bad side. Even now, he wields great influence in Republican circles, writing columns for *Christianity Today*, espousing a strict evangelical Protestant viewpoint about contemporary issues, arguing that creationism should be taught in school and that many problems in the country can be attributed to secularism.

One of my first assignments soon after I signed on regarding Vietnam and the Pentagon Papers was to interview Lieutenant Colonel Lucien Conein, an army intelligence officer who had information about the events leading up to the death of South Vietnamese premier Ngo Dinh Diem. I was the perfect person to put Conein at ease, as we had known each other in OSS and the CIA, having trained together at Catalina Island and worked with each other in Kunming before he was reassigned and parachuted into Indochina. After the French were routed out of Vietnam, Conein worked for years in both North and South Vietnam, becoming one of America's greatest authorities on the country.

Conein was happy to hear from me when I telephoned him at his home in McLean, Virginia. He was readily interested in being interviewed and expressed hope that I might help him renew his contract with the CIA as he was suffering financial problems. I told him that I would do what I could, and I reported my progress to Colson.

At the time, I did not know the degree of obsession that this White House had with recording conversations. Colson wanted to make sure this interview was secretly recorded, but as there were no facilities for this in either of our offices, he arranged for the Secret Service to set up a recorder in Ehrlichman's office, where the interview was to take place—also, apparently without the knowledge of the office's owner, who I was admonished would be furious if he ever found out.

I questioned Conein extensively in Ehrlichman's office about the circumstances surrounding the November 1, 1963, death of Premier Diem, who, along with his brother, had been assassinated in a coup by military leaders after John F. Kennedy let them know through back channels that he supported Diem's elimination (as he did not believe the South Vietnamese president was strong enough to resist the North Vietnamese). Knowing that the conversation was being recorded, I made no attempt to take notes and soon steered the conversation into another topic of interest, Pentagon Paper leaker Daniel Ellsberg, who had been assigned to Vietnam as a senior representative of the Pentagon.

If we wanted dirt on Ellsberg, we had found a good source. I broke out a bottle of scotch, poured a couple of liberal glasses, and listened to Conein tell stories. Apparently, Ellsberg was quite fond of the local Vietnamese women and had even gotten into a fight over a woman with a dangerous local bar owner and notorious narcotics trafficker named Nicolai.

Unfortunately, the next day, when I arrived with my hangover at Colson's office, his secretary, Joan Hall, informed me that the Secret Service had installed the microphones improperly and that most of the tape was inaudible. Chuck hoped I would be able to reconstruct the conversation from memory. Despite all my CIA and OSS training, however, the scotch prevailed and my memory was of little use.

Colson, getting into the idea of covert action, suggested that I call Conein and ask him to recite some of this information again to a White House security officer, "Fred Charles," in reality Colson, who had a recording device on his line. Conein agreed, and we reconstituted the conversation, with Colson interjecting various questions.

After this, I requested that my office be outfitted with microphones so that I could tape-record further interviews. The Secret Service performed the task, inserting strategically placed microphones that ran to a Sony recorder in the lower right-hand drawer of my desk. A switch was installed so I could easily turn it on and off inconspicuously. I had my first opportunity to use the device a few days later when I interviewed Major General Edward G. Lansdale, a former CIA chief in South Vietnam, about the same topics I had covered with Conein.

I enjoyed working in the White House atmosphere, which reminded me of my previous CIA experience. This was the center of power of the nation and the world, and it had an enormous effect on me. You couldn't help but feel that your work was of manifest importance, which was something I hadn't felt working in public relations.

About this time, I met Richard Nixon's counsel, John Dean, in Colson's outer office. Dean acknowledged the introduction with a dismissive nod before heading in to meet with Chuck. I was amazed at how young Dean was, just over thirty at the time, but with his hair receding even then, prompting a sort of comb-over from left to right. Still, he had an affable Kennedy-esque air and drifted through the corridors of the White House with apparent confidence. Dean would soon be called a "master manipulator" and, unfortunately, a "star witness" when Watergate broke.

On Saturday, July 10, I was called into an emergency meeting chaired by John Ehrlichman's assistant, Egil "Bud" Krogh, held in the Roosevelt, or sub-Cabinet, Room, where senior representatives from State and Defense, the FBI, and the Secret Service were assembled.

The problem in question was a prominent *New York Times* op-ed piece revealing U.S. and Soviet negotiating positions during the Strategic Arms Limitation Talks (SALT) that had just started, aiming to reduce antiballistic missiles and nuclear weapons. The information had not yet been publicized and could only have come to the writer through a leak at the State Department.

Although even younger than John Dean, Krogh, who had been a partner at Ehrlichman's Seattle law firm, handled the experienced government officials with ease. He focused the discussion on narrowing the leaker to one of two consultants for the State and Defense departments, with most suspicion falling on a man who had made previous contact with the *New York Times* reporter.

I suggested that since it was the weekend and neither suspect was likely to return to his office until Monday, the State and Defense security officers should open the suspects' safes and inventory the contents. The idea was accepted and the orders issued. The measure was effective, proving that both suspects had leaked information to the reporter, although no further sanctions were ever taken against them.

This is the environment in which we operated at the time. Every day, it seemed that more classified information was being revealed. When the holes were plugged in one area, they would burst in another. The White House was becoming more paranoid by the day.

One of the first major leaks from inside the State Department led to a May 1969 article by the *New York Times* revealing the Nixon administration's secret bombings in Cambodia (which would eventually lead to between 150,000 and 500,000 civilian deaths—definitely a blot on Nixon's résumé). Later, it came out that Nixon was also worried that further leaks might jeopardize his covert negotiations with China and the Soviet Union and peace talks with the North Vietnamese. Not only didn't Nixon want Americans to know about his under-the-table diplomacy, the other governments didn't want anybody to know about it, either, and it was possible that they would halt the dialogue if they couldn't trust the Nixon administration to keep a secret. In the minds of the administration, headed by Nixon, whose worldview had been shaped during the Cold War, leaks such as these were treasonous, whether or not they actually hurt our interests.

Ellsberg was being lionized by the press, turned into a heroic, larger-than-life figure, a David fighting the Nixon Goliath, with the nugget of truth in his sling. The questions around the White House were: What was Ellsberg's motivation? Was he a madman? A martyr?

Was he a spy being manipulated by a foreign power? Or was he something even worse—an idealist or an altruist?

Whatever the case, the White House felt that Ellsberg could not go unchallenged, lest other government officials, feeling sympathetic to the cause, follow his example. The Department of Justice drew up indictments and prepared to prosecute Ellsberg and his friend Anthony J. Russo. But the administration, Colson told me, was worried that "Ellsberg could be turned into a martyr of the New Left," concluding, "He probably will be, anyway."

One reason why the White House felt that getting to the bottom of the Ellsberg situation and stopping it at all costs was of paramount importance was described by H. R. Haldeman on June 14 in a tape-recorded conversation with Nixon the day after the initial publication of the papers: "To the ordinary guy, all this is a bunch of gobbledygook. But out of the gobbledygook comes a very clear thing: you can't trust the government; you can't believe what they say; and you can't rely on their judgment. And the implicit infallibility of presidents, which has been an accepted thing in America, is badly hurt by this, because it shows that people do things the president wants to do even though it's wrong, and the president can be wrong." A very prescient quotation if ever there was one.

Additionally, we saw Ellsberg's actions as the work of a sort of counterculture shadow government trying to unilaterally assert its right to declassify and publish top-secret government documents at its own choosing. The administration had been elected by a majority of voters, but the minority was trying to take power in a sort of slow-speed revolution, which had been fomenting over the last few years in campus uprisings, urban bombings, and mass marches.

The counterculture government was also aided by elements in the media, clergy, scientists, and lawyers who could be counted on to support the underground government with various reports, studies, and court proceedings. Added to that were moles such as Ellsberg who were deeply entrenched in government, with access to classified information, who took it upon themselves as judge and jury to leak matters of national security. In some ways, this was a mirror image of events, sans military, that the CIA had perpetuated in other countries such as Guatemala to effect regime change. Perhaps that's what seemed so frightening to the administration.

The United States was being confronted by a hostile force—it didn't matter that it was from within our own borders; it was just as

dangerous, if not more so. If Daniel Ellsberg decided that the legitimate government was criminal, then he was treasonous. Already, the
administration had lost a lot of public support for the war, and the
only way the administration could think to fight against it was to
attack the messenger.

Additional concerns were focused on all extremist elements—such
as hippies, yippies, zippies, and the SDS (Students for a Democratic
Society)—which seemed to be branches of the countergovernment
that had a clear purpose to destroy and take over where they had
failed by the elective process. So this was the charged atmosphere that
I entered at the White House, halls so deep in paranoiac sludge that
we had to wade through it with boots. It was a White House that felt
under siege, an Alamo fighting not only the surrounding army but an
internal uprising as well.

It's not exactly paranoia, however, if people really are out to get
you.

One day in the summer of 1971 when I requested a classified document from Colson, he directed me to see G. Gordon Liddy in Room
16, where sensitive documents were being filed. The quick stroll
down the halls of the Executive Office Building was as uneventful and
mundane as any I had taken before. If I had been an actor in a movie,
perhaps there would have been some kind of ominous music to signal
that something portentous was about to occur. But in life, we are not
so lucky. It seemed like any ordinary day, any ordinary moment when
I arrived at the room and introduced myself.

Liddy was a wired, wisecracking extrovert who seemed as if he
might be a candidate for decaffeinated coffee. He was a lawyer who
had been an FBI agent and, more recently, a special assistant to the
secretary of the Treasury. We formed an almost instantaneous friendship, and I soon learned that he been a prosecutor in Dutchess County,
New York, south of my former home in Albany, and was married with
several children. An unsuccessful bid for Congress had resulted in a
job with the Nixon administration in payment for trying.

Liddy was a triple-A personality, decisive and action oriented, with
no patience for paperwork or bureaucratic red tape, who had made a
name at the Treasury with Operation Intercept, catching Mexican drug
smugglers. Considered an expert on narcotics interdiction, he was
frequently consulted by Walter Minnick, another denizen of Room 16.

His supervisor was an agreeable, prematurely balding young man named David Young, who loved to play tennis. Young had a law degree from Cornell and had transferred to the National Security Council after working as an aide to Henry Kissinger. But the unit (later called the Plumbers by the press) was directed by Egil "Bud" Krogh. At that point, however, I hadn't heard the term *plumber* in any connotation except someone whom my wife needed occasionally to unclog a sink, and I was a bit mystified by the reasons for the unit's existence.

The secretary, Kathleen Chenow, had transferred from the Hill, where she had worked for a New England senator. Everyone in the unit seemed to work long hours, as I did, and we were usually among the last to leave the building at night.

I was in and out of Room 16 very often in my search for sensitive documents relating to the war, and I soon became aware that Liddy and the unit were receiving periodic reports from the FBI on Daniel Ellsberg and his colleagues. One of Krogh's offices was converted into a sort of situation room with charts lining the walls to show the status of various assignments.

It was easy to find reasons to visit the room, where Liddy was usually in good form, telling stories and jokes, providing necessary comic relief from other sections of a pretty austere White House. Even the names of his characters were funny. In his stories, there were no mundane men named John Doe; things happened to guys named Tondelayo Schwarzkopf. He definitely knew how to tell an anecdote. We soon began having lunch together in the White House cafeteria and the occasional drink at my clubs downtown.

Despite our friendship, there was a side to Liddy's personality that I could never quite understand. Documents that originated in Room 16 were stamped "ODESSA" to distinguish them from other routine classified material that circulated within the White House. I would later learn that Liddy, an aficionado of Germany, had formed the word from a German veterans organization that some of his friends belonged to, Organisation der Emerlingen Schutz Staffel Angehörigen, a group that smuggled Nazis out of Germany after World War II. I didn't know why a group like that appealed to him.

I would only find out about his affinity for Nazi Germany little by little over the course of our relationship. At one point early in our friendship, he asked if he could come over to my home in Potomac, Maryland, to play an important record. I agreed. It turned out to be a German recording of the arrival of Hitler at a massive crowd of supporters. Liddy described the scene as though he were there, his face taking on a rapturous glow.

Later, when our work for the Nixon reelection campaign (which led to Watergate) became more intense, we traveled together and socialized frequently. Dorothy was fond of Gordon's wife, Frances, but disapproved of Liddy and his penchant for Nazi Germany, especially as she had worked for the Treasury Department tracking down the regime's ill-gotten plunder. One evening, when the Liddys were dining at our home, Gordon sat down at the Steinway grand piano and belted out a lusty version of a Nazi song, which prompted Dorothy to find something urgent to do in the kitchen.

I was also told on good authority that while Liddy worked for the White House, he arranged a private showing of *The Triumph of the Will*, the most notorious of the Nazi propaganda films, made by German filmmaker Leni Riefenstahl.

The De Motte situation had been simmering in the background for a couple of weeks, and on July 22, 1971, I was summoned to CIA headquarters for a private meeting with General Cushman, during which I learned that John Ehrlichman had called to ask for the fake identification that I had requested. I told the general I needed a good disguise and a driver's license with the first name Edward, as that was how I was being introduced, and some "pocket litter" to fill it out. I would need the I.D. to check into a hotel and possibly show the "gentleman" whom I needed to contact. Cushman agreed that I would collect the material at a CIA safe house.

Before we parted, he said, "If you see John Ehrlichman, say hello for me. . . . He's a friend from previous days. How's that Domestic Council working out?"

I told him that it was working out well and observed that publication of the Pentagon Papers had the White House in a panic.

Cushman mulled that over for a moment and said, "Well, I think John is in charge of the security overhaul, isn't he?"

"That's right," I agreed.

While this exchange seems rather innocent, it does show that the upper echelon of the CIA did have a passing knowledge that even then the White House was performing its own covert ops.

Cushman was about to say something else when he thought better of it and started moving papers around on his desk. "Well, let me get to work on this. I'll get word back to you."

Wearing a brown wig, thick glasses, and a mouthpiece that changed my vocal inflection, I met Clifford De Motte a few days later in a hotel room in Providence, Rhode Island, in the guise of Edward J. Warren. De Motte was quite nervous, but he asked about Bob Bennett and mentioned that he would like to work in the upcoming presidential campaign—this time for the Republicans.

However, his information, which I tape-recorded, did not prove to be the blockbuster material that we'd hoped for. He had simply worked in public relations for the Cape Cod Inn, a favorite hotel of the Kennedys', where he had become deeply involved with the Kennedy staff. Unfortunately, his stories mostly involved Pierre Salinger; he mixed in a few rumors about the Kennedy clan's antics on Cape Cod—the biggest news being that they were notoriously late to pay their bills. This was nothing that I deemed very damaging. When pressed, it became obvious that he knew nothing about the Chappaquiddick incident, although he promised to make inquiries with friends on the island. I gave him some expense money, urged him to explore the situation, and told him to contact Bob Bennett if he needed to get a message to me.

I prepared a detailed memo of the conversation for Colson, who agreed that the only worthy material might come out of an investigation of Chappaquiddick and to keep him posted on further developments.

My contact with the people in Room 16 became increasingly frequent, and I soon learned that the group had an in-house title: the Special Investigations Unit. Liddy told me the unit had been set up because the White House was frustrated by both the FBI and the Department of Defense, which were doing a poor job investigating Ellsberg. When Liddy showed me one of the FBI reports, I had to agree.

One source had told the bureau that Ellsberg and his wife, Patricia, had taken part in orgies at the Sand Stone Club in Los Angeles. Deviate sexual behavior was often preyed on by the Soviets, so this kind of information could be crucial to finding a link between the two, yet the FBI had been too lazy to investigate further. Liddy and I tried to find out more by telephone to California but couldn't find a club of that name. We requested further details from the FBI as to the club's location, membership, and so forth, but were given no response. Then, in late 1972, a magazine article was published describing Sand Stone as a reputable institution for the group treatment of sexual dysfunction—hardly the degenerate orgy club that had been reported by the FBI.

Meanwhile, the media was idolizing Ellsberg as a disciple of truth, an audacious loner fighting against the evil, war-mongering Nixon administration. Liddy and Young, both lawyers, believed that Ellsberg might even avoid jail time, since the indictment was so sloppily drawn that it would be difficult to prosecute. Convinced that he was right, Liddy thus informed Robert Mardian, assistant attorney general in charge of the Internal Security Division of the Department of Justice under Attorney General John Mitchell.

The FBI furnished some further reports about "Saint Ellsberg" that stated that the man and his first wife had experimented with hallucinogens; that he maintained numerous mistresses; and that he had had a rich sex life between marriages. Two of his girlfriends had been foreigners—one Indonesian, the other Swedish—and he had visited the latter in Sweden before returning to the United States from Vietnam.

The word *Sweden* instantly provoked interest in any covert operations officer, as it was a favorite entry point, via Finland, to Europe by Soviet agents. Our interest was further inflamed when we read reports saying that copies of Ellsberg's Pentagon Papers had been delivered to a Soviet agent or to the Soviet embassy sometime before their publication by the *New York Times*.

The FBI report indicated that it was based on a telephone intercept of a conversation between Ellsberg and his psychiatrist, Dr. Lewis Fielding, in which the leaker told Dr. Fielding that he was immensely relieved that he had completed his task. The more we heard, the more it seemed likely that Ellsberg did not deserve his halo and that he might very well be a Soviet agent. Our suspicions were based on his involvement with foreign women while he held high-level security clearance and the alleged delivery of the documents into Soviet hands. Other factors that seemed to point to the agent theory were that Ellsberg had attended Cambridge University in England, historically a fertile hunting ground for Soviet recruiters. Discussing the situation among ourselves, since Ellsberg was being so open with his psychiatrist, we wondered whether Dr. Fielding's patient files might not verify our supposition.

One worry we had was that if the prosecution's case was strong enough, Ellsberg might get off with an insanity plea. The more we thought about it, the more we conjectured that the files were probably a treasure trove of information and would either prove that he was a spy or that there was a basis for an insanity plea, in which case the White House should recommend to the Justice Department that the charges be dropped, at least against Ellsberg, rather than proceed with such an unpopular case.

We first tried having a psychological profile on Ellsberg prepared by a CIA psychologist, similar to studies that I had once found extremely helpful when trying to determine whether to recruit a foreign asset. Two separate reports were unsatisfactory, however, giving us no insight into the target's character or motivations. So Liddy and I began discussing alternative methods of resolving the Ellsberg dilemma.

During this time, I kept a frustrated Colson informed of our progress—or lack thereof—and put together a memorandum for him on possible steps to neutralize the Ellsberg effect, one of which suggested that we somehow obtain the psychiatric material from Dr. Fielding's files, with two ultimate purposes in mind: one to determine the prosecutability of Daniel Ellsberg, the other to find something that would damage his Olympian stature.

No matter what other ideas we came up with, however, in the end we had to agree that somehow we were going to have to get a look at the doctor's confidential files. Liddy and I submitted this idea to Bud Krogh and David Young, telling them that they didn't have to make any decisions yet; we should first make a feasibility study of Dr. Fielding's office and office building to see if it was even possible.

Political savants they may have been, but neither man had any experience with this sort of operation, so I explained in detail the techniques with which I was familiar. We put together a budget for the proposed feasibility study, which amounted to the cost of travel and accommodations for a trip to Los Angeles. Bud Krogh told us the plan was approved, authorizing us to take initial action.

We obtained an additional disguise from my CIA contact, "Steve," for Liddy, who decided on an alias of George F. Leonard, consisting of a barbered black wig with longish hair, proper "flash" identification, pocket litter, and an annoying heel lift device designed to make the wearer limp, which Liddy would later discard in rage.

We flew out to Los Angeles under our aliases on August 26 and checked into the Beverly Hilton, a mere three or so blocks from Fielding's office. We took an evening stroll to case the psychiatrist's office, then returned to the hotel, where I was surprised to see Liddy drop to the floor and perform a hundred push-ups before going to bed. Throughout our friendship, I would find Liddy to be a chronic exercise enthusiast who watched his diet and drinking assiduously.

The next morning, I took the opportunity to introduce Liddy to my old navy buddy Tony Jackson, who was now a prominent lawyer in Los Angeles. We made the acquaintance using Liddy's alias, George Leonard, saying that we were in town doing research for an antinarcotics task force. While my main reason to see Tony was to discuss a possible business venture that Barker, Artime, and I had discussed earlier that year, I also wanted him to meet Liddy in case the two should ever need to make contact—in case something went wrong with our operation and we needed a lawyer immediately.

After Jackson departed, Liddy and I donned our disguises and headed over to Fielding's office with my trusty 35mm camera. During an active day, we photographed the target from all directions, posing Liddy in front of the office building as if we were taking tourist shots rather than reconnaissance photos; drove in a rental car out to Dr. Fielding's residence, which we photographed from three sides; then returned to the psychiatrist's office, where we determined that the doctor drove a white Volvo that occupied his space in the office parking lot. Later in the night, after dinner, we returned to the building to photograph the building's exterior and record which office window lights were still lit.

Noting through the building's large glass doors a single cleaning woman, we decided to reconnoiter Fielding's office on the second floor, where I prevailed on her in Spanish to open Fielding's office so that we, two of his "colleagues," could leave him an item he was expecting. Once inside, I kept her occupied in conversation while Liddy entered Fielding's inner office to photograph it with a CIA-supplied camera hidden in a tobacco pouch, which supposedly held film so sensitive that you could just about take a picture in the dark.

We had to cut short the operation when the cleaning lady started getting suspicious about Liddy's prolonged absence. Liddy exited just as I lost her attention. I gave her a nice tip for her trouble.

"Did you manage to get any shots?" I asked Liddy as we strolled back to the hotel.

"A few," he grumbled, saying that he had been sure the lady was going to come barging in on him.

We returned to the hotel, picked up our rental car, and continued our stakeout of the office building, noting with surprise and delight that when our friendly cleaning lady exited the premises, she did not lock the front or back door. Equally delightful was a lax police department that did not seem interested in cruising the area. Additionally, we discovered that a section of the hotel was in direct line of sight with Fielding's building, and his building could be monitored from a room in that wing. We returned to Washington the next day. All in all, everything went as planned, except for an amusing event in the park. Liddy told me that he had been sitting on a park bench when he was cruised by a gay "seven-foot Navajo" who apparently found Liddy so inviting in his longish wig that Liddy almost had to fight off the large, amorous suitor.

Steve, the CIA tech with whom we were dealing, delivered the photos to a safe house when we got back, and we began to plot out an operational plan. This was aborted when Liddy informed me that his "principals," meaning Krogh and Young and possibly their superiors, had okayed the operation on the proviso that neither Liddy nor I would go anywhere near the target premises, which meant that I had to find other hands to do the job.

I recruited my old friend Bernie Barker, who in turn brought in two of his Miami Cuban compatriots—Felipe De Diego, a Bay of Pigs veteran, and Rolando Martinez, a muscular commando who had led sabotage missions inside Cuba—telling them only that the target was a traitor to the country. We scheduled the break-in for Labor Day weekend, hoping that the doctor would steer clear of his office over the long weekend, when we would have plenty of time to go through his files.

Last-minute jitters intensified when Krogh was late to provide operational funds, but he finally arrived just in time for us to reach our flight. He was a bundle of nerves, hands trembling as he held out the envelope. "Here it is," he said, voice breaking as he admonished, "Now for God's sake, don't get caught!"

"We won't," Liddy assured him, confident as ever.

Krogh was not mollified, forcing upon Liddy his home number to call as soon as the operation was over. "Whatever happens, call and let me know," he said. "I'll be waiting."

Liddy replied that he would call from a pay phone. "I'll be George—honest George Leonard. What will I call you?"

Krogh looked like he was going to vomit from nervousness. "Just call me Wally."

"Wally?"

"Yeah, Wally Fear," he croaked.

Amusing as his nervousness was, we had no time to kid him, as Liddy would assuredly have done; we had to make our flight.

Barker and his cohorts flew to Los Angeles and checked in to the Beverly Hilton under pseudonyms, while Liddy and I flew west through Chicago, where we split up and purchased an array of specialized equipment that was needed to photograph documents. We were careful to buy separate pieces from different shops to keep a low profile and avoid the possibility that they could be traced back to us if the team was caught.

Once in Los Angeles, Liddy and I checked into the hotel, then went out to purchase other necessary items at different stores, including work uniforms for the three men, a large suitcase, entry tools, a length of strong nylon rope, and black muslin to cover the windows, as I might have done during my CIA days. While we expected our men to make a frontal entrance through the office door, the nylon rope could offer an emergency escape out of the window should the operation be compromised.

The photo equipment, black muslin, and nylon cord were packed into a suitcase on which I plastered some air-freight labels, which the men delivered to Fielding's office during the day. Another amicable cleaning woman placed the box inside the target for us.

We ran tests on our walkie-talkies, satisfying ourselves that they functioned, and on September 3 prepared to accomplish our job.

Barker and De Diego borrowed the disguises that Liddy and I had used previously. I called Fielding's office telephone and ascertained that he was not in, then backed myself up by phoning him at home, this time getting an answer, prompting me to hang up.

I drove a rental car to Fielding's apartment, where I would keep watch on his Volvo, while Liddy surveilled the office from another rental automobile, watching for any passing police cars, about which he would alert the team inside via radio. Parking a couple blocks from Fielding's apartment, I strolled down his block, seeing that the Volvo was just where we wanted it to be.

Over the next sixty minutes or so, I kept watch on Fielding's apartment, alternately walking or driving past. Then his apartment light went off, signaling that he was likely going to bed for the night.

It was very difficult for me to remain this far removed from the action when I had been a part of so many hair-raising operations over the years. It's something that gets into your blood, keeps your heart beating, your mind keen, and casing a dark apartment like one of my lower-ranking agents during my CIA career made me wonder how close I was to being relegated to a permanent armchair, living vicariously through characters in my books. I fought a temptation to raise Liddy on the radio, but that would have violated my own rules regarding radio silence except in case of an emergency.

I strolled back to the car, started the engine, and drove past the dark apartment once more. A pit suddenly entered my stomach. Everything looked the same as it had a few minutes ago—neighborhood quiet, a few lights on, Fielding's apartment still dark—except for the striking absence of the Volvo.

Wondering whether the doctor had somehow been alerted to the break-in, praying that nothing had gone wrong and my friends were not in handcuffs, I parked around the corner and tried to raise Liddy on the radio. "George, this is Leonard. Report," I implored and repeated the message. All I heard was static.

After repeating my attempt a few more times, I sped back to the office building, hoping to be able to warn the team that Fielding was on his way—knowing full well that I might already be too late. But when I drove slowly past the office building, I was relieved to find no sign of activity or police cars. Fielding's windows were still dark. I could see Liddy sitting in the darkened rental car nearby. He sat up when he saw me approach, and I squeezed into the passenger's seat. He wanted to know what happened.

"I put Fielding to bed," I said. "But fifteen minutes ago, his car disappeared!"

"What!"

I nodded, then asked, "Where are the boys?"

"Hell, they're inside."

It turned out that the operation was running late because the cleaning lady had locked the doors to the building this time, causing the team to break a window near an air conditioner in the rear of the building. There had been no word from the team since entry.

"I shouldn't have lost Fielding," I said, shaking my head at my amateurish failure. "The car was there; fifteen minutes later, it was gone. Where the hell would he go this time of night? If he was a general practitioner, he might be off seeing a patient, but not a shrink. After six o'clock, shrinks don't budge. Believe me, I know."

Liddy tried to transmit a message to the team, but the walkie-talkie wouldn't work. The hundred-dollar radios that we had bought, trying to keep expenses down for his superiors, were pieces of garbage.

"We'd better get them out of there," I observed.

Liddy laughed in disgust. "Yeah, I know how to do it, too. Heave one of these mothers through their window—that'll bring 'em! This Mickey Mouse gear! If we ever do another op like this, we're going to go first cabin, believe me." His face became so red that I thought he was going to follow up his words with action and hurl the radio through a window. Instead, he pushed the antenna down, though I got the impression he was trying to crush the walkie-talkie with his grip. "For two box tops, you get one of these and an Orphan Annie ring!" he said. "Let's go get them."

We were walking casually toward the building when we saw men-shaped hulks near the dark side—our boys had exfiltrated the building. I turned to Liddy and told him we were back on track and I'd meet him at the hotel.

In the hotel room, I put a bottle of champagne and five glasses on ice and waited for my friends. Soon Liddy pushed through the door, flung his coat on the bed, and said with a grin, "I bet Krogh's pissing his pants. Wally Fear, for God's sake!"

Barker and his buddies, sweaty and disheveled, soon followed. I think Martinez was bleeding, having cut himself on some broken window glass from the rear entry. We gave one another *abrazo* for a successful operation, but the elation turned sour almost immediately with Barker's report.

"Eduardo," he said, "there was nothing there!"

"Nothing?" I asked incredulously.

"We went through every goddamn file in that office, Eduardo, and there was nothing there. Nothing with the name Ellsberg on it, anyway."

"You're absolutely sure?" Liddy asked.

Barker and Martinez pulled off their wigs and mopped their perspiring faces with towels. De Diego sat defeated in a chair.

"I'm sorry, George," Barker said to Liddy. "But that's how it was." He delved into his pocket and produced some Polaroid photographs that he had taken during the operation and handed them to us. "Like you told us to do, we photographed the files before and after, and there's what it looked like."

The Polaroids showed a scene of file cabinets in disarray, pried open and savaged, but the cabinets were out of focus and it was impossible to read the headings on the individual files.

I felt a great void inside but said, "Well, I guess it's time for champagne."

The team said they had gone through a lot of files, including old tax returns, but had found nothing about Ellsberg. They had spilled some pills from a cupboard and strewn files around trying to make it look like the work of an addict looking for drugs. We figured at least nothing had gone wrong, except for having to break into the building.

We told the team to hightail it out of town on the next plane, and Liddy went to make a report to "Wally" from a pay phone. I started packing my bag and wondered if there might be any benefit to breaking into Fielding's apartment, since he might have brought Ellsberg's files there after being asked twice by the FBI for a look at them. Liddy came back and said, "Wally was so relieved he almost cried. He's so happy we weren't caught that he doesn't really care that we didn't find anything."

We caught a few hours of sleep before taking a flight back to D.C. through New York. I did not go into work on Monday, the holiday. On the following day, I brought the heavy suitcase full of photographic gear and entry equipment to my White House office. Liddy and I put in a request to perform a similar entry procedure into Fielding's apartment, but Krogh, and presumably John Ehrlichman, would not authorize it, as it was taking a large risk to obtain files that we had no information were actually there.

The office break-in was discovered on Monday. Police arrested a local drug addict, who conveniently confessed to our crime in return for a suspended sentence. Otherwise, the operation remained secret until disclosed by John Dean in April 1973. By then, of course, Liddy, Barker, Martinez, and I were incarcerated in Washington, D.C., for the Watergate mess. To this day, I have no idea where the files were being kept or if they ever existed.

In an ironic twist, charges against Ellsberg et al. were dismissed in 1973, after our break-in was revealed. Ellsberg remained free while the entry team members, trying to root out the cause of one of our county's greatest security breaches, were tried and convicted along with Ehrlichman.

While the Pentagon Papers revealed many grim machinations and subterfuge in Vietnam that portrayed our government in the most jaundiced light, questions about whether it was the right of a single person to divulge such secret documents to the world remain in limbo. In my mind, it was illegal and incorrect to unilaterally divulge such classified information to the country and our enemies. Similar situations abound in the world today with the revelations of prisoner abuse at Abu Ghraib and Guantánamo Bay and the dispute over domestic spying on terrorist suspects, which ask questions so deep and complicated that they will, no doubt, be argued among politicians and historians yet to be born.

15

Gemstone

The road to Watergate was traveled in such small, incremental steps that by the time the situation arose, the break-in would seem a natural thing to do. Aren't all vices the same? The alcoholic, be it a wino sprawled in the gutter or a power broker scoffing down martinis, has to have his first sip at some time; the drug user, be it a soccer mom gulping tranquilizers or a junky sharing needles, has her first taste of bliss; every overeater starts her progressive snacking without realizing; every criminal commits his first, usually small, crime.

The Fielding case was our first step down the low road—its necessity of enormous importance to us in getting to the bottom of what we could only conceive as a key threat to national security. None of us—not our Cuban friends doing the work out of patriotism for their adopted country; not the action-oriented, gun-toting Liddy; not me, having worked hard for my country my entire adult life—felt as if this was the beginning of a newfound employment, that this was a warm-up operation because illegal break-ins were now part of our arsenal of dirty tricks. But like the alcoholic who thinks he can stop at any time, every day there seemed reason enough to press on.

Like common drinkers, Liddy and I became covert action co-dependents. My wife and daughter Kevan thought we acted like schoolkids together, one feeding off the other.

I continued working my full-time job for Mullen & Company, but my heart was always at the White House, and I spent as much time there as possible, working weekends and after hours researching the origins of the Vietnam War. This entailed finding and requesting from the Kennedy archives thousands of cables from that administration, which I then had to collate and analyze. But many important cables, especially those close to the assassination period in 1963, seemed to be missing, which I gradually became convinced—and still believe—had to do with orders from Kennedy to have South Vietnam's premier killed. I reported these findings to Colson, saying, "Anyone who read the cables as I have could never doubt the complicity of the Kennedy administration in the death of the Vietnamese premier."

"How many cables are missing?" Colson wanted to know.

I told him it was hard to say, perhaps twenty. Maybe up to fifty.

Colson sat back in his chair and whistled. "Aren't there one or two cables that would pretty much definitely establish that the Kennedy gang was responsible for Diem's assassination?"

I shook my head. It wasn't going to be that easy. "No, you'd have to take a sequence of three or four cables, be aware of their context, and speculate on what was contained in the cables missing from the sequence."

Colson leaned forward, his gaze intensifying. This was absolutely riveting information that would completely change the attitude of people bent on bestowing sainthood on the assassinated president. "You know and I know that the New Frontier was responsible for those murders," he said. "Got any ideas?"

I told him that I was familiar enough with the language used in the directives to fabricate the missing cables, though it would be almost impossible to make them stand up under magnification without having them typed on the exact typewriters that were used to create the originals, no matter how close the typeface was to the originals. Colson nixed my idea of asking for technical assistance from the CIA or the Secret Service.

Colson then authorized me to go ahead and do my best with the equipment I had. Using Executive Office typewriters and a Xerox machine, I soon produced two "cables" that passed muster with Colson. The first was an apparent query from the Saigon embassy concerning White House policy should Diem and his brother-in-law request asylum; the second was a negative response, written in typically ambiguous, diplomatic language. The two cables looked good to the naked eye, but I knew they would quickly fail under technical examination.

At Colson's suggestion, we tried to expose the material to a Pulitzer Prize–winning journalist for *Life* magazine, Bill Lambert, with whom we had met recently on another matter. Lambert was fascinated by the cables, but his editors refused to publish the story without having the cables copied for technical examination, which we would not permit. The several hundred real cables and two concocted cables, separated from the rest, were placed in my safe. We had some success distributing the false information, however, when we learned that a TV documentary was being made on Vietnam. I showed the fake cables to Conein, who had already been interviewed for the piece. Conein in turn spoke about what he had seen during a second interview. The piece subsequently aired on television and was happily received by the White House.

Toward the end of November 1971, an elated Liddy walked into my office, sat on the corner of my desk, and told me that Attorney General John Mitchell wanted him to become general counsel for the Committee to Re-elect the President (popularly written as CRP or CREEP, usually depending on political affiliation). Most significantly, Mitchell wanted Liddy to set up an intelligence organization for the campaign that would report on the Democratic opposition. "They don't want a repetition of the last campaign," Liddy said. "They want to know everything that's going on. Everything." Apparently he had been told that at least $500,000 could be budgeted for a multitude of projects.

"I'll need you and Macho and the rest of the guys if we're going to make this work. The AG doesn't want any trouble—like Chicago—at the San Diego convention [San Diego was the planned site for the Republican convention], and he wouldn't mind causing the Democrats a little trouble in Miami [the Democratic convention site]. That's where you and the Cubans come in. We ought to be able to have informants in every hotel in Miami Beach."

Thus was born the notorious Project Gemstone.

When Liddy joined CREEP, he almost instantly came to blows with its young chairman, Jeb Magruder, the two despising each other from the start. Magruder thought Liddy was an egotistic loose cannon whose ideas about how to defeat the Democrats needed to be reined in, and Liddy thought Magruder was a senseless coward who was constantly trying to undermine his grand ideas. The two battled constantly, prompting Liddy to tell me, "If he gives me any more trouble, I'll tell him I'm going to kill him," a threat that Magruder seemed to take seriously when it was later delivered.

CREEP headquarters was coincidently and conveniently nearby, directly across the street from Mullen & Company. While Liddy moved out of Room 16, he was permitted to retain his White House pass, so we continued to lunch at the cafeteria or dining room.

During the holidays, Dorothy and I were invited to "An Evening at the White House," where we briefly met the president and his wife in the receiving line. When I told Nixon, "I'm working with Chuck Colson now, Mr. President," he smiled and replied that he "knew all about that" and passed us along to Pat.

Recognition of my work pleased me at the time. It wouldn't be until after Watergate that I would learn the full significance of those words.

That week, Gordon and Frances Liddy spent New Year's Eve at our home, and while our wives talked, we went into another room to discuss future plans and various stipulations that were being made by Jeb Magruder and Nixon counsel John Dean. While Liddy had a variety of nasty pet names for Magruder, he started using the phrase "my principals" when speaking about his superiors.

I was tasked with creating a plan to protect the Republican convention at San Diego against attacks by a mob of anti-Republican demonstrators who would likely try to disrupt the convention, establish an intelligence collection network directed against the Democratic national convention in Miami, organize groups to counterdemonstrate at the Democratic convention, and maintain in standby status the entry team that had accessed Dr. Fielding's office. Most difficult, however, was the final requirement by the principals that some kind of electronic surveillance be placed inside the office of the ultimate Democratic nominee.

We continued to meet in Room 16, where we sketched out the operation, which, in common CIA style, we named—Gemstone. It was further divided into subprojects with the names of precious or semiprecious stones such as Diamond, Ruby, Sapphire, Opal, and others. On a matching chart, each project was described with its corresponding dollar figure costs. Liddy found the technique of mapping out the covert plan very charming and hoped that his principals would have a positive reaction when he presented it.

Our highest priority, "Diamond," was the counterdemonstration plan for San Diego, where the Republican convention was scheduled to take place (it would later be moved to Miami Beach, booked just after the Democrats staged their convention in the same hotel). "Garnet" was another counterdemonstration program, in which we planned to hire various distasteful people to demonstrate *against* Republicans, with the hopeful fallout that the American public would find their antics so repulsive that they would vote for Nixon, just to thumb their noses at the demonstrators (much like how today's *American Idol* television audiences often seem to vote *for* contestants whom Simon Cowell ridicules).

"Ruby" defined our plan to infiltrate the organizations of the various Democratic candidates and their eventual presidential contender. "Quartz" was part of an ambitious eavesdropping plan, entailing the high-tech tapping of telephone lines by microwave transmitters. This worked in conjunction with "Emerald," a difficult and costly scheme utilizing a chase plane to intercept Democratic radio-phone communications from their planes and ground transportation.

The most audacious and salacious plans were dubbed "Crystal" and "Sapphire." Crystal was a project to rent a luxurious houseboat docked across from the convention site at the Fontainebleau hotel and trick it out with various electronic recording devices to listen to bugs that we hoped to plant in private Democratic convention hotel rooms. Who knows what secrets we might discover in this fashion? This operated in conjunction with Sapphire, a plan to use high-class prostitutes acting the part of Democratic political groupies to lure high-level officials into sexual excursions on the conveniently situated houseboat, where hopefully they would brag about various Democratic plans.

One adventurous project called "Opal" concerned four "black-bag ops" in which we would break in and bug the offices of various candidates, such as Senator Edward Muskie and Senator George McGovern. Watergate would eventually be an Opal-op.

There were other small jobs and dirty tricks given code names, such as "Turquoise," in which a commando team made up of my seasoned Cuban operatives would sabotage the air conditioners of the Democratic convention, a plan we thought would make the other party's tempers skyrocket in the hot summer climate, causing them to be mistake-prone.

There were some other elements that were immediately dropped for one reason or another, but the main plan, as outlined, came with a $1 million funding request, which made Liddy's principals, who had promised generous financial support, turn into misers. After Liddy presented the proposal in John Mitchell's office at the Department of Justice, complete with professionally made flowcharts created for me at the CIA, he came storming back to Room 16, where I waited to learn the outcome. "It's back to the drawing boards," he told me in disgust. Apparently, Magruder and Dean, while initially enthusiastic, had not sided with him when Mitchell said the plan was too expensive. The principals, he said, wanted us to cut the budget it half.

After much research, including a Liddy trip to San Diego, we cut out projects such as Emerald—the most expensive section, tailing the Democratic aircraft—pared down other elements to bare-bones essentials, and got the budget down to a half million. He left for the meeting in high hopes and returned like a dejected schoolboy who had been scolded by the principal. The budget was still too high.

"Magruder and Dean tell me everything's fine, then I trot in there, go through my soft-shoe dance, and get cut off at the knees by the AG. All Dean and Magruder do is nod their heads sagely. To hell with them!"

Later writings by the principals indicate that Mitchell thought Liddy was mentally unstable and no one knew what he would do under pressure. They thought some of our ideas were just too fantastic to be accomplished.

At this point, I thought that Gemstone would suffer the fate of many bold and interesting CIA plans—permanent back-burner disease. Still, we went ahead and devised a third bare-bare-bones operation that I was convinced would never be approved, going so far as to phone Bernie Barker and tell him to put the developmental work he was doing on hold.

While Gemstone was likely to be stillborn, we still needed to do what we could with current resources. One of the cheapest and easiest ideas was to have a few trusty souls infiltrate the various Democratic offices as volunteers. Through Bob Bennett's nephew, I was introduced to a likely candidate, Thomas Gregory, a disheveled-looking youth who fit in perfectly with scores of Muskie campaign volunteers. He regularly smuggled out names of Muskie contributors, financial information, and advance position papers that hadn't been made public.

We weren't the only ones up to dirty tricks. Someone high up in the White House had managed to infiltrate an agent into Muskie's headquarters to take photographs of mail and other documents, and I was asked to obtain the material through the agent's handler, "Fat Jack," a tall, portly, gray-haired man—later identified as John Buckley, an Office of Economic Opportunity official—who tendered me the material in return for envelopes of cash supplied by Liddy.

When Muskie dropped out of the race, Gregory was able to switch to front-runner McGovern's headquarters, while Fat Jack's man was not. So Gregory became our sole window into the inner workings of the McGovern campaign.

Some time had passed by now, and I had almost forgotten about Gemstone, but on April 1, 1972, Liddy informed me in buoyant tones that the project had been approved, if only for a paltry sum of $250,000. Still, if we had some incremental successes, more funds might be approved.

The important point was that we finally had the green light. I called Bernie Barker and told him the word was "*Go!*"

16

Colson and McCord

Before we could get started on Gemstone, another embarrassing revelation was made about the administration that had to be attended to. Columnist Jack Anderson had published an article on February 29, 1972, revealing a memo from International Telegraph and Telephone (ITT) lobbyist Dita Beard that promised the Nixon administration $400,000 from the company to finance the Republican convention if some annoying antitrust litigation for the multinational company was conveniently dropped. While administration officials issued the standard denials, headlines about the case were published around the country. The criminal implications aside, the investigation threatened to derail Nixon's nomination for attorney general, Richard Kleindienst, whose confirmation hearings were in session. No one could ask Beard about the memo, as she had gone into hiding. Soon there was an announcement issued saying that Beard had been admitted to a Denver hospital with a heart attack.

Colson dispatched me to Denver to interview Beard and find out whether the memo was real (or had been forged by the Democrats) and why she had left town, which I would do in my standard disguise under my assumed name. My conversation with the ailing lobbyist took place in her hospital room, where she denied writing or leaking the memo. She had left Washington, she said, to get away from the press. She expressed concern about getting her "Christmas bonus," which Colson told me to tell her would be forthcoming. I didn't think much about the "Christmas bonus" at the time, but it was obviously a code for hush money.

She must have felt reassured by Chuck's words, because she reiterated her innocence to a group of senators who met with her a short time later. Despite her denial, time has proven that the charges were correct; ITT did make the offer and antitrust charges were dropped by John Mitchell's Justice Department. That was unknown at the time, however, and John Mitchell was soon confirmed as the new director of CREEP. His deputy, Richard Kleindienst, was confirmed as the new attorney general.

Jack Anderson had been a thorn in Nixon's foot ever since 1960, when he had investigated a $205,000 loan from a Howard Hughes company to Richard Nixon's brother, F. Donald Nixon, which was never paid back. This scandal was considered by many to be the boost Kennedy needed to defeat Nixon that year. We considered more recent articles—concerning American surveillance on Soviets, for instance—to be such breaches of national security that the Nixon administration was angry, and I got the word from Colson that we needed to "stop Anderson at all costs."

I took this to mean that we were authorized to do whatever was necessary to resolve the issue. Liddy and I, feeling that Anderson had done such harm to the country by exposing foreign-based CIA agents who might be imprisoned and/or killed, spent a lot of time concocting ways to get rid of the pesky journalist, even trying to cook up a way to get him to ingest LSD through his skin from his steering wheel so that he would crash his car. A CIA specialist, however, assured me that skin was an inadequate delivery system, so the plan did not move forward. Still, Liddy was primed and ready to go it alone, planning an assassination if Mitchell would just give the word. Ultimately, the attorney general aborted the operation and the muckraker in question outlived most of his adversaries, dying in December 2005 at the age of eighty-three from Parkinson's disease.

I wrote an eight-page report on my trip and what Dita Beard had told me for Colson, then went to work for the day at my Mullen & Company office, which became a nexus point of Nixonian spin work to deny Anderson's charges with various press statements. I was still in contact with Tom Gregory and Fat Jack, and I received the occasional report from Clifton De Motte concerning his findings on Chappaquiddick. The administration was highly interested in any negative

219-6684

information about Kennedy, feeling that although the senator had not announced any intentions, all he had to do was toss his name into the ring and the Democratic nomination would be his.

De Motte had interviewed the local district attorney, among others, and had come up with a new scenario that had yet to be proved: Unknown to other members of the cottage party that Kennedy had attended, Mary Jo Kopechne had gotten into the senator's car and fallen asleep in the backseat. Later, Kennedy and another woman left the party in the car, unaware of the sleeping stowaway. When the car ran off the bridge, both Kennedy and his companion had escaped, and no one asked about Mary Jo until the sodden couple returned to the party and a frantic search for the girl began. No one was saying much, but if true, the facts were far less damaging than the conjecture.

When I reported this to Colson, he secured my memo in a drawer and showed me pictures of Kennedy escorting a couple of women other than his wife to a few nightclubs, implying they had the ammunition they needed should he get into the race. It took on less importance now, however, as it appeared that Senator McGovern was the clear leader.

On April 29, 1972, I submitted my last invoice for consultant work, as the affairs of Room 16 were accelerating, and any further investigation into the origin of the Vietnam War seemed fruitless. I still considered myself a White House consultant, however, retaining my office and continuing to work with Liddy in the affairs of Room 16.

Another fact that should be inserted here concerns my wife's .25 caliber Browning pistol, which was later found in my White House safe and about which many conspiracy theories abound. I first brought the weapon to Mullen & Company after a secretary in an office on our floor was raped in the restroom and a government official was murdered in the Executive Office Building across the street. The incidents scared our secretaries so much that they didn't want to leave the premises after dark. I brought the weapon into the office in order to escort them to their cars at night and secured it in my safe at the White House after the culprits were apprehended. The presence of the weapon at the White House would later cause a major sensation when my safe was drilled open and ransacked by the Secret Service.

Other small services I rendered to Liddy's CREEP unit included bringing an envelope of money to a foundation run by multimillionaire W. Clement Stone in Chicago, which I later figured out was probably funneled from Nixon's reelection office to Spiro Agnew's defense fund.

Liddy continued to clash with Magruder and told me that he was trying to get reassigned to the Finance Committee to Re-elect the President under Maurice Stans, a self-made millionaire whom Liddy admired. My friend also informed me of some other strange parallel operation to ours going on in New York that was being carried out by a detective of Mitchell's. When Liddy returned, he described a bizarre plot by an ex–New York policeman, later identified as Anthony Ulasewicz, to romance a Kennedy friend from the Chappaquiddick party in a tacky little apartment. The detective, otherwise known as the "Golden Greek," had siphoned off a large amount of money for his useless scheme, as the woman refused to sleep with him and impart the valuable information. Needless to say, Liddy wrote a contemptuous report on the matter that resulted in the dismantling of the electronically endowed seduction suite.

Gemstone was still treading water, and I learned from Liddy that he had paid some $30,000 to an as-yet-unidentified electronics expert for custom-made telephone surveillance equipment. "I'll tell you this about him," Liddy told me. "He was not only with your old company but with mine as well, so he ought to know what he's doing. In addition, he's been working as a bodyguard for Mitchell."

"Martha?" I asked, knowingly. The attorney general's wife was a hopeless drunk who was the subject of a lot of embarrassing gossip around the White House. It was known that Mitchell had assigned a watchdog, who I would later find out was James McCord, to Martha. She would get into a bathtub, for instance, and flounder around and drink a few more drinks and pass out. After a close call or two, Mitchell was afraid she would drown, so McCord was assigned to protect her—from herself.

I would only have personal contact with her once, in the green room of a recording studio, probably for a fund-raiser after the Watergate incident, but before my arrest. She came out, already well lubricated, dressed in lederhosen and clogs. She went on stage and performed some pretty awkward clogging, then walked over to where I was standing, looked menacingly at me, and alleged that she knew "all about Watergate."

Another incident that soon occurred would eventually be made famous by Bob Woodward and Carl Bernstein, particularly in the movie *All the President's Men*, in which the mysterious Deep Throat, now known as Mark Felt, admonishes the intrepid reporter to "follow the money," a quip made up for the moviegoing public.

Liddy was receiving dribs and drabs of development money from his principals, one payment coming in the form of a series of checks amounting to $100,000 drawn on a Mexican bank. It was later discovered that the funds, which he got from Hugh Sloan, chairman of the campaign finance committee, came from Texas CREEP chairman—and George H. W. Bush business partner—William Liedtke. The funds originated from Robert H. Allen, chairman of Gulf Resources and Chemical Corporation, a company that controlled a vital supply of lithium, an element used in the production of hydrogen bombs. The money had been laundered through a Mexican bank to make it harder to trace. A further $25,000 contribution given to Liddy was later sourced to Dwayne Andreas, chief executive of the Archer-Daniels-Midland company.

It was money that had to be kept under the table, as strict new accounting rules had gone into effect for political campaigns. Later campaign operators would find many ways around these rules, but at this point, no one had. Liddy asked me if I thought Bernie Barker would be able to negotiate the checks through his business in Miami and turn them into cash. I put in the request to Bernie, who foresaw no difficulties with the task, so we flew to Miami and gave Macho the checks. He brought them to a friend who was vice president of a bank, who charged a hefty fee for the exchange and delivered the money to us.

The next assignment handed down from the principals, Liddy informed me, was the ardent desire for a bug to be placed at McGovern's headquarters near Capitol Hill. We cased the building and received a floor diagram from our mole, Tom Gregory, along with the habits of campaign workers Gary Hart and Frank Mankiewicz.

Liddy brought his electronics expert, James McCord, to meet me at my Mullen & Company office. McCord had indeed been employed at the CIA, retiring in 1970 after being responsible for security at CIA headquarters in Langley. This, I knew, was a routine job that amounted to checking safes and desktops after hours, and it was not something that required black-ops training or experience. McCord was a thick-necked, wide-jawed man, with a prominent brow, who looked as if he was straight out of central casting—as a thug. It was hard to draw him out, and I would find him to be aloof and withdrawn during most of our acquaintance.

McCord brought me up to date on his efforts to procure the bugs and other equipment—now commercially available—that had been developed originally for the CIA. Liddy added that McCord was also commissioned to buy some expensive walkie-talkies, "not like the Mickey Mouse monsters we used in L.A.!"

I learned that McCord had also been providing other services for the cause, having rented an office adjacent to Muskie headquarters in preparation to eavesdrop on their campaign. This had become a moot point now that CREEP had determined that McGovern was ordained to be the candidate.

Here, for the first time, I was also informed that the principals considered bugging the Democratic National Headquarters at the Watergate building a priority. According to Liddy, his superiors had information from high-level sources that the Democrat National Committee was receiving illegal contributions from the North Vietnamese. In retrospect, these were probably Nixon's own paranoid delusions. But at the time, we were told that the information was fairly concrete. Additionally, Miami contacts relayed a companion rumor that Fidel Castro was clandestinely funding the Democrats, as well. If either illegality could be verified, the information could prove so damaging that it would not only derail McGovern's bid to replace Nixon, it might usher in a Democratic Armageddon and pave the way for the rapture of a majority Republican Congress.

Somewhere, we theorized, DNC books would reflect foreign contributions—and those books were most likely secreted in the files of the Democratic national chairman, Larry O'Brien, in the Watergate office building.

When John Edgar Hoover died a short time later at age seventy-seven on May 2, 1972, Liddy came to my office to tell me that another high-level request had been made of him. A "peacenik" rally featuring actors Jane Fonda and Donald Sutherland, lawyer William Kunstler, and the iconic Daniel Ellsberg was planned for the Capitol steps during the time that Hoover's body was lying in state, as the antiwar left considered the deceased FBI chief one of its main villains. Magruder and Colson apparently believed that Ellsberg planned to unfurl a North Vietnamese flag he owned, which they thought would be a great thing to steal and give to the president as a sort of war prize. Liddy wanted me to get Barker and his boys to come up from Miami to disrupt the gathering and abscond with the flag.

Three thousand dollars was allocated to fly in a group of boys, including Frank Sturgis, who disrupted Ellsberg's speech by calling him a traitor. The men were also instructed to form a shield to protect Hoover's casket if the protesters got rowdy enough to make a surge toward the rotunda to desecrate his remains.

In the end, some of our men got into fights with members of the crowd—Barker skinned his fist on someone's teeth—but no one was detained by the sympathetic police. In fact, a cop who broke up an altercation between Sturgis and one of the protesters told Frank that he was glad to see some Americans were willing to stand up to the antiestablishment crowd. A radio interviewer even recorded an interview with Sturgis. Unfortunately, Barker informed us, there had been no Vietcong flag in evidence to go after.

So that the trip wouldn't be a total waste, we took the men to case the McGovern headquarters, where we walked to the rear and determined that there were a few security floodlights that would have to be extinguished before a break-in could occur. Then we drove the men past the Watergate so that they could familiarize themselves with the massive complex: several curvaceous buildings rising along the Potomac, housing offices and a luxury hotel, connected together by an underground garage. In contrast, a shabby-looking Howard Johnson hotel cowered in its shadow across the street.

"That's our next job, Macho," I said.

"What is it?" Barker asked.

"Democratic National Headquarters," I told him. Then I launched into the reason why the principals had told us they were so hot for us to get inside. "There's a report that Castro's been sending money to the Democrats. He's Hanoi's favorite, too, and if McGovern's elected, he'll simply pull out our troops and the hell with everything else."

Barker replied, "That rumor is all over Miami. You don't have to tell me any more about it."

"The idea," I told him, "is to photograph the list of contributors the Democrats are required to keep. We can have them checked to determine whether the contributors are bona fide or whether they are just fronts for Cuban or Hanoi money."

"Just like the Fielding operation," Barker said.

"Yes," I agreed. "But this time I hope we can find what we're looking for."

The Miami contingent left the following morning, as they all had jobs and families to attend to. Unlike me and Liddy, they had refused payment for their services, believing they were involved in a patriotic duty, and they only received reimbursement for their lost wages. I, however, was being paid $3,000 per break-in, while Liddy received $2,500 per operation. James McCord earned $2,000.

In the end, the Cuban efforts at the rally had hardly caused a ripple in the pond, and we found a disappointing lack of reports about their actions in the press. Even Frank Sturgis's radio interview was in vain and never aired. The entire operation would have been entirely forgotten, except that it found new life when it was dredged up by Senator Sam Ervin's "Watergate Committee" and the Office of the Special Prosecutor the following year.

According to Liddy, McCord kept promising that he was on the trail of the needed electronics equipment. A single custom-made transmitter, costing what we thought was an appalling $30,000, was taking an extremely long time to fashion. I continued to meet with McCord to scout the Watergate offices, and, at his request, introduced him to Tom Gregory, our inside man at McGovern's headquarters. Gregory was working hard and had established a pattern of staying late at the office, which gave him opportunity to tally the contributions and copy the campaign material we asked for.

McCord also once passed himself off as Gregory's visiting uncle and got a tour of the campaign headquarters, from which he was able to make a diagram of the important offices belonging to Gary Hart and Frank Mankiewicz, where he planned to plant the listening devices. Our key to getting inside was supposed to be Gregory, who we told to conceal himself inside the offices, and, when the building was empty, to allow McCord in through one of the doors.

The event was scheduled, but Gregory was surprised in the building by a suspicious fellow employee, causing him to stutter an impromptu explanation and depart the building. While he was alert enough to call McCord to abort the operation for the night, he became such a nervous wreck that I had no recourse but to think of another way to get into the building.

I reported the failed attempt to Liddy the following day. "The problem with Gregory," I said, "is that he spooks when he has to stay alone in that little furnace room. Things that go bump in the night bother him, and so we'll plan around him."

"How?" Liddy wanted to know.

I outlined my plan. "Most of the volunteers leave around six o'clock; a few stay on until nine or after, including Gregory. Let's say sometime after nine, a delivery is made to the front door of McGovern headquarters. Gregory is in the area and indicates that he's heard something about a delivery, so the men come in: Barker and Martinez carrying a couple of heavy boxes, with McCord as their supervisor, all three of them in work uniforms. While Barker and Martinez unpack whatever is being delivered, McCord will get his five minutes—if not more—to splice in his bug. Delivery made, the three men leave, and if anything should go wrong then or later, Gregory will run little risk of being implicated."

"Sounds good to me," Liddy responded. "I'm for anything that doesn't involve that gutless little wonder of yours."

Before we could attempt the revised operation, the Gutless Wonder reported that a new twenty-four-hour Burns Agency guard had been hired in response to an attempted burglary. I wondered momentarily if there wasn't another parallel organization in place, but I didn't think there was enough money to go around.

It took a little discussion, but I finally convinced Liddy that this wasn't as bad as it seemed and that a bored guard working for his hourly wage might be even easier to trick than a paranoid Democratic volunteer. We only had to wait for McCord to assemble his gear, which was becoming increasingly frustrating.

"He swears he'll have the stuff in a week or so, but I don't know—he's been wrong before," Liddy said.

I told him to make sure that we received high-end walkie-talkies this time. "No more of those Dick Tracy marvels we used in Beverly Hills!"

On May 15, 1972, Alabama governor and presidential hopeful George Wallace was shot four times by would-be assassin Wallace Bremer at a campaign rally in Laurel, Maryland. A campaign worker, a Secret Service agent, and a state trooper were also injured in the attack. While I was certainly no admirer of Wallace's, I felt that U.S. politics was rapidly devolving and that the country had seen far too much violence. I was surprised to get a call from Chuck Colson the following morning, asking me to fly to Milwaukee, where Bremer lived, break into his home, and plant leftist literature to connect him to the Democrats.

"Are you nuts?" I exclaimed in response "How the hell am I going to get into a sealed apartment that's being watched by the FBI?"

Colson kept on insisting, however, prevailing on me to at least consider the possibility, so I went so far as to check air schedules. When I told Dorothy about it, she exploded. "He's got to be insane! Call him up and tell him you won't do it," she ordered. "This is one mission he can find somebody else to do."

I would later learn that he was so adamant because while Nixon was commenting publicly on the shooting as something "senseless and tragic," he was also leaning on Colson to assign a break-in at Bremer's apartment. "Is he a left-winger, [or a] right-winger?" Nixon asked soon after the shooting.

Colson responded, "Well, he's going to be a left-winger by the time we get through, I think."

Nixon laughed, saying, "Good. Keep at that, keep at that."

Nixon also wanted to find out if Bremer had any ties to the Republican Party, and he was concerned that the perpetrator might even have ties to his own reelection committee.

But nevertheless, Colson considered this a good opportunity to squeeze the Democrats. "Yeah, I just wish that, God, that I'd thought sooner about planting a little literature out there. It may be a little late, although I've got one source that maybe . . . ," Colson said on tape. That source, I presume, was me.

"Good," Nixon responded.

"You could think about that," Colson replied. "I mean, if they found it near his apartment, that would be helpful."

The White House then went into spin mode, conducting interviews that suggested Bremer might have ties to leftist causes and the McGovern campaign. I watched television updates and listened to radio news about George Wallace's condition and the ensuing investigation, wondering how Colson and his boss thought I could possibly pull this off. Dorothy knocked about the room angry that I would even consider it. But I told her I felt an obligation to do whatever my bosses desired. Luckily, I received a telephone call from Colson calling off the operation, as he deemed it too risky.

There were a lot of questions floating around Bremer, a crazy janitor who earned a pittance but managed to follow Wallace around to

several different cities—a trip that must have cost a few thousand dollars—prior to the shooting. Conspiracy theories were created so
instantly that it was as if they were waiting on the shelf—just add
water.

People claimed that there were more bullets fired than Bremer's
five-shot pistol was capable of, that Bremer was being financed by
unknown entities, that the FBI was hiding evidence of a conspiracy. A
conspiracy by whom? Most of these people focused on the weapons-
manufacturing industrial complex that was reaping billions from the
Vietnam War, thinking that Wallace might split a conservative vote,
ushering in a McGovern presidency.

It was later revealed that the FBI uncovered strange evidence in
Bremer's apartment, including propaganda from both left-wing and
right-wing sources: a Confederate flag and a Black Panther newspaper. Most fascinating, perhaps, was a diary in which Bremer sketched
his plans to kill either George Wallace or Richard Nixon. The first
sentence read, "Now I start my diary of my personal plot to kill by
pistol either Richard Nixon or George Wallace." Part of the bizarre
manuscript was eventually published in 1973 as *An Assassin's Diary*.

Some have suggested that I forged Bremer's diary. What a laugh.
This is completely untrue. I don't believe Colson or Nixon was in any
way involved, as Wallace was such a small blip on the electoral radar
screen that he could never have posed a threat to the Nixon jugger-
naut. Even Gore Vidal would later write a piece for the *New York
Review of Books* hypothesizing that I wrote Bremer's book, citing various literary tricks and misspellings that looked like they were deliberately created to look like the work of a hack.

So let me say here for the permanent record that not only did I
not go to Bremer's apartment, but I have never been in Milwaukee.
For conspiracy theorists who may observe "he didn't say he had never
been to Milwaukee, *Wisconsin*," let it be said that I have never been to
Milwaukee, Wisconsin, United States of America, planet Earth of the
Milky Way Galaxy. I did not write, pen, authorize, doodle on, or in
any other way create, make, or cause to be manufactured Bremer's
diary, book, manuscript, or whatever you want to call it.

Bremer was nothing more than a glory hound. After police tack-
led him at the rally and were hauling him away, he shouted, "How
much do you think I'll get for my autobiography?" His neighbors said
he was a strange fellow who wore the same clothes every day and
couldn't hold a job because of strange behavior, having been demoted

from a busboy job to a kitchen position after patrons complained that he mumbled to himself, whistled idiosyncratically, and marched to the beat of the ambient dining room music.

He was later convicted and sentenced to sixty-three years in the Maryland Correctional Institute, a term that expires in the year 2025. He should be seventy-four years old when he hits the streets again.

The strange man later served as the basis for the character Travis Bickle, portrayed by Robert De Niro in *Taxi Driver*. In a bizarre twist of fate, John Hinkley Jr. would later claim that the film inspired him to try to kill President Ronald Reagan.

17

Watergate

Accessing the DNC headquarters, which occupied the entire sixth floor of the Watergate office building, would not be easy. McCord and I scouted the complex and found only three ways to reach the offices—none of them ideal. We could mount a frontal assault by signing in with the guard at the front desk and ride up in the elevator; we could enter from the flank by parking in the garage and walking up the stairs; or we could enter from the bottom up, using a subterranean corridor connecting the office building's stairwell and elevator with a banquet room in the Watergate Hotel—the Continental Room.

My vote was for the corridor route: the floor was carpeted to smother our footsteps, we could enter the stairwell at that level without being observed, and most importantly, an elevator could be summoned to the corridor level, which we could ride directly to the sixth floor—the only risk being if a guard happened to glance at the elevator locator panel and see the lights ascending up to the sixth floor.

After giving it some thought, I came up with an idea that Liddy liked, which was to rent the Continental Room for a banquet, thus providing our men legitimate access to the building. I reconnoitered the room with McCord and found that the door between the banquet hall and the corridor was wired with a magnetic alarm system, which McCord indicated he would be able to defeat. Meanwhile, he would familiarize himself with the schedules of the various guards in the building and at what time the alarm systems were activated.

I phoned Barker to say that we would need to expand the team for our new job and flew down to Miami, where he introduced me to some candidates. Virgilio "Villo" González, a former Batista bodyguard, was now an excellent locksmith whom we would need to pick the lock. He agreed to the mission after learning that I was the famous "Eduardo" of Bay of Pigs fame. We also brought onboard Rolando Pico and Frank Sturgis, whom Barker had employed to man the recent Hoover demonstration.

I told them that in addition to their mission to photograph the DNC material, an electronics expert, "Jim," would be hitching a ride onto the operation. I stressed that his business would not impinge on their mission and that I would take responsibility to get him in and out safely on their coattails.

At some time in the past, Barker had formed a now inactive corporation named Ameritas, complete with letterhead and the legitimate address of his attorney. This, he volunteered, could become the sponsoring organization to rent the Continental Room.

When I returned to Washington, I had my wife telephone the Watergate Hotel to rent the banquet hall for Ameritas on the night of May 26, 1972, and plan a menu for between ten and twelve guests. Barker then had his secretary book several rooms for his Miami contingent. Feeling confident that everything was progressing satisfactorily, I gave Liddy a status report, only to learn that McCord had not yet procured the miniature transceivers that he expected and had not even secured the needed walkie-talkies. In fact, he was trying to get FCC (Federal Communications Commission) clearance for the frequencies.

Liddy was outraged, saying it was like "registering a gun that you're going to use in a holdup" and probably would have fired McCord if we had anybody else to turn to. Liddy was also frustrated with McCord's idiosyncrasies, such as the man's unsocial penchant for disappearing into the shadows until you needed him. Liddy distrusted quiet types and couldn't figure out if McCord was a nervous coward who might not have the gonads to conduct his assignment or if he was just cautious from years as an agent. Since McCord had never been a field agent, however, Liddy considered him to be the former.

McCord promised that he would be ready in time for the May 26 entry and brought me to a room in the Howard Johnson building across the street from the Watergate office, where he had installed an ex–FBI agent, Alfred Baldwin, to man a listening post that would monitor the electronic transmissions from the future DNC listening device. As of yet, the room was vacant. I could only cross my fingers and hope that McCord could expedite his orders.

As the date neared, Liddy passed me cash for operational funds (which later hearings would ascertain had come from CREEP) to pay for the team to travel from Florida, our proposed banquet, and lodging, plus an additional contingency fund of $10,000.

"Keep the extra money in your safe," he told me, "in case of an emergency."

"What kind of emergency?" I asked.

"Well, you know, in case the guys get picked up and jailed. . . ." The money would be used to bail them out of jail, hire a lawyer, and get them out of town. "I'll give Barker an extra few thousand to bribe any guard who might walk in on them. That way, we're covered in both directions. Any other problems?" he added.

"Yeah, I hope McCord gets his equipment on time."

"He swears he'll have it by the time we need it, but I think he's cutting it pretty thin," Liddy answered with frustration in his voice.

"So do I. We may have to use those Buck Rogers walkie-talkies again."

Liddy snorted in disgust. "I've checked the catalog. We can do better with Green Stamps."

"I think my mother has a few extra books filled out that we can borrow," I joked.

The Miami contingent arrived on May 22, and Barker, Martinez, González, De Diego, Pico, and Sturgis registered at a nearby hotel until their rooms at the Watergate became available. Frank Sturgis made a chance encounter at National Airport with our nemesis Jack Anderson, whom he happened to know, as the columnist had previously written about Sturgis as a freewheeling soldier of fortune who had mounted operations against Castro. Frank deflected Anderson's questions about why he was in town, but I did not learn of the encounter for many months.

We used the days before the planned operation to get our men familiarized with the McGovern headquarters and the Watergate office building and to introduce them to McCord and Gregory. Liddy shot out the security lights behind the McGovern offices with a Walther PPK air pistol, needing to stand on Sturgis's shoulders to get a bead on some of them. Then McCord took the men to the sixth floor of the Watergate, where they examined the DNC entrance. They did this overtly, signing in with the downstairs guard and riding the elevator to the sixth floor, as a large convention, Transpo '72, gave them reasonable cover to go in and out of the building.

For my part, I went to the glass entrance doors of the DNC and pressed a lump of Plasteline against the door lock, from which I made a plaster cast. This was for the benefit of Virgilio so that he could determine which lock-picking devices he would need.

On the twenty-sixth, our group of "Ameritas employees" checked into the Watergate Hotel. McCord finally brought four walkie-talkies to my Mullen & Company office, leaving us two shy of the six we needed. Not only that, but he had either received them too recently or forgotten to charge the ni-cad batteries, a lengthy process. It seemed extremely unprofessional. I hightailed the radios over to a room that Liddy and I had rented at the Watergate and plugged in the chargers as we waited for banquet time. McCord then announced that he had other things to do, which we figured meant installing monitor equipment in the listening post across the street at the Howard Johnson hotel.

I started to set up a travelogue film that I had rented on a projector facing a built-in screen on the wall while the banquet room was being set up. At this time, I noticed again the alarm on the corridor exit door and remembered that McCord had not communicated his plans to defeat the system. When I called him at the listening post, he told me not to worry, that the system wasn't armed until after eleven o'clock.

"By then, everyone should be out of the Continental Room and in the target offices."

"Yeah," I said. "Well, suppose someone's working there past eleven o'clock?"

"Then we'll abort for the night," he ventured nonchalantly.

"That wasn't the plan, Jim!" I exploded. "Now our flexibility's reduced."

He told me to calm down. "The last few nights there hasn't been anyone in the target office past ten o'clock, so I'm not going to worry about it."

Fine for him to say. I thought that if he had applied the same lax standards to CIA security, it was a wonder the country had any national secrets left to secure.

During the banquet, we tried to relax and enjoy ourselves, lingering over drinks and dessert. As usual, McCord excused himself early, before dinner even arrived, so we gave him a toast and ate his portion along with our own. Afterward we tipped the waiter handsomely, asking him to leave as we were about to begin our board meeting. He slipped the money into his pocket and exited, leaving us a small bar and several carafes of coffee.

We kept the travelogue on a repeating loop for the benefit of any nosy employees who might check on us through the glass door to the courtyard and took the time to go over our plans once again, altering them slightly in light of McCord's failure to obtain all of the promised walkie-talkies. Because of the communications shortage, De Diego could be excused, and the four units would be assigned to the listening post, McCord, Liddy and me in our command post room, and the last to Sturgis with the entry team.

At 10:00 p.m., most of the group dispersed, leaving only Villo and me sitting at the remains of the banquet, where we listened for McCord to announce that the DNC offices had been vacated. By 10:30, we'd heard nothing, and a guard entered the room to tell us that we would have to leave. Instead, we turned off the lights and hid in a closet where we could still communicate by radio. At 11:00, McCord said the lights were still burning in the DNC offices. We heard a click as the guard locked the door for the evening, thinking that we had already exited.

We were not worried at first, as Villo had brought his lock picks, and we expected to make an easy clandestine departure, but the lock makers proved better than Virgilio that night, because he couldn't open the door with any of his tools. We could only curse the aborted mission and assume that the rest of the party was bedded down more comfortably than we were. I mixed a highball from the bar and sat in a chair, depressed that the entire banquet subterfuge had been wasted, thinking that if McCord had been able to neutralize the alarm as he had promised, we would have been able to complete the operation. Villo and I spent a difficult night standing in the closet waiting for dawn and the scheduled deactivation of the alarm at 6:00 a.m.

After the designated hour, we waited an extra fifteen minutes for safety, opened the door, sauntered through the nearest exit, and went to our respective rooms.

I roused Liddy from his sleep. "Lucky we weren't caught, Gordon," I said. "Now we're going to have to try it another way."

"Through the garage-level door?" he queried.

Exhausted, I pulled off my clothes and dove between the sheets of my bed. "Yeah, thanks to McCord. Tell Jim to plan on a garage-level entry tonight. It's that or nothing. We can't go through that banquet routine again. Oh, and Gordon," I continued, "I know you like your scotch, but don't order it at the Watergate Hotel."

Gordon looked at me with a puzzled expression. "Why not?" he asked.

"Because last night when we were hiding in the closet, I had to take a leak in the worst way, and when I couldn't bear it any longer, I found a fairly empty bottle of Johnnie Walker Red—and now let's just say it's quite full."

Gordon joked that he hoped DNC chief Larry O'Brien would be the one served the polluted whiskey.

I laughed and gratefully got a few hours of sleep, knowing that I had spiked the scotch with ashes and cigarette butts so that it would not be served by an unsuspecting waiter.

After some shut-eye, I drove home for a change of clothes and returned to the Watergate Hotel at nightfall, parking my car in the basement. From there, I strolled underground over to the office building garage, where I located the double-wide delivery doors that McCord and I had scouted before. Making sure no one was watching, I pressed the doors' release bar and entered the building, where a hallway let in to the freight elevator and, beside it, the entry door to the stairwell. I tested the doorknob, which was not locked, swinging the door open with a gush of musty cement-smelling air. This door would have to serve our alternate plan.

I went back to my hotel room, where I waited until Liddy and McCord arrived. There we discussed plan B, which was taping the spring locks of the garage double doors and walking up the stairs to the sixth floor.

After McCord made his exit, slipping away as usual at the soonest opportunity, I called Barker and Martinez to join us, and they practiced setting up the lights and camera and photographing simulated documents. After everybody felt as if they had the process down pat, I reiterated my earlier instructions to Barker: "According to our information, there're a lot of file cabinets in the offices. Obviously, you won't go through the files until you find something with numbers on it—account books, contributor lists, that sort of thing. If you have any question, call me here, and I'll make the decision."

Barker nodded. "What about Jim? How long will he take?"

I said I didn't know, but that if McCord finished before he did, to "just let him leave. You're not responsible for his work, and he's not responsible for yours."

We waited until after the eight o'clock guard change, then McCord accessed the garage and taped the spring lock on the door. Even if a guard spotted it later, we felt that it would not look suspicious, as this was a standard method that janitorial crews and delivery men used to keep doors from locking them out. McCord then went back across the street to the listening post at the Howard Johnson, where he reported that he had accomplished his task. Liddy, the team, and I waited tensely for a few hours at the command post until a short time after 10:00 p.m., when McCord radioed that the last lights had flickered off at the DNC.

McCord met the entry team—Barker, González, Martinez, and Sturgis—at the garage-level entrance, and they climbed the stairway to the sixth floor, where they reported to us that González had started working on the DNC lock. Again, the wait was tense, and I often noticed that Liddy and I were hardly breathing for minutes at a time. After half an hour, we were getting very fidgety when Barker's voice finally crackled over the radio: "Villo can't pick the lock," he told us disgustedly. "He says he doesn't have the right tools. What do we do now?"

"Leave the building and report back here," Liddy told him, sitting back with a sigh and shaking his head. "I don't understand it. Villo even had your cast of the lock. Why the hell couldn't he get it?"

The team returned, entering with downturned faces and dejected shoulders. I was so pent up that I scolded Barker and Villo for not making sure they had the right tools, and I told them that I wanted Villo to return to Miami in the morning, pick up the necessary tools, and get back before dark. Barker said he'd have his wife meet González at the airport, drive him to his shop and back to the airport so that they didn't lose too much time.

Virgilio mentioned that he was pretty tired.

Liddy said, "I don't care how tired you are. You can sleep on the plane. This has to be done this weekend." I could see that Liddy had no intention of trying to explain to the reviled Magruder that he had failed.

Villo shrugged his shoulders resignedly.

"What about the door tapes?" I asked.

"I removed them," McCord said, then exited the room.

It was now Sunday morning, the twenty-eighth, so I got a few hours of sleep, then drove home to enjoy some time with my family. Dorothy could sense that things were not going well, but being used to my covert operations, she asked no questions. Instead, she took my mind off the work, telling me about the vacation plans she was making to take David and Kevan to Europe for the summer.

Later in the afternoon, Barker called to tell me that Villo had arrived with the needed equipment. After so many years of living like this, I'd learned to compartmentalize work and pleasure. The operation wouldn't commence until late evening, so I thrust it completely from my mind, as if it didn't exist, dined with my family, then after a mental alarm clock rang, punched my fantasy time card, got back on the job, and drove back to the Watergate Hotel, where we would again prepare to storm the Democratic castle in the air.

Back at the command post, Liddy and I got some good news. McCord reported that the DNC blinds had been conveniently raised all day, and he could see that only one employee remained inside. If this person followed the usual pattern of other Sundays, he would exit the office fairly soon. The walkie-talkie batteries were fully charged, so McCord took two of them and returned to the Listening Post to keep watch on the target windows.

The entry team now made an appearance. Villo seemed to have indeed gotten the rest he needed, seemed in good spirits, and was confident that he now had the correct tools to defeat the lock. The radio sparked to life, as McCord called to inform us that the tape was in place as before and that we were only waiting on the final DNC staffer to leave the office.

Around 9:30 p.m., McCord radioed with the update that the target was clear. We waited until 11:00 and gave the word to go.

In a case of déjà vu, the Miami group rendezvoused with McCord at the garage entrance and proceeded up the stairs, where Villo attacked the lock. This time, Barker reported success in about fifteen minutes. "We're in," came the promising words.

Liddy and I gave each other a strong Latin-style *abrazo*, then listened closely to the radio in case the team should require any assistance or have any questions. We drank Cokes for about an hour to keep alert, expecting to be there all night, but within an hour Barker called to say the team was leaving. By 1:00 a.m., all five men reappeared in our room, where McCord reported that "his business" had been concluded satisfactorily, collected the walkie-talkies from Liddy and Barker, then bade us good night and departed.

Barker explained that they had found an important-looking pile of correspondence on Lawrence O'Brien's desk, so they had commenced the operation by photographing there, while McCord went off and performed his own work elsewhere in the suite. Martinez opened the Minolta camera, took out one cartridge of 35mm film, then handed it to me with another he added from his pocket. "We shot one roll and part of another, Eduardo," he told me.

I looked at Barker with astonishment. "So what was the big rush to get out?"

Barker shrugged, looking just as perplexed as I'm sure I did. "Jim—I guess he didn't want to hang around."

I was livid, wanting to jump down Barker's throat, because he should have just let McCord leave, as was the plan. In my mind, the photography had been the priority mission, and the team had exited prematurely, with only a fraction of the amount of photographs that I had expected. Still, I reigned myself in, as I hadn't earned these men's respect by showing a temper, we might need them again, and it was McCord's fault for forcing the issue.

Barker could sense my disappointment. "Anything else?" he asked.

Liddy shook his head. "That's it, boys," he told them, slapping Barker comradely on the back. "Macho, this has been a good job." Then he shook Villo's hand. "Good man," he said, prompting Villo to smile.

"Just took the right tools, George. Me, that's all I need," he said.

There was now some accounting to be done. Barker returned the contingency money to Liddy, who in turn reimbursed Barker for the group's plane fare and hotel bill, and gave him fair compensation for the men's lost work wages.

When we were alone, Liddy took the rolls of film, saying that McCord had a man who could develop them.

The next day, Liddy reported the successful entry to Magruder, and we waited for McCord's contact to process the film. A week later, there was still no progress, and Liddy returned the film to me at my Mullen office, asking if I thought Barker could handle getting it developed.

Obviously, this was not something I was going to bring to a local film shop for development, imagining some nosy technician sneaking a look at the film and later exposing us, or even having it delivered to the wrong person in place of vacation photos. I didn't think the CIA would be happy to get this involved with my affairs, either.

I called Barker and told him that I would bring down some film for him to develop. In the meantime, he was to find a place that it could be processed promptly, as I only intended to stay overnight. Liddy had some other things to mention, as well.

"I hate to say it," he told me with difficulty, "but I think McCord screwed up."

"How?"

He shook his head. "I don't know. Put a bug in the wrong place or tapped the wrong line. All I know is, my principals are going bananas, and I've got to straighten it out with McCord. I'm praying there's something worthwhile on film. With Magruder on my ass all the time, I don't need another flap right now."

In addition, the Mitchell-Dean-Magruder triumvirate had also issued new requests for us, not only wanting progress reports on how far along Barker was in getting informants in place in the Miami Beach hotel, but adding a new twist: "They want to know if Barker can get a bunch of hippies to carry McGovern signs around the front of the Doral Hotel. The idea is to have them splash around in the pool there—maybe tear off their clothes—anything likely to attract the television cameras and outrage the country. Think he can do that?"

I laughed. Did these people have no limits? "That's a tough one, Gordon. The hippies would obviously be for McGovern. How can we get them to work against their idol?"

"Christ, I don't know," Liddy said in frustration. "Sometimes I think these guys figure we can do miracles. But ask Macho, will you? He's always come through before."

I said I'd ask him. "Have they made up their minds on the houseboat?"

Apparently the houseboat was nixed as too expensive, as was trying to bug the convention, which I had advised against, saying, "Every network in the country will be filming from morning until night. Nobody needs to bug the place. Anybody who wants to see and hear what's going on can sit in an easy chair and turn on the tube."

Liddy agreed and said he'd talked them out of that one.

On June 10, Barker and Martinez met me at the Miami airport. The men left me at a restaurant for lunch, and I gave Barker the film with instructions to have large prints made of each negative—cost was no object. Before I was even finished with lunch, Barker returned, saying that we could expect the developed film by late afternoon.

I broached the subject of the hippies, whom the ever resourceful Barker thought he could produce through a Realtor friend who rented "pads to hippies."

"Coconut Grove?"

"Yes, Eduardo. The Grove has changed since you lived here twelve years ago [in our Bay of Pigs safe house]. Now it's hippie haven. How many hippies does George want?" (In the years since Watergate, the Grove has graduated from hippies to yuppies living in McMansions, and it is no longer recognizable as the artistic enclave it once was.)

"To make any impression, I think we'll need at least a dozen. Twenty would be better, if you can get them."

We discussed the ongoing plans to get Barker's infiltrators hired at the various Miami Beach venues, with focus on the Fontainebleau and the Doral hotels. When Barker delivered the film back to me, I was surprised to find the address of a commercial developer on the envelope but shrugged it off as probably being one of Barker's insiders, who would not talk about the negatives. The blowups would have looked suspicious to almost anybody, as they showed papers with DNC letterhead being held by hands wearing surgical gloves. This detail lent a dramatic touch that, Liddy remarked, seemed to entrance his principals.

I would find out later that Barker had not fully understood that the film was from the Watergate break-in and had taken it to a local Rich's Camera Shop to be developed. When something I said triggered a mental switch at lunch, he realized what he had done, recruited Frank and Martinez to guard the door of the shop, and was apparently so relieved to get the right film that he tipped the clerk $20. According to Martinez, the man had, of course, taken a great interest in the film he had just developed, leaning over to Barker and whispering, "Real cloak-and-dagger stuff, isn't it?"

When the Watergate information started coming to light, the clerk notified the FBI about what he had seen.

On June 14, Liddy came to my Mullen office in a huff. I played the radio loud in case of any bugs and listened in aggravation to what he told me: "We have to go into the DNC headquarters again, Howard."

A pit grew in my stomach. Once had been more than enough for me. "Why, for God's sake? Wasn't the photography enough?"

According to Liddy, the photography was good, and they wanted more. The bottom line was, "McCord's screwed up somehow. Evidently he bugged the wrong telephone line. He was supposed to tap O'Brien's."

I asked if we weren't closing the barn door after the horse had already escaped. "From what McCord says, O'Brien's already in Miami. Why tap the man's phone when he's left the office?"

"I don't know," Liddy complained, plainly frustrated by the higher-up men pulling his strings. "But those are my orders. And they want a lot more photographs. Have Macho buy another camera and bring up a lot of film. They want everything in those file cabinets photographed."

"All of them?"

He told me that I had heard it correctly. I told him it was nuts, that it would take hours. He responded that we would have to do it between the eight and twelve o'clock shift changes.

"How soon are we supposed to do this?"

"As soon as possible."

I thought about it for a few minutes. "I'm against it, Gordon," I said in a forceful tone. "My men got McCord in and out of the target premises, and if he fouled up his part of the operation, I don't think we should be asked to go again."

"Makes sense to me," Liddy agreed. "Besides, Jim tells me the Democrats have even started moving out their files."

"Sure. They'll be sending them down to the Fontainebleau. If Mitchell, Dean, and Magruder want another crack at them, the Fontainebleau's the place. Not here." I took a deep breath and studied Liddy's face. He was looking a bit haggard and quite unsure of this latest turn of events. "Gordon, from the start of this Watergate operation, it's been McCord who's fouled things up. His equipment doesn't arrive when it's promised. My team gets him into the premises and gives him all the time in the world to do whatever he was supposed to do. Even then, he seems to have somehow managed to tap the wrong phone."

Liddy sighed. "It's worse that that. "He put a bug in an office, and it's not transmitting properly. Or if it is, the building's too well shielded and they can't pick it up across the street."

"Meaning McCord has to repeat the work he's already done?"

Then he dropped the next bomb—the principals wanted the McGovern office operation completed, too. "We can do it the night after the Watergate," he said. "If we get it done between eight and twelve, they can do McGovern the same night."

"The boys'll be exhausted!" I exploded.

"I agree with you—we shouldn't be asked for a repeat on this, but I'm under pressure. I'll argue against, but I'm not hopeful."

I told him to do what he could and try to get them to change the venue for another break-in to Miami, where there would be confusion to cover us. Later that day, Liddy called back to say his principals were insisting on another Watergate entry.

"Will McCord have enough walkie-talkies—the minimum six?" I asked.

"He says he will."

"These are my men, Gordon, and I'm the one who's responsible for them. I don't have my heart in this operation, and you're putting me in the position of ordering them into something I don't believe in."

"The Big Man [Mitchell] says he wants the operation."

"What about McCord?"

"Jim doesn't like it, either. He's mad about having to repeat his work, but damn it, if he'd done his work right the first time, we wouldn't have to do it a second."

I hesitated, and Liddy knew me well enough to sense that I was about to "include myself out."

"Look," he cajoled, "we're soldiers in this thing, Howard. If I've got a future, it's in government, and when the Big Man tells me to do something, either I do it for him or he gets someone else who can."

"Like who?" I asked.

"Caulfield, maybe."

"Or the Golden Greek?" I added.

We laughed, letting off some tension.

I told him that I'd put Bernie and the others on standby, but we weren't going to go unless McCord came through with the rest of the electronics equipment. When I told Bernie about the next job, he responded with his customary sense of unquestioning calm and duty. "Okay, Eduardo. I'll get in touch with the boys, get the hotel rooms, and call you back. Not much notice, is it?"

He went on to tell me that the hippies were all set up. "These guys are some of the filthiest people you've ever seen," Bernie told me. Not only had they agreed to invade a McGovern press conference as pro-Democrats, they would announce their backing of the candidate by pulling down their pants and urinating in front of the cameras. Anything that McGovern had to say would get lost in the swirl of hippie coverage and, we hoped, outrage voters into withdrawing support for the candidate and the Democrats in general.

Usually able to compartmentalize my duties from my life, I tossed and turned all night debating the merits of another entry. To me it had no sound basis. O'Brien was in Miami, and the important files we were supposed to photograph most likely had been shipped down there with him. When I saw Liddy the following day, I expressed my concerns again.

"Barker confirms that O'Brien's in Miami. Why in hell should we tap the phone in his Washington office? If O'Brien has already taken offices in the Fontainebleau, chances are his files are with him. What's the rationale? As a friend, colleague, and fellow professional, I'm asking you to go back to Mitchell, Dean, and Magruder and reargue the case. If you want to get off the hook, tell them you're having problems with me. I've never dealt with them, so I'm an unknown entity. You can put it that I'm jumpy or truculent or however you want to describe my resistance."

But Gordon had met with his principals and said they didn't want an argument. In his book, *Will*, Liddy referred to this specifically, writing, "The purpose of the second Watergate break-in was to find out what O'Brien had of a derogatory nature about us, not for us to get something on him or the Democrats."

Much would be made of this concept, culminating in the 1991 publication of an excremental exercise of revisionist history called *Silent Coup*, whose authors, Len Colodny and Robert Gettlin, wrote that the information in question named John Dean's future wife, Maureen Biner, and her roommate as call girls working with the Democratic National Committee. Thus, the theory said, DNC would have records with "Mo's" name on them, which could be used to blackmail her, and through her, John—thus derailing his fast-rising legal-political career. Therefore, John sent an entry team into the DNC offices in the Watergate to retrieve all files with Maureen's name on them.

Even given the wild allegations, a *Washington Post* reviewer called *Silent Coup* one of "the most boring conspiracy books ever written." The *New York Times Book Review* observed that it showed "a stunning ignorance of how the Government under Mr. Nixon operated." And Sam Dash, the chief counsel for the Senate Watergate Committee, denounced it as "a fraud . . . contradicted by everything on the White House tapes and by the evidence."

Needless to say, there was no semblance of truth to this version of history. But the impact of the book on Maureen Dean, a financial consultant for Shearson-Lehman Bros., was devastating. She became seriously depressed, unable to function well in her career, and, as I recall, unable to venture forth from her house for a period of weeks or even months.

As the Deans were considering a lawsuit, my lawyer Bill Snyder and I gently reminded John of the high hurdles a "public figure" faced in winning a libel case, having by this date already gone through my ordeal with the Liberty Lobby and the JFK assassination allegations. John chivalrously replied that he didn't care how much time, effort, expense, or heartache it entailed—Maureen had stood by him during the darkest days of his life, and he was going to stand by her during hers.

My heart went out to Maureen. I was happy to be a deposition witness (and trial witness, if the case had gone to trial) for her. I testified at length about the true provenance of Watergate—that it was a political intelligence–gathering operation from start to finish, very possibly ordered personally by the president himself.

The authors and the publisher of *Silent Coup* crumbled—settling with John and Maureen. Gordon Liddy, who had trumpeted the false version of Watergate on his radio program, said that he would never settle and demanded a full trial in federal court. In the end, he did cave—but only after the Deans had spent thousands of dollars to secure some justice. Libel defendants often ask that the terms of the settlement be sealed by the court—to protect the guilty. The terms of these settlements were all sealed, so I'll never know the particulars. I only hope and trust that the Deans made a boatload of money.

When a reporter asked about the financial rewards of the settlement, Dean said that he was limited to two words, "We're satisfied."

Maureen eventually wrote her own memoir, *Mo: A Woman's View of Watergate*, and two novels, *Washington Wives* and *Capitol Secrets*.

So as far as Liddy's and Ehrlichman's quotes go, saying that the second break-in was in response to some dirty Republican linen that the DNC was holding, no one mentioned it to me at the time, and the Cubans who would have been tasked with finding it were not briefed, so the break-in would not have succeeded in that purpose.

On Friday, June 16, I met Thomas Gregory in the lobby of the Roger Smith Hotel to discuss ways of getting the team into the McGovern offices. As we conversed, we strolled outside to the nearby park, where McCord was waiting on a bench to discuss Gregory's part in the plan. But Tom looked at me in confusion.

"You didn't get my note?" he asked.

"What note?" I said in a low growl as we neared McCord.

"I gave Bob Bennett a note for you. He was going to give it to you this morning."

"What was in the note, Tom?" I asked.

"I'm resigning," he told me hesitantly. "This is getting too deep for me."

I was disgusted, but in a way relieved, thinking that this might be a way out for us. "I've sort of sensed it," I responded. "Okay. I don't want any unwilling workers."

We reached Jim, who rose from the bench and reached to shake Gregory's hand.

"Jim," I said, "Tom's copping out." Then, to Gregory: "Did you bother to write up a report of your week's activities?"

He sheepishly handed me a slip of folded paper from his shirt pocket. It seemed to me as if his heart had gone out of the operation. He wasn't scared of getting caught; he was exhibiting signs of what would later be called Stockholm syndrome, after a 1973 bank robbery in Sweden in which the hostages began to identify with their captors. I had seen it happen with some of our agents years earlier and figured that working so closely with the zealous campaign workers, Gregory wasn't spying on the enemies anymore; he had been taken over by them.

What we didn't need was him getting so remorseful that he spilled his guts. I said I'd pay him what was owed and give him plane fare home, hoping that he would quickly leave town.

McCord and I watched Gregory shuffle disconsolately away toward the bus stop. As an aside, I said to Jim, "I hate to pay the little son of a bitch anything, but if there's one thing I've learned over the years of agent handling, it's always leave them smiling."

"Couldn't agree more," McCord said. Then we forgot about Gregory and altered our entry plan to compensate for the loss of our inside man. We finally agreed that the best strategy was the delivery operation that relied on being able to con the rent-a-cop guarding the office. Jim confirmed that the other two walkie-talkies were now in his possession, and we would have the full count of six for the next task. Even he gritted his teeth and said he wished we didn't have to go in again.

"I've been arguing against it for days," I told him. "But Liddy's boss is adamant."

Midday, Barker called to say that he and the team were lodged in Rooms 214 and 314 awaiting further orders. I suggested he get some rest in preparation for a long night's work. He assured me that they would get some sleep and that they had all the necessary equipment, including cameras and fifty rolls of film. I told him that I'd see him after 9:00 p.m. At this point, I didn't mention that the team would also be asked to enter the McGovern headquarters the following night, as I wanted to delay that information as long as possible. It would not be well received, no matter how patriotic and optimistic Barker and the team were. They were still human.

I updated Liddy on the telephone, telling him that the boys had gotten to "the location," then, after a full day's work, I left my Mullen office and drove home through heavy rush-hour traffic. It was always great to finally turn off the road, drive through the gates of our wooded six-acre property, and forget the world behind—which I certainly wanted to do that day. Dorothy, Kevan, and David had left for Europe, so that night I dined with just St. John and Lisa.

It was a normal night, the quiet broken only by the background sounds of our horses whinnying for some attention from their stables. If anybody should have developed a second sense by now, it should have been me—after all I'd been through in my life. And maybe I had to some extent, because that little voice had been gnawing at me ever since Liddy had called for an encore presentation, which had made me voice my concerns so vociferously. But if I felt uneasy, I suppressed it, kissing my children good night and telling them that I was seeing Mr. Liddy that evening and would be back on Saturday morning. I could not have guessed how great a lie I was telling them, for my actions of the night would tear apart our lives forever.

18

Watergate Redux

The summer night air was thick and sticky, making me blast the air conditioner in my Pontiac Firebird to evaporate the sweat on my forehead. I made sure to drive the speed limit to the Watergate Hotel, as a Firebird always attracted some police attention, and the last thing I wanted was to hold up the operation because I was stuck getting a ticket. Once at the hotel, I parked in the underground garage and walked over to the office entry doors to make sure that everything looked like it had when we had made our previous ascent.

From there, I met up with Barker and Martinez in Room 214, where we were soon joined by Liddy, who was a little late because he had been stopped and issued a verbal warning by a traffic cop after accelerating his green Jeep through a yellow light. He parked on the street in front of the Watergate complex as well. "You have the right tools this time?" he kidded Martinez, who assured him that he did. Then González and Sturgis came down from 314 while we waited for McCord.

Barker and Martinez took the time to demonstrate a new technique for taking the necessary amount of pictures that the principals had requested. With two Minolta cameras loaded, one man would photograph the documents while the other reloaded the spare camera. They were stocked for all contingencies, with spare bulbs for the high-intensity lights and a Polaroid with film to take photos before the operation so that they could put everything back in place correctly and show Liddy's bosses that the work had been accomplished.

When McCord arrived, it turned out that the two extra walkie-talkies were not functional, as the batteries had not been charged, so we were stuck with four again. That would not be a problem this time, as Rolando Pico and Felipe De Diego had been excused from this team because the principals, in their wisdom, had decided to cut the budget for this operation that they deemed so important. Previously, the two had hidden in the hallway as guards. McCord informed us that people were still at work in the target office and that he had already taped the locks on the garage entrance doors and on the sixth and eighth floors, as he had before. This time, he had something that looked like a run-of-the-mill smoke alarm device that presumably had an electronic listening device in it, which he planned to install in O'Brien's office.

Everyone seemed a bit on edge about the assignment. For some reason, it was like putting dirty clothes back on, and it just didn't feel right. I gave McCord some old alias identification documents that had once been created for me at the CIA and another set to Barker. Liddy lent another team member his George Leonard papers and gave Barker a wad of hundred-dollar bills to bribe a guard or use as bail money in case of an emergency.

This action would, unfortunately for us, turn into a serious mistake, as it was the same money that Barker had tendered to us after cashing the large series of checks that Liddy had given him in Miami. For some reason, Barker left in his hotel room a portion of the sequentially numbered emergency funds, which the FBI would trace to Barker's bank in Miami and find out that they had been issued on the proceeds of the Mexican check, which would in turn lead the FBI to the illegal political contribution at the Finance Committee to Re-elect the President.

Liddy and I remained in the room for a while, discussing the defection of the Gutless Wonder, and how we would have to change plans for the McGovern entry. Then we crossed the street to have a snack at the Howard Johnson restaurant, where we could easily walk outside to check if the DNC lights were still illuminated. The Democrats were nothing if not dedicated to the cause, however, as the lights stayed frustratingly on. The air was still viscous as I took the opportunity to repark my car on the street in case we needed a quick getaway, positioning it conveniently in front of the hotel. On my way back to the room, I rode the elevator with the acclaimed French film actor Alain Delon, who was ironically in town filming the movie *Scorpio*, a story about a fictitious CIA agent.

Like so many operations, it was a case of hurry up and wait. We had all broken our backs to get here, set up, and get ready, but now we could only sit anxiously waiting for the devoted Democrats to finish their work. What were they doing up there, anyway? Didn't they know the action was down in Miami? Finally, after we drank a few cans of Coke, making my veins sing from the caffeine, McCord broke the tension in the room, reporting over the radio at about 12:45 a.m. that the last lights had been extinguished, and he was on his way over from the listening post to join us.

Liddy, the team, and I jumped to alert status while we waited for McCord to appear. When he arrived, he said that he had checked the tape on the doors and found that it had been torn off. He had retaped the locks so that the team could proceed with the task.

I got a bad feeling as soon as I heard the tape had been removed. "Let's junk it," I said, meaning to abort the operation.

McCord shook his head. "I don't think the building guard took off the tape. There was a big stack of mailbags nearby, and I think when they were taken out, the mailman took the tape off the doors."

Liddy studied my face, hoping to see me change my mind. "Scratch it," I repeated. But Liddy and McCord discussed the issue at length, with McCord saying it was unlikely that a guard had taken off the tape, and even if it was a guard, it shouldn't cause any undue alarm, as it was common for maintenance crews to tape locks. The Cubans were completely unflustered and indicated that they were willing to proceed.

As project manager, Liddy had to decide whether to continue. He came over to me and said that it was necessary for McCord to plant his bug. It was "his show." Liddy's face was grim and set, and I could tell that he was thinking how difficult it would be to face the administration officials who were pressuring him.

"We're doing this because McCord did a lousy job last time," I reminded him. "It may be 'his show,' but there are four others with him who are my responsibility."

Somehow, in silence, the decision was obviously made. Barker walked over to me, shook my hand without a word, and the Miami men filed out of the door, which Liddy locked behind them.

Liddy took a car radio antenna from McCord's black attaché case, extended it, jacked it into the walkie-talkie with a long wire, and set it up on the outside balcony to get better radio reception. To ease the tension, he turned on the television, then sat down in an armchair. I drank more Coke and settled down with the evening paper. It was now extremely late, well after 1:00 a.m.

The five-man team traversed the garage, found the tape in place, and made their way stealthily up the stairway. It was McCord's duty to take the tape off at this point. It would no longer be needed for the exit, as the door would open from the inside. The "experienced" CIA security expert failed, leaving the tape, which would raise the suspicion of security guard Frank Wills. Once inside the DNC offices, Martinez even asked McCord if he had removed the tape, receiving an affirmative reply in response.

Liddy switched the television channel to a late-night film classic, and we started to calm down, as there was no word from the team, which I took as being good news in this situation. They obviously were making the entrance. But after a while, the radio silence had gone on for too long. Liddy said, "They ought to be inside by now. Wonder why Macho doesn't contact us?"

"He probably figures McCord will let us know when they've made the entry," I mused.

We didn't know it then, but the team had successfully entered the DNC offices, where McCord asked Bernie to turn down the gain on his walkie-talkie, as the slight hissing noise might be heard in the hallway if a guard passed. We hunkered down and continued to watch the movie.

In the meantime, outside the focused cocoon of our conspiracy, the world spun on. Unbeknownst to us, security guard Frank Wills had removed the tape earlier at 12:30 a.m. before shuffling over to the Howard Johnson—maybe even standing next to us there—before going back to the hotel and finding the doors retaped an hour later. He had, in fact, assumed that the tape had been placed earlier by the maintenance crew, as we had hoped. But the second taping raised alarm, causing him to call the D.C. police.

Just minutes away, three undercover officers, Sergeant Paul Leeper, Carl Shoffler, and John Barrett, happened to be heading toward Georgetown when a dispatcher broadcast an alert that there were "doors open" at the Watergate complex, signaling a possible burglary in progress. Leeper, at the wheel, executed a U-turn and drove quickly to the office building. The three officers were not particularly worried, with Leeper telling the *Washington Post* later, "We didn't jump out of the car and go running up there. You get so many calls like that—burglary in progress—and 90 to 95 percent of them aren't anything."

However, when the anxious Wills showed the cops the black-taped door latches, the seasoned officers became instantly suspicious. They deactivated the elevators, then Leeper vaulted up the stairs, calling down that he had found more tape on the sixth- and eighth-floor stairwell doors. This was looking serious. Still, when they checked out the eighth floor, they found no signs of nefarious activity.

We were unaware of these events when the walkie-talkie finally hissed to life at 2:00 a.m. Only it wasn't McCord's voice, as we had been expecting to hear. Instead, it was his listening post agent, Alfred Baldwin, with a message: "There's flashlights on the eighth floor."

Liddy and I discussed the statement and decided that it must be a guard, so there was little cause for concern. Liddy got on the walkie-talkie and tried to raise the Miami men: "One to two, did you read that?" Organizationally, we were "one," the team was "two," and the listening post was "three."

There was no answer, as Bernie couldn't hear us due to the walkie-talkie's being turned down. Liddy returned the radio call to Baldwin: "One to three, keep us advised."

Baldwin's next radio transmission was: "Now they're on the seventh floor."

Liddy and I shrugged. It wasn't the most welcome news, though it supported our previous conjecture that it was simply a guard dutifully making his rounds. But the next communication was laced with an urgent yet puzzled quality: "Any of your guys wearing hippie clothes?" he asked.

Now we were alarmed. Liddy sat up and squawked into the transceiver: "One to three, repeat."

But the message hadn't changed. "Any of your guys wearing hippie clothes?"

We both jumped to our feet. Liddy replied: "One to three, negative. Our guys are in business suits. Why? Over."

Baldwin answered from the listening post. "There's four, maybe five guys running around the sixth floor. Lights are going on. One's wearing a cowboy hat, another a sweatshirt. Uh-oh, they've got *guns*. Looks like trouble."

I pounded my fist into my palm in frustration.

"Keep reporting," Liddy said, giving me a "we're screwed" look. "One to two," he barked into the radio, calling the entry team. "Come in. This is an order. Repeat, *come in!*"

Meanwhile, the cops had checked out the seventh floor, quickly ascertained that it was quiet, and moved down to the sixth-floor glass doors of the DNC headquarters, which looked like they had been tampered with.

The men drew guns and funneled inside. File drawers were askew with papers jutting awkwardly out of them. The three moved stealth-ily forward, finding a door to a terrace propped open by a chair. Def-initely not the way workers would leave their offices. Leeper and Shoffler stepped outside, guns ready, but found nobody waiting. Shof-fler even crawled out on a ledge to see if a burglar was hiding out there in the shadows and noticed a man staring at him from a balcony at Howard Johnson across the street.

Meanwhile, Barrett scouted the offices inside, switching on lights as he progressed. His partners were outside, however, so if he met up with a burglar, he was on his own. Then, as he was turning a corner, a man's arm accidentally hit the glass partition next to his face.

While it may sound like the stuff of a hundred television cop shows, on the twentieth anniversary of the break-in, Barrett vividly described this moment to a *Washington Post* reporter: "It scared the shit out of me!" First he yelled, "Back here!" over his shoulder to alert his partners, then shouted toward the intruder, "Police! Come out with your hands up!"

Surprisingly, not one but five men wearing business suits and sur-gical gloves rose to their feet. Outnumbered five to one, the cop jumped on top of a desk with his gun pointed at the men. Villo was carrying a black bag filled with his lock picks and a trench coat draped over his arm, which for all the cop knew might be hiding a pistol.

He shouted for González to drop the bag and raise his hands, but the Cuban didn't understand. Barrett almost shot the poor locksmith, but his life was spared when Bernie translated the command into Spanish and González promptly complied.

Leeper and Shoffler rushed in, ordered the men against the wall, and patted them down. Barker tried to sneak his hand into his pocket to activate the walkie-talkie to inform us that the unit had been com-promised, but Shoffler slammed him against the wall, ordering Bernie to show him what was in his pocket. Cleverly, Macho grabbed a note-book and slowly revealed it, leaving the radio behind. The cop snatched it out of his hand. Luckily, the cops only had two sets of handcuffs with them, so Bernie would get another chance to alert us.

In the hotel room, Liddy and I were frantic. There was no doubt about it—my worst fears had been realized. Muscles throughout my body tensed, my heart started slamming around in my chest, and my throat went dry. We had to act fast ourselves. I scanned the 214 command post room, making a quick mental calculation on how much incriminating evidence we had to evacuate.

The monitor came to life in Liddy's hand. Barker was finally able to reply in a whisper, *"They've got us!"*

Baldwin again: "Now I see our people. They've got their hands up. Must be cops!"

That was all I needed to hear. I strode out onto the balcony to get a firsthand look. Lights were on across the top floors of the office building. I jumped back inside, where Liddy was receiving play-by-play action: ". . . filing out with them now, guns drawn. Police wagon pulling up at the entrance below, also some marked police cars . . ."

Liddy told him to keep talking. I threw the suitcases on the bed, spread them open, and began packing the operational litter from the room. McCord had left behind his extra electronics gear, which I now crammed back into his black attaché case.

Liddy was glued to the radio and looked at me with a bit of confusion. "Let's go," I told him. "The police will be here any moment."

"Why?" he asked.

"Barker has our room key," I answered bluntly. Liddy looked alarmed.

Baldwin's plaintive voice emanated from the radio. "What should I do?"

Liddy had jumped into action and now had his hands full, so I picked up the radio. "Keep your lights out and stay out of sight," I ordered. "I'll come over as soon as I can. We're signing off."

I retrieved the antenna from the balcony, telescoped it to its shortest length, and jammed it down my pant leg since it was too long to fit into a bag. By this time, Liddy had finished packing. "Let's go," I said, walking stiffly out of the room, as the antenna kept me from bending my knee. We sweated our way downstairs in the elevator, half expecting to be met by a SWAT team when the doors opened. But all was tranquil when we hit the lobby, and we walked calmly past the drowsy front desk clerk, who obviously had no idea of the historic events taking place around her. The antenna was a problem, as it started to slide down my leg, making me hitch my pants up, but I kept walking as we reached the front door.

Outside, we were hit by a flood of warm air and the jarring blue and red lights of police cars splashing against the glass-walled buildings from a half block away. There was a lot of unwelcome activity down there that we needed to avoid. "Where are you parked?" I asked.

"Down the street," Liddy replied.

My Firebird was just a few cars down. "I'll drive you around, and you can walk up to it from the other direction," I told him.

"Good idea," he agreed, then gestured at the Howard Johnson listening post across the street. "What about him?"

"I'll come back. Go home and get yourself an alibi."

I drove him a safe distance and let him out. "Got the emergency money?" he asked.

"I'm going to get it now," I told him.

"Okay," Liddy said, his voice still decisive, strong, and undefeated. "Good night, Howard. I'll be in touch tomorrow." It was as if the chaos around us didn't exist. We shook hands, I watched him trudge toward his green Jeep, then I made a quick U-turn and parked two blocks from the motel.

The Howard Johnson hotel was a far cry from the executive-style Watergate. The elevator was either interminably slow or my mind was just racing too fast, because it seemed to take a year to get up to the seventh-floor listening post, where I finally knocked on the door and was admitted into the room by Alfred Baldwin, who handed me the binoculars. "Take a look," he said. "The cops are leading them out."

There wasn't time. "Listen," I said. "It's all over. Pack up and get going."

He looked at me like I was crazy. "Lotta heavy gear here. What do I do with it?"

"Load the goddamn van and shove off," I snapped impatiently.

"Where should I go—McCord's house?"

The guy was supposed to be a former FBI agent but was acting like the worst amateur. "That's the last place to go. I don't care if you drive the van into the river. Just get the stuff out of here. Understood?" I strode purposefully toward the door.

Baldwin's plaintive voice wafted from behind me. "What's going to happen?"

"I don't know," I said. "But you'll be contacted."

Then, as I was closing the door, Baldwin asked, "Does this mean we're not going to Miami?"

All I could do was stare at him coldly for a second before slamming the door.

Downstairs, I joined a few other casual rubberneckers on the sidewalk, where I watched the police load my guys into a white paddy wagon across the street. It was sickening. I cursed McCord, the principals, Liddy—saving the worst admonitions for myself for not voicing a strong enough dissent. This was one time my life experience should have really told me to abort the operation. The small voice had nagged, but it should have blared the order in my brain with a megaphone.

I walked to my car and drove over to my White House office in the Executive Office Building, where I flashed my pass to the guard and entered with three heavy attaché cases. I unlocked the door to Room 338, went in, and opened my two-drawer safe, then took out my operational notebook and dialed a number.

It was 2:13 in the morning. Five of our guys had been arrested and presumably taken to D.C. Jail. I had recruited them, and it was my responsibility to get them out. I started making calls. My first was to lawyer Douglas Caddy, who had resigned from Mullen & Company when the promised transferal to our stewardship had failed to take place. His sleepy voice didn't sound too happy. "Yes?" he said.

"Doug? This is Howard. I hate to wake you up, but I've got a tough situation and I need to talk to you. Can I come over?"

That was the beginning of Watergate—a scandal that would bring down a president and destroy my life in the process.

19

Fallout

I fetched Liddy's emergency ten grand from the safe, putting $1,500 in my wallet and the other $8,500 in my coat pocket. I stashed McCord's black attaché case in a safe drawer that held my operational notebooks, then locked the safe and left the office after positioning the other two cases of equipment in the corner, feeling that this was probably one of the most secure rooms in the country in which to hide the evidence.

From the Executive Office Building, I crossed the street to the Mullen & Company office at 1700 Pennsylvania Avenue and signed in under an alias, not wanting a written record that I had entered the building at such a late hour. Then I went to my office, gritted my teeth, and made a difficult telephone call to Barker's wife, Clara, in Miami.

She was obviously hoping to hear her husband's voice when she picked up. "Clarita," I started.

She took in a breath, knowing that I could not be calling with good news.

"Things have gone wrong," I told her in a calm voice. "Macho's been arrested."

She let out a shriek. "Oh my God!" she exploded.

"He's got bail money with him," I continued. "So maybe he'll be able to get out before dawn. I don't know how these things work, but I think he ought to have an attorney. I've already called one, and I want you to call him, too."

I gave her Caddy's name and number, telling her to call him from a pay phone and retain him for Barker. She calmed down and started asking questions, like, "What the hell was Bernie doing in Washington anyway?"

"I don't have time for questions," I told her. "Just call Caddy. That's all you or anybody can do."

Afterward, I looked to see if any evidence was laying around my office, found some notes that should be destroyed, stuck them in my pocket, and turned off the light. It would be the last time I saw the office for several weeks.

From there, I met Caddy at his high-rise apartment.

"Coffee?" he asked.

"Any milk?" I answered. "My ulcer's acting up."

He shook his head negatively and apologized.

"Then I'll take some coffee," I said, sitting down. "There was an operation tonight, Doug, and five men were arrested. You know one of them, Bernie Barker."

"I remember him," Caddy said, continuing skeptically: "What do you mean 'operation'?"

I sat back, feeling older than my years, then recounted the details of the operation to Caddy. "Five people are going to need legal representation," I finished, giving him the $8,500 emergency funds from my pocket. "Could you go down to police headquarters or wherever they take men after they're arrested and see if you can bail them out?"

It was amazing, even to me, that at this point in my life, I had no real idea where the District of Columbia Police Department would bring a robbery suspect. Caddy looked at me with the same sort of doubt that I had. "I'm not a criminal attorney, Howard. You know that. I don't have the faintest idea where police take arrested men."

He had to call one of the partners at his firm, who in turn had a criminal lawyer, Joe Rafferty, call us back. Rafferty explained that the men would probably be taken to D.C. Jail and that he would make some phone calls.

After he hung up, Caddy turned back to me. "Any idea what the charges will be?" he asked.

"Whatever they are, they can't be very heavy," I said, ignorant at the time about modern conspiracy law. "Maybe something like being on the premises without permission, trespassing. The door lock was picked, so there shouldn't be anything like breaking and entering or burglary. They weren't going to steal anything, just photograph some documents. One other thing . . ." I explained that Bernie and one of the others would be listed under the names of some false documentation they carried, which made him curious as to where they obtained the documents. "In CIA, it's a need-to-know basis," I told him. "There are things you don't need to know to bail them out. I want them out of jail and out of town before dawn."

We also called Liddy, who, I was amazed to find, was already asleep at home in bed and seemed a bit annoyed at being woken up. I explained to him what was happening. He didn't seem all that bothered, so taking my cue from him—since he was a former prosecutor—I figured that maybe the water wasn't as hot as I had imagined. While the situation was unfortunate, maybe everything was containable. The men would get bailed out and disappear. The electronic surveillance had been conducted under the authority of Attorney General John Mitchell, who had also approved Gemstone. If anybody had the clout to get this thing swept conveniently under the rug, it was Mitchell.

I also figured that Liddy would have informed the principals by now and gotten the White House to apply pressure to have the five men released. I didn't know it then, but with the exception of John Dean, all senior White House officials were in San Clemente, California, that weekend. Even so, I would have thought Dean, as the president's counsel, was powerful enough to arrange our team's release.

Caddy took a call from Rafferty, then informed me, "Rafferty thinks this may take a little time, Howard, so I'm going to get dressed and stand by to meet him. You can stay here if you want."

I told him I'd rather go home and to reach me there. We shook hands, and I thanked Caddy for his help. Strangely, I would never see him in person again.

Meanwhile, down at Second Precinct headquarters, the Miami quartet mixed up their aliases, with both Barker and Sturgis offering the same name.

Barrett told them, "Wait a minute, fellas. You guys got to get your stories straight."

Something about the way the perplexed cop spoke the words made two of the experienced ex-commandos laugh. To them, it was probably like being scolded by a child.

Later, the police would become even more confused when their prisoners mysteriously declined to call any lawyers. In hindsight, we should have practiced this possible scenario in greater detail, as the police considered this a pretty strange development for their five well-dressed burglars—white-collar criminals are normally quite happy to be given an opportunity to alert their attorneys. The police kept questioning the burglars about their lawyers until Barker volunteered that the appropriate people had already been notified.

This, of course, made the police even more suspicious that they had stumbled onto something larger than it appeared. Stoffler remembered the man on the other balcony staring at him. Maybe he had been part of it, too. It was worth checking. Additionally, the interesting array of electronics, cameras, lock-picking paraphernalia, and wads of brand-new hundred-dollar bills galvanized the police like hunting dogs on the trail of a wounded animal.

The next morning, their suspicions would blossom when a police detective reporting for duty recognized one of the culprits who had been calling himself Edward Martin, shocking his colleagues with the correct identification. "That's Jim McCord! He's security chief at the Committee to Re-elect the President!"

Dawn was a spreading fire on the horizon as I drove the Firebird home, feeling empty and fatigued to my bones. I parked the car outside our home and walked leadenly toward the front door in a semi-daze, feeling as if I was in a dream, trying to move forward but slogging through some sort of viscous liquid or strong current. I took a sleeping pill and went to bed as the sky was brightening and the pleasant sounds of chirping birds came from outside. The world was going on just as it always did, and that somehow gave me a sense of well-being, making me think that I was overreacting and that everything would be inconvenient but all right. The Miami men had clean records, especially the ones with aliases, and it wasn't like they were being held on murder charges. I was confident that the attorneys would arrange bail for the men, as that's what attorneys did.

The maid woke me up at 11:00 a.m. "I'm sorry, Mr. Hunt, but there's someone on the telephone for you."

Great, I thought. This was probably Liddy giving me an update. I walked groggily to the telephone in the kitchen and picked up the receiver. "Yes?" I said.

"Mr. Hunt?" Definitely not Liddy, I thought, my mind still hazy.

"Yes," I said.

"Mr. Hunt, this is Bob Woodward from the *Washington Post*. Some men have been arrested, and one of them had your name in his notebook. His name is Barker. Is he a friend of yours?"

For a moment, in my daze, I thought of Robert Woodward, the ambassador in Uruguay and later in Spain who had caused me so much trouble, and I wondered what the hell he was calling me for. But I shook my head. He'd said the *Washington Post*!

"Oh my God," I replied without thinking, then hung up. The phone rang again moments later. It was Woodward.

"Mr. Hunt, is Barker a friend of yours?"

"Sorry, I have no comment," I said, then hung up the phone again.

I told the maid that a reporter had called and that I didn't want to speak to him or any other. "The only calls I'll take are from Mr. Caddy or Mr. Liddy."

I decided to get dressed and face the day like a good soldier, no matter if there might be people outside with their metaphoric gunsights trained on me. My mind quickly cleared, and I wondered just how much the reporter knew. He'd said that Barker had my name in his notebook. Did he mean phone book? If so, why hadn't Barker left it at home in Miami? These guys knew my contact numbers by heart. They didn't need to bring them along. But whatever the case, it was too late for that. I wondered how Liddy and Caddy were faring nine hours after the event.

Unfortunately, neither was at home, giving my ulcer a twinge. Woodward called again, making it react some more. Acid bile started to collect in my throat and I could barely taste breakfast. Still, I reasoned that the men might even now have posted bail, as there was no reason to deny it. Then my mind wandered back to the operation, making me wonder how we could have lacked the foresight to think the building guard might call the police. All of our scenarios had assumed that if alerted, he would confront the intruders himself, giving them the opportunity to pay him off. That was why Liddy had given Barker so much money to take in with him. Additionally, and perhaps most importantly, since McCord was an employee of John Mitchell's, we figured the former AG would move the earth to secure McCord's release, so as to avoid implication himself.

Liddy finally called, speaking in a somber voice. "The boys are still in jail," he told me. "There are reporters all over the place, and I've just seen the noon paper. It's got Bernie's name in it."

"I'm not surprised," I told him. "A reporter from the *Post* named Woodward told me that a little earlier."

"He did?"

"My name was in Barker's address book. I don't know whether they found it on him or in his room. Do you?"

"No. But it doesn't make any difference. Did Caddy come through?"

"Well, he got a lawyer named Rafferty to go down to the jail. I thought by now they'd have been able to get the men out. Where are you calling from?"

"My office. All hell's breaking loose around here. I'm shredding everything I've got. What did you do with the stuff you took from the room?"

I told him I'd stashed it in my office at the White House. "Colson once remarked that it was the safest place in town, so let's hope it is."

Liddy then told me that he was having trouble getting in touch with his principals, as they were all out on the West Coast and had full schedules. Nothing could be done until he could speak to Mitchell personally. But so far, he hadn't had any luck. We promised to call each other if we got any news.

Then, toward afternoon, the doorbell rang. The maid found me in my study, where she informed me that two government men were at the door.

"What kind of government men?" I asked hopefully, expecting that they were emissaries from the White House.

"They say they're from the FBI," she said.

My ulcer almost howled. "Did you tell them I was here?"

"Yes."

There was nothing I could do but go to the door, where I found two youngish men who presented FBI credentials and asked if they could talk to me.

"About what?" I asked.

"Some burglars were arrested last night, and one of them had your name in his address book. We'd like to talk to you about it."

I shook my head. "Sorry, but before I talk to you, I'd want to talk to counsel."

The agent shrugged but wasn't about to walk away. "After you've talked to your attorney, Mr. Hunt, would you talk to us then?"

"It depends on what my attorney recommends."

The agent let out a sigh. "You *will* call your attorney, won't you?"

I assured them that I would and closed the door. Caddy had already explained that he knew nothing about criminal law, so I tracked down Liddy, the former prosecutor, at his CREEP office for some advice. He told me to tell them that on the advice of my attorney I was choosing not to speak with them. While well within my legal rights, I knew that this wasn't going to go over too well with law enforcement.

There wasn't a second of peace that day, however. The phone started to ring constantly, and the property came under siege by reporters camping outside the house. I couldn't believe that the situation had blown up like this. When my children returned from school, they wanted to know what all the reporters were doing outside their home. I had to explain that Bernie had been arrested, my name was found in his address book, but that it had nothing to do with me.

I turned on the radio and television to find out what I could. News broadcasts said that five men had been arrested in Democratic National Headquarters. Cameras and electronic devices had been confiscated, and the name of E. Howard Hunt, a White House aide, had been found in a notebook belonging to one of the men. I kept hoping that this was the extent of the information, but new details kept being added as the hours ticked by. The men were Cubans from Miami, they had been staying at the Watergate Hotel, James McCord had been with the CIA . . .

I escaped with the children to my country club for dinner, then told everyone not to answer the phone or the door. Liddy's phone was busy. I hoped that at any moment the White House would exert the proper pressure on the police chief, a political appointee, to release the men and stop talking to the press. But this belief was a fantasy.

On Sunday, June 18, 1972, the first *Washington Post* article, with a byline by staffer Alfred E. Lewis, was published, describing the arrest of five men wearing surgical gloves and carrying a large amount of cash, electronics, and photographic equipment who had broken into the DNC. The Cubans and Sturgis were all identified by name, with disconcerting one-paragraph biographies. Even González's boss at the Missing Link Key Shop had been contacted, offering the quote that his employee occasionally missed a day without calling in. Worse, bail was set at a stratospheric $50,000 per man, with $30,000 for McCord, since he was local. This was about ten times the going rate for a normal B&E.

I left the house early, drove to my office at the Executive Office Building, and put the contents of the attaché cases in my safe, then drove home. Television cameras were stationed along River Road to catch me, and reporters followed my car up the drive on foot. Again, I asked them to leave or I would let the dog out.

The FBI agents appeared again, and I explained that my lawyer, a former FBI agent himself, had advised me not to speak. They seemed very disappointed, but there was nothing they could do but leave. I telephoned Liddy and filled him in, then asked about "the boys."

"Still in jail," he told me.

"Christ, when are our people going to get them out?"

"Frankly, there have been some problems I didn't anticipate. You gave Caddy the ten grand?"

"I kept out fifteen hundred, thinking you or I might need it."

"We may at that, Howard. I shredded all the green I had in my office."

Apparently, he realized that the sequentially numbered bills could be traced and that he had numbers corresponding to ones that Barker had in his pocket. It must have been hard to shred a mass of hundred-dollar bills, especially when he knew we would need the cash.

Caddy called me later in the day with the news that he and Rafferty had met the boys in jail, and they weren't too happy about being there. "What do we need to bail them out?" I asked.

"The charges are too heavy. I don't think they're going to be able to get bail."

Mr. Ulcer came back with a bang and performed a few painful somersaults in my stomach. I almost threw up. "I never heard of anything you couldn't get bail for except murder, and the boys haven't done that or anything close to it."

"Well, they've got hold of your name and found out you were at the White House, so the thing is getting a lot of publicity. Besides, the Democrats are getting interested in this, and things are likely to get worse before they get better."

"Listen, Doug, I want to go down there and see them. That's the least I can do. Just tell me where they are."

"I don't advise that," he said. Besides, it didn't matter, as the men were only permitted to speak to their lawyers. He then informed me that Mrs. Barker was on her way up from Miami. Again, something that would just complicate matters, as there was nothing she could do, and she might be set on by reporters.

Worse, Caddy told me that his firm's extremely conservative partners were so angry about seeing his name in the paper in association with this investigation that they had suggested he resign. It didn't make him feel one iota better when I told him about my two visits from the FBI and the advice that Liddy had given me. He signed off after reiterating his admonition to keep away from my imprisoned colleagues.

I could not remember ever feeling so alone and powerless, isolated from both my superiors and my subordinates, under siege by enemies, praying for some kind of White House cavalry to come riding triumphantly over the proverbial ridge to help me in my direst hour. While I could no longer keep myself under the delusion that the crisis was easily containable, I could only hole up and hope to outlast and outwit my opponents until help arrived.

Instead, when the White House backup did appear, they would do everything to the contrary—they were the anticavalry.

While this was a time I really needed Dorothy's advice and support, she was in Europe. Still, perhaps it was better; she and the other children weren't here to suffer along with me, fending off reporters and FBI agents at our home. In fact, the reporters, sensing blood, had gotten so ravenous and plentiful that I allowed our Afghan hound outdoors to keep them away.

On Monday, June 19, the *Washington Post* came out with the second story about the break-in—this one featuring bylines by Carl Bernstein and Bob Woodward—with the salivating lead that tied James McCord to the Committee to Re-elect the President, quoting John Mitchell as saying that the five arrested men "were not operating either in our behalf or with our consent." Just as unsettling was information from "Miami sources," saying that Barker and Sturgis had been searching for recruits to demonstrate against the Democratic national convention.

I didn't feel hurt by Mitchell's statement, which was standard operating procedure in any covert operation. But whether the administration was far enough removed from the situation to offer an explanation of "plausible denial" remained to be seen.

I didn't know it at the time, but Woodward was already meeting with FBI deputy director Mark Felt—later, "Deep Throat"—who told him that I was a prime suspect in the Watergate burglary. This led to a nasty little article headlined "White House Consultant Linked to Bugging Suspects," which mentioned that my name had been found in the burglars' address books.

This would be the first time that White House press secretary Ronald Ziegler would comment on the subject, saying, "Certain elements may try to stretch this beyond what it is," but the operation was "a third-rate burglary" that the White House felt was beneath them to comment on.

Also, unbeknownst to me at the time, Liddy had met with Attorney General Kleindienst at the Burning Tree Golf Club on Sunday the eighteenth, where he told Kleindienst that the DNC break-in had been engineered by CREEP and that Mitchell wanted him to have the arrested men released at once. Kleindienst nearly had a heart attack when he heard the story, said Liddy, who reported in *Will* that Kleindienst responded, "What the fuck did you people think you were *doing* there?" Furthermore, he refused to do anything to spring the prisoners, as it was sure to come back to harm the president.

That morning, I drove to my EOB office and ascertained that nothing looked disturbed since I'd been there last. The safe was still in place, and the few papers on my desk were reassuringly undisturbed. I decided that as long as I was in the building, I should go up to see what Chuck Colson thought about the news. He hadn't arrived yet, but I saw his secretary, Joan Hall, who exclaimed, "I'm surprised to see *you* here!"

The tone of her voice annoyed me, as if she were already placing the blame or guilt on my shoulders. "Why shouldn't I be here?" I asked, sitting down in a chair. My temper suddenly started to soar, and I continued, "There's one thing I want to tell you. You can pass it along to Chuck." I gestured toward the ceiling. "That safe of mine upstairs is loaded."

She nodded her head gravely. "I sort of thought it might be," she said.

When I left the Executive Office Building shortly afterward, I didn't know that I would never enter it again, so I gave my departure no second thoughts.

Across the street at my Mullen office, the secretaries and my colleagues were gossiping about seeing my name in the paper. I didn't let it get to me, closed the door to my office, and sat down to work on the nearly completed Julie Eisenhower public service television commercial. The piece still needed some postproduction work in New York, but the positive and negative prints were there, awaiting my consultation.

During the day, I received a visit from Bob Bennett, who remarked that the papers seemed to be full of my name and that reporters had been calling to get information about me. While he had told the media that he knew nothing about anything that I did outside the office, he implied that maybe my being there was getting to be a liability. I reminded him that not long before, he had been connected in the press to a couple of hundred political fund-raising committees that were fronts for processing money from the milk-producing industry, so negative publicity was not something foreign to the firm. His face went ashen, his jaw tensed, but he left me alone after that. Bennett, now a twice-elected senator from Utah, would later be fingered as "Deep Throat" in a book by Leonard Garment, published in 2000, which argued that my former boss was probably trying to keep reporters from finding out that Mullen & Company was in bed with the CIA.

Before noon, I received a call from Liddy. His voice sounded hoarse, either from stress or arguing, I didn't know. I got the message that he suspected the lines might be tapped. "Howard," he said quickly, "this is George. Go down to the street and walk west on Pennsylvania Avenue as far as the corner. Turn left, and I'll meet you there. We'll keep walking."

"How soon?"

"Right away. Get going."

I was glad to do it, as I felt as if I was in an information vacuum. I did as he asked and caught up to my friend. He was ostensibly reading a newspaper at the corner of the U.S. Information Agency Building. As I walked toward him, he fell casually into step next to me, and we walked down the street. His voice was tense, his lips almost not moving, as if he thought lip readers might be watching. "They want you to get out of town," he said. "They," in this case, I would later find out meant John Dean.

We argued about it for a minute, Liddy saying that "they" wanted me to go on vacation to Europe to meet Dorothy; me saying, "If I leave town now, it will look as though I'm a fugitive—particularly after two visits by the FBI—and I don't like it. I don't need a vacation. What I *do* need is a lawyer. Can you get me one?"

"We'll work that out later," he said tersely. "I'm due back in a few minutes. Are you going to go?"

I blew out a breath. "If that's what *they* want," I said. "But let's get a lawyer for me, hey Gordon?"

He told me to use the $1,500 I had left in the safe and he'd get more money to me later. Then he gripped my hand, "*Adiós, amigo!*" he said, as if we might never see each other again, gave me a quick half-*abrazo*, and strode away.

When he had disappeared into the crowd, I turned and walked back to my office, where I informed Bennett that I would be leaving town for a while. He simply nodded. I put a dustcover over my typewriter and let myself out by the side exit that Liddy and McCord often used to visit me.

A short while later, at home, I was angrily tossing some clothes into a suitcase when Liddy called. "Howard, the orders have been changed. You don't have to leave."

I told him that canceling important orders like that made me uneasy, and it made me realize that the principals weren't so smart and had no plan. I had some work to do on a television spot in New York, so I would go up there, and it wouldn't look like I was hightailing it out of town. I figured my absence would keep the press from hounding the kids, as well. They were savvy young adults by this time and could take care of themselves pretty well, but it certainly wasn't good for them to go through this. I told him that I'd call him from New York.

"Do one thing for me, will you? And do it now," I said when we finished the conversation. "Get me a lawyer. When I call you tonight or tomorrow, I'll want that lawyer's name, Gordon."

"Okay, *amigo*. I'll get with it."

The Watergate break-in topped the Monday evening news again, ballooning out of all proportion. The Tuesday morning papers continued the barrage, with articles now telling me the unhappy news that my White House safe had been opened and that a pistol (the one I had borrowed from my wife to protect my secretaries) had been found there. The insinuation was clear. I was a pistol-packing fugitive.

My greatest concern, however, was the disposition of my files. I had made a pointed warning to Joan Hall that my safe was loaded. She, as well as the Secret Service, had the combination, so I hoped that she or Colson had spirited away the papers and Colson's briefcase before it was discovered by the FBI.

Feeling as if I really needed a lawyer now, I tried calling Liddy but couldn't manage to get him on the phone. Failing that, I called Bob

Bennett, told him I was in New York doing production work on our public service commercial, and asked him what the atmosphere in Washington was like.

He whistled, describing it as extremely excited and ominous, mentioning that the opening of my White House safe was heading the news.

"Bob," I said, "I feel I've been put in a false position and made to look like a fugitive—which I'm not. All I want is an attorney. Liddy said he'd find one for me, but I haven't been able to reach him. Would you call Liddy for me? Or, failing that, Doug Caddy?"

Bennett said he'd do what he could, and I told him I'd be at the postproduction facility for the next few hours. Later, I called London and found my wife in her hotel room. She sounded very unhappy, telling me that my name was in the London papers, too.

I tried to calm her down. "The important thing is for you not to cut short your vacation. I'm sure this whole thing will blow away just as soon as the right people do what they're supposed to do."

"Was Gordon arrested?" she wanted to know.

"No. So far, his name hasn't even been mentioned. Just me—and, of course, Bernie, McCord, and the other men. I don't know why they've let the thing reach the dimensions that it has, but it makes me more than a little unhappy. Liddy said he'd get me a lawyer, but I haven't been able to reach him. My photo's in all the papers, and it won't be long before I'm recognized in New York. The night it happened, I went to Doug Caddy, and he found a lawyer to represent the arrested men, but there's no lawyer for me. The press has been all over the house, and we've been like prisoners."

She wanted to know what I was going to do.

Suddenly, the thought came to me that I could go to my old navy pal Tony Jackson's home in Los Angeles. He was a lawyer, and at least I would have the benefit of a friend's advice. I told her that I was very sorry to worry her but to stay in Europe.

"All right, darling," she said skeptically. "We've been having a wonderful time, and if you don't need us, we'll stay and continue the trip."

I continued working that afternoon on the postproduction part, then left for Kennedy airport and caught a plane to Los Angeles, where I phoned Jackson from a telephone booth and asked him for a place to stay, assuring him that I wasn't a fugitive. He welcomed me to the house, which, as luck would have it, was fairly empty. His wife and kids were out of town to attend a wedding, and he would soon be joining them.

He was happy to see me and to consult but reminded me that he hadn't handled criminal law in years, suggesting that I talk to one of his partners. Whatever the case, I was welcome to stay at his home: a lovely pool house, situated high on a crest in Beverly Hills, furnished with carved teak from Bangkok.

From there, I called Liddy and explained where I was. "Have you found an attorney for me yet?"

"It's in the works. Tony can take care of you for now, can't he?"

I told him Jackson was leaving town.

"Sit tight, *amigo*, and I'll get back to you."

"Great," I said. "Opening my safe was a charming affair, and I'm delighted to be known as a gunslinger. Whose idea was that? Who the hell's in charge back there?"

Liddy said to take it easy. "All hell's breaking loose here in Washington." He had no good news. Bennett had never called him, and the boys were still in jail and he didn't know when they were going to get out. "You can't imagine what this thing's like, Howard. It's ballooning all over the place. The office is crawling with reporters, and I haven't had any sleep in two nights. If you think you've got troubles, think of mine."

I complained that it didn't seem like anyone was in charge and the principals hadn't done anything. We would later find out that Nixon was trying to get the CIA to make the FBI stand down on the investigation for national security reasons but hadn't gotten anywhere.

Over the course of a few days, newspapers reported that I was being sought in all fifty states and had been spotted simultaneously in Spain and Mexico and shopping the grand boulevards of Paris. I also learned from the papers that Bob Bennett announced that I was fired.

Liddy flew out from Washington, delivered a thousand dollars, and told me that the "action officer" in charge of what would later be known as the cover-up had changed from John Dean to Bob Mardian—something he seemed highly pleased with, saying that the former assistant attorney general of the United States should be able to smooth out the rough roads ahead. I didn't know Mardian from Moses but hoped Liddy was right, telling him it looked like the White House was cooperating with the investigation instead of impeding it.

We would eventually find out that someone was leaking information from inside the FBI. An apoplectic John Ehrlichman called the new FBI director, L. Patrick Gray, and ordered him to stop the leaks, which were juicing up newspaper stories, especially ones by Woodward and Bernstein. The ineffectual Gray was unable to do anything about them, however, and the leaks would continue, as his second in command was the purveyor of the information.

Behind the scenes: Attacking from a different flank, Haldeman met with Richard Helms at the CIA, demanding that he notify the FBI that further investigation into tracing the Watergate burglars' money would expose a national security operation. Haldeman and Nixon's tape-recorded conversation from June 23, in which Nixon approved the plan, would later become the publicly termed "smoking gun" that prosecutors needed to ascertain what the president knew and when he knew it, which would lead to his resignation. To increase pressure on Helms, Haldeman suggested that Richard Nixon had information that the CIA had been involved in the JFK assassination.

Richard Helms did in fact instruct Gray to derail the investigation, but by the beginning of July, Mark Felt had already proceeded with the inquiry, telling Gray that unless the bureau received an official written CIA request to halt, it needed to continue the investigation into the money trail. Bob Woodward reports in The Secret Man *that the enterprising Felt told his superior, "I am convinced we will be going much higher than these seven. These men are pawns. We want the ones who moved the pawns."*

Liddy dropped another bombshell on me—he would soon announce his resignation from the committee. The FBI had found his name in Macho's notebook, too, and the news would hit the papers the next day.

"They're abandoning you?" I asked.

He assured me that they weren't, that we would all be taken care of "company style," meaning in the manner of the CIA. They might disown us publicly, but Dean and Mardian assured him that we and our jailed colleagues would all be taken care of monetarily. I reminded him to get me a lawyer. "I want competent counsel to represent me. Highly competent!"

He said to be careful talking on the telephone, as he had good information that both our lines were tapped. He suggested that I fly to Miami to soothe Clara Barker, who was "going bananas."

I flew to Miami, but when I got to Barker's house in the evening, it was completely lit up and surrounded by reporters. Clara didn't answer the telephone, and I certainly wasn't going to knock on her front door, so I flew back to Los Angeles, where I called Caddy. He told me that my wife and kids had returned from Europe and that he would relay a message to them about where I was.

Then I called Bennett, telling him I didn't want to talk about his firing me but to get me the names of some competent attorneys. He muttered something vaguely about not wanting to get mixed up in the affair, but I insisted, asking him to call John Dean. "If anybody should know Republican lawyers, it's the president's counsel, right?"

He said he would try but couldn't make any promises. The parameters of the grim situation were finally starting to sink in to my thick brain. I was essentially a fugitive, Liddy was fired from the committee, and the Gemstone pals—Mitchell, Dean, and Magruder—had disassociated themselves, and were running for the shadows. Nevertheless, Liddy assured me that everything would be taken care of company style, which I took to mean heroic efforts made to right the situation, financing a strong legal defense, and paying for lost wages. That's what it meant to me.

The principals hadn't been in the CIA, however, and they were deeply in standard CYA—cover-your-ass—mode.

20

Disaster Strikes Twice

For all his hospitality, I couldn't impose on Tony after his wife and children came home, so I flew to Chicago to stay with Dorothy's cousin, Phyllis, who phoned my wife and suggested she come to Chicago for a brief visit. Dorothy, married to an undercover agent for so long, understood the hint at once and soon joined me at her relative's home.

Our reunion was if not joyous—given the circumstances—warm, loving, and without recrimination on her part. I described the sequence of events, finishing with Liddy's assertion that we were going to be taken care of company style and my belief that either he or John Dean would find appropriate counsel for me. In turn, Dorothy told me that she had been in contact with Doug Caddy, who had not been helpful to her, but she had been unable to reach Liddy.

She couldn't stay longer than one night, as that might have caused the FBI to look for her, so she returned to Washington in the morning. As short a visit as it was, her positive reinforcement gave me the morale boost that I needed and renewed energy to confront the situation.

Even with my tank refilled, however, I hit a brick wall in regard to getting an attorney, as I couldn't reach any of my Washington, D.C., contacts. Finally, on July 2, Jackson gave me the names of two Washington attorneys. Alphabetically, the first name on the list was William O. Bittman, so I called him first and asked if he would be willing to represent me. Bittman was a partner in the large, prestigious D.C. firm of Hogan & Hartson. Considering everything that would happen later, I bet Bittman wished his name began with a Z.

As Jackson had made a preliminary introduction, Bittman was expecting my call. I explained to him that I resented being cast in the role of a fugitive and had only been awaiting the retention of competent counsel before I agreed to speak to whatever government agencies were looking for me. On that proviso, Bittman agreed to represent me and told me to meet him at his home the following night.

Dorothy and Kevan met me at O'Hare airport and dropped me off at Bittman's residence, which was only about a mile away from our own home in Potomac, Maryland. With Bittman was his associate Austin Mittler. Bittman was a type A personality if ever there was one and had worked both sides of the criminal law, making me feel as if my case was in good hands.

Over the next several hours, I ran through the story and gave Bittman $1,000 of the $1,500 emergency funds as a retainer. Bittman then called the assistant U.S. attorney, Earl Silbert, and explained that he was representing me and that I would consent to an interview without prosecutors resorting to the power of subpoena.

Afterward, we discussed the situation until late into the night, then I returned home to enjoy the comfort of my own bed, sleeping next to my wife for the first time in what seemed like years. I closed my eyes fearing, but not daring to think, the worst.

Liddy hadn't been kidding that all hell was breaking loose in Washington. We were getting blasted from every direction. Unbeknownst to us, Alfred Baldwin had been traced to Room 733 at the Howard Johnson hotel and was cooperating with the government. The outraged Democratic National Committee had initiated a dramatic lawsuit against the Republican Party, CREEP, me, and the five arrested men, four of whom were now out of jail and at their homes. A federal grand jury was looking into the allegations and had threatened Douglas Caddy with contempt when he declined an invitation to discuss my conversations with him. He himself had now retained counsel to keep himself out of jail while defending our rights of attorney–client confidentiality. At this point, I took Bittman's advice and claimed my constitutional Fifth Amendment rights when answering a very frustrated and angry Silbert at the prosecutor's office.

On July 7, Bittman gave me the good news that he had received $25,000 as a retainer for my representation. I didn't ask where it came from and he didn't tell me. My wife happened to be with us at the time, and the lawyer mentioned as an afterthought a curious telephone call he had received: "Some guy—I don't know who he was—said he wanted to talk to the 'writer's wife.' He said his name was Mr. Rivers and that he wanted to talk only to the writer's wife."

I was the only writer whom Bittman knew, so he deduced that it was Dorothy to whom Mr. Rivers wanted to speak. "Is there any reason why he wouldn't just call your house?"

Of course: if he was an agent of Liddy's principals—Mitchell, Dean, or Magruder—he would assume my telephone had been tapped by the feds!

Dorothy then informed me that when she had gotten to Washington and had been unable to talk with Caddy or Liddy, she had gone to CREEP headquarters and spoken with their general counsel, Paul O'Brien, whose blood had drained from his face when she told him of my involvement with Liddy. He had promised her that he would look into the circumstances at once. Mr. Rivers's call, we conjectured, was probably in response to her visit.

Bittman was able to confirm with CREEP lawyers that Mr. Rivers was an appropriate person for him or Dorothy to deal with. So on the following evening, when Dorothy received a call from a man identifying himself as Mr. Rivers, she agreed to go to a particular phone booth in Potomac Village to receive his call.

When she returned, she told me that Mr. Rivers had asked for an estimate of each arrested man's monthly living expenses and attorneys' fees, including Liddy and myself. He would get the information from her the next day at a different telephone. She called McCord, then Barker, who in turn would get a combined estimate of the rest of the Miami men. The following day, she gave the amount to the disembodied voice of Mr. Rivers, who replied, "Well, let's multiply that by five to cut down on the number of deliveries."

My astute Dorothy immediately wondered why Mr. Rivers would use a multiple of five—aware that five months represented about the amount of time to the presidential election—to which the man replied that it was just a convenient figure for him to multiply by.

Within a couple of days, Mr. Rivers instructed Dorothy to drive to National Airport and go to a particular wall pay phone, where she would find a locker key taped to the bottom. This she did, opening a nearby locker that contained a blue plastic airline bag, which she brought home.

Instead of the promised five months of expenses, there was only enough for three, although Mr. Rivers had informed her that Liddy would receive his funds through a separate channel. She divided the money and distributed the funds to the parties involved.

While I obviously felt very terrible that my wife had been drawn into this situation at all, I was relieved that Liddy's promise that everything would be taken care of did seem to be panning out, which gave me renewed confidence that the situation would ultimately be resolved and obligations would be met.

Behind the scenes: In fact, John Dean had met with Vernon Walters at the CIA to ask if the agency could provide financial assistance to the Watergate Seven. A couple of days later, Walters opted out of doing things company style and denied the request. On June 29, Haldeman rode to the rescue, telling his staff assistant, Gordon Strachan, to deliver some $75,000 to the defendants. This was given to Frank LeRue and routed to us through Nixon's lawyer Herbert Kalmbach and the "Golden Greek," Anthony Ulasewicz, who came back into our lives as "Mr. Rivers."

Unfortunately, the principals' powers did not extend to the media, as the plague of Watergate coverage continued to spread and grow into an epidemic. And the situation grew darker. On July 13, every member of my family except David, who was only eight, was served with a summons, then interrogated by the grand jury on the eighteenth. I was hauled down to the federal courthouse, fingerprinted by the FBI, and made to submit handwriting samples. Douglas Caddy was forced to testify in front of the grand jury after being held briefly in jail. Each day, I spent long hours conferring with my attorneys.

Over the weekend, Gordon and Frances Liddy dined with us and discussed our rapidly deteriorating situation. It turned out that Gordon had received $8,000, just a little more than three months' salary, at a National Airport locker through a Mr. Waters, who we assumed was another permutation of our Mr. Rivers. Legally, he was being represented by an old chum from Poughkeepsie, New York, Peter Maroulis.

With his typical wry humor, Liddy characterized the lead prosecutor, Earl Silbert, as oily and obsequious, later describing the man as
a "world-class ass kisser" in his autobiography. But the guy was cultured and articulate; you had to give him that, and he would no doubt
present a good case should we come to trial. Also, he seemed extremely
angry and passionate about the case, as if we had personally insulted
him by breaking into his home instead of the DNC. He was assisted
by fraud chief Seymour Glanzer and Donald Campbell, who was the
in-house wiretap expert. Glanzer was an aggressive, rough New York
bulldog, the polar opposite of the polished Silbert. Athough an effective team, they were duking it out to be considered next in line for
U.S. attorney.

Amazingly, the outraged Silbert would later become a famous
criminal attorney, specializing in corporate litigation, white-collar
crime, and legal ethics. Recently, he represented Kenneth Lay of
Enron infamy. Glanzer went into private practice in 1974, also
becoming a major criminal attorney.

Chief Judge John Sirica had assigned himself the case. While a
Republican, he was widely considered to be influenced by the political
wind and had a reputation as one of the most frequently reversed
judges in the district. We didn't know whether that was good or bad
for us. What we didn't like was his nickname, "Maximum John." He
had already made some questionable rulings, such as compelling
Caddy to testify. As an indication of just how personal and dirty the
trial would get, prosecutors tried to intimidate Caddy by subpoenaing
his bank accounts and credit card records, prompting a Woodward-
bylined story, "Jury Probes Lawyer in 'Bug Case.'"

The media exposure wasn't getting any quieter. On August 1,
Woodward and Bernstein published one of the first follow-the-money
articles, "Bug Suspect Got Campaign Funds," with a lead saying that
a $25,000 check deposited in Bernie's account had originally been
made out to CREEP by Midwest finance chairman Kenneth H.
Dahlberg. This was one of the first direct connections to the Nixon
campaign and started Washington buzzing like a beehive. The article,
of course, did not specify how the reporters had obtained such information, but Carl Bernstein had flown to Miami, where he had whee-
dled the information out of a local FBI agent.

Knowing that such information had to be coming from inside law
enforcement, Nixon went ballistic. Mitchell called Mark Felt, who
was supposed to be trying to plug the FBI leaks, and told him in no

uncertain terms to find the leakers. As would only recently be revealed, since Felt was the leaker himself, the fox had been put in charge of the henhouse.

Sometime in early August, I wrote a letter to Chuck Colson, apologizing for having put him in a difficult position, and, as his employee, thrusting his name into unwanted prominence. I felt worse when my good friend failed to reply.

We didn't know when we'd get time to vacation as a family again, so on August 10, Dorothy and I took Lisa and David to Walt Disney World in Orlando. Then we met the Barkers in Miami and drove down to do a little fishing in Marathon in the Florida Keys. I gazed out at the water, thinking how easy it would be to just put everyone aboard a fishing boat and keep on going. I knew a few little airstrips in the Everglades and Mexico where one of our Cuban friends could land a plane and take us all down to Nicaragua, where I felt certain we would be welcomed by President Samoza. I had broached the idea to Liddy as well, but we decided that such a move, living life on the lam, would eventually turn out to be much more problematic than facing our problems in Washington.

While in Miami, we got a message to call Colson's secretary, Joan Hall. We called from a pay phone along US-1. Joan told me that Chuck had received my letter and wanted me to know that he regarded me as a friend and a loyal, patriotic American, and he was shocked at the recent course of events. I, in turn, told her that I had argued against the second Watergate break-in, but had been over-ruled by Liddy and to relay the message that "my lips would be sealed, even if I had to go to jail."

Colson told her to say that after the election, he would do the best he could do to help me. This gave me a great sense of relief, as it made me think that the situation was being tended to, albeit slowly, at the highest levels of government and that the wheel of fortune would soon be turning in our favor. This is one of the conversations that I would repeatedly perjure myself on during later inquires, as it plainly shows that Colson had basically implied a quid pro quo for my continued silence.

We returned home on August 17, and I resumed my consultations with Bittman. Then, on August 29, I went to one of the DNC lawyers' offices for a deposition. I tried to sneak in, but the press and television corps filling the lobby were like a school of hungry piranhas—and I was bait. The whole place came alive in a frenzy as I tried to get to the elevators. Flashbulbs popped, reporters called my name asking questions, and the whole place turned into a blur for me. After I gave my deposition, I tried to leave by a rear exit, only to find television reporters camped there, as well. Pursued by cameramen and reporters, I walked briskly across the street to the Army and Navy Club, where I dawdled over lunch until the midday news was over and the reporters had dispersed.

Even poor Tony Jackson from Los Angeles and Mañuel Artime, whose name had been found in Barker's address book, were dragged in front of the grand jury. Prosecutors were obviously fishing and casting the widest net imaginable. I joked acidly that next I'd see my first-grade teacher dug up from her grave and her skeleton paraded into the courtroom. Amid this tumult, my daughter Kevan began her sophomore year at Smith, and we sent her off hoping that my problems wouldn't interfere with her studies too much.

The following day, on August 30, Nixon announced that John Dean had completed a Watergate probe and determined that no one from the administration was involved.

On September 15, the seven of us were indicted on multiple counts and compelled to appear at the U.S. courthouse on Capitol Hill for arraignment on the 19. For someone like me, who had spent his life in the shadows, this was a nightmare. The media had multiplied logarithmically, with news crews flying in from across the world. Hundreds of print and television reporters thronged in front of the building, generating a thundering buzz made of whirring 16mm motion picture cameras and the heavy clap of still-camera shutters releasing amid a cacophony of shouted questions and people yelling our names, hoping we would raise our heads so that they could get better shots.

We traipsed into Judge Sirica's courtroom, where we were charged with multiple counts of wiretapping and conspiracy, with my bond set at $10,000, of which I needed to pay $1,000 cash to the courthouse clerk. From then on, I was required to call the bail agency once a week and give a full account of my movements if I planned to do any traveling.

The taps on my telephone line were so obvious that I could hear the eavesdroppers muttering to themselves in the background of the call. And it wasn't cross-talk with another line, as one guy clearly said, "That's Bittman," to another when I was on the phone speaking with my lawyer. Of course, the government denied it was intruding on our private conversations. My attorney fees exceeded the $26,000 retainer, and we were proceeding on financial fumes.

Sirica soon entered a gag order against all sides. But somehow this didn't keep Alfred Baldwin from giving a full account of his activities in the listening post to the *Los Angeles Times*, including information that he had personally delivered transcripts of the intercepted telephone conversations to CREEP headquarters.

I called McCord to complain about Baldwin's disclosures, but surprisingly he defended his partner's conduct, saying that under advisement from his attorney, Baldwin had asked to consult with CREEP lawyers, but they had turned him away, saying they didn't know who he was and didn't know how he was involved with McCord. This reaction, McCord said, freed Baldwin to act on his own. Then he had the gall to ask me when I thought more money would be forthcoming. Angrily, I told him that since Baldwin had violated my orders and taken the van to McCord's home, the van, which McCord had purchased with Gordon Liddy's cash, should be sold if he needed money. I took a breath, calmed down, and finished by saying that I was sure he would not be forgotten.

There were other wheels within wheels turning, as well. McCord struck out into uncharted and dangerous territory by writing mysterious letters to a friend of his in the CIA's Office of Security. Then, in another strategic move, he called the Chilean embassy and requested a visa, identifying himself as a Watergate defendant. This request was not made because he was actually thinking of fleeing the country but because he believed the CIA was tapping the phones of the Chilean embassy; he thought the government would drop his case rather than reveal that they knew he was trying to leave the country through the wiretap. The ruse failed, and the government denied wiretapping the embassy.

Dorothy never liked McCord, saying that he made her feel uneasy. There was just "something wrong" about him, and the less she had to do with him, the better.

About this time, Bittman tried to arrange a deal with U.S. Attorney Silbert, saying that I would give a full account of the events if he would recommend a suspended sentence. Silbert laughed in his face, saying that he didn't need my testimony and was, in fact, going to compel all of us to testify to the grand jury anyway, by immunizing us after our jury trial was finished.

On September 29, a Woodward and Bernstein article reported that while serving as attorney general, John Mitchell had controlled a secret fund used to finance "widespread intelligence-gathering operations" against Democrats. Needless to say, this headline did not come as welcome news to those of us dependent on it, as its revelation would serve to dry up our funds.

My fifty-fourth birthday in the beginning of October was one of the worst of my life, especially when Sirica denied a motion to disqualify himself from presiding over our trial, since, as chief judge, he was also presiding over the Watergate grand jury. This was basically unheard of. Sirica then set a trial date for November 15, scarcely a month away.

On October 15, a Woodward and Bernstein story revealed that Donald Segretti had been paid $20,000 a year to run a White House operation to sabotage various Democratic campaigns. This worried me, as I did not believe that Segretti had the stamina and fortitude to ride out this hellacious storm.

On October 20, I told Bittman about my call to Colson, saying that I would love to get my lawyer the money he deserved but that I didn't feel it was in my best interest to sell or mortgage my home to meet the defense costs. Instead, I would rather face trial without an attorney than deprive my family of a home or mortgage my children's future.

The money stream had dried up, with no word from Mr. Rivers for some time. On October 22, Dorothy called Joan Hall to ask Colson to find out what was happening. Hall told her to call back a couple of days later, but when she did, there was no answer. We thought we were being thrown to the wolves, but then we received a call from Mr. Rivers, who told Dorothy that he would call her on the following day.

The next day, on the advice of his physician, Sirica postponed the impending trial until January 8, 1973, which was, we guessed, something positive. Dorothy waited fruitlessly for Mr. Rivers. There was no further news from him until a telephone call on the thirtieth, with a man's voice saying he was a friend of Mr. Rivers's and wanted to speak to "the writer's wife." So contact was resumed.

That week, when I was at Bittman's office one evening, a package of money was delivered. I don't remember how much was there, but it was hardly enough to pay the attorney's fees, and there was nothing left over to support my family, much less for Liddy, McCord, and the Miami men.

On November 7, President Nixon swept to a landslide victory. We thought this was great, as all our mistakes had not jeopardized the campaign, and we hoped that the president's continued reign would mean that our case would somehow be controlled. Instead, the opposite happened.

The day after the election, I accompanied Bittman and Mittler to the U.S. courthouse, where I was allowed to examine evidence that had been confiscated from my White House safe. To my surprise, my operational notebook, files, and telephone list were not among the seized material.

This material was sufficient for my conviction, but any documents that could have been used to construct my defense were missing: namely, my operational notebooks, telephone lists, and documents recording the details of Gemstone from its inception. While the notebook did not specify Mitchell, Dean, and Magruder by name, they could be inferred from Liddy's "principals." Bittman asked Silbert if he was holding more seized material in another location, but the prosecutor claimed this was everything that had been found.

Dorothy now began to complain about the position that Mr. Rivers had put her in—not for involving her but for not coming up with enough money to help out all of the people involved. It was she who had to call the families and tell them that needed funds hadn't arrived—fund amounts that had never fulfilled the initial commitments, anyway. She was now dealing with a "friend" of Mr. Rivers's, and she was worried that with the election won, the White House would no longer feel obligated to live up to its assurances. Moreover, she felt that because she was a woman, her arguments were falling on deaf ears. She suggested that I call Colson and tell him what was happening. On instructions from Mr. Rivers, she had given specific financial promises to the Miami defendants, but the money had never been fully paid, and their lawyers were starting to grumble.

Accordingly, I made an appointment through his secretary and called Colson from a pay phone. After a few minutes of initial pleasantries, congratulating him on the president's victory, I attempted to present a few facts, but he cut me off, saying that the only way he could be of any assistance to me was if he stayed apart from the imbroglio; he did not want to know any more, because he did not want to be put in a position of perjuring himself.

"Well, John Mitchell has already done that," I told him, referring to the fact that the attorney general had already gone before the grand jury and testified that he knew nothing about Watergate. I then went on to explain that certain "commitments" had been made and that they had only been partially kept, and now the money was coming in small dribs and drabs. Kenneth Parkinson, CREEP's attorney and our current go-between, was becoming increasingly less effective in getting us the needed funds.

I explained our present situation, adding that I hoped that now that the election was over, the powers-that-be could concentrate on the fates of the Watergate defendants. I informed him that despite all assurances—some of which had been met—financial support was in dire arrears, leaving high legal fees unpaid. I believed that the seven of us had behaved manfully and remarked that this was a "two-way street"; that money could be replaced, but the men—the defendants—couldn't and should not be considered expendable. Money was sorely needed for the support of families and to pay for legal defenses.

At one point, Dorothy had suggested that I write a memorandum to Kenneth Parkinson, summarizing the financial needs of all seven men. I had not done so yet, but I told Colson that I was planning to write such a memo and "lay it on Parkinson" in the near future. I expressed hope that a week or ten days should be sufficient time for Liddy's principals to make up the arrears.

This conversation and the memo I subsequently wrote would all come to haunt me later, becoming part of the great Watergate mythos. My argument was later constituted to be a "blackmail" demand, and the memo I wrote would go down in history as the "Parkinson memo," one of the smoking guns that would lead to the conviction of Mitchell, Ehrlichman, and Magruder.

Colson was cagey, arguing that he had not been involved, was not involved, and did not want to be involved. Somehow, he said, his non-involvement would be of more assistance to me than if he tried to come to my aid. It wasn't until later that I would find out the reason for his strange behavior: Colson taped the call and had it transcribed—I guess as some kind of proof of his innocence. Right then, however, it sounded like complete nonsense, and I hung up feeling that the White House had not only thrown us to the wolves but basted us so that we would be a more tasty treat.

Ten days later, the monetary stream was still as dry as Death Valley. McCord called Dorothy for a meeting, but she was unable to give him much hope that the principals had any concern about us. She returned home saying that McCord had taken the news calmly and seemed strangely resigned to the devolving situation.

Behind the scenes: On November 11, Carl Bernstein interviewed Segretti, who confessed that Gordon Liddy and I were behind the dirty tricks campaign against the Democratic Party. By the fifteenth, Nixon, Colson, Haldeman, and Ehrlichman were sequestered at Camp David, discussing my latest "blackmail threat." A decision was made to keep funding us for the time being. On the twentieth, Nixon summoned Richard Helms to Camp David and demanded his resignation from the CIA for failing to suppress the FBI investigation. On December 1, John Mitchell told John Dean to get a portion of $350,000, acquired from CREEP treasurer Hugh Sloan, to pay our arrears. The money was delivered to Frank LeRue to be sent down the food chain through "Mr. Rivers."

On December 4, all defense lawyers met at Bittman's office for a pretrial strategy meeting. I saw Bernie for the first time in a while and told him that Dorothy and I were going to take the children to Key West before Christmas. He said that he and his wife might join us for a day or two.

On the seventh, I received a threatening letter from McCord, accusing me of planting news stories that charged him with being the recruiter of the Miami men. I took it over to Bittman, who said he had received a similar telegram from the unstable McCord but had refused to accept it, saying anyone could have signed it. Barker's attorneys had also received a similar message, giving everyone jitters as we tried to interpret the significance of this enigmatic new development.

Meanwhile, Dorothy and I had been discussing our shaky financial future and decided to make a $10,000 investment in a company controlled by Dorothy's cousin-in-law, Hal Carlstead, who operated two Holiday Inns in Chicago, with a third under construction. Our investment was obviously small, but it was a bit of a Hail Mary pass, as I hadn't drawn a paycheck in six months and, after all this negative publicity, did not feel as if my prospects for future employment could be described as anything but grim. The investment, we hoped, would lead to a paying position after my trial.

With the Christmas season in full swing, Dorothy suggested that she fly to her cousin's home in suburban Chicago and deliver the money, along with various Christmas presents for the family. She called United Airlines to make a reservation. Finding out there were no economy-class tickets available, she turned to me from the phone, asking, "Could I travel first class, Papa, just this once?"

"Of course," I answered. "I don't even know why you bothered to ask."

I had been working on a spy novel, *The Berlin Ending*, for some months, and I was having some problems with a suitable ending. Dorothy, who had been reading and typing up the final manuscript, had finally come to the end of the book the morning of the eighth, the day that I drove her to National Airport.

"The way you have it," she said, "the good guys win. But Howard, you know it isn't always the way in real life. More often than not, the good guys lose—so why not end it that way?"

"What are your ideas?"

"Well, the girl, for one thing. The hero doesn't get the girl. And the villain, well, he gets away. That's how I'd end it if I were you." She smiled. "Besides, if you don't do it that way, I won't type it for you."

"That's the clinching argument," I said with a chuckle, as I drove up to the United Airlines entrance. "Shall I come in?"

She said that she wanted to do some shopping in the concourse to pick up some last-minute gifts. We kissed good-bye and the skycap picked up her bags. This was a familiar scene, as we had said countless airport good-byes since that first time at Charles de Gaulle Airport so many years before when the unintelligible French announcer had called my plane. It seemed of no special significance. She waved, I waved back, and she entered the doors of the airline ticket office. Once inside, she did her shopping, and, apparently as an afterthought, she bought $250,000 in accident insurance from an airport vending machine.

I drove home pondering Dorothy's idea about the ending and liked it more and more. So when I got home, I went straight to my study and started rewriting the ending, staying engrossed in the work for a few hours, until I heard David running down the stairs and realized he was home from school.

"Papa, Papa!" he called, running to my desk.

This was no happy child, though. "What's the matter?"

"Papa, in the car radio coming home, I heard that Mama's plane crashed and she's dead!"

I took a quick glance at my watch, seeing that Dorothy's plane should have landed in Chicago by now. Frantically, I dialed Phyllis Carlstead. "There's been a crash at Midway Airport," I said when she answered. "Is Dorothy all right? Is she with you?"

Her voice was strained. "Oh, Howard, Hal's at the airport, and he just called. There's been a crash, and he thinks it's Dorothy's plane. He said he'd call back."

"Can you call the airport and find out what's happened?"

"I'll try, dear. Oh, Howard, this is awful!"

"I'm going to start for the airport here," I told her, hung up, then dialed United Airlines, but the lines were busy. Helplessly, I stared at David, who turned and strode toward the steps, starting to sob. I hurried after him, snatched him into my arms, and carried him upstairs, trying to comfort him. My heart and mind were rocked by the news, and I had to join my son in grief. Unquenchable tears fell from my eyes, I broke down sobbing, and David, in turn, tried to comfort me. He looked up at me, drying his tears and patting my arm consolingly. I kissed his forehead and hugged him. I would never see him cry again.

I turned on the radio and told the servants what had happened. Kevan called from college. I told her that I was leaving for Chicago, and she said she was coming home. I left David in the charge of Lisa and St. John, who could hardly see through their own tears, and began driving through a heavy rainstorm toward National Airport, not knowing whether my wife was dead, alive, or injured. Her seat was in the first-class section at the front of the plane, I told myself, and she might have survived anything but a nose-first crash. For a second, all the close calls I had had with airplane crashes over the years spun through my head. It seemed like whatever fate I had avoided all those times had decided that if it couldn't get me, it would get someone I loved.

The rain slowed traffic to a maddening crawl, and when I finally reached the airport, the United Airlines concourse was awash in worried relatives. I identified myself to a service agent and asked for a seat on the next flight to Chicago. While he made arrangements, I called home, then our cousins in Chicago, learning that a morgue had been set up in a nearby hangar, where attempts were being made to identify the bodies. Hal was there now, and Phyllis, manning the telephone at home, had not yet heard from him, giving her a slim hope that Dorothy had survived.

We landed at Midway after dark. From the air, you could see burning embers being doused by fire engines at the edge of the field, with police car lights flashing across the darkness. Hal was waiting for me as I got off the plane.

"I don't know yet, Howard," he said before I could speak. "There are too many bodies, and most of them are burned beyond recognition."

"What about the injured?"

"They've been taken to hospitals. No one knows where they are."

United Airlines agents said the best thing we could do was go home, where they would call us with any new information, as there was nothing else we could do. At the Carlstead home, Phyllis and I embraced tearfully. She was hit as hard as I was, as she and Dorothy had been raised almost as sisters, and she was the only one in the world who knew Dorothy better than I did. We called the airline all night long but could not gather any further information, so we finally fell asleep with the lingering hope that Dorothy was one of the lucky survivors who had been taken to a hospital, and we might find her alive the next day.

In the morning, however, there was still little additional information. Few of the dead had been identified, nor had many of the injured.

At midday, an attorney partner of Hal's joined us. I told them that Dorothy was traveling with $10,000 in cash for the investment and probably had another $700 in her purse. He suggested practically that I sketch some of the jewelry that she had been wearing, such as her wedding ring, family signet ring, engagement ring, and finally a large solitaire diamond that had been my mother's.

During the miserable wait, Phyllis sadly telephoned guests who had been invited to a party for Dorothy, canceling the affair. I was unable to eat, could barely sleep, and had uncontrollable outbursts of weeping. I was unable to tell my children at home whether their mother was dead or alive. Their highly emotional states reverberated inside me, magnifying my own already unimaginable fear and sorrow.

Toward midafternoon, we rode over to the Cook County morgue with the sketches I had made of Dorothy's jewelry. It was an interminable ride through a grim, wintry dusk to the hulking, solitary building, where we identified ourselves and sat down for a lengthy wait. Finally, an unsmiling clerk returned holding a plastic bag, emptying several pieces of scattered jewelry unceremoniously across the surface of the table.

I stared at the blackened pieces with bile surging in my throat and tears clawing my eyes. Everything I had sketched was there—except my mother's diamond solitaire, presumably stolen. I focused on Dorothy's wedding ring, picked it up, and held the cold metal in my hand. Ashes dropped from it, leaving black smudges on my hand. It felt so final. Her charm bracelet had been half melted from the heat, though her signet ring appeared unharmed.

The functionary's voice was unsympathetic. "Can you identify these, Mr. Hunt?"

I choked on my words and could only nod agreement. The man turned to another worker and said, "That takes care of body eighteen." He slipped a form in front of me to sign. "Where was she born?" he asked me. "What year?"

But I couldn't answer, forcing Phyllis to give him the information.

That night, reports that my wife was carrying $10,000 in hundred-dollar bills spewed across radio and television airwaves, catching me completely unprepared for the level of innuendo and insinuation that followed. The FBI checked the bills' serial numbers against lists they had created when cataloging all the bills that had been paid to Barker in return for the Mexican checks, but no connection was established, as these were not CREEP funds but rainy-day money that we had put away over the years. One of the bills happened to have the words "Good Luck, Frank" written across it, which was interpreted by the press to be a reference to Frank Sturgis, one of the arrested Miami men. This money would form the core of conspiracy theories that would spin and grow for a generation.

Dorothy was an extremely resourceful individual, and it is possible that she could have taken matters into her own hands without my knowledge. There are stories that she was meeting with CBS reporter Michelle Clark, who was also a passenger on the flight. Also aboard the plane were a number of political people who had ties to Watergate figures such as Attorney General John Mitchell—not too strange, considering the plane was flying from Washington, the capital of the United States, to Chicago, the capital of American unionism.

One journalist wrote that Dorothy and I were a CIA couple who had information connecting Nixon to the assassination of John F. Kennedy, and we were planning to flee the country with $2 million in cash, which we were going to invest with fugitive investor Robert Vesco. While my lawyer would later report to me after Dorothy's death that she had once told him rather emphatically, "Howard is never going to go to jail," this tale is, as far as I know, completely inaccurate. If we'd had $2 million, I would have hired the best attorney in the United States to represent me, and we would have planned to appeal the case on a host of Judge Sirica's strange courtroom antics.

In addition, if we had owned such blockbuster material, I would have revealed it immediately, despite my former admiration for the president. The theory is also ridiculous because if we had been so inclined to use the information against the White House, we certainly wouldn't have been so stupid as not to have made and retained photocopies in a safe place before Dorothy boarded an airplane with the originals. Also, I'm quite sure that if we had had such outrageous information in our possession, the White House would never have been late on a single payment!

21

After the Crash

L ooking at myself in the mirror, shaving only because it was
something I had done almost every day of my life, I saw sunken
cheeks and dark circles under empty, defeated eyes. I'd seen junkies
and near-dead men who looked like they had more flame in their soul
than I did. Flying back to Washington, I felt like a piñata in the shape
of a man, someone who had been battered until his insides spilled out,
leaving only a sorrowful and empty shell.

Depression crept into what was left of me, making me realize that
I could not stand the stress of a lengthy trial, now less than a month
away. I was also convinced that the only exculpatory evidence that I
had—from which I could prove that I was acting in good faith, directed
from above—had been spirited away by the higher powers (in fact, it
would later be revealed that John Dean and acting FBI director
L. Patrick Gray *had* destroyed the material). I decided to plead guilty
in the hope that "Sirica Maxima" would give me a lenient sentence.

I have little recollection of my homecoming or the next few days,
but my daughters, even in this low tide of their young lives, showed
amazing character and fortitude, taking over the house, filling it with
friends, relatives, and sympathetic visitors. To my surprise, even
James McCord stopped by to express his condolences.

Worried that the FBI might sweep into my house with a search
warrant, I gathered up all the incriminating material I could to dispose

of it. I packaged all of Dorothy's notes, containing memos about financial disbursements to the Miami men and other related material, and gave them to my daughter Kevan. I didn't tell her the contents of the material, only to "take it away and burn it." Luckily, she was unable to destroy her mother's papers and failed to heed my instructions, taking the envelope with her back to Smith, where she taped it behind her dorm-room bookshelf.

I would have done the dirty deed myself but had been equally disturbed to burn my wife's notes, and I also knew that I could not allow myself to be spotted in the act by investigators or reporters who might be following me. Still, on one dark night, I drove out to a bridge and heaved the typewriter I had used to forge the Kennedy/Diem cables into the Potomac.

When I came up for air, I informed my attorney of my intention to plead guilty, which was met with strange indifference and no efforts to dissuade me. Bittman said he would inform the prosecutors and see if the electronic charges could be dropped.

We buried my wife of twenty-three years, three months, and one day in a small Catholic cemetery near our home. Anybody who has lost a loved one knows the misery of throwing that first shovelful of dirt against the coffin. Still, I stayed as strong as I could for the children, who were shortly to be virtually orphaned, without a mother and without a father, should I go to jail. I could only imagine how afraid they were for their futures. After the funeral, I took our four children to visit their mother's cousin in Largo, Florida, for the holidays, as staying in our home over Christmas would have required more strength than I had at the time.

Bittman was so alarmed by my depression that he summoned me back to Washington to undergo physical and psychiatric evaluation. And while my doctor of many years concluded that I was not healthy enough to go to court, government physicians declared otherwise, and I was ordered to appear at the federal district court on Monday, January 8, 1973, one month to the day after Dorothy's death. My decision to plead guilty caused a sensation among my codefendants, and Bernie flew up to Washington a few days before the trial.

"What else can I do?" I asked him dolefully. "They have everything in the safe that incriminates me, and everything that would have substantiated a defense that I was following orders from above is missing. If I fight the charges and lose, the judge will hit me like a

Mack truck. I'll be roadkill on the Sirica Highway. If I plead guilty, I may get a minor sentence or even probation."

"I see you're depressed," Barker told me. "But what about us? You're pleading guilty and weren't even arrested. The five of us were caught red-handed in the office, and I haven't been able to find out yet from our attorney what our defense is going to be. He tells us he's a law technician, and he'll get the judge so mad that he'll commit reversible errors and we can have the case thrown out on appeal." Barker looked at me with questioning eyes. "Does that make sense to you?"

I sighed and sat down in a chair with my head in my hands, hating the fact that my actions would make it harder for Barker and the others. "I don't know enough about law to even guess," I told him finally. "Besides, my situation is different from yours. I've got four children to take care of, Bernie, and if I go to prison, I'd rather spend the last few weeks with them rather than in a courtroom every day. I've got to provide for their future, and there's no way I can do it with so many other things on my mind."

Accordingly, I sent a letter to Colson, dated December 31, 1972:

> Dear Chuck,
> The children and myself were touched by your letters, and we deeply appreciate your sympathy. I am unable to reconcile myself to Dorothy's death, much less accept it. For years I depended on Dorothy, but only now do I realize how profound that dependence was. Her death, of course, changes my personal equation entirely, and I believe that my paramount duty now and in the future is to my children, particularly to my nine-year-old son, who was unusually dependent on his mother, particularly since last June's tumult began.
> I had understood you to say that you would be willing to see my attorney, Bill Bittman, at any time. After my wife's death, I asked him to see you, but his efforts were unavailing. And though I believe I understand the delicacy of your overt position, I nevertheless feel myself even more isolated than before. My wife's death, the imminent trial, my present situation, all contribute to a sense of abandonment by friends on whom I had in good faith relied. I can't tell you how important it is, under the circumstances, for Bill Bittman to have the opportunity to meet with you, and I trust that you will do me that favor.
> There is a limit to the endurance of any man trapped in a hostile situation, and mine was reached on December 8. I do believe in God—not necessarily a Just God, but in the governance of a Divine

Being. His Will, however, is often enacted through human hands, and human adversaries are arraigned against me.

Sincerely, and in friendship,

E. Howard

I wanted Colson to allow my attorney to meet with him so that he could explain the reasons for my guilty plea and ask for help in saving my CIA pension, which the prosecutors were trying to terminate. Bittman also needed to discuss our motion to obtain the contents of my White House safe that were missing. Without the documents, it was hopeless to proceed with anything but a guilty plea, so we had to find out if the White House would fight us and make it necessary for us to file a motion to suppress all of the safe's contents. Most important, the principal reason for the meeting was to confront Colson about getting the White House to do something in relation to the intolerable charges against me.

In due course, Bittman was received in Colson's office, where they discussed the matters at hand. Colson explained to my lawyer that "they" had discussed my guilty plea and decided that given my exemplary character, my long years of government service, and my recent bereavement, it was "their" joint consensus that I would probably receive a relatively light sentence, possibly even probation, and in the event of a longer sentence, "Well, Christmas comes around every year."

This was the type of subtlety and care that was often invoked. The words sound innocuous, but they contained a specific reference to the prior prosecution by Bill Bittman of Teamster boss Jimmy Hoffa, who had been paroled at Christmastime approximately two years earlier. It was generally known that Colson was the man behind the scenes who arranged Hoffa's pardon.

I would later find out that Colson had indeed expected to live up to his promise, because when the White House recordings were revealed, Nixon told Colson during one tape-recorded conversation that it would be easy to make excuses for my pardon, given that my wife had been killed.

To me that meant that even if I went to jail, under any sentence, I could look forward to an executive intervention by Christmas 1973. This simple statement would play a vitally important part in the way I conducted myself over the ensuing months of grand jury and subcommittee investigations.

The motion to suppress the safe's contents was also significant because anybody who had touched the safe in the White House might be called into court to state his connection with it. We thought this was putting the thumb screws on Colson. In reality, it was Dean and L. Patrick Gray who had gotten a group of bully boys together and taken my loaded safe down to the basement of the White House, where they had attacked it with mallets and sledgehammers to open it up. All they had to do, if it was a legitimate opening—and in this case, even I had to admit it was—was have the Secret Service representative either give Dean the combination or open the safe himself. That was a great example of amateur overkill. I suppose they did not want the Secret Service to witness the event.

After researching the issues, Colson informed us that the White House was taking the position that I had abandoned my office and safe; therefore, the White House had every reason to enter and appropriate my abandoned property. Their argument was unfounded, as I had never resigned or been fired from my position as a White House consultant, had visited my office frequently, and still retained my White House pass, which the Secret Service never requested me to return.

Colson added that he would continue to be my friend and would help me in any way he could in a personal capacity, even taking my children into his home should that be necessary. Colson was the king of nice words, however, and the full extent of his help would amount to sending an unsolicited letter to my probation officer, who was conducting my presentence investigation.

Thinking about it, I realized that Colson had not even bothered to attend Dorothy's funeral, deputizing Joan Hall to make the appearance in his stead, sending only a short handwritten letter of sympathy. While I appreciated the precarious position he was in, I was also aware that our "friendship" would not survive much more inclement weather.

My guilty plea had a domino effect, causing Barker and the Miami men to fall after me. Barker called me, saying his attorney was resisting the change and wanted to discuss it further, but I couldn't give him advice either way. The difficult decision was theirs alone.

"What about our financial support?" he wanted to know. "Will it continue if we're in prison?"

"I hope so," I responded. "I can only go on the fact that the promises they made have been reasonably well honored."

Behind the scenes: To back up my statement, the always reliable Jack Ander-
son reported on January 6, 1973, that I had arranged for the defendants to
be paid $1,000 a month during whatever prison sentences they would receive.
While an extremely nice promise, he was much more sure of it than I was, as
it was news to me.

On Sunday, the day before the trial, my depression seemed to
lighten a bit. My family had gone through a tragedy and no doubt
would face some difficulties ahead. But I also realized that Dorothy
would never have wanted me to give up, so I determined to forge
ahead as if she were still standing behind me. It was good I came to
that realization, because Sirica entered the ring with a one-two punch
designed to knock me out in the first round.

Bittman called, his voice like a doctor telling a patient that he has
a fatal disease: "When Silbert told Sirica about your plea deal, he
went crazy, saying, 'If Hunt wants to plead guilty, let him plead guilty
to everything.'"

Sirica had dealt a few heavy body blows, and there was nothing I
could do but fall down, pleading guilty to all seven counts. We hoped
a quick capitulation would turn into leniency if it was done before
prosecutors submitted their indictment. But Sirica wasn't content to
be a judge. He wanted to be prosecutor and jury as well. Even many
of the nation's most liberal law experts have written that what was
soon to transpire was not only a blow to me but to the American justice system, starting with, according to Douglas Caddy, the prosecutorial team's alteration of the transcripts of the grand jury investigation.

Monday morning before the trial, I gave myself a close shave,
careful not to nick myself as I often did, and put on my best, freshly
dry-cleaned suit, a spotless shirt with starched collar, and a new
business-looking tie. Today, they'd call it my power suit. For my children and friends, who would no doubt see my face splashed across the
news, I did not want to look like the pathetic creature I felt like.

A moist, bitter wind blew from the north, with accompanying
overcast skies that could easily have made me feel suicidal if I had
allowed the depression to set in. Bittman and Mittler walked beside
me, elbowing reporters and cameramen out of our path, expertly
negotiating me to the ceremonial courtroom on the fourth floor. I
took my place with the other defendants and our attorneys at the
enormous old wooden table that looked as if it had been crafted dur-

ing Colonial times, and I wondered how many people had sat behind it waiting to hear their fate.

The people in the courtroom rose when Chief Judge John Sirica strode up to the bench at 10:00 a.m., then banged his gavel to bring the court into session. Bittman approached the bench, stating that I wished to change my plea to guilty. Sirica brushed it off, saying he would not entertain any deviation from set procedure until the jury had been selected and the prosecution had outlined its case. It was obvious that he was basking in the limelight and had no desire to have it turned off prematurely.

Unfortunately, this would be the first of many courtroom skirmishes that would go against me over the ensuing eleven months. As if some preternatural knowledge of the future had been revealed to me, a chill settled on my skin like a cold, wet cloth. The courtroom was filled with semifamiliar faces of television reporters and journalists who had been camping out near my house, salted with the friendly faces of the Miami men's relatives and, of course, the stoic federal marshals who guarded the door.

I guessed what was happening here was important to my future, but I still had trouble focusing on it. I was pleading guilty, and the machinations of the court just weren't important. Instead, in my mind, I ran through a series of chores and other matters pertaining to my children, which had to be attended to. Barker said he was still having trouble with his lawyer, who did not want the men to plead guilty.

"Bernie," I said, "you know I can't tell you what to do, but you saw what happened in court this morning. Sirica not only repudiated the agreement Silbert made with Bittman, but he's twisting the knife by refusing to let me plead guilty until after the government's presented its case. That makes it look as though I didn't decide to plead guilty until I was overwhelmed by what Silbert intends to prove."

"I heard it," Bernie said. "But I guess I really didn't understand what was going on. Bad, huh?"

"It's certainly not good!"

The rest of the day was spent in the dreary process of jury selection, featuring a seemingly endless line of faces of people who really didn't want to be there. Gratefully, the court recessed at about 4:35 p.m., and my attorneys and I shoved our way through the mobs of reporters. I went to Bittman's office, where we discussed all of Sirica's negative directives for the day before I drove home.

If anyone had asked, I would have told them there was little that could bring a smile to my face that day, but that night Mañuel Artime visited to give his support and reassurance, doing the best he could to comfort my children. Over the next year, he would prove his mettle, remaining an ever-reliable friend, as close as a blood brother, for whom I would be deeply grateful.

At this point, I found out that Jack Anderson's information was indeed correct and received assurances from the powers above that if the boys all pled guilty and kept quiet, the White House would provide for their families while they were in prison. I met with the Miami men at the Arlington Towers Hotel to tell them the good news.

A jury was finally seated on Tuesday, Janury 9, with proceedings resuming on Wednesday, whereupon Silbert began presenting the government's case. He showed blowups of the Watergate complex, along with renderings of DNC floor plans, then itemized a list of evidence that had been captured at the scene, such as the photographic and electronic equipment. After all was said and done, Sirica finally allowed me to enter my plea of guilty.

One of the problems with the ensuing trials began right then, as Sirica became personally involved in questioning, interrupting the proceedings to ask me about my involvement in the case. My attorney protested, explaining that such questions should have been addressed at the grand jury, which had handed down the indictments.

Sirica looked as if he had suddenly tasted something sour, then announced that he would consider the matter overnight. In the morning, after opening the court, he declared that he was accepting my plea on all seven counts and instantly proved his vindictiveness by ordering me jailed in lieu of a $100,000 cash bond. He added that he would want to know the source of any monies that might be raised for such a bond, implying that he would do his best to prove it was dirty money and thus unacceptable.

A bond of that size, in cash rather than in collateral, as was customary, seemed a gratuitous slap in the face. It was unprecedented except in murder cases.

Marshals grabbed me by the arms and led me into a small elevator reserved for a select group—prisoners. Taken below, I was frisked, fingerprinted, handcuffed, photographed, and booked, finally being brought into a holding cell with a metal bench—the felony tank. The marshal removed my handcuffs, leaving me alone for the first time in jail.

The cell had one of its desired effects, seeming to suck out my life energy, replacing it with a deadly fatigue. I rolled up my coat for a pillow and lay down on the cold, hard bench, taking a look at my desolate surroundings. There was a bare washbasin and a seatless toilet surrounded by piss-yellow-colored tile. As ugly as it was, as much as I hated it at that moment, this place would prove to be the largest and cleanest of any of the cells in the various jails and penitentiaries in which I was imprisoned over the next year.

Law enforcement would be glad to know that I thought back to the moment when Liddy first approached me in the White House, telling me about the attorney general's desire to establish the program Gemstone and its ensuing consequences that had ended here in this cell. That's what punishment is supposed to make you do—repent. And it did so here, though I still felt like we had done the wrong things for the right reasons—trying to determine if foreign Communists were trying to influence U.S. elections. To this day, it is publicly unknown whether this is true, as Watergate and the cover-up overshadowed the causes for the operation. Still, with Nixon's proven paranoia, I think it can pretty much be considered a figment of his imagination.

My mind was chaos for a while, with a thousand fragments of thoughts smashing against one another, each one seemingly more important than the other—what would happen to my children, our home, my friends, their families, the president? And on and on. Then suddenly a weird sense of peace descended on me, and I fell asleep.

The sound of keys rattling in the lock woke me up. The hearty voice of the first friendly marshal I had met so far said, "Wake up, Mr. Hunt. Your lawyer is here."

I sat up, taking a minute to realize where I was.

"Are you okay, Mr. Hunt?"

My back was stiff and my mouth dry, but I muttered that I was okay. I put on my coat and followed the marshal down the hall to meet Bittman, Mittler, and their company's notary in the interview room.

"Howard," Bittman said, "we'll have you out of here in a little while. Just sign these checks from Dorothy's insurance proceeds. We'll deposit them to a joint account with the surety company. After that's done, we'll go with you to the clerk's office and you'll be released."

With all the technicalities out of the way and the appropriate papers signed, I was soon released until sentencing. Even at this later hour, the press was massed in front of the courthouse. Microphones jabbed in my direction, flashbulbs exploded in my eyes, and bright camera lights centered on me as the press pleaded with me to make a statement.

Squinting painfully into the lights after four hours in a dim cell, I thanked them for the opportunity and said, "Anything I may have done, I did for what I believed to be in the best interests of my country." Then I stepped back from the microphones.

"That's all there is," Bittman told them, then took me by the arm and guided me to a waiting car.

Sentencing was scheduled for March 23, so I had a couple of months of freedom before my life would take another turn for the worse.

22

Sentencing

The next several weeks were tumultuous. I tried to spend as much time with my four children as possible, but I gave a few brief interviews to *Time* and other publications, made an appearance on Bill Buckley's *Firing Line*, though not about Watergate, met my probation officer, and started tidying up my affairs for a long absence, not knowing how long a jail term the unpredictable Sirica might hand down. From the beginning, there had been attempted malfeasance by the judge and prosecutors, and it continued, with my probation officer, Frank Saunders, apparently deputized by the court to try to wheedle more Watergate information out of me, although he was unsuccessful.

The days flickered by like white striping on a highway. After a three-day trial and a brief deliberation, the Watergate jury found Gordon Liddy and James McCord guilty of six and eight counts, respectively. Despite the convictions, the Senate voted unanimously to establish a select committee to investigate the Watergate break-in and the related dirty tricks campaign tactics that surrounded it. Bittman assured me it was inevitable that I would be called as a witness, though he couldn't know when. Also, on Bittman's advice, I hired a Chicago attorney to represent my wife's estate in suing United Airlines for her wrongful death. Since I was now a convicted felon, stripped of many legal rights, I would be unable to remain executor of her estate, so Bill Buckley kindly filled the role.

The Miami contingent fired their lawyer, who refused to allow them to enter a guilty plea, and did so with a court-appointed lawyer on January 15. They were sent to D.C. Jail, notorious as one of the worst in the country, to await sentencing.

President Richard M. Nixon was duly inaugurated for his second term on January 20, 1973. I was not invited to the inauguration festivities, but Mañuel Artime was. While I can't say I was happy at this point, I felt that at least my actions had not been in vain and that the president would have four more years to get the country back on track.

Recent revelations show that at this time reporter Bob Woodward was receiving a lot of leads from FBI deputy director Mark "Deep Throat" Felt, who on January 24 relayed the information that Charles Colson and John Mitchell had instigated the Watergate operation. That was erroneous, as Colson had nothing to do with it, but the report got the facts mostly right.

On February 7, the Senate voted to create the Select Committee on Presidential Campaign Activities, a panel that I would come to know intimately. Then, on the tenth, the *Washington Post* kindly revealed that I had been investigating Edward Kennedy during the summer of 1972. As my sentencing was coming up the following month, these continued revelations couldn't do anything but harm my chances for probation.

On February 17, the president nominated L. Patrick Gray, who had dutifully helped the administration as much as he could so far, as permanent director of the FBI, subject to Senate confirmation. Senator Byrd was opposed to the confirmation because of the bureau's alleged failure to investigate the Watergate case. That day, I wrote the nominee a somewhat scathing letter, saying that I would be happy to be a witness testifying on his behalf that:

> The Bureau left no grain of sand unturned in its investigation. My late wife and children were interrogated, blackmailed, threatened and harassed by Special Agents of the Bureau. . . . My relatives, friends, acquaintances, however remote, were interviewed exhaustively and embarrassingly by FBI personnel across the country, their inquiries extending as far back as my primary school days. Threats and intimidation were not the least of the investigative tools employed by SAs under your direction.
>
> For whatever assistance the above might be to you in realizing your professional desire of being confirmed in your present post,

feel free to utilize it. Should the occasion arise during my projected appearance before the Ervin Sub-Committee, I will be eager to make the thoroughness and savagery of the FBI's Watergate investigation a matter of public record.

While this letter was obviously a futile exercise, simply venting some internal pressure before it led to a heart attack or brain death was worthwhile. L. Patrick Gray would, in fact, turn from Nixonian lapdog to attack dog, biting the hand that had fed him. On February 28, Sam Ervin arrived at Gray's nomination hearing carrying a folder of newspaper articles about Watergate. This was not supposed to be a Watergate hearing, and it took Gray by surprise when Ervin began questioning what the acting FBI director knew about the cover-up.

Gray must have been harboring a deep sense of guilt, as without much provocation, he stated that he had relayed confidential reports and discussed the ongoing investigation with John Dean. Needless to say, his nomination to head the FBI failed, and Dean was now directly linked to the cover-up.

Despite my guilty plea, legal fees were mounting and would continue to escalate during the coming subcommittee hearing. We weren't destitute, thanks to Dorothy's insurance settlement, but I did not feel as if her blood money should be going to pay my legal fees. That money was needed to pay a governess to come live with the family in Washington during my absence, pay the mortgage, insurance, college tuition for both daughters, and private school tuition for David. Two hundred fifty thousand dollars would not go far. I felt as if the principals needed to get their act together and make due on their promises. I was never privy to the total support money provided so far but was later stunned by John Dean's admission that he had used some of it for his honeymoon.

No further payments had been made since Dorothy's death, and there had been no further contact with Mr. Rivers. Therefore, I asked Bittman to arrange a meeting with CREEP counsel Paul O'Brien so that we could review the financial situation, O'Brien having been the official whom we had first approached when Dorothy had returned from Europe.

O'Brien and I met in early March. I explained to him that Mr. Rivers's funds had never been enough to meet the original figures that had been agreed to and that the debt was steadily mounting.

Now that I was going to prison rather than testify against the higher-ups, I hoped funds would be forthcoming. While I didn't know if he was privy to the entire story of seamy affairs—alluding to but not naming the Fielding break-in, forging State Department cables, and Donald Segretti—since he was the sole remaining contact with the source of funds, I had no one else to go to. But in regarding said affairs, I was deserving of support, and if the White House was going to abandon me, I would have "no recourse but to consider my options."

O'Brien told me that he would relay my conversation but said that I should write a memo to Colson. This suggestion was surprising, as Colson had never been the conduit to Mitchell as had O'Brien.

"Why should I do that?" I asked.

"Because some of us feel it's time that Colson got his feet into it—got his feet wet like the rest of us," O'Brien said snidely.

I later told Bittman what O'Brien had said. I did not think it was wise to put my words into writing, so Bittman made an appointment for me with Colson's law partner, David Shapiro, on March 16. I was under the impression that this was going to be a thinly disguised way for me to achieve a face-to-face meeting with Colson, who would magically appear at the meeting through a back door, but Shapiro declared that he was acting as Colson's attorney, and I should state my business. His manner seemed arrogant and offensive, and I told him that I had expected to see Chuck and not a surrogate. Shapiro's manner softened, and he said that Colson admired me and wanted to help any way he could in a private capacity. But I had had my fill of this coy nonsense and told him in no uncertain terms that our payments needed to be made.

Shapiro did not want to hear anything about payments, but I insisted on telling him that I wanted two years of family support plus legal fees in hand before my sentencing on March 23. Shapiro grimaced but said he would pass along such parts of the conversation as he saw fit. My temper boiled over, and I shouted at him that he should pass along the entire conversation or none of it; that between my attorney's fees and two years of expenses, I felt that I was owed $120,000.

"Tell him that I can bring John Ehrlichman to his knees," I spat at him. "If I reveal the seamy things I've done for Ehrlichman and Krogh, they couldn't survive it."

Then I walked out of the office and slammed the door on the shaken lawyer behind me. My display was uncharacteristic and a bit theatrical, as no one seemed to understand the enormity of the problem. Still, when I left his office, I feared that little to nothing had probably been accomplished.

I didn't hear anything back for some time. As the days passed with no news, I learned that Liddy and Barker were in the Federal Correctional Institution in Danbury, Connecticut, pending sentencing. I wrote them both, receiving strained replies, since all prisoner mail was censored.

As March 23 came nearer, my ulcer flared, as I had heard nothing further about funds and was increasingly worried about my family. Bittman remained somewhat hopeful that I would be sentenced to probation, given my previous military service and government career, but having witnessed the judge's dark demeanor, I was not optimistic.

On March 21, I received a phone call from Bittman, saying that he had received an envelope for me. I picked it up from his home in the morning and found that it contained a total of $75,000—$45,000 less than my estimate of $60,000 for two years of expenses and $60,000 owed to my lawyers.

Somehow, this payment seemed to have all the finality of a Dear John letter, and I felt that since I had had to pull teeth to get this amount delivered, I could probably count on no further assistance from Liddy's principals—Mitchell, Dean, Magruder—or their successors. With the investigations going on, checks would be harder to cash than ever. I hoped that provisions had been made for Liddy and the Miami men but had no way of knowing if they were being provided for.

White House tapes would later reveal that John Dean told Richard Nixon that the Watergaters were "going to cost a million dollars over the next two years." Nixon replied that he knew "where it could be gotten." So I suppose we were not being abandoned.

I doubt anybody sleeps well the night before sentencing, and I was certainly no exception. Visions of that stark cell below the courthouse wafted through my consciousness every time I closed my eyes. And I knew that there were much worse places out there. In the morning, feeling numb and enervated, I did some light packing then removed the family signet ring that I had worn since I was twelve years old and left it in my bureau drawer.

Good-byes to the children were tearful and a bit strained, as they felt a strange mixture of grief, trepidation, and resentment that I was leaving just when they needed me most—on top of which, I told them that I couldn't bear for them to be in the courtroom. It was not a happy moment when Bill Bittman drove up to take me to the federal courthouse.

At 10:00 a.m. on March 23, 1973, Judge Sirica appeared, and McCord's lawyer asked to approach the bench. When he did so, he handed Sirica a sealed letter from McCord. The unexpected move should have been no surprise to the defendants, as it was the culmination of McCord's strange behavior over recent weeks, but it sent a murmur through the courtroom as reporters asked each other what this could mean. Sirica quickly silenced the uproar, then announced that he would suspend sentencing on McCord. We didn't know it then, but the letter stated that the defendants had pled guilty under pressure from the White House and that perjury had been committed during the trial.

Sirica then read a bland statement saying that he had considered the defendants' presentence reports and ordered Liddy, Barker, Martinez, González, Sturgis, and me to stand and come up before him. McCord stayed mysteriously seated. Sirica looked down from his bench, a little man on top of a mountain, and explained that he was going to hand down provisional sentences pending further evaluation of our cases—sentences that might be lightened depending on our cooperation with the Senate committee and grand jury.

Unfortunately, Sirica was livid with Liddy's completely legal but annoying antics before the grand jury and at trial, so he pointed out that Liddy's sentence—a stunning twenty years—was not provisional. My mind was still reeling when Bittman nudged me in the ribs. Sirica was asking the pro forma question if anyone wished to make a statement. Having just seen a glaring example of Maximum John's behavior, my attorney urged me to plead for leniency. I had a feeling that any such plea would fall on deaf ears and possibly even spur the vindictive jurist to increase my pain, but I had to take a chance on behalf of my children, whose fate weighed heavily on my mind. Besides, I thought, it was a possibility—however remote—that this prosecutorial judge, who had not shown the least interest in the defendants as human beings, might exhibit a semblance of humanity. So with the court's permission, I stepped forward and began reading from a statement I had prepared:

Your honor, I stand before you, a man convicted first by the press, then by my own admissions, freely made even before the beginning of the trial. For twenty-six years, I served my country honorably and with devotion: first as a naval officer on the wartime North Atlantic, then as an air force officer in China. And finally as an officer of the Central Intelligence Agency combating our country's enemies abroad. In my entire life, I was never charged with a crime, much less convicted of one. Since the seventeenth of June 1972, I lost my employment, then my beloved wife, both in consequence of my involvement in the Watergate affair. Today I stand before the bar of justice alone, nearly friendless, ridiculed, disgraced, destroyed as a man. These have been a few of the many tragic consequences of my participation in the Watergate affair, and they have been visited upon me in overwhelming measure.

What I did was wrong, unquestionably wrong in the eyes of the law, and I can accept that. For the last eight months, I have suffered an ever-deepening consciousness of guilt, of responsibility for my acts, and of the drastic penalties they entail. I pray, however, that this court—and the American people—can accept my statement today that my motives were not evil.

The court is about to impose sentence on me. It is my understanding that three principal factors are taken into consideration in arriving at the appropriate sentence. The first is the character of the offender—whether his life represents a cycle of criminality or whether he is a first-time offender. The second factor, as I understand it, is the extent to which the offender represents or is likely to represent a danger to society. Third is the deterrent effect—whether the offender is likely to repeat his offense and whether his fate serves as a deterrent to others who might consider a like offense.

As to myself, Your Honor, the offenses I have freely admitted are the first in a life of blameless and honorable conduct. As a man already destroyed by the consequences of his acts, I can represent no threat to our society, now or at any conceivable future time. And as to the factor of deterrence, Your Honor, the Watergate case has been so publicized that I believe it fair to say the American public knows that political offenses are not to be tolerated by our society within our democratic system. The American public knows also that because of what I did, I have lost virtually everything that I cherished in life—my wife, my job, my reputation. Surely, these tragic consequences will serve as an effective deterrent to anyone else who might contemplate engaging in a similar activity.

I am entirely conscious, Your Honor, that what is done to me from this time on is in your hands alone. The offenses to which I pleaded guilty even before the trial began were not crimes of violence. To be sure, they were an affront to the state, but not to the body of a man or to his property. The real victims of the Watergate conspiracy, Your Honor, as it has turned out, are the conspirators themselves. But there are other prospective victims.

Your Honor, I am the father of four children, the youngest a boy of nine. Had my wife and I not lost our employment because of Watergate involvement, she would not have sought investment security for our family in Chicago, where she was killed last December. My children's knowledge of the reason for her death is ineradicable—as is mine. Four children without a mother. I ask that they not lose their father, as well.

Your Honor, I cannot believe the ends of justice would be well served by incarcerating me. To do so would add four more victims, young and innocent victims, to the disastrous train of events in which I was involved. I say to you, in all candor, that my family desperately needs me at this time. My problems are unique and real, and Your Honor knows what they are. My probation officer has discussed them with me at some length.

I have spent almost an entire lifetime helping and serving my country, in war and peace. I am the one who now needs help. Throughout the civilized world, we are renowned for our American system of justice. Especially honored is our judicial concept of justice tempered with mercy. Mercy, Your Honor, not vengeance and reprisal, as in some lands. It is this revered tradition of mercy that I ask Your Honor to remember while you ponder my fate.

I have lost everything, Your Honor—friends, reputation, everything a man holds dear—except my children, who are all that remain of a once-happy family.

Since the Watergate case began, I have suffered agonies I never believed a man could endure and still survive. I have pled guilty as charged, of my own free will. Humbly, with profound contrition, I ask now that Your Honor look beyond the Howard Hunt of last June 17 to my life as a whole. And if it please this court, to temper justice with mercy.

My fate—and that of my family—my children—is in your hands.

Bernie Barker and Rolando Martinez both contributed moving statements for the record that would have softened the hardest heart. But for all our efforts, we might as well have walked up to the judge and slapped him in the face instead.

Maximum John looked at me with a severe expression and pronounced a five-year sentence for each of the seven counts, to run consecutively—a total of thirty-five years. The four Miami men were handed an appalling forty years each. This was so over and beyond anything I had conceived possible that I sat in stunned, nauseated silence. I had little time to gather my wits, as Sirica revoked my bond and marshals led me away. Maximum John had struck again. What we were not told at that point was that under a particular statute, the judge had no discretion as to what sentence to impose. All provisional sentences were automatically set to the maximum. At this point, however, all it made us do was consider Judge Sirica to be some kind of maximalist Inquisitional figure to be hated.

I was reacquainted with the courthouse Felony Tank, then taken in a locked, guarded van to the old stone complex near RFK Stadium—D.C. Jail. I knew it by reputation as being only a step above a gulag, with brutal, deeply entrenched gangs ruling the cell blocks, kept in check only by a cadre of vicious guards. Recently, there had been a prisoner revolt with a number of guards taken hostage.

The van stopped outside the gates, where marshals surrendered their firearms to a guard. Then the van was driven past the watchtowers to another gate, where a marshal got out and phoned ahead. The gate slid open, the van entered, and the gate closed solidly behind us.

I was ordered to exit the van once we arrived inside a courtyard and marched to a steel door that opened into a corridor made from black steel bars, one side of which formed the central control office, with guards sitting at desks watching grainy black-and-white security monitors. A guard removed my handcuffs and left. I stood there wondering what would happen next when a voice blared over a loudspeaker commanding me to enter the next section of the corridor. It was like going through a succession of canal locks. Walk, stop, wait for the door to close behind you, then move forward through the next. Guards, officers, and trustees stared at me through scratched Plexiglas windows, their lips occasionally moving mutely, as nothing they said could be heard in the hall.

At one point, a waiting guard motioned me to follow him. I did as ordered, following him down a series of steps into the hot, fetid bowels of the enormous complex. We stopped in a low-ceilinged room, painted some kind of greenish gray, browned with years of nicotine sweat from cigarette smoke, where sneering guards wearing khaki suits lorded it over convicts wearing blue dungarees and denim shirts who were seated at old, scarred metal tables. Behind a wire mesh screen, a line of convicts waited their turns at four grungy pay phones. Barker had told me about these, and I had brought a few dimes so that I could call out if I ever got a chance.

A guard shoved me in front of a camera, positioning my head straight, while another one snapped a few quick photographs. I was fingerprinted again, commanded to strip in front of two guards, then told to step to a yellow line, where I was ordered to raise my arms, open my mouth, extend my tongue, run my fingers through my hair, bend and turn, spread my buttocks, raise my testicles, show the bottoms of my feet, then have my clothing inventoried by a convict speaking in such hip ghetto jive that I couldn't understand a word he said.

A guard said, "Okay, burn him," which scared me, until I realized that it meant adding a lighter to my inventory.

They searched my shoes, rifled through my tobacco pouch, and knocked my pipe against the table before returning them to me.

I was issued wrinkled denim jeans, white socks, two sheets, a blanket, and a pillowcase at a counter. Strangely, except for the unabashed crudity, it was pretty similar to what I'd gone through years earlier in the service at Annapolis and Fort Dix.

I was then taken to R&D—Receiving and Discharge—after which I was taken to the "hospital," where after a long wait a nurse took samples of my blood and urine. I filled out a couple of forms indicating that I had an ulcer and some skin cancers, and turned them over to a disinterested doctor before I was led away.

Finally, I was led to Cell Block 4 on the third floor, where I knew Liddy and the four Miami men were incarcerated. Somehow, they knew I was coming and met me with strong *abrazos* and handshakes.

"Welcome, *amigo*," Liddy said bluntly.

The deck guard pointed out an empty cell not far from the guard desk, where my friends helped me make the bed to prison regulations. I mopped the floor and cleaned the basin and toilet.

"The canteen's about to open, Eduardo," Martinez said. "What do you need?"

"Toothpaste, a brush, soap, and writing paper would be good," I told him.

"Get some candy bars," Barker suggested. "It's a long time between meals, Eduardo."

I nodded, grateful to be among friends in this hellhole, then went down the corridor to shake hands with twenty to thirty mostly African American fellow prisoners. By now, I noted that in contrast to the greater prison population, Liddy and the Miami men were wearing starched, pressed denims. Liddy told me that he had a contact who could get me clothing in my size and deliver it pressed and starched twice a week for a couple of packs of cigarettes. If black opium and gold had been the preferred currency back in my OSS days in China, I would find that cigarettes were the main currency in prison.

"It's not bad here," Sturgis told me, then took me to a large corner cell with two double bunks and a makeshift card table. "Here's our home—the Watergate Hilton."

Villo handed me an orange, which I began to eat, starting to relax for the first time in days.

Then the deck guard shouted my name.

I jumped to my feet, then strode down the corridor to where a gray-shirted man from central control was standing by the guard desk. "Let's go," he snapped.

"Where?" I asked.

"C'mon, get going. Bring your bedding," he said.

I certainly wasn't going to argue, but my friends repeated the question. Finally, the guard said, "CB-One."

Sturgis made a disgusted sound. "That's where we were last summer. It's rough, Eduardo."

Liddy came forward and took me by the arm. "There's got to be a mistake. Listen, I'll try to work something out. This is the only place to be."

In a daze, I unmade my bed, rolled up the bedding, then followed the guard through a maze of doors that he locked and unlocked as we forged back into the deepest intestines of the prison—the Lower Depths. We finally arrived at a small steel doorway, behind which was CB-1, where we found another desk manned by another guard and convict assistant. "This here's Hunt," my escort pronounced. The desk guard glanced at me with no interest whatsoever and said, "Cell Seven."

I walked to the cell. The barred door slid open electrically, then closed with a clang after I entered. Inside was a double bunk, both mattresses filthy, no pillow. I selected the cleaner mattress, that perception probably only a figment of my imagination, and started to make my bed on the upper bunk, as far from the disgusting cement floor as possible. Up until this point, tension or denial must have been masking some of my senses, because suddenly I was taken by a sensory overload, with the sounds of raucous yells and arguments drumming against my ears and the stench of urine and old vomit filling my nostrils. This thick, dirty air was sucked into my lungs, making me feel slimy inside and out.

My cell faced a room as large as a basketball court with six television sets stationed on the walls, all tuned to the same discordant, staticky channel. I looked around for a lightbulb, but the socket was empty. But maybe that was a bit of a blessing, because even in the dim light I could see the accumulated filth on the basin and on the cracked, chipped, seatless toilet. Moving forward, I stepped on something that squashed under my foot—my first roach victim.

Psychological fatigue overcame me. I climbed to the upper bunk and stretched out, but the noise was deafening as dinner was being served to prisoners who were not in deadlock, as I was. I molded some wet toilet paper into earplugs and lay down again. After a while, a paper plate was shoved at me through a slot in the bars, along with a plastic spoon and a paper cup of Kool-Aid. A sorrowful-looking frankfurter with a few strands of sauerkraut dripping across it was on the plate. "No, thanks, not really hungry," I muttered. But a dish of vanilla ice cream came later, which I gulped gratefully before laying down again.

Even with the earplugs, the noise was at a much higher decibel than normal people are used to. I sat on the edge of my bunk for a half-hour trying to meditate the atmosphere away. It helped a bit, making me feel a little less exhausted, my mind an iota more clear.

An inmate sweeping the catwalk in front of my bars paused. *"Pssst! You Hunt?"*

"Yeah."

"The cats in CB-Four want to know what you need."

"Soap and a towel. A lightbulb. Toothpaste and a brush." It seemed a large order.

"I'll see what I can do, man." He grinned at me. "Don' go 'way."

"I'll be here. What about showers?"

"Once a day. Too late now. Tomorrow afternoon." He swept on, and in an hour returned with everything I'd asked for.

Using the towel for insulation, I got the metal base of a former bulb out of the socket, then screwed in the new one. Maybe it was a mistake. I blinked in the sudden light, seeing a strange phenomenon—

the walls appeared to melt, then turned from brown to green as a coating of roaches scurried away. My nostrils were acclimating to the rancid odors of my cell, but the TV sets blared on. I lay facedown on the bunk, peering through the bars and trying to watch television on the far wall, but the angle was wrong. A guard paused and peered at me, then kept going, satisfied that I was alive.

I heard voices in a high-pitched chatter, then a half-dozen female-appearing creatures swished along the catwalk. They wore towel skirts and turbans; two appeared to have breasts. They stared in at me and giggled, stopped at the next cell, and made sexual propositions to the two occupants.

Late that night the TV sets were silenced and the noise level lowered enough that I could sleep. But before then, I pondered McCord's private letter to Sirica and felt betrayed. Unwilling to accept his conviction and desperately grasping at anything that might save him, my onetime CIA colleague had chosen to step to the head of the line instead of waiting, as the rest of us were, to tell the grand jury those facts of which we had knowledge. In most circles, McCord was a hero, but I wondered how history would finally view him. McCord had become the most practical one of us all, for his letter set down the record as he knew it, preventing him from serving another day in prison. Doing this had never occurred to me, as I had said I would provide testimony in front of the grand jury.

The meal attendant woke me before dawn. "Diet tray," he called and shoved a plate through the slot in my bars. The plate held a cold fried egg, pears, and bread, reasonably close to the bland diet I had been following for years. As I ate, I reflected that apparently the physician's letter had had some effect on the jail sawbones.

The lightbulb kept the roaches at bay while I meditated, then made my bunk and anticipated the luxury of a shower. Today was Saturday, and the TV sets were turned on while other inmates breakfasted in the area beyond my catwalk. The queens were out there in all their makeshift glory, being goosed unresistingly from time to time by interested inmates. By now, I realized that I was in the jail's disciplinary section under deadlock, something reserved normally for only the most hardened and refractory prisoners. It was like the hold of a slave ship.

I made fresh earplugs from toilet paper and tried to sleep, but the cacophony was far too great, so I lay in a half-conscious daze until midmorning, when without notice my cell door slid open. I stepped onto the catwalk, and the guard beckoned me toward him.

"You got a visitor," he said. "Wait here for a convoy."

The rotunda was a high-domed room with windowed booths along one end and rows of tables where attorneys consulted with their clients. I was led into a booth occupied by four other prisoners and told my visitors were allowed one-half hour.

After a prolonged wait—something I was getting mighty used to—Lisa and St. John appeared looking fresh and cheerful. I tried to suppress my emotions as I picked up the telephone to communicate with them. They told me that David was doing well, and we talked about some household problems for a while. They wanted to know how bad it was in jail, but I wouldn't give them the details, as I knew it would be horrifying. Then I asked them to inform Bittman that for some reason I had been placed in solitary, and to somehow get me back with my five friends in CB-4. Then a guard came up and ended my first family visit.

When I returned to CB-1, the shower period was over, and I would have to wait another day. The TV sets now featured an Aretha Franklin concert, followed by *Soul Train* through the long afternoon. A prisoner stopped by and leered at me. "Well, Dad, you done joined the Blue Denim Brigade. Right on. How you like them motha-fuckas?"

"Not much," I told him and turned over on my bunk.

"You'll like 'em less when you been here long as me," he called.

True words, I was to find, but hardly a revelation even then. I began to muse—as I did every day of my prison term—on the singular cruelty of Judge Sirica's sentence. First offense, a spotless record, twenty-six years of service to the government, my wife dead less than four months, four motherless children—the sentence was nightmarish, unbelievable. But it might be lessened, depending on my cooperation. Only that had been decided long ago—in October, when the prosecutor told Bittman all of us would be immunized and taken before the grand jury. When would that be? How soon would I be called? Hell, I was *eager* to talk.

I gazed at my filthy surroundings and saw scratched on the wall: *If I was God, I'd quit!*

It was almost as if the words had been placed there by psyops to depress me. If so, the words did their duty. To rouse myself from total despondency, I got up, pulled off one of my shoes, and began killing roaches. It was a task for Tantalus, but it focused my mind and kept me physically active. The futility of trying to eradicate a never-ending supply of roaches was all too evident, and after a while, I surrendered.

A steam hose was needed to clean the cell, rid it of its long-accumulated filth—and so far I had not even managed a shower.

23

The Web Unweaves

B ittman was able to get me transferred back to CB-4 a few days later, on March 26. I was sure that stuffing me in the worst cell was all part of a carefully choreographed scenario, along with the provisional thirty-five-year sentence, to make me squawk as loud as I could in front of the grand jury.

Even so, I was so happy to get back to my friends that I couldn't help but break into a huge grin when I saw them. The group was missing Liddy, however; he had gotten into a brawl with another inmate who had stolen some of his things. Liddy was in the hospital getting medical treatment.

At this point, my days in front of the grand jury began and would go on for about two months, ushering in a nearly daily routine that meant waking up at 4:30 a.m., getting washed and shaved, donning my civilian clothes, and around 7:00 a.m. taking a bus to the federal courthouse, where I would wait in the Felony Tank until called for.

My guilty plea had kept prosecutors from being able to call many Nixon administration officials who they had reason to believe were involved to the stand. Still, at this point, they not only had McCord's mysterious letter, which claimed that we had all pled guilty under pressure from John Dean and John Mitchell—who had committed perjury when they had testified in front of the grand jury that they had no prior knowledge of the Watergate break-in—but McCord himself had testified in detail before the Ervin Committee and the grand jury in so-called secret sessions. But there were so many leaks that nearly whole sessions had appeared in the press and in Jack Anderson's column. Such leaking was normally a criminal offense.

Since McCord's testimony was hearsay and he had never spoken to anyone but me and Liddy, the grand jury basically wanted me to reiterate what McCord had already told them and name the higher-ups. Still, since I had never spoken directly to the principals, either, even my testimony was hearsay—though perhaps less removed. Only Gordon Liddy could give direct testimony, and he had steadfastly declined to do so. For this, he was held in contempt by Judge Sirica, who sentenced him to an additional eighteen months.

Liddy, however, was appealing his case, basically saying that the trial had been a mockery of justice, peppered with many reversible errors, so it was premature for him to testify before the outcome of his appeal. Gordon seemed to relish any hardship, physical or mental, so the more they threw at him, the more he rebelled. Even as late as May 1974, when the White House was mired in Watergate muck, he maintained his tight lips, receiving an additional year's sentence for contempt of Congress.

To further the prosecutor's investigation, Judge Sirica bestowed "use immunity" upon me and my five fellow Watergaters—whether we wanted it or not—meaning that our testimony could not be used against us. However, we could be held in contempt if we did not testify truthfully, so it was a bit of a double-edged sword, since I had no plans to do so. The judge's provisional sentence of thirty-five years, meant to pressure me into revealing my superiors, had had the opposite effect, as I now believed that my only recourse was to lie and obfuscate, protecting the people in power for two reasons: First, as a good soldier, I was falling on my sword to protect them, as promised. Second, I felt that if I kept my end of the bargain, Nixon would come through and grant me the promised pardon.

"Christmas comes around once a year," Colson had said.

The grand jury room was roughly a 20- by 20-foot smoke-filled chamber, with a long wooden table down the center. On one side sat twenty-three jurors comprised of a cross-section of the D.C. population. Facing them sat U.S. attorneys Silbert, Glanzer, and Campbell. The foreman would administer my oath, then I would be parked at the end of the table near the court stenographer, facing the long line of jurors and prosecutors down the table. While I was alone, Silbert informed me that at any time I wished, I could ask the grand jury foreman for permission to consult my attorney—a right I was to avail myself of frequently during my many interrogations.

I was always tired and hungry, as the grueling schedule left little time to sleep and often made me miss the regimented mealtimes of prison. So there were many nights that I was forced to go to bed without dinner. There were a lot of times I wondered if I was indeed taking the right course of action, as there were reports that John Dean and Jeb Magruder were making deals with the prosecutors. McCord seemed to enjoy the spotlight and his role of repentant conspirator, so he and his lawyer, F. Lee Bailey, were often in the media.

Another thing that irked me was my constant search for pen and paper to continue writing a journal that I kept throughout my prison experience. While Black Panthers and murderers in my cell blocks were allowed typewriters, ribbons, and paper to bang out their political screeds, I had to hoard writing materials as if they were made of gold.

On April 5, 1973, the White House withdrew the nomination of L. Patrick Gray as director of the FBI. It was still secret at the time, but we now know that he and John Dean took my Hermes notebook— in which the details of Gemstone were written—the forged Kennedy cables, and other materials out of my safe, whereupon Gray took the material home and burned it.

On April 9, the *New York Times* reported McCord's allegations to the grand jury that my late wife had delivered cash to the Watergate Seven in return for their silence and pleas of guilty. These statements made me apoplectic, as it implied that Dorothy had been involved in the cover-up. Indeed, such testimony gave prosecutors ammunition to name her as an unindicted coconspirator. In my mind, all my wife had done was undertake a humanitarian mission to supply defense and family support funds to the defendants.

Most important, McCord later alleged that Dorothy had spoken to him about clemency and pardons, which I thought would be completely out of character, as she was not authorized to do so and had never spoken to me about it. Instead, it was John Dean who had offered McCord clemency through private investigator Jack Caulfield, not my wife, and for the White House to have employed a channel to

McCord less official than Caulfield seemed unlikely. Easy to pin these things on someone who was resting six feet underground. During this period, while the conspirators' pact was falling apart around me, I dodged all questions regarding higher-ups, saying that I had had no knowledge of anybody else's involvement, and I lied when I said that I was not expecting any quid pro quo for my silence.

Bill Bittman brought galley proofs of *The Berlin Ending* to me at D.C. Jail, remaining in the rotunda while I read and corrected them. Even under the difficult circumstances of its writing, the book was eventually published to good reviews, including a full-page positive profile in *Time* magazine.

A rather important event happened around now: John Dean revealed both our entry into Fielding's offices in Beverly Hills and that Gray had destroyed some incriminating contents from my safe. I was rushed before the grand jury to give a lengthy statement about the Fielding operation, which Silbert sent to Judge Matthew Byrne, who was presiding over the trials of Daniel Ellsberg and Anthony Russo. In yet another ironic twist, the judge dismissed all charges against the two after reading the grand jury transcript.

Apparently, Mark Felt, in his "Deep Throat" guise, confirmed the Gray story to Bob Woodward, saying the missing papers were "political dynamite," and that on June 28, 1972, Ehrlichman and Dean told Gray that my documents "should never see the light of day."

On April 22, 1973, while Dean was cooperating with the Watergate Committee, Nixon invited him to Camp David to write a detailed report about his knowledge of the crime. The wary Dean, however, refused, sensing that he was being set up as a scapegoat for the crime and the cover-up.

On April 30, President Nixon addressed the nation on television, taking general responsibility for Watergate, though denying any personal knowledge of it. He then announced the dismissal of John Dean and the resignations of his old friends H. R. Haldeman and John Ehrlichman. Also, he revealed that Attorney General Richard Kleindienst was stepping down. This official acknowledgment, I thought, would absolve us, but the president's statement was carefully couched to establish his own innocence rather than ours. During the statement, the president indicated that he was aware that there had been some attempt to conceal the facts surrounding the case and announced that he had given Acting Attorney General Richardson power to appoint a special prosecutor. This, of course, would create a precedent that would later hound various presidents, including Ronald Reagan and Bill Clinton.

Then, on May 2, I returned to CB-4 and informed my brethren that it was no use holding out any longer, that prosecutors knew all about ODESSA and had showed me the files. When I told Gordon that I had made a decision to cooperate fully, he turned on his heel and walked out, then apparently said something to the guard that got him transferred to deadlock in CB-1. We would never speak again. I didn't know it at the time, but my friend would later write that he had formed an elaborate plot to have me poisoned in jail if the White House ordered, and going into deadlock was part of the plan.

And the soldiers kept falling. On May 5, *Newsweek* published a story claiming that John Dean was about to reveal that President Nixon was involved in the Watergate cover-up. On the ninth, Bud Krogh assumed responsibility for the Fielding entry and resigned as under-secretary of the Department of Transportation. Still, he denied that any of his White House superiors had knowledge of the operation.

Behind the scenes: On the sixteenth, Bob Woodward sent editor Ben Bradlee a memo saying that "Deep Throat" had confirmed that the cover-up went all the way to Nixon. Oh, yes, and that I was "blackmailing" the president.

On May 18, the historic Senate Watergate hearings began, with Archibald Cox named special prosecutor. Then, the following week, the four Miami men and I were transferred to the Federal Correctional Institution in Danbury, Connecticut. With its sports facilities, green grass, and liberal visiting policies, it seemed like a paradise after D.C. Jail.

My grand jury testimony continued, with even longer drives down from Connecticut to Washington, where I was reintroduced to D.C. Jail. After a bad episode with another inmate there, whenever I was in Washington, authorities housed me at the Arlington County Jail and the Montgomery County Detention Center—a ten-minute drive from my Potomac Home.

During this time, despite my "use immunity," I was still waiting for "Christmas" and still protecting the president, so I continued to frustrate prosecutors by making false and evasive statements concerning who knew what. But on June 3, John Dean told investigators that he had discussed the Watergate cover-up with the president at least thirty-five times. That caused large *Washington Post* headlines, which were followed up with the uncovering of a memo addressed to Ehrlichman that detailed our Fielding operation.

Los Angeles prosecutors then subpoenaed Bernie Barker, Rolando Martinez, and me to appear in front of their own grand jury. We were housed in the same maximum security cells in which the killers Charles Manson and Sirhan Sirhan had once been incarcerated. Unbelievably, the accommodations and treatment were far better than anything we had received on the East Coast. After a week in L.A., we returned to Danbury, were assigned prison jobs—I was made a librarian—and hunkered down for what appeared to be a long stay.

One day in the library, I was rereading *Judgment at Deltchev* by one of my favorite spy novelists, Eric Ambler, and came across this quote describing a prisoner who "must be discredited and destroyed as a man so that he may safely be dealt with as a criminal." Those words resonated inside my head, as the same thing was happening to me. At the end of June, I learned that Silbert, Glanzer, and Campbell had withdrawn from the Watergate inquiry. That was a happy day for me, as I was convinced that their unwillingness to plea bargain with me was responsible for my incarceration. I also couldn't forgive them for their hostile interrogations of my wife, daughter, and son.

At night, we were allowed to watch the occasional rebroadcast of the televised Senate hearings; I watched John Dean and James McCord testify, giving embroidered accounts of what had transpired. It was as if they were trying to create a legend to be told by people thousands of years later, like the *Iliad*.

On July 4, while the country was celebrating its anniversary, I hosted a wonderful visit by my children and was emotionally overcome by having them see me in my prison garb. At least we were able to sit together and embrace, much different than speaking over a telephone in D.C. Still, when they left, I felt more depressed than before, as I worried about our various futures.

On July 13, Alexander Butterfield, Nixon's former appointments secretary, revealed for the first time that President Nixon taped all conversations and telephone calls in his office. This was an explosive development. Special Prosecutor Archibald Cox and Sam Ervin naturally demanded the tapes, which Nixon naturally refused, prompting prosecutors to take their request to the Supreme Court.

The strain of my weekly trips to Washington, being grilled hour after hour, the daily uncertainties of location, difficulty sleeping in different jails, and frequent loss of meals added to my sad mental state. Then Bill Bittman announced to me that he had been asked by Special Prosecutor Cox to cease representing me. While this angered me to no end, the reason would eventually come out: Cox now included Bittman as an unindicted coconspirator whose testimony was a conflict of interest with my own. Bill's services, especially those involving passing messages to CREEP attorneys O'Brien and Parkinson, were being considered as helping further the cover-up. (He was ultimately named as an unindicted coconspirator in the cover-up conspiracy case that went to trial in the fall of 1974: *U.S. v. Mitchell, Haldeman, Ehrlichman, Parkinson, and Mardian.*)

I was recommended to a former U.S. attorney and onetime president of the D.C. Bar, Sidney Sachs, who continued to serve me throughout the televised Senate hearings, after which I could no longer afford his fees. By then, I had spent nearly $70,000 of my personal savings on litigation—money derived from Dorothy's flight insurance—and had resolved not to spend any more of my own money, as it would have a negative effect on my children's future.

As hot summer days gave way to showers of golden autumn leaves, the intensive regimen became so demanding that even the Senate staff saw that I was going to collapse. At the request of my attorney, the Ervin Committee pressed the Marshal Service to keep me in a safe house in Fort Holabird, Maryland, near Baltimore, only a forty-five-minute drive from the U.S. Senate.

There I had my first semblance of normality in what seemed like a lifetime. I had my own motel-like room with a bed, a shower, and a writing table. The place was populated by sixteen white-collar criminals, con men, and mafiosi who were serving brief sentences while they testified in various cases as government witnesses. Cooking and cleaning chores were shared among the safe-house occupants, so the food was actually very good. When I bedded down for the evening on a thin but serviceable mattress, it was with the first decent dinner I had enjoyed in many weeks. A brief scare occurred when my location was leaked by an unfriendly senator, but my lawyer negotiated my return to the safe house, where I was to stay until my final sentencing by Judge Sirica in November.

On September 17, Sachs petitioned the U.S. District Court to withdraw my guilty plea and dismiss all charges against me. In yet another ironic turn, my attorney was basing the petition on the actions of L. Patrick Gray and John Dean, who had confessed their destruction of the documents in my White House safe. If the case against Ellsberg had to be dismissed because the Fielding break-in had violated his constitutional rights, then the burning and destruction of my White House safe materials violated mine, as well.

A week later, I was again paraded in front of the glare of camera lights to testify before the Ervin Committee. The senators took their places around the high, curved podium before me, and Senator Ervin called the session to order and swore me in. I was then allowed to read an opening statement, which my attorneys and I had prepared, hoping to place my life in reasonable perspective to my interrogators.

I gave a brief summary of my childhood and my military and government service. I continued with my retirement from the CIA, my work for Mullen and then the White House, giving full details about Gemstone, the Fielding entry, and the Watergate operation; the reasons behind it; and the officials who had authorized it. I reminded the committee that I had asked for the contents of the safe, which were withheld, and that I had answered thousands of questions on more than twenty-five occasions, saying, "I have answered all questions, even those which involved confidential communications between my attorney and myself."

I told the committee that after my pleas, I learned of obstruction of justice by government officials who had destroyed and withheld evidence, perjured themselves, and suborned perjury before the Watergate grand jury—official misconduct that deprived me of evidence that would have supported my position that (a) my participation in Watergate was an activity authorized within the power of the president of the United States, and (b) if my participation was not so authorized, I justifiably believed that it was.

I maintained that the charges against me should be dismissed based on facts made public since my plea, which proved my actions were not unlawful, citing Judge Byrne's admonition in the Ellsberg case: "The totality of the circumstances of this case . . . offend a 'sense of justice.' The bizarre events have incurably infected the prosecution of this case."

I said that although I had asked for promised funds to be made available, I had not "blackmailed" the parties involved, and made no threats. I recounted how I had been attacked and robbed in jail, suffered a stroke, kept in solitary, manacled and chained hand to foot, and isolated from four motherless children. I added that I was faced with enormous financial strain caused by my defense fees.

"In conclusion," I said, "I want to emphasize that at the time of the Watergate operation, I considered my participation a duty to my country. I thought it was an unwise operation, but I viewed it as lawful. I hope the court will sustain my view, but whatever that outcome, I deeply regret that I had any part in this affair. I think it was an unfortunate use of executive power, and I am sorry that I did not have the wisdom to withdraw. At the same time, I cannot escape feeling that the country I have served my entire life and which directed me to carry out the Watergate entry is punishing me for doing the very things it trained and directed me to do."

I thanked the senators for listening to me and said I would answer their questions to the best of my ability. The senators asked the same familiar questions they had been asking from the beginning, more guiding perhaps, just having me outline the whole story beginning with my friendship with Charles Colson. It was an arduous experience, being grilled under the painfully bright lights, and would have been difficult under the best of circumstances, let alone after having been in jail for a while. As the morning wore on, I became exhausted and light-headed, and have little recollection of that day and the next. I remember that Senator Ervin had a disconcertingly uninflected voice, leaving me in doubt as to whether he was asking me a question or making a statement. Senators Baker and Inouye seemed very astute, and Republican senator Gurney seemed bored by the proceedings. I slept at Holabird again that night in a bed in a noise-free room, which gave me the power to face the next day.

There were a few things that stick out in my mind from the next round of questioning. Senator Weicker savagely attacked my theory that Alfred Baldwin might have informed DNC officials of the pending entry. But, in general, these days seem to have melted together into a homogeneous soup that is difficult to recall.

During the time that I was being hauled in front of this or that hearing, the only person in my family of age on the outside that Sachs could send a bill to was Kevan at Smith College. At one point, my poor daughter received a particularly fat statement from Sachs's office, with an accompanying letter offering her a couple of payment choices. The enterprising lawyer would take an assignment of all of my book royalties or a mortgage on my house, which I had already turned down, or Kevan could make payments of $10,000 per month until he was satisfied.

Kevan called Bill Buckley, who, after calling me, fired Sachs that afternoon and put me together with a lawyer from Baltimore, William Snyder. He was managing some of my wife's affairs and our wrongful death lawsuit against United Airlines. Snyder had never handled anything of this magnitude before, but he jumped in and met me the next day for my first debriefing in front of the new Watergate special prosecutor. Except for my appeal, which would be handled by Dickerson Williams, Snyder would represent me with great ability through more than five years of criminal proceedings (including the Fielding break-in, etc.), countless civil suits, tax cases, clemency proceedings, several criminal investigations (e.g., into the White House Plumbers' activities), and meetings with the likes of the CIA's chief of counterespionage and counterintelligence, and he still represents me to this day.

At this point, getting to the truth of Watergate had become a national obsession, with the Watergate Special Prosecution Force (WSPF) getting more intense every day. The office was like a small fortress—which even had combination locks on the bathrooms—and was divided into several sections, each dealing with a different subject matter. The main one focused on the Watergate cover-up, a group that interrogated me several days a week. Another dealt with the John Connelly "milk producers" scandal—illegal quid pro quo campaign contributions. Still another dealt with the activities of the White House Plumbers.

By October, Nixon was under such pressure that on the twentieth, he ordered Attorney General Elliot Richardson to fire Archibald Cox. Richardson refused, resigning in protest. This was the beginning of the famous "Saturday Night Massacre." Nixon then ordered Deputy Attorney General William Ruckelshaus to fire Cox, but he also refused and was promptly fired. Nixon then appointed Robert Bork, the solicitor general, as acting attorney general, and Bork complied with the order (this, of course, would help fuel his detractors when he was later nominated for the Supreme Court by Ronald Reagan in 1987). In turn, these tumultuous actions would spur pressure for impeachment in Congress.

My treatment by marshals varied greatly and was always a mystery to me and Snyder. One day, I would be led into the special prosecutor's

office in handcuffs, and we would have to lunch on take-out sand-
wiches eaten in an empty office room. The next day, I would be
allowed to dress in a business suit and was simply dropped off by the
marshals at the WSPF offices. On those occasions, Snyder would take
me to dine at Chez François, Duke Zeibert's, Paul Young's, or another
of the fabulous expense-account restaurants that K Street offered.

Snyder remembers that although I gave the prosecutors a host of
useful information about the White House Plumbers, Watergate, and
a variety of subjects, there was a palpable tension in the air, as it was
clear that they knew I was covering for other people: "Usually," Snyder says, "the tension was expressed by one of the assistant prosecutors to me privately at the end of a long day of question-and-answer
sessions. The prosecutor would exhort me to 'work with Howard' and
get him to 'be more forthcoming' and to see that truthfully cooperating with the special prosecutor was his ticket to freedom."

As antagonistic as Silbert had been toward me, the proceedings
had always at least bordered on the realm of civility. In contrast,
Richard Ben-Veniste, a federal prosecutor from New York, badgered
and intimidated me angrily. The prosecutors wanted to use me as a
key witness in the forthcoming trial (in the fall of 1974) of the president's top lieutenants (Mitchell, Haldeman, Ehrlichman, Mardian,
and Parkinson). At that time, the government had to vouch for the
truthfulness of *all* of the testimony its witnesses would give—or else
not use the witness at all. The prosecutors could not put me on the
stand as a government witness and cherry-pick the good parts of my
testimony and simply ignore the bad. They had to guarantee the
truthfulness of *everything*.

I, however, was worried that my truthfulness would conflict with
my earlier testimony, giving Maximum John the right to incarcerate
me for a total of thirty-five years, so I continued equivocating. At one
point, I was giving a series of evasive answers to Ben-Veniste's questions about whether I had been promised a presidential pardon. He
seemed obsessed with this point, demanding to know over and over
again whether I was still expecting clemency.

When I said no, he replied, "Bullshit!" and hammered on me
some more. While this was evasive on my part, I was speaking the
truth, as I had never out and out been promised a deal. You had to
read between the lines of Colson's carefully worded message to con-
strue the meaning. *"Well, Christmas comes around once a year."*

Almost apoplectic with rage, Ben-Veniste wheeled on me and told me that if I was put on the stand as a government witness and gave an answer like that, I would probably be prosecuted for perjury and wind up at Leavenworth. *Leavenworth!* After all the terrible places I had been, I almost had a heart attack when I heard that name. I beckoned Snyder for a private conference outside of the interrogation room. "Bill, did you hear *that?*" I exclaimed angrily. "That little prick just threatened me with *Leavenworth!* What are you going to do about it?"

Snyder replied that as long as they thought I was holding back, the tension would continue and indeed grow, as the cover-up conspiracy trial set for fall 1974 drew near.

Later, in 1974, when I was called as a witness against Mitchell, Haldeman, Ehrlichman, Mardian, and Parkinson, this testimony would rear its ugly head again.

While much of the various trials blend together, interestingly the joys of Holabird stick out. I began to regain some weight. I was allowed to wear my own clothing and use a portable typewriter, with which I began to attack piles of unanswered mail. I guess my appearance before the committee must have touched a spark in the audience, as the Senate received several thousand telegrams and letters in the wake of my testimony. Bill Buckley had to get together a small committee of people at the *National Review* offices to help answer them. We hoped that this interest might be transformed into some financial assistance for my legal bills, but the results were disappointing, so Buckley generously suggested that I retain his personal attorney at no cost to me.

On November 9, 1973, the Miami men and I were called into Judge Sirica's courtroom for our final sentencing. Now we would find out just how much all of our help was appreciated. McCord, still free but also awaiting sentencing, tried to shake my hand, but I turned away. I stood with my companions in front of the bench and listened to Sirica hand down our sentences: one to three years for the Miami contingent, deferred sentencing for James McCord (as we had expected). . . . My heart jabbed my ribs, and my pulse pounded in my ears. I barely heard his words through the noise of my own body. . . . What was that? A staggering eight years plus a $10,000 fine for me!

No parole before serving thirty months! I was too dazed to make any statement. Rolando Martinez, however, made a strong speech, which everyone in the courtroom besides Sirica seemed to think was very moving. Now I was glad that I had lied and evaded, as all the hundreds of hours testifying and months in jail that I had endured were obviously meaningless. It was all I could do to keep from raising my fist or my finger to the judge on the way out of the courtroom. He would have loved it, though, as it would have given him ammunition to increase my jail term with a contempt of court citation.

I was taken to the Felony Tank and joined in the dank depths by Sid Sachs, whose normally unshakable attitude had been crushed by the sentence. All I could do was thank him for all the hard work he had done and reiterate that I could no longer afford his services. At the end of the day, I was returned to the Fort Holabird safe house.

Almost as if I was preparing to die, I took care of long-suffering family business, resigned from several clubs, and spent as much time talking with St. John and Lisa and old friends like Bill Buckley and Mañuel Artime as I could. Family-wise, things were not going well. St. John and Lisa were furious at me and were threatening to run off with David. Buckley had to intervene so that Artime could fetch David and take him to Miami, per my wishes. Things between us were so strained that no one came to spend Thanksgiving with me, though Kevan arrived that night for a long, affectionate talk.

During all this time, Nixon maintained his innocence, and on November 17 declared famously, "I am not a crook!" thereby giving a generation of stand-up comics and other impersonators years of easy jokes.

The Supreme Court had decided that Nixon had to comply with the Watergate prosecutor's subpoena for the White House tapes. On the twenty-first, the infamous eighteen-minute gap that would obsess people for the rest of the century appeared. Nixon's secretary, Rose Mary Woods, denied deliberate erasure.

On the twenty-ninth, I was abruptly transferred from Holabird to Federal Prison Camp at Allenwood, Pennsylvania. This place was popularly called one of the "country clubs" of the federal prison system, but the term was highly inaccurate. While it did not have the walls and bars of a high-security prison and prisoners could walk freely in the vicinity of camp buildings, it was nothing more than a forced-labor camp. As a new arrival, I was housed in a large, decaying, World

War II–era wooden dormitory with broken showers and drafty windows. Rations were just a step above the rotten food at D.C. Jail, with heavy emphasis on large volumes of pasta with thin, ketchupy sauce.

Despite my experience as a writer, I was denied work in the library or the education area, and despite my health, arthritis, and age of fifty-six years, was compelled to work on the cattle farm shoveling dung, digging postholes, and stringing barbed wire for the twelve-hundred-head herd. After my health became worse, I was reassigned to work as a clerk in the farmhouse, where at least there was some protection from the cold winter winds.

Three days after Christmas, I returned a call from Bill Snyder.

"I've got some good news," Bill said. "The court of appeals has ordered your release pending formal arguments in your case."

I was speechless. Tears sprung into my eyes. After all these months, I could hardly bring myself to believe what I was hearing. I could see my children again, live at home—at least until the court of appeals, which had reversed many of Sirica's contemptuous rulings, decided the merits of my case. "That's incredible," I said in a broken voice.

When the news filtered out to the prison populace, I received congratulations from prisoners I didn't even know. While the order came down on a Friday, the bureaucratic molasses was slow, and official notification of my release would not arrive at Allenwood until mail resumed after the New Year's holiday. It was agonizing, but at least I had a release date, only four days away. With the exception of the time I'd spent in solitary at D.C. Jail, those were the longest days of my prison life.

Even though I should have already been out, I still had to work on the farm until the marshals came for me on Tuesday, January 2, 1974. Of course, they got lost and arrived late on a day that I was due in a Washington court no later than 4:00 p.m. Having said my good-byes over the last few days, I walked down the hall to central control, was issued an ill-fitting suit of street clothes, then was turned over to two marshals, who manacled me hand and foot for the eighty- and ninety-mile-an-hour drive to the federal courthouse. A crowd of photographers swarmed around us there, making it impossible for the embarrassed marshals to remove my leg irons and handcuffs without being noticed. A few of the vigilant press corps made note of the fact and remarked on the paradox in their stories.

I was led into the office of the clerk of the court of appeals, where I was read the court's decision and the terms of my release: no bond, report monthly to the probation officer, and no travel outside the metropolitan area without the officer's permission. When Bill Snyder arrived, I took an oath to comply with my parole. Next, we met the chief probation officer, who found a space for me to compose a brief statement to give the press. They were storming the building like zombies in a horror film, flinging themselves indiscriminately at us, hungry for their pound of living flesh.

I walked to the courthouse steps, proclaimed my happiness that the court of appeals had found sufficient merit in my case to warrant my release, then thanked my attorneys and the thousands of well-wishers whose telegrams and letters had made the long prison months more endurable. I finished by saying that I was eager to be reunited with my children. With that, Snyder helped me push through the crowd to his waiting car.

As we drove, we were followed by two carloads of reporters and a cameraman filming dangerously from a motorcycle. Snyder told me that there was also a media battalion covering my home in Potomac, so we probably shouldn't go there. He had clothes for me at his home in Baltimore and thought I should go to Bill Buckley's in New York, where Kevan was waiting for me. He had already received permission from my parole officer to go there. Later, I could visit David at Artime's in Miami.

Even at the Snyder home, the press banged on the door asking for further statements, which we declined. We took the ringing phone off the hook while Bill's wife prepared a gourmet meal and allowed me to indulge in the first highball I had enjoyed in nearly eleven months. Later, I placed phone calls to friends, wrote out checks for accumulated bills, and rolled into bed for a dreamless sleep.

The next morning, I took the Metroliner to New York, where I reunited with Kevan at Bill and Pat Buckley's house. We were joined by lawyer Dickerson Williams, who would handle my appeal. After a notable lunch and much discussion, we decided that I should make no more statements or appearances for the time being. Then Kevan and I took a plane to Miami, where we found another mob scene of photographers waiting at the airport. Artime met us, not allowing the hubbub to annoy him in the slightest, and took us to his car, then to a motel near his home, where we registered under aliases to avoid the media.

Even Mañuel's home was staked out by the press, who were convinced that I would have to go there to see my son. Instead, Artime snuck David out the back door and brought him to see me in the motel, where he stayed with me for several days until the media finally drifted away.

It was amazing and almost mind-numbing to be able to go anywhere and do anything I wanted. I didn't know what I wanted to do first. We went to the beach and enjoyed a general sense of freedom, which I had lacked for so long. After a week of sunshine and good food, I left Miami for Potomac, where I thanked our housekeeper for staying so long and took back the keys. She returned to Argentina a few days later.

Lisa and St. John were still not speaking with me and were living in a nearby rental, as I had told them that I was planning to sell the house and had gone so far as to get a friend of Snyder's to pose as a possible buyer—it had been the only way to get them to relinquish control of David to Mañuel. It was incredibly lonely staying there by myself, and everything reminded me of Dorothy, so it was a difficult adjustment. Even the silence was disconcerting, as I had spent so much time being bludgeoned by the din of prison.

For several days, the only thing I could do was shuffle around the house and feed the joyful Afghan hound who followed my every footstep and the mewling Siamese cat that had been suffering from a deficit of belly-scratching. Then I gradually opened up, responded to invitations from my neighbors, and found the energy to open and read correspondence that had been piling up for months.

Over the next few months, I dictated a highly revisionist book manuscript about my life—in which I had to hide some of my CIA past, use agents' code names, and reiterate the many misstatements that I had made before various Watergate investigations. I appeared on television shows such as Buckley's *Firing Line* and ABC News, and gave interviews to various press.

In February 1974, Congress authorized the House Judiciary Committee to investigate whether there was ample ground to impeach the president. At the end of April, the White House tried to get out of releasing more tapes by sending the committee twelve hundred pages of edited transcripts, but the committee demanded the original tapes.

Dickerson Williams argued my appeal on June 14, 1974, with other attorneys from the Watergate Seven, but two of the court's more conservative judges recused themselves, which destroyed the panel's nine-judge liberal-conservative balance. The remaining judges would not permit Williams to utter more than a few words before firing questions at him, subtracting from his allotted twenty-five-minute presentation. Later in the year, all of our appeals were denied, 5–2, and I was sent back to prison. The Miami men would all serve one year in jail. I would serve thirty-three months.

24

The Memo Bites Back

Washington was the hottest place in the country in the summer of 1974—if you were President Nixon or anybody connected to Watergate. The Supreme Court ordered the White House to produce and hand over to prosecutors all secret tapes that had been recorded. On July 27, the House Judiciary Committee adopted the first article of impeachment, charging Nixon with obstruction of justice regarding the investigation of the Watergate entry.

On August 8, Richard Nixon became the first U.S president to resign, announcing his intentions by a televised address to the nation. On or just after the day on which Nixon resigned the presidency, my lawyer, Bill Snyder, was in the courtroom of Judge Gerhard Gesell, a federal judge in D.C., representing me in one of the nasty spawn of litigations brought on by Watergate. Federal marshals brought in Gordon Liddy and sat him down right next to Bill.

At the time, Liddy had not yet published his book, *Will*, and was reveling in being the only stand-up, strong, silent-type guy. Consequently, Bill asked him, "Well, Mr. Liddy, are you going to continue to remain silent now that your leader has resigned?" Liddy replied that the soldier owed his allegiance to the prince, no matter whom the prince may be. Poor man's Machiavelli.

A day or so later, Liddy was hauled before the Nedzi Committee—the House Armed Services Committee. When asked if he would tell the truth, the whole truth, and nothing but the truth, Liddy replied, "No!" He was subsequently cited for contempt of Congress and returned for sentencing to Judge Sirica, who angrily added an additional eighteen months to his sentence.

A month later, on September 8, President Gerald Ford announced a "full, free, and absolute" pardon of the former president for "all offenses against the United States" committed between January 20, 1969, and August 9, 1974. Nixon, the man who was conspirator in chief, would somehow rise like a phoenix from the ashes of his ignominy and become an elder statesman whose funeral would draw every living American president, including President Clinton. No other Watergate figure would fare quite as well.

The presidential pardon did not cover other conspirators named in the indictment, so the trial of John Mitchell, H. R. Haldeman, John Ehrlichman, Kenneth Parkinson, and Robert Mardian proceeded at the end of September 1974. One important prosecution witness would be John Dean, who was serving one to four years in prison. I would be considered another blockbuster witness, technically brought to the stand by Judge Sirica in a controversial move so that prosecutors would have more leeway to question me.

This unconventional move had been orchestrated by Ben-Veniste to help conceal from the defendants' lawyers that I was now cooperating fully with prosecutors. Up until very recently, I had steadfastly maintained my earlier fallacious testimony concerning my superiors, which had angered prosecutors so much that Ben-Veniste had uttered his disturbing Leavenworth threat. Even my own lawyer, Bill Snyder, had threatened to part ways if I continued prevaricating.

We were of two minds. He thought my best hope of having Sirica cut my draconian thirty-five-year sentence was to fully cooperate with the government. I, however, had no trust in Sirica by this time and thought that if I admitted to perjury, the angered judge would use it as a weapon to uphold the entire provisional sentence hovering above my head like the sword of Damacles. Even Snyder, however, did not know that I was lying—he could only suspect it.

Kevan produced the envelope of papers I had given her to destroy shortly after her mother's death. Our relationship had not been warm since the Watergate revelations, as she blamed me for involving Dorothy (and her, by proxy) in such a high-stakes game. One night, after discussing with Snyder how they could get me to recant my testimony, she had given him the long-secreted envelope that had weighed so heavily on her mind. Then the two confronted me like family members going through an intervention one evening when I had been allowed by marshals to prepare for court at Snyder's Baltimore home.

My reaction was just as violent as that of an alcoholic in denial. I cursed them and called them betrayers—but eventually conceded defeat. Snyder turned the papers over to overjoyed prosecutors with great fanfare about my "conversion." The effect was almost magical, flipping the stormy climate of animosity into balmy geniality. Now they had weapons they would need in the oncoming trial, including the amounts and dates of monies received and disbursed by my wife to my coconspirators. Still, they wished to conceal my sudden born-again transformation as long as possible, so they had Sirica call me as a special witness.

During opening statements, each of the defendants' lawyers tried to paint his client in the best possible light. Parkinson's attorney said he was simply in awe of John Mitchell, just "like a ballplayer who wants to meet Babe Ruth or Hank Aaron." So it was easy to see how the poor gullible Parkinson believed Mitchell when his boss told him that CREEP had nothing to do with the break-in. Haldeman and Ehrlichman also both pointed at John Mitchell as the man in charge of the cover-up and any payment scheme that might have existed. Everybody was pointing fingers at everyone else.

While John Dean was supposedly the star witness at this trial, I was brought in to testify on October 29 and would create the biggest splash. By this time, the jury had listened to so many hours of scratchy White House tapes that certain members were often falling asleep. Despite all of this very graphic testimony, including the treasury of my papers, there was no smoking gun to which prosecutors could point to say that any of the principals had absolutely full knowledge of the break-ins and that the total of $429,000 that we had received for lawyers and living expenses had been in return for our silence.

Ben-Veniste questioned me several times on the whereabouts of the missing memo that I had "laid on Parkinson." I had given it to Bittman, who said he had read it to Parkinson over the telephone and put it in a folder that had later been destroyed. Now Bittman suddenly came up with a copy of the confidential memo, which he gave to prosecutors to keep from being indicted. Ben-Veniste had kept it from defense attorneys for over a month, allowing them to question and harangue various defendants, believing that it did not exist or possibly had never existed. Now I dutifully testified that the copy was a true and correct photocopy of the original, and Ben-Veniste read it to the jury very dramatically. It had a chilling effect on the defendants and their lawyer.

The one-and-a-half-page memo had been typed in a crisp, businesslike font on my IBM Selectric typewriter. I started by noting that the Watergate operation had been planned against my better judgment.

> The seven Watergate defendants, and others not yet indicted, bugged D.N.C. offices initially against their better judgment, knowing that Larry O'Brien was seldom there and that many items of interest were being moved to Florida. Furthermore, the defendants pressed an alternate plan to bug O'Brien's Fontainebleau convention suite, before occupancy, a low-risk, high-gain operation, which was rejected.
>
> The seven defendants again protested further bugging of D.N.C. headquarters on June 16–17, the intercepted conversations by then having shown clearly that O'Brien was not using his office.
>
> Again, objections were overridden and the attempt was loyally made even though money for outside guards was struck from the operational budget by Jeb Magruder. In fact, the entire history of Gemstone was characterized by diminishing funding coupled with increasing demands by those who conceived and sponsored the acitivity.
>
> If initial orders to bug D.N.C. headquarters were ill advised, the defendants' sponsors compounded the fiasco by the following acts:
>
> 1. Indecisiveness at the moment of crisis.
> 2. Failure to quash the investigation while that option was still open.
> 3. Allowing Hunt's safe to be opened and selected contents handed to the F.B.I.
> 4. Permitting an F.B.I. investigation whose unprecedented scope and vigor caused humiliation to families, friends, and the defendants themselves.
> 5. Granting immunity to Baldwin.
> 6. Permitting defendants to fall into the hands of a paranoid judge and three self-admitted liberal Democrat prosecutors.
> 7. Failure to provide promised funds on a timely and adequate basis; continued postponements and consequent avoidance of commitments.
> 8. An apparent wash-hands attitude now that the election had been won, heightening the sense of unease among all the defendants who have grown increasingly to feel that they are being offered up as scapegoats ultimately to be abandoned.

Items for Consideration

1. Once the criminal trial ends, the D.N.C. civil suit resumes. In his deposition John Mitchell may well have perjured himself.
2. Pending are three investigations by Congressional committees. The Democratic Congress is not going to simply let the Watergate affair die away.
3. The media are offering huge sums for defendants' stories, for example an offer to one defendant for his "autobiography" now stands at $745,000.
4. The Watergate bugging is only one of a number of highly illegal conspiracies engaged in by one or more of the defendants at the behest of senior White House officials. These as yet undisclosed crimes can be proved.
5. Immunity from prosecution and/or judicial clemency for cooperating defendants is a standing offer.
6. Congressional elections will take place in less than two years.

Defendants' Position

The defendants have followed all instructions meticulously, keeping their part of the bargain by maintaining silence. They have not, until now, attempted to contact persons still in positions of responsibility in an effort to obtain relief and reassurance, believing pre-election security to be a primary consideration.

The Administration, however, remains deficient in living up to its commitments. These commitments were and are:

1. Financial support.
2. Legal defense fees.
3. Pardons.
4. Rehabilitation.

Having recovered from post-election euphoria, the Administration should now attach high priority to keeping its commitments and taking affirmative action in behalf of the defendants.

To end further misunderstandings, the seven defendants have set Nov. 27 at 5:00 p.m. as the date by which all past and current financial requirements are to be paid, and credible assurances given of continued resolve to honor all commitments. Half measures will be unacceptable.

Accordingly, the defendants are meeting on Nov. 25 to determine our joint and automatic response to evidence of continued indifference on the part of those in whose behalf we suffered the loss of our employment, our futures, and our reputations as honorable men.

The foregoing should not be misinterpreted as a threat. It is among other things a reminder that loyalty has always been a two-way street.

Looking back, my lawyer comments, "To a prosecutor, this was *gold*—a clear road map of the cover-up, of quid pro quo. 'We continue to keep silent; you pay the money you owe.'" Snyder also remembers that he was watching Sirica when Ben-Veniste read the section about the paranoid judge but that the man in question sat stonefaced, giving no indication of his thoughts.

The memo had two immediate effects. First, it added immense credibility to my current testimony, as I had previously testified in front of the Senate subcommittee saying the opposite to what the memo contained, and I was now "coming clean." Second, it pointed directly to higher-ups, specifically naming Jeb Magruder and John Mitchell. Attorneys for Mitchell and Parkinson thought that the letter, which had been withheld from them, was so damaging to their clients that they filed for a mistrial.

Parkinson's lawyer, Jacob Stein, argued, "I am now stuck with a cross-examination that is harmful to my client. I have now a cover-up within a cover-up. I'm caught between the blades of scissors in a play within a play."

I could have told them how far that would go in front of the paranoid, railroading judge in charge of the case.

On January 1, 1975, after sixty-four days of trial, the jury deliberated for fifteen hours and five minutes, delivering a guilty verdict on all counts of the cover-up to Mitchell, Haldeman, Ehrlichman, and Mardian—four men who had once been some of the most powerful officials in the land. Parkinson's argument that he had been misled by his superiors was apparently believable, as he was acquitted.

John Mitchell served nineteen months at the minimum-security institution at Maxwell Air Force Base in Alabama before being released early because of bad health. He was a man who was accustomed to having his orders obeyed without question and did not take no for an answer. His subsequent courses of action after our arrests showed that he had little sensitivity for those whom he ordered around.

He did, however, make an apologetic statement to Judge Sirica: "My reflections since the trial upon my acts and deeds and the events in which I participated, my reflections have led me to considerable remorse and regret that they occurred, and, of course, that they resulted in such distress to my family and friends and associates and all other people who were affected by them. . . ." He promised never to perform such deeds in the future.

After being released from prison, Mitchell settled with his companion, Mary Gore Dean, in Georgetown, where he attempted unsuccessfully to write a memoir. It's too bad that he never finished, because as the "Big Man," he must have had some very juicy tidbits to reveal. The failure to deliver prompted Simon & Schuster to sue him to recover the large advance they had tendered, making him the only conspirator to never publish a book about Watergate. He took his last breath on November 9, 1988, and was buried in Arlington National Cemetery.

H. R. Haldeman was sentenced to eighteen months in Lompoc Federal Prison in California. In 1978, he published *The Ends of Power*, taking responsibility for creating the atmosphere that allowed an operation like Watergate to flourish. The book also engendered more conspiracy theories, as it alleged a CIA plot to cover up facts surrounding the Kennedy assassination, which Oliver Stone used in his movie *Nixon*, speculating that the missing eighteen-and-a-half minutes of Nixonian tape concerned the cover-up. Haldeman became a successful entrepreneur before dying of abdominal cancer in California on November 12, 1993.

Haldeman also prepared a statement to the judge. To his credit, he spent most of his time repeating that he would like to contribute to society in the future and apologizing: "I do totally accept responsibility for my actions and I recognize my responsibility to atone for those actions. I have in a religious sense as well as in a legal sense a very strong feeling of repentance."

Robert Mardian was convicted on the basis of Magruder's testimony and sentenced to ten months to three years in prison, before his conviction was reversed on appeal on grounds that his lawyer had fallen ill two weeks into the trial. Before Mark Felt's "Deep Throat" revelation, many people believed the Watergate leaker to be Mardian, who would have been a perfect person, as he was Liddy's "action officer."

Ehrlichman had the most to lose, as he had already been convicted in the plumbers trial and could receive twenty years. In the end, the mean and vindictive counsel to the president was sentenced to twenty months to five years in prison. He ended up serving eighteen months in a minimum-security Arizona prison camp.

After his release from prison in 1977, he issued a statement to Judge Sirica rationalizing his actions, saying, "I now realize that I had an exaggerated sense of my obligation to do as I was bidden, without exercising independent judgment in the way I might have if it had been an attorney-client relationship. And I hope that people who are in the White House now and in the coming years will have a different sense of that relationship. It's almost a metaphysical kind of relationship.

It's very hard to define, but see you're asked to do all kinds of thing—out of your loyalty to the institution, out of your loyalty to the man, as your essential relationship—you're kind of an extension of his arm." He finished with perhaps his least self-serving and truest words: "I went and lied; and I'm paying the price for that lack of willpower. I, in effect, abdicated my moral judgments and turned them over to somebody else. And if I had any advice for my kids, it would be to never ever defer your moral judgments to anybody—your parents, your wife, anybody. That's something that's very personal. And it's what a man has to hang onto."

He clearly could have been speaking for all of us. Afterward, Ehrlichman settled for a while in New Mexico, where he wrote two novels and two nonfiction accounts of his time with Richard Nixon. Ehrlichman died of diabetes complications in Atlanta, Georgia, on Feburary 14, 1999.

All in all, nineteen administration officials would be convicted, with Liddy doing the most time, a total of four years, before President Carter ordered his release. Despite the Democratic president's mercy, Liddy gave thanks by parleying his notoriety into a "successful," ultraconservative radio talk show.

In his book, *Blind Ambition*, John Dean recounts a conversation with Chuck Colson, who said: "I tell you, John, . . . I turned into something of a CIA freak on Watergate for a while, you know, and I still think there's something there. I haven't figured out how it all adds up, but I know one thing: the people with CIA connections sure did better than the rest of us. Paul O'Brien's an old CIA man, and he walked. David Young was Kissinger's CIA liaison, and he ran off to England when he got immunity. Bennett worked for the CIA, and he ran back to Hughes. And Dick Helms skated through the whole thing somehow. Maybe those guys just knew how to play the game better than we did." Dean did pretty well, though. After he testifed, Sirica sentenced him to time served, which totaled four months.

Despite Colson's observations, my CIA connection was not much help to me. I ended up serving thirty-three months in prison. It wasn't pleasant, but there was one good aspect: it was in prison at Eglin Air Force Base that I met my wife, Laura.

Eglin is another one of those country club prisons that sounds better than it is. While it was superior to D.C. Jail, you never forgot that you were in prison. Yes, it is for nonviolent, short-term prisoners, and you can play tennis, but it's still not a place you want to go back to once you've been released.

I didn't have a wife to visit me, so one of the other prisoners, a man by the name of Hughes, who is now deceased, told me that he wanted me to meet a young divorcée from his old town in Georgia. I told him that I preferred not to meet anybody, because usually when I did, they gave me a stack of Bibles. I had so many of them that I had become a major source of Bibles for the prison converts. The givers were all quite well intentioned, but I was comfortable with my own level of interest in religion.

Then I received a nice letter from a woman who said she had seen me interviewed by Tom Snyder on the *Tomorrow Show*, and would like to meet me.

I wrote back a terse reply:

Dear Miss Martin:
Thank you for your letter and your interest in visiting me, but I am not interested in meeting strangers. Every time I am on network television, I get hundreds of marriage proposals. Again, I am not interested in meeting someone who saw me on television.
Sincerely,
Howard Hunt

She was amused by the letter and kept it on her dining room table for several days before writing back:

Dear Mr. Hunt,
I am not the least bit interested in proposing marriage to you. You are five years younger than my father! I merely have admired you from afar and thought you might enjoy a picnic lunch from this teacher who, believe me, has NO designs on you. Perish the thought. I am not offended, since we do not know one another; in fact, I had to grin when I read your letter.

You are a WONDERFUL patriot who has done so much good for this country, and how ironic that your country sent you to prison over so small a thing. If Nixon (whom I thought was an excellent president) had taken responsibility for the whole affair, he likely would have enjoyed a very successful second term. How tragic that you and your children suffered so terribly in the loss of your wife/their mother in that plane crash.

Good-bye, Mr. Hunt. Stay well.

Sincerely,
Laura Martin

By chance, Laura was, in fact, the woman whom Hughes wanted me to meet. "She's a former Miss Georgia," he prompted enticingly.

So I agreed to the meeting the following Sunday; on Sundays families usually came to visit in a large hall with minimal guards.

"The lady I mentioned to you is right over there," Hughes said, gesturing toward a very charming young lady.

To make a long story short, it turned out to be Laura. She visited me on weekends and would bring me fried chicken and things like that. When I got out of prison, I continued seeing her for six to eight months while I got my life straightened out, because there were still many loose ends to tie up. Once I was clear, I asked Laura to marry me.

The wedding was planned for Thanksgiving 1977 but had to be postponed because my great old friend Mañuel Artime was dying from recently diagnosed pancreatic cancer.

Mañuel liked Laura instantly and told me, "Don't let this one get away, *hermano*."

Unfortunately, he died before Laura could get to know him, but she fell in love with his wife, Adelaida, and their children.

On our honeymoon, Laura had to laugh when I told her that the only reason I agreed to meet her was because Hughes had told me she was a former Miss Georgia.

"I've never been in a beauty pageant in my life!" she told me.

At first, we moved to Guadalajara, Mexico. Laura was (and still is) a Spanish teacher, so she was excited by the idea. Accordingly, we bought a trailer and loaded it with essential items, and headed south across the border, where countless expatriates have gone to get away from their reputations.

I knew a couple of CIA people who had resettled in Guadalajara, and I had gone down there before to check it out with them. So when Laura and I got to Guadalajara, we had a circle of ready-made friends, which expanded rapidly in the American colony. We enjoyed a very good life and sent the two children we had together to a reputable American school. All in all, it was a good move, and I was able to write a couple of books there. But after five years, it became as expensive to live in Mexico as in the United States, so we moved to the other major city in the United States where you can usually leave the past behind—Miami.

I realized that not only had I successfully left my past behind but had acquired a different identity altogether. One day in a supermarket, a middle-aged lady rushed up to shake my hand. "Oh, it's so nice to see you here. . . . We were wondering for a long time what happened to you, Mr. Liddy!" she said.

I don't like to be misidentified with him. We're totally different, to say the least. But there you go.

As of this writing Laura and I have been married for twenty-eight years, and our children, Austin and Hollis, are twenty-seven and twenty-one, respectively. Sometimes it amazes me that these two fine human beings would never have arrived on this earth except for the terrible trials of Watergate. I now have six children, some of whom have their own children, so I've made my mark on the eastern part of the United States.

I suppose the genesis of Watergate is to be found in the Vietnam War. The Nixon White House was deeply disturbed and baffled by mass antiwar demonstrations, spreading campus unrest and destruction, the Kent State killings, and publication of the Pentagon Papers. Their cumulative effect produced in the White House a bunker mentality— Us against Them—prompting the nefarious actions detailed in this book.

Nixon's impeachment turned on the crucial question of whether he thought that he was paying blackmail for my and the others' silence. So for the rest of my life, I will probably be known as the man who tried to blackmail the White House, even though all I was trying to do was collect on promised debts.

Still, it's clear that at least from the time of Alger Hiss, Nixon was accustomed to spinning his own paranoid reality and had been somewhat successful in foisting it upon a willing public—to which I belonged. And so it was that a bodyguard of otherwise honorable men began shielding private Nixonian truth with public lies. That was the beginning of the cover-up and the fall of Richard Nixon.

I was one of those liars, and the subterfuge cost me everything I held dear, except my life. I lied to protect the presidency—until it became clear that the president was frantically trying to preserve himself, not his high office. In the end, my involvement in Watergate cost me the disruption of my family; legal fees of nearly $800,000; the fall of the Cubans who trusted me; publishers' resistance to my books after a long, successful writing career; the permanent labels of "Watergater" and "burglar"; and thirty-three months in prison. Collaterally, my name, published photographs, and CIA background attracted the unwelcome attention of assassination buffs who fantasized that a Watergate conspirator could have conspired to murder John Fitzgerald Kennedy.

This for a man who had only contempt for me and those he sacrificed to lighten his sinking boat—intimate friends, longtime supporters, and advisers—until all were gone and he sank alone, rejected and unregretful. In the spring of 1974, I read transcripts of Nixon's Oval Office tapes and realized that the president whom I had so long admired and for whom I had sacrificed so much was indifferent to our fate. For me that was a turning point, and I resolved to testify truthfully, and did so from then on.

Still, here's one example of the surreal atmosphere that suffused the White House—and how much Nixon was living in his own reality: at the time he was fighting impeachment, Nixon's attorney telephoned, asking if I would come to the White House to help prepare the president's defense. The invitation was so incredible that it took me a few moments to comprehend what was being asked. Finally, I managed to decline civilly, though outrage and profanity were on the tip of my tongue.

Nixon's legacy of misfeasance is found in diminished respect for the presidency and suspicion of government itself: an imprint as enduring as it is unforgivable.

Classical Greek dramatists focused on hubris, the tragic flaw in a man's character that inevitably brings him from high to low estate. Nixon's flaws were paranoia, vanity, pride, and obsession with self-preservation at the expense of the public's governance.

As Richard Nixon lay on his deathbed, I uncharitably recalled Shelley's words on George III: "an old, mad, blind, despised, and dying king."

25

The Problem with Langley

Watergate set off a blood feud between Democrats and Republicans that may continue for generations. Since then, each party resurrects the fight with every transgression by the other party, each shout spiced by the indignant echoes of the past. Americans now suffer from political fatigue, lacking faith in the leadership of both parties.

And we never seem to learn. Lessons taken from the Bay of Pigs should have kept us out of Vietnam, but they didn't. The "quagmire" of Vietnam should have kept us from invading Iraq, but it didn't. Watergate should have made each successive administration more transparent and mindful of the law, but it didn't. Instead, almost every administration has had some scandal important enough to hang a "gate" on, such as Iran-Contragate under Ronald Reagan and Monica-gate under Bill Clinton.

Long before Watergate, Richard Nixon discovered early in his administration that he was not above the law when he tried to order the warrantless wiretapping of Americans, focusing on antiwar activists. Even the über-snoop J. Edgar Hoover disapproved, and Congress shouted down the plan early in its inception.

George W. Bush could have learned a lesson from Nixon's folly, but instead he chose not only to resurrect the policy with a "Warrantless Lite" procedure in which we only spy on Americans if a call is international, but has now upped the ante with a "New Improved" version in which the administration is defending government's inalienable right to monitor the conversations of Americans inside our borders—or, at the very least, keep a database of who has talked to whom.

I truly don't know what to say about this. While I agree with the president's intentions, and think that we must use every strategy in our power to defeat terrorism, the heavy-handed implementation of this policy has a good chance of being found unconstitutional by the courts regardless of any positive results that may be attributed to it. Surely there was some way to accomplish the same results with less political risk, or at least the tried-and-true method of "plausible denial." A shotgun was used when we really needed a sharpshooter.

The difference between the *abuse* of power and the *use* of power continues to dance around the fine line of semantics and chance. If our Watergate team had found that the Democrats were indeed being financed by Communist enemies, then our criminal actions might have been judged heroic. Like those who were advised that there were weapons of mass destruction in Iraq, our Watergate team was subject to faulty intelligence. We were wrong, and we took our punishment. Bush should have admitted his mistakes early on and taken the rap. His blind defiance will have ramifications on the Republican Party for at least several election cycles—not to mention on the families of all those who have died in Iraq.

It is a cliché that during wartime ordinary people find that they are capable of extraordinary things. Just so, our ordinary Constitution proves itself most extraordinary when it is under attack, and its ideals must be upheld for the good of the country. We must do everything within our power to defend it.

But, some would ask, what if a domestic communication is warrantlessly intercepted by the National Security Agency and this eavesdropping in turn saves lives—as it might have on 9/11 or during our homegrown bombing of the Murrah Federal Building in Oklahoma City in 1996? In that case, should ordinary principles give way to extraordinary ones?

These are like questions posed in Philosophy 101. If someone told you to kill a baby, you wouldn't. But what if you knew the baby was Adolf Hitler? Hands get raised very quickly. Of course, you still don't kill the baby because there *is* no way of knowing whether anyone will grow up to be a doctor or a mass murderer—or if their children, in turn, will be saviors or sinners. So as a society we do our best to ensure the life of every baby born, provide him the framework of an education, and teach him a set of values to live by. Still, while we provide a decent public education, no one has a right to the very *best* education, or everyone would attend the private school and college of their choice.

Likewise, every American citizen is protected by the rights provided in the Constitution. But that wonderful document, which we do so much to protect, does not provide us *unlimited* rights. We have the right to privacy but not an *unlimited* right. Our rights of free speech are so broad that even the most reprehensible views of the most twisted minds are protected. But the courts have also reasoned that while we each have a right to free speech, no one has the right to yell fire in a crowded theater—except when there actually *is* a fire. In that case, you might be found criminally negligent for *failing* to yell fire if you saw one. Again, the difference is between use and abuse.

You have the right to defend yourself, your family, and your property, but most states limit the use of deadly force: for instance, making it illegal to set a deadly booby trap to catch a burglar. It is up to a judge and jury to decide the fate of an individual—not a frustrated store owner.

Of course, authorities must have the right to put citizens under surveillance (and surveillance by any other name is still spying), but the Foreign Intelligence Surveillance Act of 1978 already provides for this, allowing investigators to obtain legal warrants from a special court with minimal evidence (if any at all), even up to seventy-two hours after initiating the interception. Spy first—ask later. In the words of a golden-oldie song that was commandeered for a famous commercial campaign: "Who could ask for anything more?"

Congressional subcommittees have already started investigating the administration's actions, saying it all comes back to oversight and keeping the abuses of power to a minimum. Yes, it is perfectly all right to spy on our citizens – as long as it is done within the law—with suitable oversight and checks and balances.

As far as the "New Improved," *purely domestic* spying goes, perhaps the president just went too far too fast. Maybe society hasn't caught up yet.

Judging from today's culture, the nature of privacy seems to be shifting by the nanosecond. While generalizing always leaves somebody out, we squawk about privacy, while exposing everything anyway. Our democracy is full of such devilish inconsistencies. Perhaps if our society seemed more concerned about our citizens' privacy instead of celebrating and exploiting our exposé culture, then government and the courts would treat our privacy with greater respect.

With all the amazing high-tech gadgets that are available on the open market or on the black market from other countries (or with the help of foreign powers), well-financed terrorists, like drug lords before them, have an amazing array of surveillance capabilities at their disposal, a veritable smorgasbord of choices to learn how much we know about them. The only way to combat their technology is to keep at least a half step ahead. To coin a phrase: "If spying is outlawed, only outlaws will be spies." Just like failing to yell fire when there is one would be criminally negligent, perhaps the government should be censured for *not* spying, because their failure to capture a potential terrorist puts us all in jeopardy. Americans must simply accept that liberty is not absolute, and right now must be paid for with increased surveillance.

I am often asked what I think about how to improve today's CIA. Well, there's a reason I never aspired to become anything close to the director of Central Intelligence. Even the best of us has never truly had a good grasp of what to do. What do I think? We should get a genius to run the CIA. But that doesn't work, because we've had a couple of geniuses, or at least some of the best minds in the land, and we've still had monumental failures. We still almost had a third World War; we still discovered spies and moles in the highest places; we still didn't know what was in the hearts and minds of the citizens and governments of other countries. We still don't and never will. You can stare into the eyes of a Vladimir Putin all you want, but all you will ever see is your reflection. The best we can do is guess.

What usually *doesn't* work, however, is bringing in people to head the agency who have had no intelligence experience. George "Slam Dunk" Tenet was an academic before being made director of one of the largest, most powerful intelligence-gathering agencies on earth. It was like the college kid who dives off a pier and drowns after saying, "Don't worry, I've read all the books about how to swim." Field experience cannot be duplicated in the classroom. But Tenet, who assured President Bush that there was a "slam-dunk case" for weapons of mass destruction in Iraq, was still awarded the Presidential Medal of Freedom despite his failed analysis.

One of the problems in the CIA has been the political nature of its appointments. The agency has *always* been a political swamp that has *always* needed to be completely reconstructed on an ongoing basis. It's one reason why no director has ever lasted very long. Each is set up to fail because of the dichotomy between the covert and overt agendas of the United States. We want foreign nations to believe that we are a peaceful nation that will never attack anybody without provocation, so we do it clandestinely, through third parties, just far enough away to provide a veil of plausible deniability to the most gullible—or to those who wish to turn a blind eye. We never fool the skeptical.

But there's a reason for doing things that way. President Bush has found that once you've crossed the line that you drew in the sand, you can't just draw another line. Broad actions invoked on marginal intelligence, analyzed by people with a blind eye, will only get you into trouble. A creative, subtle, strategic covert campaign to remove Hussein from power in a country where he was already imprisoned and marginalized by world standards might have had some success and been better rewarded. Perhaps—just thinking creatively here for a second—we might have actually funneled weapons to him that made him *feel* safe, *feel* powerful, but that had a severely short shelflife, or that could be deactivated by satellite, or that would self-destruct if he ever tried to use them. Still, we probably would have gone into Iraq anyway, as I believe that the case for weapons of mass destruction was just a pretext to invade the country in an attempt to establish a lawful democracy in a region devoid of it.

While it is often said that the world has become a more complicated place than it was when I was in the agency, it has always been complicated. Surviving World War II and its consequences, trying to keep people from destroying the world with nuclear missiles, was never a simple task.

While 9/11 occurred under the administration of George Tenet, the terrorist attack and the ensuing war in Iraq, based on faulty intelligence, might still have happened under the most experienced, most capable director, because the CIA did not have the proper underlying structure beneath it. By Tenet's time, the "company," as it is often called, had become just that, a corporation whose real mandate was to perpetuate itself—like Project Samurai back in my Japan days. Like a company when its main competitor (in this case, the KGB) folded after the Cold War, many reasons for the agency's existence became obsolete. Under President Clinton, its budget and personnel were cut by a third and the CIA was expected to rely on the newest technology, which in turn propagated a flood of information to be analyzed. The agency became one of the largest consumers of paper in the world, pushing pages back and forth, finally content to stamp them TOP SECRET and file them in massive storerooms, with only about 5 percent of the information ever undergoing analysis. The CIA just didn't have the personnel to keep up with the flow.

The agency's failures were ones of imagination, of analysis, of staying politically safe. Where intelligence was correct, where imagination rose to the occasion, where reports cried out that terrorists were planning to use air transportation as bombs, *that* information should have been rammed down the Bush administration's throat. Instead, like Richard Bissel complaining that he should have taken a stronger stance with JFK, not wanting to step on toes during the Bay of Pigs assault, CIA administrators were too protective of their jobs to stress the importance of this information to the president and his staff. Where were our intrepid whistleblowers then?

I have rewritten this chapter twice as events keep catching up to me. In previous versions, I called for the resignations of CIA director Porter Goss and Secretary of Defense Donald Rumsfeld, both of which occurred while the book was still in production. So now, while I may not look quite as prescient as I might have, let's look at some of the factors that led up to their ousters and see what lessons can be learned. By mid-2006, a revolt of top military brass occurred, with at least half a dozen current and retired generals drumming a beat for Rumsfeld to resign over his handling of the Iraq war. They said they were often unable to express their views, pointing out the case of General Eric Shinseki, former army chief of staff, who testified to Congress a month before the 2003 invasion of Iraq that the United States would need "several hundred thousand troops" to successfully occupy the country, a much larger force than was eventually supplied. General Shinseki's estimate was summarily dismissed by Secretary of Defense Donald Rumsfeld and Deputy Defense Secretary Paul Wolfowitz, who called Shinseki's estimates "wildly off the mark." The dynamic duo quickly marginalized him and any other opposing voices before the war.

An April 14, 2006, *New York Times* article quoted Thomas E. White, the former army secretary, as saying, "Rumsfeld has been contemptuous of the views of senior military officers since the day he walked in as Secretary of Defense. It's about time they got sick and tired." White was forced out of his job by Rumsfeld in April 2003.

On April 17, *Time* magazine published an essay by retired lieutenant general Greg Newbold, the former operations director for the Joint Chiefs of Staff, who argued that the Bush administration and higher powers at the Pentagon used the 9/11 tragedy to "hijack our security policy." While I believe this smells of revisionism, he makes some valid points.

He wrote, "Inside the military family, I made no secret of my view that the zealots' rationale for war made no sense. But I now regret that I did not more openly challenge those who were determined to invade a country whose actions were peripheral to the real threat—al-Qaeda."

Pentagon leaders, he stated, "with few exceptions, acted timidly when their voices urgently needed to be heard. When they knew the plan was flawed, saw intelligence distorted to justify a rationale for war, or witnessed arrogant micromanagement that at times crippled the military's effectiveness, many leaders who wore the uniform chose inaction."

While Newbold also notes Congress's culpability and gullibility with the war, he ends with the forceful observation: "It is time for senior military leaders to discard caution in expressing their views and ensure that the president hears them clearly. And that we won't be fooled again."

This is exactly right. The yes-man mentality must give way to the dictum to question authority, with dissenting opinions properly thought out, communicated, and, most important, listened to in the intelligence agencies such as the CIA, throughout the branches of the military, and especially in the Executive Branch halls of power. This may cause inaction in some cases, but it need not cause catatonia. The headstrong macho plan plays well on TV; but a carefully constructed, well-thought-out strategy provides more positive results.

A case in point: President Bush proclaimed that Iran, Iraq, and North Korea were all part of an "axis of evil." This sort of cowboy statement makes a great sound bite, but it only galvanized the citizens of those countries (many of whom had nothing against us) and others to oppose our policies. These are people with long memories and enmities that stretch back thousands of years. When the president uses the word *crusade* as a verb, they interpret it as a noun with a big C—Crusade. They will not forget the president's little quips. Today's sound bite is tomorrow's war cry.

A much more productive and subtle way to deal with terrorist countries is to co-opt them. The ancient Chinese general Sun-Tzu said, "Keep your friends close, your enemies closer." We shouldn't bomb Al Jazeera television, as Bush once suggested; we need to buy it—through a third party, of course. Then slowly and subtly change the news slant to deprogram all the negative brainwashing that has occurred. Until then, we should do exactly what the military was doing in Iraq—pay for good news PR. It just needs to be done with greater élan so that what we are doing is never discovered.

It takes around five years to train agents to truly understand their objectives and form worthwhile opinions about them, so it will probably take at least a decade before the CIA is back up to fighting weight. Maybe longer, because a lot of people will retire in that amount of time. In fact, after Porter Goss took over and seeded the upper eschelon of the agency with his self-serving cronies, experienced operatives left in droves. We'll need a lot of energetic, intelligent Generation X, Y, and Zers to consider joining the CIA.

So, in the meantime, if you are going to think like my old friend Frank Wisner might have, what do you do? You have to start indoctrinating the youth. There's hardly a NASA engineer who doesn't trace his or her interest in space exploration to *Star Trek*. Likewise, the CIA needs to clandestinely produce television programs, movies, and electronic games that make people want to grow up to serve their country and enter the intelligence community. Television shows like Fox's *24* are doing a bang-up job of reinventing the spy genre for modern times, even promoting previously untenable acts such as torture to gain information, precariously arguing that the means justifies the ends—especially when desperate times call for desperate measures. Is there a *24* video game around the corner? I could not have come up with a better piece of continuing propaganda myself. This show follows a loyal cadre of friends who are defying authority for the greater good, led by a charismatic protagonist who fights against terrorists. No doubt a loyal following of young viewers will one day join the ranks of law enforcement and intelligence because they were first inspired by a television show, much like the generation who grew up watching *Mission: Impossible*.

The military has done a stunning job of revamping its image to entice people to enlist. Before the insurgency took its toll in Iraq, making our soldiers look worn out and morally defeated, the living-room war broadcast from Afghanistan was an absolutely mind-bogglingly well-accomplished piece of propaganda that filled the enlistment offices with America's best and brightest. The same journalists who had been promoting weapons of mass destruction, who helped the president launch the war, were then given preferred seating as "embedded" reporters, who breathlessly informed the public about the brave deeds of the military. Donald Rumsfeld and General Tommy Franks became media darlings, quipping and spinning on a national stage.

The CIA should hire the same advertising firm as the Pentagon, since the country would be better off hiring more agents than soldiers. For a fraction of the cost of waging war, we can train a thousand operatives to infiltrate terrorist organizations, pay foreign journalists to write favorable stories, influence religious leaders, and quiet the hysteria being built against the West. When we were fighting Communism, the most useful weapons didn't explode—they had pages, a volume control, or a great personality. They still do.

In today's world, the CIA leadership must engender a more creative workforce, giving staff the opportunity to form and communicate dissenting opinions. The worst decisions being made today have come from group-think, from self-protection and self-propagation. Also, intelligence is not a commodity to be hoarded; it must be shared among agencies and personnel. Our homegrown terrorist, Unabomber Theodore Kaczynski, was caught because his manifesto was printed for millions of people, including his brother, to read. Likewise, something that seems like an innocuous crumb to an analyst in one agency may be a treasure trove to another. And yes, our intelligence agencies must work hand-in-hand with today's military.

Some of this is being done under first-year director of National Intelligence John Negroponte, a career diplomat with no real intelligence resume. He has been put in charge of organizing a sort of clearinghouse for FBI, CIA, and Pentagon intelligence, none of whom show him a grain of respect. His year hiding out as U.S. ambassador in Iraq was plagued by violence, which continues to this day. Basically, he was another yes-man, put in to replace the dissenting voice of Ambassador Paul Bremer, who was and continues to be critical of the administration. Under Negroponte's watch, we have now failed to predict that Hamas would win the Palestinian elections and that Iran would be able to enrich uranium so soon. Who knows what other lapses will occur? Despite more than a hundred intelligence briefings in Negroponte's first year, Congress has complained that the agency has actually slowed the flow of intelligence. Still, a tanker needs a lot of room to slow down and turn, and any changes made by Negroponte will take time to prove themselves.

In April 2006, a year after the National Intelligence Agency was founded, lawmakers are stunned at the lack of progress and have criticized the new super-spook Negroponte for failing to fulfill his mission. The office of the director of National Intelligence is "not adding any value" by enlarging the bureaucracy, Representative Pete Hoekstra, a Michigan Republican who leads the House Intelligence Committee, told *USA Today*. "They're lengthening the time to make things happen. . . . We want them to be lean and mean." He told the newspaper that the "agency does some tasks well, but is only slowly improving the quality of intelligence."

Hoekstra's bipartisan committee was so critical of the new agency that they requested that Congress freeze some of the department's budget until it replied to lawmakers' concerns, which included a massive staff that has not increased intelligence analysis. Again, shades of Project Samurai. "Once a bureaucracy takes root," Hoekstra said, "it's awfully hard to get rid of."

Now Negroponte's deputy, General Michael V. Hayden—the former NSA chief who initiated the controversial domestic eavesdropping program—has been named the new director of Central Intelligence after Porter Goss was summarily fired. While at first glance he doesn't seem to have the personal charisma necessary to inspire people to follow him, he does seem to have the experience and Machiavellian instincts required for the job.

What we don't need is another political hack at the top. We need to find a leader like Wild Bill Donovan in spirit, a few more Frank Wisners in vision. We need to hire more energetic and aggressive operatives—members of the PlayStation generation—to get the most out of the hi-tech marvels inside the walls at Langley, with a corresponding need for dynamic X-Gamers out in the field—think Bode Miller with a Princeton education and a Middle Eastern genealogy. We must go back to the principals and ideals not of the early CIA but of its forerunner; we must find people with imagination and will, reaching back toward the personalities of the Office of Strategic Services—back to the heart and souls of the "daring amateurs."

Index